AN INTRODUCTION
TO SYSTEMS SCIENCE

AN INTRODUCTION TO SYSTEMS SCIENCE

John N. Warfield

Professor Emeritus, George Mason University, USA

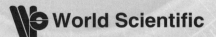
World Scientific

NEW JERSEY · LONDON · SINGAPORE · BEIJING · SHANGHAI · HONG KONG · TAIPEI · CHENNAI

MER
003 WAR

Published by

World Scientific Publishing Co. Pte. Ltd.
5 Toh Tuck Link, Singapore 596224
USA office: 27 Warren Street, Suite 401-402, Hackensack, NJ 07601
UK office: 57 Shelton Street, Covent Garden, London WC2H 9HE

British Library Cataloguing-in-Publication Data
A catalogue record for this book is available from the British Library.

AN INTRODUCTION TO SYSTEMS SCIENCE

ISBN 981-256-702-X

Printed by FuIsland Offset Printing (S) Pte Ltd, Singapore

Preface

Many changes are in store for the systems community in coming years, if it is to meet the challenges imposed by the many problematic situations extant in the world today. This community must rise to these challenges or it will deservedly pass away. I seek to provide the basis for stopping some of the bad practices, including the following:

- **Underscoping the Systems Domain**. Various devices are used that implicitly underscope the systems domain. Among these are representing this domain as coincident with particular methods, such as "systems dynamics" or coincident with the work of particular individuals, such as L. von Bertalanffy; or coincident with a particular academic program; or what is represented in the language of a particular marketplace such as information technology. This is particularly troublesome in education, since people are placed in public positions with weak understanding of the possibilities, and with tendencies to mis-formulate problematic situations and mis-apply both public and private resources.

- **Unimaginative Workspaces.** Workspaces tailored to the complexity of problematic situations are far too unimaginative. Workspaces that are not tailored to match the complexity of the problematic situations, and which do not provide opportunity to scan the extensive products of description and design work, and to keep such work constantly updated and available for inspection, updating, and learning by project personnel, virtually assure that errors will be introduced into systems designs that will engender failures, some of which will cause loss of life, and all of which will cause major expense; sometimes extending into many billions of dollars.

- **Mismatched Media.** Habitual usage of small-scale media in small-scale problem-solving is carried over into systems domains. Typical mismatched media include, e.g., small computer screens, conventional textbook sizes, conventional blackboards and overhead projections; when present-day problematic situations require very large wall displays and wide-scanning capabilities with physical movement along the wall displays to allow for back-and-forth discussions among groups.

- **Linguistic Pollution.** The systems language is heavily polluted. It is necessary to dispense with outmoded and ambiguous language like "systems approach" and "problem-solving", which are not serviceable and replace them with well-defined terms like "systems science" and "resolution of complexity"[1]. Worst of all, the desecration of such terms as "science", and the willingness of universities to succumb to and sponsor such desecration in order to enable the coffers to be enlarged, is unforgivable, and must eventually be corrected.

- **Premature Quantification.** An entirely unjustifiable false sense of security arises out of premature quantification. Put an end to the practice of leaping prematurely into application of numerically-based methods that are well-known to the user, long before a problematic situation has been adequately defined and its attributes organized in a way that is responsive to, e.g., Ashby's Law of Requisite Variety.

- **Insensitivity to Discovered Behavioral Pathologies.** Human fallibility can now be explicitly recognized in methodology.

---

[1] The systems community is not alone in its linguistic barbarism. In governmental circles one constantly hears such phrases as "address the whole question" and deal with "both sides of the equation", so that presumably all will be well "at the end of the day". One might describe such practices as "government by metaphor".

Recognize, pay tribute to, and factor into systems science the discoveries of behavioral pathologies that have been made in the last half of the twentieth century; and which have now been demonstrated to be the basis for serious errors in systems made by human beings; errors that could have been avoided by responsible design practices.

- **Inadequacy of Comparisons of Alternatives.** For those who feel an earnest need for numbers, alternatives can now be assessed in terms of complexity metrics. Alternative designs are almost never compared on the basis of relative complexity, and quantitative measures of complexity based on known human behavioral pathologies are almost never taken into account in system design; which explains much of the difficulty faced by consumers in using systems designed with such inadequacy.

- **Blindness to History.** Some people thought about systems long ago. There seems to be a strongly entrenched belief that systems thinking originated in the last half of the twentieth century. Virtually every important concept that backs up the key ideas emergent in systems literature are found in ancient literature and in the centuries to follow. It is time to recognize the contributions of these elder scholars and factor them into systems science where their presence is absolutely essential to a mature science.

- **Monotonous Bifurcation.** Systems literature cannot be valued properly by weight. Too much of the systems literature is bifurcated. It offers either theory with no empirical evidence or (less commonly) empirical evidence with no supporting theory or, now and then, sheer fantasy with neither theory nor evidence; thereby at least giving some relief from the monotonous bifurcation.

It would be of no use merely to rail against bad practices if nothing were offered to replace the practices. I offer to replace these practices with systems science and what the application of systems science yields. The name "science" has been misused often in recent decades. I strive constantly to honor it, and I do my best to use it in the way it was used by those noble souls so often treated badly in previous centuries. In this quest, we can draw some solace from such things as the words of C. S. Peirce that "truth, crushed to earth, shall rise again", and from noting that even though it took 400 years for the Church to acknowledge that Galileo had been correct, it did eventually acknowledge it. Perhaps even the university, as a generic institutional type, can find the strength ultimately to look to its integrity now and then and restore some of the linguistic integrity associated with the terminology describing its offerings.

Before I explain the organization of the book, I will describe first my perspective on what constitutes systems science and how I have presented this subject. The reader who is familiar with a significant part of the systems literature will soon realize that this presentation is relatively novel, although it does not ignore prevailing concepts. That is because this perspective has only arisen in my mind in the past year or so as I have been working to integrate over three decades of research and publications on systems, and it is only as a result of that effort that I have finally been able to arrive at a concept of what constitutes systems science. I have explained thoroughly the odyssey that produced this concept in **Appendix 3** of this book titled "Discovering Systems Science".

Systems science is best seen as a science that consists of nested sub-sciences. It is presented most compactly using the notation of set theory.

Let **A** represent a science of description. Let **B** represent a science of design. Let **C** represent a science of complexity. Let **D** represent a science of action (praxiology). Let **E** represent systems science. Then

$$\mathbf{A} \subset \mathbf{B} \subset \mathbf{C} \subset \mathbf{D} \subset \mathbf{E} \qquad (1)$$

Eq. (1) illustrates the concept that we can learn something of systems science by first learning a science of description. Then we can learn a science of design which includes a science of description. Next we can learn a science of complexity which includes a science of description and a science of design, and so on.

I have published books on **A**, **B**, **C**, and **D**, having only recently becoming clearly aware that what I was doing at the time was constructing portions of Eq. (1). The present book is **E**. It cannot include **A, B, C**, and **D**, but it can incorporate them by reference, and it can provide necessary links.

Table 1 offers some of the linkages. Others will be made clear in the ensuing chapters and appendixes. The tables and figures in the last book cited in Table 1 are duplicates of identical tables and figures in the first book in the table and their numbers are subtracted from the totals to give a more accurate picture of the totals.

In light of what is shown in Table 1, the reader may begin to understand that the main purpose of the present book is to provide the glue that links together the work presented in these other books. In order to do this, the foundations that link these other works must be tightly constructed, and the empirical evidence that supports the use of the foundations and the linkages that form systems science are to be made evident here.

Table 1. Books That Describe Sub-Sciences of Systems Science

Science	Citation	Pages	Tables	Figures
Description	J. N. Warfield (1976) *Societal Systems: Planning, Policy, and Complexity*, New York: Wiley Interscience.	490	46	115
Design	J. N. Warfield *A Science of Generic Design: Managing Complexity Through Systems Design*, 1st Ed (1990) Seaside, CA; Intersystems. 2nd Ed. (1994) Ames, IA: Iowa State University Press.	635	46	132
Complexity	J. N. Warfield (2002): *Understanding Complexity: Thought and Behavior*, Palm Harbor, FL: Ajar.	278	16	52
Action	J. N. Warfield and A. Roxana Cárdenas (1994): *A Handbook of Interactive Management*, 2nd Edition, Ames, IA: Iowa State University Press.	353	18	8
Description	J. N. Warfield (2003) *The Mathematics of Structure*, Palm Harbor, FL: Ajar.	164	21	24
Totals		1,920	147 - 21 = 126	331 - 24 = 307

What is Needed to Present Systems Science? To a first approximation, taking into account the 1920 pages in the books listed in Table 1, and the 400 or so pages in the present book, one could say that about 2,300 pages are required to present systems science. This would be misleading, because text alone is insufficient. **Appendix 2** of the present book describes the "Warfield Special Collection" in the George Mason University Fenwick Library in Fairfax, Virginia. This collection occupies over 90 linear feet (a measure used by librarians to indicate the size of such a collection). A computer link to the collection appears in **Appendix 2**. Following this link one can find on the Internet the contents of the collection. Included there are titles of more than 100 VHS videotapes, more than 20 DVDs, lots of audio cassettes, and hundreds of overhead transparencies. All of these audio-visuals have been used at one time or another to help convey the material that is described using text in this book. The behavioral aspects are among the materials most difficult to convey using text alone, and most readily perceived when one is cued as to what to look for on the videotapes or DVDs.

With this background, I am now ready to describe the organization of the present book. As the contents indicate, the book has five "Parts" which include 20 Chapters, and seven "Appendixes". I will explain briefly the purpose(s) of each Chapter and make some comments about their relationship to systems science, as I have defined it in Eq. (1). The comments will then be summarized in Table 2.

Foundations. Part 1, consists of a discussion of the foundations of systems science. It is argued here that all science, including systems science shares three common foundations, and that a distinguishing feature of systems science is that it must be neutral; i.e., not be attached to any particular arena, in order that it can be applicable to any problematic situation. This means further that it can be quite frugal in terms of methodology, having as its principal purpose to provide a service to local practitioners to describe their problematic situation in a viable language. For this to occur the systems science itself must have a high-quality discursivity founded in the theory of relations, since any system model will be comprised of relational descriptors. The history of the development of such a viable language is recounted here in terms of thought explorers; and the evolution of the process that enables the local group to describe its situation and, ultimately to design a system for resolving it, is suggested.

Key concepts of quality control in modeling are described, and the authors of these concepts are identified. The importance of the work space and its layout as a factor in getting good work done is stated.

The discussion in Part 1 aims to strike a complementary balance between the removal of the negatives and the achievement of the positives as the essential foundational aspects of systems science, bypassing conventional ways of approaching systems issues by starting with well-known methods.

The Work Program of Complexity. The Work Program of Complexity has two main parts: Discovery and Resolution. Part 2 of the book deals with the Discovery portion. The Discovery contains two parts, Description and Diagnosis. Incorporated here are considerations of metrics of complexity which can be computed from the work of Description. The local group does the Description, and a person highly experienced with the action component of systems science called Interactive Management does the Diagnosis (without introducing new concepts, but merely feeding back to the group what their work has produced). What is described in Part 2 in a relatively few pages is detailed in books with many pages, hence the purpose of Part 2 is to provide overview to the Discovery portion of the Work Program of Complexity; not to generate expertise in carrying out the first part of the Program.

The second part of the Work Program of Complexity is Resolution. Part 3 of the book deals with Resolution. The Resolution contains two parts: Design and Implementation. Once again, books are available that deal with these parts, so again only a relatively few pages are required to provide overview, not to generate expertise in carrying out the second part of the Program.

Empirical Evidence of Effectiveness. One of the unique features of this book is a collection of contributions by authors from various countries who have experiences to relate that connect to systems science as presented here. It was my intention in inviting these authors to try to obtain a sufficient variety both in locale and in subject matter to help show that the idea of systems science as a neutral science was a valid concept, and that what was being presented was also society-neutral in that the processes would work as well in one society as in another society, because the processes involved sensitivity to deeply-felt, universal human aspects. I feel that the authors have satisfied this intention, and I hope that you do too.

As I explain in my introduction to Part 4, I chose to place the contributions of the authors in four categories: the private sector, the government sector, the education sector, and the social arena. There is overlap among these, and the authors contribute to more than one sector, but I think their contributions shown here relate mainly to the topic of the Chapter in which I have placed them. Several of the authors could have made contributions to more than one Chapter, but I didn't feel that I could ask them to do more. I thank them very much for what they have done to help make this book more valuable. I have included the contributions of Carmen Moreno and Graciela Caffarel in both Spanish and English.

Part 5 on Systems Science. The discussion of systems science really occupies more than Part 5, although I have titled Part 5 "Systems Science". The subject is also the topic of the Appendices, so I am able only to deal with the subject in an overview way in Part 5. In Chapter 19 I give a quick overview of the subject, and in Chapter 20 I offer a few thoughts on a possible future for this subject.

The Appendices. Appendix 1 gives either photographs or drawings of people whose work helped me greatly in developing systems science. I describe briefly the relevant work of these individuals, and provide some information on the status of some of them.

Appendix 2 provides linkages to the "Warfield Special Collection" which is very large, and which offers a great deal of supporting research material for the scholar who wishes to spend some time in the library reviewing particular parts of the background, or watching videotapes of work as it progressed in particular applications.

Appendix 3 describes how the systems science was discovered, as a kind of odyssey through time, and Appendix 4 complements that by going into more detail on the linguistic aspects of systems science.

Appendix 5 discusses the two key neutral processes which I feel are sufficient to fill the needs of systems science. As I explain in several places, a well-carried out application of systems science will reveal what, if any, other methods may be needed to complete a project.

Appendix 6 offers three different ways to view this subject.

Appendix 7 is a short summary of the importance of structural graphics as a special kind of literacy requirement to help portray and understand complexity in particular problematic situations.

Table 2. Book Parts, Negatives–Positives Table

Part 1. **Foundations**–An overview of the severe negatives in the systems domain and ways of exorcising these negatives			
Division	Division Title	Negative(s) Attacked	Positive(s) Given
Chap 1	Unlimited Scope of Systems Science	Underscoping the systems domain	Constructing systems science as a neutral science, unconstrained by premature choices of methodology, while recognizing and accounting for those natural constraints which cannot be removed, but which can be taken into account in designing processes
Chap 2	The Human Being (Creative & Fallible)	Insensitivity to discovered behavioral pathologies	Designing processes to circumvent behavioral pathologies
Chap 3	Language (Overpromising, Underperforming)	Linguistic pollution	Founding discursivity for systems science, and applying the language of systems science locally to enable local language construction by local practitioners for local problematic situations
Chap 4	Second-Order Thought	Blindness to history, Premature quantification	Defining second-order thought as thought about thought itself, and what this means in terms of the development of science

Chap 5	The Thought Explorers	Blindness to history, Premature quantification	Identifying the key mathematics of systems science, explaining why that is the key mathematics, and revealing its historical development
Chap 6	Quality Control in Modeling Structure	Blindness to history, Premature quantification	Showing how to control quality in model development, and explaining why this method is appropriate
Chap 7	The Situation Room	Unimaginative workspace, Mismatched media	Showing how to tailor space for high-quality model development, and explaining why this type of space is required

Part 2. **Discovery**–how systems science itself is discovered, and how it provides the means of discovery in problematic situations

Division	Division Title	Negative(s) Attacked	Positive(s) Given
Chap 8	Describing a Problematic Situation	Mismatched media	Explaining how a problematic situation is described, the process used, the products of the process, the nature of the description, and the use of the products as inputs to the design process
Chap 9	Metrics of Complexity	Insensitivity to behavioral pathologies, Inadequacy of comparisons of alternative designs	Describing a variety of numerical metrics of complexity, showing how the data are obtained, how they are computed, and mentioning links to sources of application of such metrics in making system design choices
Chap 10	Diagnosing	No clear picture in the systems literature of how diagnosis is done.	Diagnosis is carried out by a person who is highly experienced in "reading" the products of prior work; and who tests that reading against the perceptions of those who created the products. The diagnosis renders a verbal description to accompany the graphical products, thereby rendering a more complete description.

	Part 3. **Resolution**–how systems science provides the means of resolving problematic situations through systems design and implementation		
Division	Division Title	Negative(s) Attacked	Positive(s) Given
Chap 11	System Design	Insensitivity to behavioral pathologies, Inadequacy of comparisons of alternative designs	Processes for generating design options to match dimensions in the description of the problematic situation are given, using Ashby's Law of Requisite Variety as a disciplining agent.
Chap 12	Choosing from the Alternatives	Insensitivity to behavioral pathologies, Inadequacy of comparisons of alternative designs	Complexity metrics are computed using information produced to this point, and these metrics become part of the information used in choosing from the design alternatives that are developed.
Chap 13	Implementing the Design	Insensitivity to behavioral pathologies, Inadequacy of comparisons of alternative designs	A large amount of information is developed which culminates in developing a detailed plan for implementing a system design.
Chap 14	The Corporate Observatorium	Insensitivity to behavioral pathologies, Inadequacy of comparisons of alternative designs, Unimaginative workspace	A system design having been produced by a relatively small team, there is a significant educational task to enable a larger body of individuals who will be involved in implementation. This requires additional physical plant, called the corporate observatorium, where large graphical displays are laid out and maintained (NOT Pert Charts), showing the full development of the description, design, and work plan, which is kept up to date, and which precedes (NOT FOLLOWS) activities carried out in work programs.

Part 4. **The Practitioners**–offering empirical evidence of application of systems science in four major domains of humanity

Division	Division Title	Negative(s) Attacked	Positive(s) Given
Chap 15	The Private Sector	Lack of empirical evidence from sector	Empirical evidence either as direct discussion of specific applications, or as opinions based on direct experience of the reporter; with various reporters from different parts of the world, having to do with different types of applications; coming from individuals who may be available to furnish additional evidence if required; some of whom have already made significant contributions to the "Warfield Special Collection" described in Appendix 2.
Chap 16	The Government Sector	Lack of empirical evidence from sector	Empirical evidence either as direct discussion of specific applications, or as opinions based on direct experience of the reporter; with various reporters from different parts of the world, having to do with different types of applications; coming from individuals who may be available to furnish additional evidence if required; some of whom have already made significant contributions to the "Warfield Special Collection" described in Appendix 2.
Chap 17	The Social Arena	Lack of empirical evidence from sector	Empirical evidence either as direct discussion of specific applications, or as opinions based on direct experience of the reporter; with various reporters from different parts of the world, having to do with different types of applications; coming from individuals who may be available to furnish additional evidence if required; some of whom have already made significant contributions to the "Warfield Special Collection" described in Appendix 2.

| Chap 18 | The Education Sector | Lack of empirical evidence from sector | Empirical evidence either as direct discussion of specific applications, or as opinions based on direct experience of the reporter; with various reporters from different parts of the world, having to do with different types of applications; coming from individuals who may be available to furnish additional evidence if required; some of whom have already made significant contributions to the "Warfield Special Collection" described in Appendix 2. |

Part 5. **Systems Science**–expounding on the nature of systems science and speculating on a possible future for systems science

Division	Division Title	Negative(s) Attacked	Positive(s) Given
Chap 19	Systems Science	Underscoping the systems domain	More detailed discussion of systems science.
Chap 20	Reflections and Speculations	No clear future picture for systems science	Personalized discussion of a possible future for the systems domain.

Appendixes–adding depth and perspective in selected areas, as well as links to extensive additional resources

Division	Division Title	Negative(s) Attacked	Positive(s) Given
App 1	Gallery	Blindness to history	Pictures and descriptions of the older contributors and the living ones
App 2	The Warfield Special Collection	Blindness to history, Underscoping the systems domain	Showing the great variety inherent in the systems domain, and furnishing many examples of applications in great detail, including complete videos, DVDs, books, and reports.

App 3	Discovering Systems Science	Underscoping the systems domain; Monotonous bifurcation	Detailing the odyssey by means of which the systems science reported in this book was discovered.
App 4	Linguistic Adjustments	Linguistic Pollution	Explaining why the language that grew artificially in the systems domain is not serviceable, what some of the changes are that are required and why; and what terminology can replace the present language.
App 5	The Two Neutral Processes of Systems Science	Premature Quantification	Explains why only two processes are required for systems science, and why all the many other processes can be seen as possibly among those which would be shown to be required as an outcome of the application of systems science in specific problematic situations.
App 6	Statements, Themes Findings, Structure	Linguistic Pollution	Aggregative outlines of systems science portrayed in various ways, to show linkages.
App 7	Literacy in Structural Graphics	Linguistic Pollution	The importance of structural graphics in establishing discursivity in the domain of complexity.

ACKNOWLEDGMENTS

I thank journal publishers for permission to include papers which make up Appendixes 3 and 4 (details appearing in the Appendixes).

I thank Greg Thomas of Vanderbilt University for permission to include sketches of the following people in Appendix 1:

Peter Abelard, Aristotle, George Boole, Kenneth Boulding, Georg Cantor, Arthur Cayley, Alexander Christakis, Augustus De Morgan, Michael Foucault, Frank Harary, Friedrich Hayek, David Hilbert, Irving Janis, Harold Lasswell, Antoine Lavoisier, Gottfried Leibniz, Charles

Sanders Peirce, Alexander Pope, Bertrand Russell, Herbert A. Simon, and Sir Geoffrey Vickers.

I thank these people for sending photographs to me which I include in Appendix 1:

Henry C. Alberts, the son of W. Ross Ashby, Chris Argyris, Moses N. B. Ayiku,, the son of Bela H. Banathy, Surinder Batra, Benjamin Broome, Graciela Caffarel, Alda Roxana Cárdenas, G. S. Chandy, Andre Delbecq, George J. Friedman, Arthur D. Hall III, Koichi Haruna, F. Ross Janes, Carol Jeffrey, Wan Jiangping, Yang Jianmei, Iannis Kapelouzos, Robert McDonald, Jorge Rodriguez, Roy Smith, XueFeng Song, Scott M. Staley, Maria Carmen Temblador, Reynaldo Treviño, Bruce W. Tuckman, and Li Da Xu.

I thank the following people for extending written permission to show pictures of them in Appendix 1:

Graham Allison, Chris Argyris, Andre Delbecq, Anthony Downs, George J. Friedman, James G. March, Robert McDonald, George A. Miller, Carmen Moreno, Paul Rabinow, Jorge Rodriguez, Scott M. Staley, Maria Carmen Temblador, Reynaldo Trevino, Bruce W. Tuckman, and Li Da Xu.

I thank Ms. Denise Napolie and Ms. Carmen Moreno for helping to collect permissions for this manuscript.

Finally I thank all those whose kindnesses along the way helped me in countless ways to make this work possible.

John N. Warfield
Palm Harbor, Florida

Contents

List of Figures

Figures in Appendix 3: Discovering Systems Science

Part 1

Foundations: The Chapters

In this Part, I begin **(Chapter 1)** by insisting that **systems science must have unlimited scope**. Many of the methods that have been offered in the past as part of systems science are very specialized, hence one must reflect a doubt and a concern: doubt that what has been available to guide the resolution of complexity in problematic situations is up to the task; and concern that unless a neutral systems science is articulated, accepted, and applied, the number of such situations will continue to grow to the detriment of people everywhere. To ease this apparent conflict of perspective, it is best to distinguish a science from its domain. A neutral science, free of speciality restrictions, may call upon speciality methods when properly applied, calling them into its domain of application.

Systems science has the same foundations as all sciences, involving three components that are necessary for any science: the human being who creates the science, the thought which gives it form, and the language in which it is expressed.

Still, systems science necessarily must differ from other sciences. While sharing the foundations with those sciences, systems science must not veer off into a narrow territory; but rather **must be neutral**. The necessity of being neutral arises because of the unlimited scope of application that systems science must offer, if it is to fulfill the aspirations of offering utility in all problematic situations.

The three components of the foundation of all science are explored separately.

Human beings everywhere appear to share certain behavioral pathologies that are not removable **(Chapter 2)**. It is necessary to identify those pathologies and to design processes for systems science that circumvent these pathologies. If it were not possible to do so, there could not be any neutral systems science. As the behavioral pathologies demonstrate, circumvention demands that people work in groups. But when working in groups new pathologies accrue, because of the human surround arising from the presence of others. Then because of the complexity involved in problematic situations, organizations must be involved in financing activity required to discover and resolve the complexity. But the presence of organizations induces still more pathologies. Most, but not all, of these can be circumvented by following the pathways of systems science.

Substantial empirical evidence tells us that the way time is allocated in striving to resolve problematic situations is grossly defective. A much greater percentage of available time must be used for clarification in a facilitated group activity. The common assumption that one-way communication is highly effective is intolerable in working with complexity, as can readily and repeatedly be discovered by applying the Nominal Group Technique (NGT). Development of a language that is unique to each local problematic situation is necessary in order to enable effective local communication about that situation. The systems science must make this possible **(Chapter 3)**.

Thought about thought ("second-order thought") **(Chapter 4)** by "Thought Explorers", is factored into the design of processes for working with complexity through group activity, in a way that circumvents pathologies. The initial thematic approach of problemization is supported by more than ten years of study by Michel Foucault. Once generated, clarified, and filtered, through NGT, ideas can be organized using Interpretive Structural Modeling (ISM) which provides substantial computer assistance, both in sequencing the organizing processes and in organizing the large amounts of information that are generated.

The products of the Thought Explorers are traced through time in reverse order. It is easier to start at the end and work backwards, as this helps with the focus that is involved in tracing almost 2500 years of thought **(Chapter 5)**. I tell you the end result, and work backwards to the beginning with Aristotle.

The first initiative in moving toward the resolution of complexity through group work is to organize ideas emanating from the informed group. This work benefits from understanding how to control quality in structural modeling. Modeling the structure of a problematic situation incorporates and integrates results from the work of Ross Ashby, George Friedman, and Frank Harary. Each of them offers a theorem to guide the task of organizing ideas **(Chapter 6)**.

The processes that are carried out are much more effective when done in an environment designed specifically to enhance their effectiveness, and to allow a highly-experienced staff who carry out the processes to do their work effectively. The situation room design **(Chapter 7)** has been tested for more than two decades and found to be a very favorable environment for effective group work.

The Pictures

Throughout my long research on systems science and complexity, I have found it has helped me a great deal to spend literary time in the company of scholars from the past. For me it has not been enough merely to read the words. Today's computers and elegant library work enable us to see the images of these stalwart individuals, whose work was often carried out under more difficult conditions than we face today. So I have felt an urgent requirement to share this visual experience with those who read this book. For some of these pioneers, photographs are available. For others, sketches have been provided by Greg Thomas of Vanderbilt University. I refer to the photographs and sketches as "pictures" or "images".

For a time I felt that I would insert each image at an appropriate point in the book, but this proved to be just too difficult, and would have delayed the publication unduly. So I decided to put all pictures in a gallery in **Appendix 1**. In this gallery, I identify each pictured individual, assign a figure number to the picture, and give enough associated text to provide a context with the picture.

But it would be wrong merely to portray legacy scholars. There are also living scholars, many of them practitioners, whose work has been very important in helping to make possible this book. Rather than separate the pictures into two groups, I have just merged them into the one gallery, and have followed the same procedure of describing the individuals and indicating their relevance to the context of systems science.

Two of the Appendices are essentially the same as two of my prior publications. One (**Appendix 3**) presents the history of the development of my work. My debt to George J. Klir and his journal is acknowledged there. The other (**Appendix 4**) went into great detail on the critical linguistic difficulties that beset the systems community, and I have acknowledged my debt to the publishing journal there. These and other Appendices are intended to add depth to the Chapters, and have permitted me to keep some of the Chapters quite short in order to sustain continuity.

Chapter 1

Unlimited Scope of System Science

Like many scientists, the system scientist is driven by the irritation of **doubt**:

- **Doubt about methods.** I doubt that those methods which are promoted for use in working with systems are adequate to cope with the complexity inherent in most or any of the problematic situations of this era
- **Doubt about biases.** I doubt that it will be possible to overcome biases of people educated in academic disciplines, to enable them to accept the breadth and neutrality necessary for systems science, without which it must inevitably fall short in many critical problematic situations

Sir Geoffrey Vickers gave a metaphor that describes well the nature of the second doubt:

> *"Even the dogs may eat of the crumbs which fall from the rich man's table; and in these days, when the rich in knowledge eat such specialized food at such separate tables, only the dogs have a chance of a balanced diet."*

Sir Geoffrey Vickers (1965, 1983), *The Art of Judgment*, London: Chapman, Harper & Row, p11.

The Practitioner's Struggle. The practitioner who struggles with problematic situations in government, in industry, in the private sector, in education, is driven by **concern** for the potential consequences of allowing affairs to proceed along current lines, and about the inadequate apparatus with which to mount an organized effort to resolve the situation.

Of the various barriers to effective communication that are erected in our world, that between a system scientist and a practitioner may be as troublesome as any.

Language. Success in the development of an accepted science or a component of a science seems always to involve a narrower and narrower focus; and growing right along with the information gained is a specialized language that has to be developed as a previously-not-understood domain begins to be conquered. It has always been so. Leibniz (lawyer, turned librarian) emphasized the *necessity* of developing specialized languages to support communication merely among the denizens of a particular domain of science. Hilbert recognized that ordinary language, while inadequate to serve a domain of science would, nonetheless, form an intermediate linguistic arena between practitioner and scientist.

A Requirement for the Systems Scientist. But taking these ideas at face value, a difficulty remains. To the extent that developments in science have potential for the systems practitioner, the local practitioner will also need a specialized language as will the various cooperating individuals and groups. The local practitioner's language, untutored in the ways of the science, and frequently foreign to the system scientist, requires winnowing and organizing in order to place the fragments of information stemming from a particular venue into a form where systems science can offer a way to gain insight into the local problematic situation. It is unreasonable to expect that this activity can proceed unless the systems scientist offers a process that will make it happen, and will achieve the desired result. **The systems scientist must enable the practitioner to construct a local language that is adequate to describe and diagnose the local problematic situation.**

Another Requirement for the Systems Scientist. The practitioner needs a high-quality local language. But the systems scientist can hardly claim to have a meritorious product unless it is possible to demonstrate its value to practitioners. This means that the language of the local practitioner, weakly suited even to communication among fellow practitioners, must also become friendly to the language of the systems scientist. It is unreasonable to expect that this activity can proceed without the benefit of a process to make it happen—a process that the systems scientist must provide. **While helping the practitioner to develop a high quality local language, the systems scientist must enable a tight connection between the local language and those algorithms of systems science that are essential to assist the practitioner to structure the local problematic situation.**

Biased and Neutral Science. Virtually any science can be said to be biased in the sense that it pertains to a particular sphere, and only to a particular sphere. It is this bias, this focus, that ultimately makes the science useful to a practitioner; and allows the work of the practitioner to help test and hone the science. Systems science, on the other hand, is expected to be applicable to virtually *any* problematic situation. Three consequences flow from this:

- Systems science cannot be biased; it must be **neutral**
- But a neutral science alone can hardly be expected to be **sufficient** to resolve most or perhaps any problematic situation, hence
- Systems science must be powerful in bringing the state of an exploration to the point where the specific needs for specialized methods are identified and, if such methods are not available, to specify the requirements for their development, in order to be useful

If the application of systems science reveals the need for further exploration in a biased domain, it serves that domain by posing a scientific challenge. If the application of systems science clarifies adequately how existing science can be applied, it serves the practitioner. If, in the application of systems science, the practitioner identifies weaknesses in the methods drawn from systems science, the practitioner thereby offers insights to help develop systems science more fully.

Having said these things, obvious questions arise: what constitutes a neutral science? If a neutral science is formed from components, must these components be neutral? From what sources, if any, can neutral components arise? These must be among the key concerns of the systems scientist. To speak to these concerns, it is appropriate to ask whether there can be any overlap between systems science and any other science, or whether systems science is entirely unique with nothing in common with other sciences.

A very common way of describing a science is to say that the scientist begins with a hypothesis, devises a means to test it and, if the hypothesis stands up to this test, and to any other tests that may be posed as time passes, the hypothesis joins other parts of the science until such time (if ever) that it may be invalidated by experiment or in practice. This common description, while acceptable, is not sufficient to respond to the key concerns of the systems scientist.

Common Foundations of All Science: The Fundamental Triangle. Three components form the foundations of **any** science whether it be biased or neutral. These are:

- **The Human Being** (creative, but fallible) who constructs the science
- **Thought** (the principal activity of the human being in constructing the science)
- **Language** (the means whereby the scientist documents the findings that make up the science)

I will strive to show that whatever may be involved in resolving a problematic situation will necessarily be a derivative (i.e., have foundational roots in) one or more of these three components. This is not a terribly difficult thing to show, since the same foundations also apply to the local practitioner. But a significant distinction must be made. Unless the three foundations are assiduously developed to form a systems science, the practitioner will be left to operate his ship without a rudder, placing upon the practitioner the requirement to reinvent a kind of localized science for every localized problematic situation. This is an untenable situation for the local practitioner who is usually under fire and should be well-served by systems science so that all available time and resources can be dedicated to the local situation.

Derivatives

As suggested by Michel Foucault, and emphasized by the anthropologist Paul Rabinow, the human sciences have always been difficult to discuss because of the difficulty in constructing for them a language having adequate discursivity. Perhaps this is partly because of long strings of dependency which are very difficult to describe and remember using only prose. One concept that seems not to have been applied to that purpose is the "derivative". To introduce this idea, I begin with the mathematical derivative, proceed to the financial derivative, and then apply the term by analogy to systems science in a way that can be applied also to any of the human sciences.

The Derivative in Mathematics. The mathematical concept of derivative arises in the calculus of continuous functions. If a function f of a single variable x, i.e., $f(x)$ is continuous at some point, then it is possible to find, at that point, a derivative of the function. For example, if $f(x) = x$, then the derivative at that point is $f'(x) = 1$ which, for this particular function, is valid at every point.

It is also possible to find the derivative of the derivative, i.e., the second derivative of $f(x)$. For the example with $f(x) = x$, the second derivative is $f''(x) = 0$.

While the derivative can be discussed without any graphical reference, it is often taught to students by noting that the first derivative is the slope of the curve of $f(x)$ at a particular point, and the second derivative is the slope of the slope at that point. For our example, the first derivative is 1 at all points and the second derivative is zero at all points. The graph of $f(x)$ is a straight line, so the slope is constant, and the slope of the slope is constant.

Derivatives of all higher orders also exist for our example, and are all equal to zero.

The Derivative in Financial Markets. In the past few decades, the concept of derivative has come to play a major role in financial markets. While perhaps not often so imagined, the financial derivative has much in common with the mathematical derivative. Just as the mathematical derivative depends on another variable that we might call the "base" of the derivative, so does the financial derivative. For example, a "wheat future" can be purchased that derives its value from the value of wheat, a commodity, which might be called the "base" of the derivative. In financial markets, some derivatives are based in a single commodity, while others are based in bundles of commodities or, more generally, bundles of securities. One may purchase a derivative based on the future of the Standard and Poor's Average, the latter being a measure of the value of a bundle of securities.

The Derivative in Systems Science. I have indicated that all sciences have three foundations in common, these being the human being, thought, and language. I will now proceed directly to a discussion of derivatives of each of these. Each will serve as the base for a first derivative. To be a first derivative, the topic must be directly connected conceptually to the base. Hopefully this concept of direct connection will be clear from the examples.

First Derivatives of the Human Being. I believe that almost no one will doubt that a human being exhibits both creativity and fallibility (and sometimes both of them in concert). Since these are both attributes of the human being, they are examples of first derivatives.

Second Derivatives of the Human Being. An example of a second derivative of the human being would be Da Vinci's *Mona Lisa*. It is not a first derivative, because it is not a component of Da Vinci's corpus; but it is a product of the creativity of Da Vinci and actions of Da Vinci, and thus becomes a second derivative. One test to establish that it is a second derivative of Da Vinci is to show first that it required Da Vinci himself in order to create it and second that it would not have been created if Da Vinci had not been a creative artist. While this form of reasoning may not have the absolute precision of the mathematical and financial forms of derivative, it seems that it certainly passes muster in terms of what might be considered as somewhat looser language that is typical of the human sciences.

First Derivatives of Language. I believe that most would agree that language is a vehicle both for communication and mis-communication. This being the case, both of these are first derivatives of language.

Second Derivatives of Language. Actions that ensue as a direct consequence of a communication or a mis-communication can be thought of as second derivatives of language.

First Derivatives of Thought. If thought is seen as a process founded in biology or physiology, then an idea could be seen as a first derivative of thought. Perhaps an idea is the generic first derivative, but since ideas could be categorized into a variety of types, each type could be thought of as a first derivative of thought.

Second Derivatives of Thought. In our work with groups, ideas often are followed by silent writing, where the person who generated the idea writes it on paper to help preserve and edit it. It is also often true that ideas are voiced, as in "brainstorming". These ideas, once expressed, become second derivatives of thought, and first derivatives of the mental operations that produced them in the body.

Derivatives as Concepts in Process Design. If one sets out deliberately to use these ideas of derivatives of the three foundation concepts in process design, very early in the work it must be imagined that there is a question of how far the derivatives of those three ideas can go. I have illustrated first derivatives and second derivatives of each of them. Can there be third derivatives, fourth derivatives, fifth derivatives, and so on? In the mathematical example, once the second derivative was reached, all higher-order derivatives had the same value; but this was only because of the simple nature of the base that was chosen. A term that might be used to discuss this subject in overview is "structural length".

If a structural length is 7 this would mean that, beginning with one or more of the foundations as a base, there would follow first, second, third, fourth, fifth, sixth, and seventh derivatives. The second would be the first derivative of the first. The third would be the first derivative of the second, and so on. Reasoning in this way, one may begin to imagine the difficulties involved in striving to delineate for systems science and, for the human sciences, structural schemes of unknown length.

The situation just introduced can become more complicated rather quickly. Suppose that one discovers a first derivative of the combination of thought and language; or of mis-communication and voiced thought, and so on. The possibility of generalizing to include all combinations may be apparent, but the desirability of trying to do so with routine tools may be overwhelming.

Abelard's Formulation of Inference. In his scholarly investigations, Bochenski discovered an Abelard formulation of inference as follows:

> *"Whatever follows from the consequent follows also from the antecedent"*

The base, in this formulation, is implied. The implied base has a consequent. And the implied base has an antecedent. Furthermore, if the consequent implies something, so does the antecedent. And, by implication, so does the base.

Placing these ideas in the language of derivatives:
The base is a first derivative of its antecedent. The consequent is a first derivative of the base. The consequent is a second derivative of the antecedent. There is a third derivative of the antecedent, which is the second derivative of the base, and is the first derivative of the consequent, and it is implied by any of the three.

I have chosen here to mix together the concepts of derivatives and inference. This has been done deliberately in anticipation of the idea that, **whenever structural lengths exceed what might be thought of as reasonable values for analysis or design, it could be extremely helpful or even essential to take advantage of inference in developing the structures of problematic situations.**

To connect derivatives of the Fundamental Triangle to systems science and, ultimately, to the practitioner, each of the components of the Fundamental Triangle must be explored in turn.

The use of the computer to develop structural models is equivalent to finding the various derivatives of more basic concepts. That this is possible comes about by following the results of persons who have assiduously studied human thought, as will be shown in later Chapters in this work.

Chapter 2

The Human Being (Creative and Fallible)

Systems science must be neutral. Virtually all who call themselves systems scientists, or who identify others as systems scientists, passed at an earlier time through the surrounds of some biased academic discipline that has evolved inwardly, becoming more and more specialized and self-perpetuating in the hands of academia; where hope for individual and collective survival rests largely upon adherence to a narrowing, if deepening, body of literature that is offered as scientific; but often is devoid of the kind of empirical evidence that would lend credence to the contents of the archives.

The human being who works within the vineyard of the biased science must be creative to continue to develop material that will be declared suitable for publication in the face of a steadily enlarging literature.

But I am not concerned here with human creativity so much as with human fallibility. The former attribute must return to my text eventually, in the form of a participant in resolution of complexity in local problematic situations. But for now it is fallibility that will be the focus of interest.

Systems science must incorporate provisions that on the one hand recognize fallibility of the human being and on the other hand incorporate means of overcoming that fallibility. To lay the groundwork for achieving this end, two requirements from **Chapter 1** must be recalled. For the sake of facilitating discussion, I will now begin to label requirements as constraints on the systems scientist and, hence, on systems science.

Constraint 1. Local Language Construction. The systems scientist must enable the practitioner to construct a local language that is adequate to describe and diagnose the local problematic situation when embedded in an appropriate enabling process.

Constraint 2. Connecting Local Construction to Algorithms of Systems Science. While helping the practitioner to develop a high quality local language, the systems scientist must enable a tight connection between the local language and those algorithms of systems science that are essential to assist local practitioners to structure the local problematic situation.

In recognition of the fallibility both of systems scientists and of local practitioners, the methods applied to describing the local situation should, on the one hand, make provision for honing the local language rather than merely accepting it as it arises from fallible human beings and, on the other hand, should incorporate quality-control discoveries that relate to working with complexity, whether engaged in description or design, and not simply accept as inviolate recommendations emanating from systems scholars.

In order to achieve these desirable results, it is necessary to understand more about the fallibility of the human being and, especially, as it is manifested when working with complexity. While complexity itself is the subject of a variety of definitions, at this point in my manuscript I will be content with saying that it involves many different concepts and relationships, and those attributes of the human being that become critical when working with the problematic situation are the ones that I must now discuss.

Behavioral Pathologies

A behavioral pathology, as described here, is some human condition, generally beyond the powers of the human being, working alone, to overcome. It cannot be eliminated. It is supposed that a pathology can be overcome, but that some kind of deliberate action is required to overcome it. Such an action will normally have to be based in the kind of evidence that comes from behavioral science with mutually supportive theory and empirical evidence.

I will discuss pathologies as they may relate to one person, to several persons in a group, and to collections of individuals in organizations larger than what we normally think of as a group. One must anticipate that whatever pathologies are present in the individual will accompany that individual into a group where the collective pathologies of the members may take hold. One must also anticipate that action in a group will demonstrate pathologies merely because the group is acting together in some way; and that individual pathologies may be uncovered in group work that could not be seen in the absence of means of comparison that arise from group action.

It must also be supposed that membership by an individual in an organization can induce pathologies in the individual that could not be seen in the absence of means of comparison that arise from what goes on in the organization.

While all of the pathologies I will discuss are manifested in the individual, it is both convenient and conducive to easier reading to describe these pathologies as follows:

- **Individual Pathologies:** Pathologies that are detectable in an individual, without regard to the surround of the individual; not depending upon any local conditions, but arising out of either the history of the individual or the physiology of the individual. These pathologies are found to arise in the entire human population. If there are instances where a particular individual lacks these pathologies, we do not expect such instances to arise sufficiently often to treat them other than as common to the human race. Please see Appendix 1: Gallery, for pictures of persons who provided insights into individual behavioral pathologies.

- **Group Pathologies:** Pathologies affecting individual behavior, which can only take place when the individual is a member of an interacting group of people (and which do not always necessarily take place, but are sufficiently commonplace to suppose that any group can exhibit them). Please see Appendix 1: Gallery, for pictures of persons who provided insights into group behavioral pathologies.

- **Organization Pathologies:** Pathologies affecting individual behavior, which can only take place when the individual is a member of an organization (normally thought of as larger than a group, with actions going on that sometimes involve the individual in direct interaction, but in other times go on without individual participation of the affected individual). Please see Appendix 1: Gallery, for pictures of persons who provided insights into organization behavioral pathologies.

It is remarkable that much, if not most, existing treatises on systems ignore or merely mention these pathologies in passing, without discussing the implications of them for either the development of systems science, or for the work of practitioners. In most instances involving formal attacks on local problematic situations, all of these pathologies are found in the surround of the practitioner.

I shall now discuss each of these pathologies in turn, keeping in mind that all types are found in the organization; two of the three are found in groups; and all of them affect individual behavior, whether in constructing systems science (or any other kind of science) or practicing systems science (or any other science) in striving to resolve complexity in local problematic situations.

Individual Pathologies

Keeping in mind that individual pathologies inhere to the individual whether alone, in a group, or in an organization, we identify just two pathologies.

Instinct for Survival. The instinct for survival is scarcely something that needs to be pointed out. Yet it is worthwhile to recognize it because of the impact it may have on individual behavior when the individual is working in a group or organizational setting. I suspect that the impact of this pathology can often be annulled if the individual has faith that whatever the individual is involved in can be dealt with adequately by institutional action. If, however, the individual lacks faith in the institution, this instinct will surface and be reflected in whatever action the individual may take.

Processing Limit (the "Magical Number"). It is widely accepted that the individual can only cope with a small number of ideas at a time. This limitation has been called the "Magical Number". Different authors have said that this number is "seven, plus or minus two", "nearer five than seven", and "three, plus or minus zero". Whatever it may be, within these numerical limits, it has a profound implication for systems science. Any involvement of an individual in developing systems science that involves many variables should be regarded as suspect in the absence of stated quality controls on the processes that are used. A similar caution must also be accepted for practitioners, whether in a leadership role or in a subordinate role.

These two individual pathologies focus upon a new constraint for systems science.

Constraint 3. Overcoming the Individual Behavioral Pathologies. In its construction, systems science should be so designed as to overcome the impact of the Individual Behavioral Pathologies.

As I proceed, I will focus first upon how these limits affect two types of activity: **description** of a problematic situation, and **design** of a system for resolving that situation. Later I will describe how these pathologies are overcome.

Group Pathologies

Keeping in mind that individual pathologies are portable, and go along with the individual who interacts with a group, three group pathologies that contribute to fallibility can be discussed: clanthink, groupthink, and spreadthink.

Clanthink. I suppose the best-known example of Clanthink is belief in a flat earth. Another would be that taking a significant amount of blood from a patient will heal the patient. Clanthink refers to a situation where everyone in a group believes the same thing, and that same thing is wrong. This is a group pathology that does not surface often, which makes it all the more important to recognize that it might be active. One of the most powerful ways to annul the impact of Clanthink is to make it possible for a group to discover on their own that a universally-held belief is incorrect.

Groupthink. Groupthink has become so prominent in the social sciences that many who have heard the name tend to apply it indiscriminately as though it simply means what a group thinks, as if there could be such a thing. Two types of excellent discussions of Groupthink appear in the literature.

- Literature that explains the many dimensions of Groupthink
- Literature that discusses case studies of Groupthink in action

For our purposes, it is sufficient to understand that it is a phenomenon wherein people exhibit unanimous agreement in spite of contrary facts pointing to another conclusion: facts that may be known, in part, or in entirety to each of the members of the group. An Internet search to find more information about Groupthink will encounter the name of Irving Janis, who has described it in detail and several prominent instances where it was exhibited in high-profile situations, including the Bay of Pigs and the Challenger disasters.

Spreadthink. Spreadthink is not nearly as well known as Clanthink or Groupthink. It is, however, just as prevalent, and just as important in understanding group processes. It refers to a condition where every member of a group assesses differently from others the relative importance of those problems that have been uncovered as part of a problematic situation.

The Collective Concern. Keeping in mind that all members of a group are subject to the Individual Pathologies cited previously, now a triple threat to effective work by a group is encountered in the aggregate form of Clanthink, Groupthink, and Spreadthink. This enables us to state a fourth constraint on systems science.

Constraint 4. Overcoming the Three Group Pathologies. The products of a group potentially should be suspect from the impact of any of the behavioral pathologies discussed so far. Even if systems science has made it possible to overcome the impact of the Individual Behavioral Pathologies, neglect of the three Group Pathologies will almost certainly assure that group products will be unsatisfactory.

As I proceed, I will describe the consequences of ignoring these pathologies and a way in which they may be overcome through application of a sound systems science.

Organizational Pathologies

Keeping in mind that both the Individual Pathologies and the Group Pathologies are inherently part of the pathologies that are active in organizations, additional pathologies arise in the organization. Many of these have been discussed at length by Anthony Downs, and will not be repeated here. One pathology that is critical to working with complexity in problematic situations is found in the unwillingness of top managers to accept high-quality studies emanating from lower levels in the organization. Much of this can be attributed to a common component in the education of high-level managers, in which "the decision maker" is prominent. It is rare that such education assigns to high-level managers these functions:

- **Enabling Effective Practices in Subordinates.** As the complexity in situations grows, a point is reached where the organization must change its practices to accommodate the demands of complexity. These changes include installing infrastructure that has been demonstrated to be highly effective in enabling effective practices in small group activity—practices about which the highest-level executives display inconsistent views. These changes also involve a need for staff (whether in-house or contracted) that are educated in effective participatory processes for resolving complexity—means that are tailored to overcome the Individual and Group Pathologies.

- **Accepting Results from Subordinates Who Have Used Effective Practices.** Once the efficacy of such processes has been highlighted in the organization, high-level management typically resorts to the use of such processes when they are unable to arrive at sound strategies or activities; but, perhaps in order to avoid an appearance of inadequacy, may choose to reshape, rather than accept, those products that have been developed from a sound base in systems science.

Exploring the Possibilities

Is it possible to overcome the collective impact of these pathologies? What are the resources that hold opportunities to overcome them? These questions drive the content of succeeding chapters, as the possibility of overcoming them in aggregate is explored. I can tell you now that all of these pathologies have already been demonstrated to be correctable through the application of systems science as presented in this work, with the exception of the organizational pathology associated with arrogance and non-receptivity at the highest level of the organization.

The latter presumably is correctable only through the exercise of power at high levels in the organization to remove executives who are not aware of their own limitations, as they make decisions that are indifferent to their own behavioral pathologies.

Chapter 3

Language (Overpromising, Underperforming)

In the mid-1970s, three faculty members, then at Kent State University, designed a process which they called the Nominal Group Technique (NGT), with the goal of enhancing the quality of the products of group interaction. In observing many applications of NGT with many different groups working on many different local issues, I have learned how ineffective group communication is when allowed to flow in an undisciplined way, whenever the subject is difficult. When NGT is applied to assist in moving toward an ultimate resolution of a problematic situation, it offers significant opportunity for learning along the way about group process, as well as offering an opportunity to understand better the problematic situation.

The learning about group process has been made possible by the well-designed sequence in which NGT is carried out. Before the group activity begins, a question is formulated to which the members of the group are expected to respond. This question is formulated in an effort to satisfy these conditions:

- **Solicit Individual Responses.** Engender replies from each member of the group that reflect that member's response to the question
- **Focus Responses Toward Action.** Get replies that are not so general as to preclude any definition of appropriate action in response to the problematic situation
- **Focus Responses Toward the Context.** Get replies that are not so remotely connected to the problematic situation that their significance would pale in comparison with other replies

- **Promote Insight, in Aggregate.** In aggregate, enable a much better understanding of the problematic situation than any participant could have had before the NGT was applied
- **Promote Comprehensiveness of Aggregate Response.** If it should turn out that a system design proved to be feasible, to be sufficiently representative in aggregate of the situation, that some design based on what is uncovered during the use of NGT could be sufficiently responsive to the situation

When compared with other ways of eliciting beliefs from members of a group, NGT proves to be superior for several reasons, but this is not the place to describe in detail all of the merits or demerits of NGT. Instead I focus here upon the linguistic aspects of the application of NGT.

Initially, each member of the group is asked to respond silently to the triggering question, by writing responses on paper. When all members cease writing, a round-robin exercise is carried out by a group facilitator, in which each individual, in turn, states one response which is then written on a flip-chart page, and eventually posted on the wall, where it is in sight continuously to the group. Members sometimes attempt to clarify a response as it is offered, but this attempt is postponed by the facilitator until it can be done systematically for all responses.

Following the posting of all the responses on the wall, the next step in NGT is known as the "clarification" step. In clarification, each of the previously-offered ideas is clarified, one by one. During this clarification section of NGT, it always becomes abundantly clear that confusion concerning what the originator meant is very common. Sometimes even the originator of an idea becomes confused about the idea. While it often takes only about 30 minutes to generate and post all of the ideas, it typically requires 3 hours or so to clarify all of the ideas. It is very common, when an individual is called upon to clarify an idea the individual says "This one surely is very clear", only to find that someone else in the group asserts the contrary.

Having observed many such NGT sessions, I can say that it is only a slight exaggeration to say that participants "don't know what they are talking about", even though they are almost always chosen because of highly-relevant experience and what is regarded as deep knowledge about aspects of the problematic situation.

The connection to language is inescapable. Language does not have the property most commonly attributed to it of being a good vehicle for communication–at least not without significant exchanges back and forth between the generator of the concept and the recipient of the concept.

Perhaps the most important conclusion that can be reached is that, whenever a small group of "experts" is convened to discuss a problematic situation, and whenever that group proceeds with unregulated discussion, the opportunity for very significant misunderstanding permeates the activity; and the likelihood of misinterpreting what was said as though it were some kind of semi-consensus is high.

Inescapably, then, one finds that in any group activity where a problematic situation is to be discussed, the use of NGT will reveal many mis-communications. Ultimately, it will provide a collection of clarified responses that offer information suitable for designing a corrective system which, if implemented, could resolve the problematic situation in a way that would be viewed as favorable by local practitioners.

Could the results of an NGT be taken as the basis for resolution of the problematic situation? My answer is "not until further work is done, which structures the elements that are accrued through the use of NGT." To help explain this view, I call on some ideas from the late Sir Geoffrey Vickers. In his book titled *Human Systems are Different*, Vickers provides the following thoughts:

- **Systems.** Systems "consist of relationships...that are more basic than the entities related." In fact, they are "nets of relations which are sustained through time...by a process of regulation." "Systems are...tools of understanding devised by human minds for understanding situations, including situations in which human beings appear as constituents."

- **Situation.** The concept of "system" must include "the minimum number of relationships needed to constitute the situation which is to be understood." This "is defined by its relevance to the *concern* of some human minds."

If one accepts these ideas, the work to be done following the use of NGT should appear clearly: the ideas developed through NGT should be structured to display key relationships among the members. This is not to say that NGT develops no relationships; but rather that NGT develops a particular kind of relationship, which can be firmly stated as follows:

"x **is a response to** question y"

where y is the specific question (the "triggering question") to which the participants in the NGT session responded, and x refers to any response that remains (often in edited form) following the completion of the clarification session of NGT. I have highlighted the relationship in order to introduce a style of writing that emphasizes the relationship more than the elements being related. Whether this is a universally important idea is not the point; what **is** the point is that the relationship is often assigned a much lower level of attention than the elements being related. **At the very least, the relationship should have as much attention as the elements being related.**

What Kind of Question? What Kind of Response?

For about three decades, or almost from the time NGT was published, my colleagues and I have been using two prototypical triggering questions for NGT. Here is the most prominent question type that is asked:

"What problems do you see that lie ahead in the
problematic situation Y?"

Available data show that the average number of problems identified by those who respond to this question is around 70. The smallest number ever noted is 36. The largest number recorded for a single group was around 160. With a single problematic situation that was attacked intermittently by different groups over a 5-year period, a total of 678 problems was identified. If one is reminded of the behavioral pathologies, i.e., the limits on the ability of human beings to cope with such large numbers, one surely will understand why computer assistance in **structuring** such large numbers of problems is not merely desirable, but absolutely essential. It was to help groups structure such large numbers that I developed a computer-assisted method called Interpretive Structural Modeling (ISM). When the sequence NGT, followed by ISM, is used, a high-quality structural type is typically developed by an informed group.

The use of ISM to structure problematic situations will be discussed in Chapter 4 but the linguistic aspects of this usage can be discussed now. In using ISM a typical question that would be put before the group is:

Will problem x **significantly aggravate** problem y?

Here x and y would be a selected pair of problems accrued from the use of NGT. Note that the relationship "significantly aggravates" asks the members of the group to consider whether some problem, say y, is made more intense (worse) by the presence of problem x.

One should recall that a problem is a human construct, stemming from an individual's aggregate experience with a problematic situation. When ISM is carried out following NGT, the two problems involved in the question are pretty well understood as a result of the clarification section of NGT. Nonetheless it has been found in experience that there is some small occurrence where the comparison of two elements (problems or other elements) invokes ideas about the elements themselves that may require still further clarification. This type of event merely reinforces the previous remarks about the poor quality of human communication.

The term "polysemy" does not appear often in English texts. It means a word or phrase that has multiple meanings. The derivation of the word from "poly" and "semantics" is probably evident. While this phenomenon of language is often the basis for comic strips, it is seldom the cause of confusion in NGT or ISM. Rather the cause seems to lie in the different life experiences of human beings; so that one person calls upon one life experience to construe a meaning different from that construed by another person. It is a fact that ordinary communication is beset with polysemys.

ISM can be seen as a kind of linguistic honing process on the understandings developed in the clarification session of NGT. While this is important in itself, other attributes of ISM are the most notable, as will be discussed in **Chapter 4**.

One might ask whether usage of NGT and ISM is particularly suited to one culture, but not suited to other cultures. The combination of NGT and ISM within a larger process cluster called "Interactive Management (IM)" has been used in numerous countries on a wide variety of problematic situations, with software written in different languages. Experience has shown that it is safe to assume that virtually everything said about IM is portable from one culture to another. Moreover the use of the computer is especially appreciated by groups that have made a practice of consensus-seeking through dialog, because this use makes much more efficient a practice that was already highly-valued for its political utility, in spite of its often lengthy discussions.

While the interpretation of individual terms is greatly enhanced in quality by the use of NGT and, in a somewhat augmented way by the use of ISM, it is the structural benefit obtained from the use of ISM that is most notable and most unique in the world of problematic situations. The use of ISM will be discussed under the heading of "Second-Order Thought". A word of explanation is in order. Almost all of science and, for that matter, almost all of human thought seems to be "thought about x" where the one "value" assumed by x is NOT thought itself. If we say that "thought about x" can be categorized either as first-order thought or as second-order thought; where first-order thought is the common usage of thought; the relatively unfamiliar and less common idea of thought about thought itself may justifiably be called "second order thought."

Second-order thought becomes important as a component of systems science. As has already been indicated, one of the three components of all science is thought. Anything that can be shown to enhance the quality of thought deserves attention in all of the sciences, and certainly deserves it in systems science where the neutrality of second-order thought commends itself to our concept of neutral science.

Systems scientists may now be grateful to those hardy pioneers who devoted many years of their lives to the study of thought about thought. I have identified the most prominent of these, and noted their contributions. Their pictures appear in the Gallery, **Appendix 1**, along with brief descriptions of their contributions.

Chapter 4

Second-Order Thought
(The Stuff Reason is Made of)

I suppose that anyone who ridiculed Sir Isaac Newton's calculus because of his views of the occult would hardly be taken seriously. Yet I have personally encountered several times the strange phenomenon of denying or downplaying Aristotle's contributions to logic and linguistics on the grounds that he was a male chauvinist. Aristotle's concept of science was recently highlighted in a publication of the Center for Disease Control and Prevention (CDC) in (Atlanta, Georgia):

> *"Aristotle repeatedly pointed out that his predecessors' work and conclusions were often marred by insufficient observation. He himself, after a remarkable analysis of the reproduction of bees, states that he cannot arrive at certain conclusions because 'the facts have not yet been sufficiently ascertained. And if at any future time they are ascertained, then credence must be given to the direct evidence rather than to the theories; and to the theories also, provided that the results which they show agree with what is observed.' This, indeed, is the principle upon which his work is based. It is also the definition of the scientific method, which was later broadened in scope, especially by Bacon, and by and large constitutes the basis of the scientific method we practice today. Note the subtle yet critical point: Aristotle does not say 'the results prove the theory,' but 'the results agree with the observations.' Today, we take this reasoning for granted, that science proceeds and progresses not by proving hypotheses, but by disproving them. If the*

observations do not agree with a hypothesis, we shelve it; if it does agree with a high enough level of certainty and consistent repetition of the results, we accept it. We can never prove it."

N. C. Myrianthopoulos (2000) *The Philosophic Origins of Science and the Evolution of the Two Cultures*, CDC 6(1), 80.

Ironically, in using ISM to structure a problematic situation, one is using beliefs based upon past experience to presume the continuation of relationships among constituent problems unless some action is taken to moderate or eliminate those problems.   But as Aristotle's thought illustrates, one can only use evidence that is at hand.   There are some who have argued in favor of muddling through.   There is even a term "dynamic programming" to represent the idea that one progresses step by step, always observing the result of the most recent step before undertaking a new step.   But even this idea, which may be used as an argument to counter planning, does not foreclose the utility of planning. Planning, in its most excellent sense, involves an understanding of relationships that are observed in the problematic situation.

To enable relationships among a large number of elements to be studied systematically, learning along the way, I developed a computer-assisted process for structuring.   Aided by a group facilitator, a group of well-informed participants responds to a steady stream of computer-generated questions, each having to do with how a computer-selected pair of elements is related in a way chosen to focus the dialog.

I first announced ISM in a publication in 1974.   In that year, a software program became available for using the process on a mainframe.   It was put to work immediately in two different urban settings.   Since then it has been applied frequently in many settings around the world.   This is not the place to dwell on the history of its successful use, since that subject has been dealt with frequently in literature that can be discovered by using the search engines of the Internet. Instead the focus in this Chapter shall be on the use of formal logic, the major extension of Aristotle's syllogism to link many syllogisms in one structure, and the necessity of this kind of help in resolving problematic situations.

Videotape and DVD records of entire ISM applications are available in the George Mason University Fenwick Library (see Appendix 3 for links). (The reader who is computer-oriented may find it useful at this point to download an old software program for ISM, made available free on the Internet along with a User Guide. This reader is forewarned that the program is not user-friendly and that it requires the DOS operating system. These defects are partly overcome by following the detailed examples in the User Guide. For those who are interested, http://www.gmu.edu/departments/t-iasis offers a locale from which the software and User Guide may be downloaded, at least at this writing.)

The Essence of the ISM Process

The observer who has never seen an ISM process underway with a group, would probably describe it this way: A group of people sits around a table with a large screen before them. A computer that holds the problems previously clarified by the group now causes a question to appear on a wall or screen before the group. An example of the **form** of such a question is:

Does problem x *significantly aggravate* problem y?

where x and y are two problems from the set of problems that has been saved in the computer and "significantly aggravate" is the relationship chosen for model construction. After this question appears, some members may say "yes" and some may say "no", while others may appear to be lost in thought. The facilitator encourages discussion if there is no consensus. Occasionally a problem statement may be edited as a result of the discussion, to make sure that the integrity of the vote is not compromised by inadequate semantic construction. After the discussion has ended, the facilitator calls for a "yes" or "no" vote on the question. The majority vote is entered in the computer. (A tie vote corresponds to a "no".)

Immediately another question of the same form appears. The process of group discussion is repeated, and a vote is taken, with the majority vote entered in the computer. This process continues until such time as the computer recognizes that all the questions that are required by the ISM algorithm have been asked, discussed if necessary, and voted on by the group.

The observer will note that the supporting staff will then tabulate the voting results and display them to the group. The staff will provide a written record of what transpired later.

The Problematique. The staff will develop and display the structure corresponding to the group's majority votes on the wall of the room, with each problem statement printed in very large font on standard size paper, and with lines that house arrows joining the individual bits of paper, so that it is possible to inspect the large structural model and see which problems aggravate other problems. The description just given yields a structural type called a "problematique".

The Problems Field. If some other relationship is chosen, a different type of structure can be produced. One question type that is commonly used is:

Is problem x *in the same category as* problem y?

This question is used to produce what is called a "Problems Field", in which the problems are sorted into categories, with the categories later being named. This process facilitates two-level discussions of the problems. Sometimes the categories are sorted into still higher-level categories called "areas". This process facilitates three-level discussions. In one project that advanced intermittently over a period of five years, the total number of problems that survived the NGT processes was 678. These problems were sorted into 20 categories. The categories were sorted into 6 areas. In this way, a highly-organized structural model was created, which not only facilitated discussion but enabled major correlation between higher-level categories and organizational components to be seen. For example, one person who is responsible for an area may also be seen to be responsible for, e.g., six categories, which encompass, e.g., two-hundred problems. Through this type of structure, an organization gains substantial transparency for management purposes.

While it is true that problems change with time (hopefully being eliminated in significant part because of the insights that enabled corrective measures to be applied), one suspects that the categories and areas do not change very often. In any case, once displayed prominently, occasional upgrades to the structure can be made, normally without further use of ISM.

The Options Field.

Another type of question that is commonly used is:

Is option x, *if carried out, likely to assist in carrying out* option y?

This type of question would be used after a group has produced and internalized a problematique and a problems field. For each category in the problems field, the group could use NGT to generate and clarify options that are responsive to that particular category of problem. This enables an Options Field to be created that is in correspondence with the Problems Field. By this means, continuity is achieved between the analysis of the situation and the initiation of the synthesis that is intended to culminate in the resolution of the situation.

At that point, questions of how well some options would help other options can arise, as the answers will help determine which options are finally chosen for action.

Unknowns and Variables

Analysts are accustomed to working with applications of mathematics in which the number of variables or unknowns is between one and seven. There are in existence econometric models for which the number is in the thousands, and I am sure that there are other models with the numbers in the thousands, but these models do not and cannot exhibit any transparency.   These models typically involve the production of numbers.

As the late Richard Hamming, a mathematician at the late Bell Telephone Laboratories remarked "the purpose of computing is insight, not numbers". There is little evidence that the numbers flowing from such models produce insight, although it is quite likely that decisions are made based on the algorithms used, and involving the numbers that are obtained from using the models. I call models of this type numerant models and I have adopted the British term "numeracy" to represent people who are comfortable in using numbers. It is the numerical partner to the common term "literacy".

I have mentioned numeracy and numerant models, in order to contrast these familiar subjects with the type of model created by using ISM. The models created with ISM are called structural models. The function of ISM is to enable persons who have partial informed belief about problematic situations to provide order to those problematic situations and, in turn, to gain very substantial insight into those situations—insight sufficient to enable effective designs to be produced and implemented.

In a typical application of ISM the number of unknowns will range from a few hundred up to several thousand. Unlike the unknowns in numerant models, the unknowns in structural models are logic variables which correspond to "yes" or "no", because they represent answers to questions that can be answered in one of those two ways. Those familiar with Boolean algebra will probably anticipate that these answers correspond to Boolean arithmetic and can, therefore, be represented in a computer by 1 or 0. In logic such possibilities are often referred to as "true" or "false".

If the ISM software required that every participant in an session involving ISM know all of the unknowns, the software would be of no value, because it is almost always true that no one knows all of the unknowns. Accordingly, the algebra in the ISM algorithms is designed as follows:

- **The Meaning of "Yes".** A "yes" answer to a question corresponds to entering a 1 in the computer, and is intended to mean that the individual who says "yes" in response to the question believes strongly in that answer
- **The Meanings of "No".** A "no" answer to a question corresponds to entering a 0 in the computer, but it is interpreted to mean one of two possibilities: a) that the individual who says

"no" believes strongly in that answer OR b) that the individual who says "no" lacks enough experience or knowledge to render an informed judgment

This plan is somewhat foreign to the analyst who normally assumes either that a datum put into a model is known, or that it has been found to lie within certain limits, or that it is characterized by probability data that enable numerant results to be obtained from the model.

Four points will make clear why the "double meaning of no strategy" is reasonable:

- **Not Asking the Impossible.** There is no reason to embarrass anyone by asking for a definite opinion on a question for which no adequate background is available from which to respond. By allowing a "no" to be ambiguous, issues of adequacy need not arise when a "no" answer is given

- **Using Group Time Wisely.** In view of the first point, a lot of fruitless discussion is bypassed in a group setting. This is very important in saving expensive group time, in the light of higher-level management's common reluctance to allocate several consecutive days for group work

- **Facilitating the "Reading" and Amendment (if Needed) of the Models Produced.** When the structural model is completed, the only relationships that appear are those corresponding to answers of "yes". This is a great convenience, because structural models are unfamiliar to most people, and anything that can enhance the readability without diminishing the utility of the model is much to be desired. This is particularly true, in light of the fact that since no one has previously seen the just-produced structural model, the new insights that it brings become an asset in carrying out any amendment that might be viewed as desirable. Experience with hundreds of instances shows that amendments to structural models produced with ISM are very rare except for those which involve placing elements into categories. But for those models, it is easy to make amendments, once an adequate framework has been developed with the help of ISM.

- **Portraying Majority Views.** Because the structural model represents only the results of majority voting (more than half of the group has responded with a "yes" to a question that represents one unknown), it can be said that **every structural model produced with ISM reflects a majority view.** The significance of this result is best understood if one understands the spreadthink phenomenon. It has been found that there is almost never a majority viewpoint when members of a group are asked to decide which of the problems they have produced and clarified are the most important. If asked to choose the five most important problems from the collection, it is very rare that any problem is chosen by at least half of the members of the group. Yet the structural model portrays a majority view on hundreds or thousands of relationships among the problems. This is a major reason why the products from ISM enable management to move forward knowingly, rather than to impose a strategy which, typically, represents one more component of the spreadthink milieu that exists before the ISM work is carried out.

Judge Iannis Kapelouzos, retired from a Supreme Court in Greece, studied the views of participants in many projects before and after the use of ISM to structure the problematic situations. He drew two conclusions:

- **No Correlation Before ISM.** He found that the views of participants before the use of ISM and after the use of ISM were uncorrelated!
- **Substantial Learning During ISM.** He concluded that the only explanation for the absence of correlation before ISM, but majority view after ISM was the substantial learning that took place during the ISM session. Since the staff who facilitate the ISM work and who operate the computing equipment never inject opinions on the content of whatever is being discussed (in contrast to the work of some facilitators who see their role as one

of aggregating and interpreting the results of group discussions), the only explanation for the learning is that the members of the group educate one another through the discussion and voting process that takes place as a consequence of the problem sequencing produced by the ISM computer software, with such minimal intervention by the facilitator as may be required to keep the discussion moving, and to oversee the voting process whereby the majority vote is determined for each question posed.

What the ISM Software Does

The ISM software receives, as inputs, the clarified ideas generated by the group using NGT. These ideas may be, e.g., problems or options or categories. The software is programmed to start producing questions to display to the group, and to accept their majority answers under the supervision of the facilitator.

At some point the computer will be in a position to begin to generate responses to questions that it will **not** ask the group. In order to do this the computer will apply the Aristotle syllogism stemming from about 350 BC in the form amended by Abelard in the 12th century, to infer responses based on the responses given previously by the group voting process. Once it is able to begin to infer, the computer will perform all possible inferences after each response is given. After it has inferred whatever it can infer, it will then compute and count the number of possible inferences it **could** make for every question that has not been answered by the group. It then uses what is called a "maximin criterion" to choose the next question to be asked.

A maximin criterion allows the computer to look at the inference that would be possible for all unanswered questions and to count how many inferences could be made if the answer were "yes" and if the answer were "no". Sometimes huge amounts of inference will be possible for one of the answers, and no inference will be possible for the other answer. If the maximum inference were allowed, the computer might not have to ask nearly as many questions of the group. This would make the final result much more dependent on inference than on group discussion and voting. In developing ISM, I felt that a more conservative approach would be to choose the next question in a way that would **maximize the minimum inference** chosen from the set of all possible answers to unasked questions. This is the criterion that has been incorporated in the ISM software.

One way to describe what the computer is doing is to say that it is filling in 1s and 0s in a square matrix in which the main diagonal is always filled with 1s. It is doing this by a combination of responses from the group and from its own inference. In a typical application, the group may supply 20% of the responses, and the computer may infer the remaining 80%; although these numbers will vary from application to application.

Once the matrix is entirely filled, the computer is able to calculate the structure, using an algorithm that will assign each element to a stage in a stage representation or to a level in a level representation. It will determine if there are any subsets of elements that are symmetrically related (cycles; i.e., x is related to y; and y is related to x), and list for each of the cycles which elements are contained in those cycles.

The computer can then print this information and the staff can use it to place the structure on the wall as described previously.

The Contributors to Second-Order Thought

The computer, in its application of ISM, is using second-order thought processes. These processes represent the work of several individuals whose lives were separated by centuries. The most prominent among them are Aristotle, Abelard, Leibniz, De Morgan, Boole, C. S. Peirce, and Harary. I will describe each of these individuals briefly in **Chapter 5**, and explain how each is, in a certain sense, dependent on others from among this group. As mentioned earlier, their pictures appear in **Appendix 1**.

Chapter 5

The Thought Explorers
(Working Backward Through Time)

In planning this Chapter, I decided to use a stylistic method that I have not seen before in its entirety. I decided that I would show the history of the development of Interpretive Structural Modeling (ISM) in reverse order. I would show this history in terms of the individuals whose work was instrumental in its achievement. Pictures of these individuals appear in **Appendix 1**: Glossary.

In presenting this material I was amazed, as I have always been in thinking about it, to see once again that it represented milestones extending over a period of about 2,400 years. If this period of development is typical of scientific progress, one can expect some of the current areas of study to become mature around the year 4400. Very likely things will move faster now.

John N. Warfield (1925-   ). Interpretive Structural Modeling. I developed ISM during the period 1971-73. The first formal presentation was in the "Battelle Monograph Number 4", published in 1974, and titled "Structuring Complex Systems". In recent years, I have regretted the choice of title. If I could do it over again I would call it "Structural Modeling of Problematic Situations". I wrote the next formal publication in my 1976 book titled "Societal Systems: Planning, Policy, and Complexity". In recent years, I believe it was unfortunate that the mathematical developments were not evident from the title of the book. I chose to republish the chapters from that book in 2003, under the title "The Mathematics of Structure". At least this made prominent the fundamental mathematics underlying ISM.

Some authors have used the term ISM to refer also to computer software that has been developed to enable ISM to be used in applications. Still others have used ISM to refer to the products as "ISM's".

I chose the name "Interpretive Structural Modeling" after studying a book by Frank Harary and his colleagues on structural models. That book offered numerous abstractions. My work built a bridge between those abstractions and the interpretation of problematic situations. My work produced mathematical algorithms whereby groups could develop, with computer assistance, structural models that could be interpreted to shed light on problematic situations.

Eventually (circa 1980) I would make ISM a part of the development called "Interactive Management". An entire book was devoted to Interactive Management (1994). This book can now be downloaded free from the Internet by going to the web site: http://www.jnwarfield.com thanks to the generosity of my co-author, A. Roxana Cárdenas who is the copyright holder.

Frank Harary (1921-   ). The Mathematics of Directed Graphs. In a book titled "Structural Modeling: The Theory of Directed Graphs", Harary, along with Norman and Cartwright, two associates at the University of Michigan, developed the theory of directed graphs (digraphs). Harary is one of the top graph theorists in the world. In this work, Harary merged into graph theory several results from previous scholars, whose work I will describe later in this chapter, including Cayley, Boole, and De Morgan.

Harary showed the close connection between sets, matrices, algebra, and digraphs. Earlier he had developed a theorem which I call "Harary's Theorem of Assured Model Consistency". The algorithms of ISM are largely based in this theorem.

Father I. M. ("Joseph") Bochenski (1902-1995). History of Formal Logic. A Polish priest, Bochenski served as faculty member in various departments of philosophy in Europe, and also served as a visiting faculty member at Notre Dame University and the University of Kansas in the United States. As I learned later, he and I had been simultaneously on the faculty at the University of Kansas for one year, and I have often wished that I had been able to talk with this man. Those who do not know his book might find the title foreboding. Actually the book is extremely readable, and is one of the most remarkable works of scholarship that I have ever seen. Bochenski traces the evolution of logic through the centuries, beginning around 600 B. C., and continuing to around 1930. The style of the work is outstanding. Intermixed with but distinguished from direct quotations from philosophers are Bochenski's own interpretive comments in which frequent comparisons are made among the various works of logic developed over the more than two millennia dealt with in his work.

Having seen the work of Harary *et al*, and having discovered the American philosopher, Charles Sanders Peirce, I became very interested in answering for myself the question of why, after having spent about 16 years in various universities as a student, and several more as a faculty member, I had never heard of Peirce nor of Bochenski. I was particularly fascinated by the lack of emphasis given to relationships in formal education. As editor of a journal, I had encountered the outstanding dissertation of George J. Friedman, who had emphasized the unity that could be brought to various branches of mathematics through "constraint theory", in which relationships and bipartite graphs played a key unifying role.

After asking (in vain) various mathematicians to enlighten me on the history of those developments, I finally ran across Bochenski's work, which answered virtually all of the questions that had come to mind. Because of the wide swath of his work, Bochenski could not spend too much time and space on any one logician. Hence I became determined to do further background study into the developments outlined in his book.

Charles Sanders Peirce (1839-1914). "America's Greatest Thinker". My first introduction to Peirce came from a small volume called "The Practical Cogitator: The Thinker's Anthology" by Curtis and Greenslet. This book was given to me by a friend in 1950. It distilled and categorized thoughts of many scholars and offered wisdom to me that I have valued ever since first reading.

I am not sure if the readings in that book, which included several from Peirce, are what caused me to begin to take an interest in him. But in any case, I am sure that a book called "The Thought of C. S. Peirce" by the late Professor Thomas A. Goudge, a Canadian philosopher, is what first made me recognize the outstanding scholarship of this man. Often reviled, often abused by people whom he trusted, it appears that even today Peirce is much better known outside the United States than inside. The title "America's Greatest Thinker" was assigned to him by the contemporary German philosopher, Karl-Otto Apel. The very well-known Sir Karl Popper described him as "one of the greatest philosophers of all time". The Peirce Project being carried on at Indiana-Purdue University seeks to edit and present chronologically about 30 volumes of his work which has been said to represent about half of his work. A modern biography by Joseph Brent was suppressed for many years by an American university.

Peirce called attention, in one of his papers, to the work of Augustus De Morgan, whom Peirce showered with praise. I was delighted to learn more about De Morgan from Bochenski's work.

In later years, I visited Peirce's residence ("Arisbe") in Pennsylvania, where a small sign on the side of U. S. Highway 6 noted the location, and a laundry hanging on the line testified to the maintenance of the property by the U. S. National Park Service.

Arthur Cayley (1821-1895). Matrices. "In 1863 Cayley was appointed Sadleirian professor of Pure Mathematics at Cambridge. This involved a very large decrease in income for Cayley who now had to manage on a salary only a fraction of that which he had earned as a skilled lawyer. However Cayley was very happy to have the chance to devote himself entirely to mathematics. As Sadleirian professor of Pure Mathematics his duties were

> *to explain and teach the principles of pure mathematics and to apply himself to the advancement of that science.*

Cayley was to more than fulfill these conditions. He published over 900 papers and notes covering nearly every aspect of modern mathematics.

The most important of his work is in developing the algebra of matrices, work in non-euclidean geometry and n-dimensional geometry."

I quote these remarks from a web site devoted to Cayley to emphasize that Cayley earlier had a career as a lawyer. The importance of this stems from knowing that several other key figures in the history of science began their careers as lawyers, and migrated into scientific areas. These include Leibniz (who became a librarian and logician) and Lavoisier (who became a chemist). **All of these individuals recognized the criticality of designed language, and contributed mightily to that recognition.**

Cayley's work on matrices, when married to Boole's work on propositional calculus and De Morgan's work on the theory of relations were the principal antecedents of Harary's work, discussed previously in this Chapter. Cayley's contribution was to extend what had been looked upon as low-dimensional mathematics into higher dimensions, enabling many variables to be treated in one context, and enabling mathematical operations on those many variables in the form of matrix operations. It is probably fair to say that Cayley was a direct intellectual ancestor of Albert Einstein, whose work on tensors represents an extension of matrix theory.

George Boole (1815-1864), Developer of Propositional Calculus (the Algebra of Logic). Boole and De Morgan were known to each other, and it seems likely that Boole's work was significantly influenced by De Morgan. In any case, Boole developed an algebra that emphasized the representation of a proposition by a symbol. For example, the proposition " it is raining outside" can be represented by the letter x. The truth or falsity of the proposition can then be represented by what logicians sometimes call "truth values", such as:

If it is raining, x has the "value" "true"; and if it is not raining, x has the "value" "false". Boole also recognized that numerical symbols could be assigned to "true" and "false", so if it **is** raining, $x = 1$; while if it is **not** raining, $x = 0$.

The late American mathematician, Claude Shannon, working at the late Bell Telephone Laboratories, popularized Boole's work, while emphasizing to the Bell Telephone researchers that a one-to-one correspondence could be had between the symbols from the algebra and the status of a pair of contacts on an electromagnetic relay. [This was known to C. S. Peirce, as drawings in his notebooks clearly show.] Other researchers at the Bell Telephone Laboratories were then encouraged to develop algorithms for minimizing the number of contacts on relays required to do switching operations. With tens of thousands or perhaps millions of similar relays in use, reduction of a small amount on one relay translated into reduction of thousands or perhaps millions of dollars over the life of relays in the Bell system.

But shortly the algebra would be recognized as the basis for switching theory in general, and made applicable to the design of minimized circuitry in digital computers. While various institutions are happy to claim a place in the history of this development, Charles Sanders Peirce portrayed a relay-operated switching circuit in one of his papers on logic, and one of his students built a small digital computer while on the faculty at Princeton University, though he was not encouraged by his faculty colleagues to pursue that line of research.

This historical record was communicated to me by Professor Kenneth L. Ketner of Texas Tech University, who holds the Peirce Chair at that institution, and has made notable contributions to the history and recognition of Peirce's work.

Augustus De Morgan (1806-1871). Developer of the Theory of Relations and Discoverer of the Concept of Transitivity, and its Importance in Understanding Aristotle's Syllogism. Appointed as Chair of the Department of Mathematics at the University of London at age 22, De Morgan developed the theory of relations—a fundamental body of mathematics which became the foundation for Harary's work on structural models. He observed that Aristotle's syllogism, often thought of as merely a structural concept, was only valid when the relationship that was used had the property of being "transitive". This discovery was noted by Bochenski, and its importance was emphasized by Charles Sanders Peirce, who had visited with De Morgan during one of his European visits.

In developing ISM, I used Boolean algebra to represent propositions by symbols, and I used a proposition that involves two elements and a relationship, as follows:

Proposition: $z = x$ is related to y (where a relationship is specified as part of the proposition). The notation $z =$ xRy is also used as a mathematical simplification. In ISM, the proposition is treated as a question, in abstract form being like "is the proposition $z = xRy$ true?" [OR is it false or do you not know the answer?] where the portion in brackets is not displayed on the screen.

If the answer is "yes", the digit 1 is entered in the computer. If the answer is "no", the digit 0 is entered.

Whatever digit is entered, it becomes an entry in a matrix. Suppose there are 30 elements being related. Then the matrix is *30 x 30*, and the number of entries to be filled in before the matrix is completely specified is *30 x 30 = 900*. You can see how important Cayley's contribution is to scholarly study involving many unknowns, how important Boole's contribution is to formulating expressions and, ultimately, how important De Morgan's contribution is to understanding how to work with relationships. Finally, Harary's contribution in developing the key conditions required for consistency of the logic in filling such large matrices forms that piece of the puzzle required to pull all these mathematical fragments together.

Gottfried Leibniz (1646-1716). Lawyer, Librarian, Mathematician, Logician. According to Bochenski, following the Middle Ages, Leibniz restored and upgraded the study of logic. He went unrecognized as co-inventor of calculus (along with Isaac Newton) until his many manuscripts were discovered in the nineteenth century. Like Cayley and Lavoisier, he was educated as a lawyer.

Pierre ("Peter") Abelard (1079-1142). Antecedents and Succedents. The outstanding logician of his time, credited by Bochenski with finding a single propositional statement to replace the 3-statement syllogism. Abelard introduced the concept of antecedent and succedent that replaced the "major premiss" and "minor premiss" of Aristotle, permitting one to make a single statement that later was important in the recognition of the importance of the transitive relationship, and other developments used by Harary to develop the theory of digraphs; the theory that was the direct predecessor of ISM.

As a teacher at the University of Paris, students flocked to hear his teachings. His personal life was not as successful.

Aristotle (385 B. C. to 322 B. C.) Syllogism and Categories. The creative use of language in reasoning is the greatest contribution made by Aristotle. He recognized the importance of categories in forming structured levels of language. Thus one could speak, e.g., of "fish" as well as "trout" and of "human being" as well as "Pontius Pilate".

He invented the foundational form of inference with the syllogism. The syllogism was studied and taught for hundreds of years before Abelard recognized the importance of presenting it in a single statement instead of the threefold statement of Aristotle. Then, following Abelard, several hundred years later, Leibniz invented the concept of representing statements by graphical figures (which came to be known today as "Venn diagrams" and occasionally as Euler's circles, even though Leibniz was using them many years earlier, as shown by Bochenski). The further development of representing logic statements by graphics was carried out by Frege in Europe and C. S. Peirce in the U. S. A., but never in a form that lent itself to practical applications to problematic situations until finally presented by Harary and his associates.

Perhaps we can look forward to the day when the academy will give recognition to these developments, modernizing the teaching of logic and restoring it to its rightful place as a key component of an education.

Should this recognition be a part of the study of resolution of problematic situations, it can take place in the context of the application of systems science, through the use of Interactive Management!

Chapter 6

Quality Control In Modeling Structure

This book is not intended to furnish significant content related to numerant models. But when quality control of modeling is discussed, the discussion can be applied both to numerant models and to the structural models that are the core of the foundations of systems science.

An unknown number of people construct and apply models. Often models incorporate large data bases that are refreshed from time to time as new data become available. The large models typically are applied to represent economics systems or physical systems. At one time the Brookings Econometric Model contained about 2,000 variables. A model of a large aircraft may contain thousands of equations. Some modelers try to model cities, corporations and\or the economics of the entire world.

Manufacturing practices have benefitted greatly by the introduction of methods of quality control, using methods that have their roots in the work of Shewhart in the 1930s and which are much more commonly associated with the name of Deming.   In contrast, most modeling activities lack any clear-cut philosophy or methodology for controlling quality. In this chapter, the work of three authors is highlighted in explaining how their work provides the basis for quality control in modeling. These authors are W. Ross Ashby, George J. Friedman, and Frank Harary. There is relatively little overlap among the works of these three authors, so quality control in modeling can benefit from the combined recognition of all three.

W. Ross Ashby (1903-1972).   Ashby's Law of Requisite Variety. (See **Appendix 1**: Gallery, for a picture of Ashby.) If a problematic situation is to be resolved, the variety available to the designer of a means of resolving the situation must have controlling access to the same variety as that found in the situation. This is a broad statement of Ashby's Law of Requisite Variety. Applied to aircraft design, since an aircraft in flight must move at one and the same time in three spatial dimensions, the aircraft designer must make available to the pilot the ability to control the motion of the plane in all three dimensions. One may readily imagine that if motion control was had in only two dimensions, the best the plane could hope for is to taxi on the ground. If the designer tried to exercise control in four spatial dimensions, one does not know what could be expected, but one supposes that strange things might happen.

Nothing in Ashby's Law is restrictive to physical motion. In theory, it applies to any number of dimensions, since it recognizes that as long as some dimension in the problematic situation is free to cause difficulty, control exercised in the other dimensions probably will not be adequate to resolve the situation; and if an attempt is made to "overcontrol" as in the case of the aircraft designer who tries to design for controlling four spatial dimensions, only the foolhardy will venture to predict an outcome.

The Law does not specify how to determine dimensionality in general. In my own work, I have construed dimensionality to be discovered in each situation. Until a better definition arises, I take the dimensionality to be the number of distinct categories found in the Problems Field and thereafter used in an Options Field, where each dimension in the Problems Field has a corresponding design requirement coming from the Options Field.

George J. Friedman (1928-   ).   Friedman's Law of Non-Conservation of Consistency in Aggregate Modeling. (See **Appendix 1**: Gallery, for a picture of Friedman.) In the late 20th century, George J. Friedman contributed greatly to the science of modeling by introducing what he called "constraint theory". Other authors have used a similar name for something quite different. When I use this term, the reader should understand that I am referring to Friedman's work.

Friedman's work is of very general applicability. It is supported by extensive theoretical development. While it was not intended to be used for developing structural models, it used structure as the foundation for the rest of the work. Specifically, Friedman used what are called bipartite graphs to represent the structure of the models that he was discussing.

Both Friedman and Harary contributed to analytical ways of dealing with modeling. Harary's models, called "digraphs", employ vertices–which represent the elements and arrows–which represent relationships. Friedman's models, called "bipartite graphs", employ two types of vertices–one type, called "knots", represent the model's variables, and the other type, called "nodes", represent relationships. An arc or "edge"–connects each node (relationship) to all its relevant knots (variables). When direction is given to these arcs, they become arrows (similar to the digraph) and computational flow can be modeled. Thus a separation of the concepts of mathematical model and computational flow across that model is attained.

As part of his work, Friedman considered a situation where the development of a large model was to be carried out by partitioning the model into submodels. Each submodel would be developed by a different group, each of which would be found to be consistent. Then the large model would be formed by simply aggregating (i.e., interconnecting) the submodels. Friedman's Theorem, as stated here, says that even if all of the submodels are consistent, there is no assurance that the model formed in the manner just stated will be consistent. In short, consistency is not necessarily preserved in interconnecting a family of consistent submodels.

Additionally, Friedman applied constraint theory to investigate other aspects of the traditional "well-posed" problem in mathematics. If a model is found to be inconsistent, constraint theory can offer specific advice regarding how to render it consistent. Even on consistent models however, most computational requests are not allowable–i.e., the computational flow is either overconstrained or underconstrained. Constraint theory can detect the computational allowability of any given computational request and if not allowable, alternative allowable computational requests in the "neighborhood" of the original request can be provided to the mathematical model manager and his analysts.

Harary's Theorem of Assured Model Consistency (See **Appendix 1**: Gallery, for a picture of Harary). Harary developed a theorem which shows how a model can be constructed to follow a certain set of conditions which assure that it will be consistent. These are the conditions that are incorporated in ISM.

Three Questions About a Model. Three questions that may be raised in connection with modeling activity are these:

- **Completeness.** How can I be sure that this model is complete?
- **Correctness.** How can I be sure that this model is correct?
- **Consistency.** How can I be sure that this model is consistent?

Model Completeness. If model completeness is to be assured, it is necessary to know what is called a "stopping rule". By a stopping rule one means that there is some condition that enables one to say: "now I can stop adding elements and relationships to my model because I have applied the rule and it has been satisfied'. But it is seldom (perhaps never) true that a stopping rule can be based in knowledge of the system that is being modeled.

For that reason, the systems science explained here incorporates, as a stopping rule, the pragmatic concept that when a group of people chosen for their intimacy with a particular problematic situation can no longer add any more elements or relationships in their description of the situation, the modeling effort stops.

This rule recognizes the limitations of human beings and, at the same time, their creativity. It is consistent with Charles Sanders Peirce's view of science as an asymptotic approach to the truth. It is easy to append another of his ideas; the existence of a "community of scholars" who, over time, strive to enhance the quality of what is incorporated in a science. Thus, and only thus, does a science grow in quality; and thus, and only thus, does a model grow in quality. The quest for model completeness involves questioning of individuals who might be able to add something to what has been assiduously found up to a point in time, at which time some action to apply or discard the model becomes a point of investigation.

Model Correctness.   Correctness of a model is judged by whether it represents totally a problematic situation. But a model cannot represent totally a problematic situation unless it is complete.   But as I have already indicated, model completeness relies on a stopping rule, consequently correctness does also.

The quest for correctness involves the quest for completeness.

Model Consistency. While model completeness and model correctness can be sought, model consistency can be achieved. There is no way to prove, in general, that a consistent model is either complete or correct. On the other hand, an inconsistent model cannot be correct, hence its completeness becomes irrelevant.

A Quality Control Philosophy for Model Development

Acceptance of a quality control philosophy for model development may be hampered by historical developments. The sometimes-accepted view of science as the ultimate truth is not consistent with the idea that, while a model is consistent, it may be neither correct nor complete.

The quest for more and more precision in measurement also may lead to a point of view that consistency is an inadequate criterion for model development.

But even in physics, which along with chemistry seems to offer the greatest precision in measurement, and the most reliable predictions, most watches that people rely on lack the precision of the atomic clocks.

The idea that finding highly qualified people, involving them in structuring a problematic situation, keeping the involvement open until their supply of ideas has been exhausted, could be a prescription for quality control in modeling may be hard to accept. But one cannot deny what has been found in practice. As I will discuss in **Part 2**, there are some strong reasons for relying on this type of process to provide the structure of a high-quality model. Structure alone is often insufficient to complete a model, hence further work may often be required to make a structural model more specific. But it should be clear that if a numerant model is made it will always embody some kind of structure. If that structure has not been developed on its own, who is to say if the numerant model recognizes the conditions of the three scholars whose work has been described briefly in this chapter?

The Behavioral Side of Quality Control in Modeling Structure

I have mentioned what I call behavioral pathologies—human limitations that affect the ability of individuals, groups, and organizations to develop and apply high-quality models. In giving more attention now to the behavioral side of quality control, I wish to go into greater detail on the nature of the behavioral pathologies and the ways that have been applied to overcome them. I will also suggest that work remains to be done in connection with the organization pathologies. In this discussion, I will follow the same style that I followed in Chapter 5, where I described those individuals that played a role in the development of ISM.

John Warfield (1925-   ) Spreadthink. It was not quite 30 years after the beginning of the work on structural modeling that the concept of "Spreadthink" finally dawned. Already in place were the behaviorally-based ideas of Groupthink and Clanthink, each referring to some kind of defect in thought that would be exhibited in group sessions; and the ideas of Brainstorming and Ideawriting, each referring to a concept of generating ideas in group sessions.

Furthermore it was well-known to anyone who had sat in on and/or participated in group work that it is very difficult to gain consensus in a group by any means other than autocratic resolution.

But it was only after watching many groups in diverse locations struggling with complexity, and after data were taken on the voting procedure using in the Nominal Group Technique (NGT) that it became clear that members of working groups seldom agreed on the most basic aspects of the problematic situation.

After members of a group have generated and clarified ideas in response to a triggering question aimed at eliciting key ideas from them, the NGT process asks that each member vote silently by selecting what that person considers to be the five most important ideas, and ranking them in order of importance.

Criteria for what is meant by "importance" are not specified, leaving that to the intuitive makeup and background information of each participant. So when all data are gathered and tabulated, what is seen in the data reflect the values of each individual in the group. I have long believed that individual values are too deep and too ambiguous to become the foundation for analytical work; but I also believe that these values get incorporated in work done in groups, and value differences are reflected in the voting results from NGT. But it is not values alone that are so represented. In spite of the extensive clarification, linguistic differences always remain, and these also become part of the rationale leading to voting results. Some will think that the voting reflects self-interests, which they believe will explain the fact that the voting results are all over the map, with little correlation from one individual to another. While I cannot prove that this is not correct, I am convinced that individual value systems are broader than generally imagined, and that linguistic differences are seldom ironed out. Not only do the data from NGT voting show quite different results from one individual to the next, but they also reveal that it is rare to find that a single element gets a majority vote from the group.

The implications of Spreadthink are great:

- **Autocratic Behavior.** A manager who insists on pressing on with his own viewpoint is incurring, at least, differences with every member of the group and, at most, animosity from each member, who invariably will find his importance ranking to be different from that member's own.
- **Requirement for Further Structuring.** Consensus is absent at the time of NGT voting. Further structuring is indicated, in order to reach some form of consensus. Such structuring must convert, if possible, the varied individual structuring into a

coherent group structure that reflects consensus among the members, providing a basis for moving ahead into a design situation.

Clanthink. I am not sure who described the concept that I call "Clanthink". It has certainly been evident historically as I have described previously. It means that all members of a group accept as correct the same idea, and that idea is wrong. I believe that a very good way to annul the effects of Clanthink is to do the kind of detailed structuring that is found to annul Spreadthink.

Irving Janis (1918-1990) Groupthink. (See **Appendix 1**: Gallery, for a picture of Janis.) Regrettably, the term "groupthink" is often misapplied to mean anything that emerged from group discussions, or any belief that is shared by a group. In conceiving groupthink, Irving Janis noted that it was a multidimensional concept in which groups exhibited a kind of behavior that inevitably produced results that did not represent what individual members of a group believed about a problematic situation; but could represent the fear of the individual members of being ostracized from the group, and which represented many other factors detailed by Janis.

When striving to resolve a problematic situation by involving groups in collective work, it is important that the processes used by the groups annul any opportunity for groupthink.

Chris Argyris (1923-   ). Organizational Difficulties. (See **Appendix 1**: Gallery, for a picture of Argyris.) In his prolonged study of organizations, Chris Argyris offered several conclusions about organizational behavior which ought to be taken into account in designing and choosing processes to resolve problematic situations. Among other things, he stressed the unwillingness and inability of managers in organizations to discuss certain "undiscussables". He indicated that managers often do not know that they do not know, and consequently proceed to act on what could be described as "ignorance of ignorance" and remain mute when discussion is called for.

Awareness of these organizational factors is often critical in resolving complexity in organizations, and can only be partly dealt with in systems science.

An advertising executive named Alex F. Osborne introduced "Brainstorming" about sixty years ago. He saw people in groups generating ideas and other people shooting them down before they could gain a foothold. (He realized that it was important not to place obstacles in the path of generation of ideas.) Nowadays the term is often used to represent any kind of group activity. To get effective results from a group it is often desirable to incorporate the principles of brainstorming. But it is also important to understand that brainstorming is not the same as NGT. It is a fact that NGT has superseded brainstorming, while incorporating its most important ideas.

Anthony Downs (1930-   ). Bureaucratic Behavior. (See **Appendix 1**: Gallery, for a picture of Downs.) Anthony Downs is that rare combination of theoretician and practitioner. His path-breaking study of bureaucratic behavior titled "Inside Bureaucracy" explains much bureaucratic behavior.

Any effort to resolve problematic situations in organizations can benefit from a study of his work, and any processes that claim to be effective in resolving problematic situations in organizations should embody the means to overcome as much of the bureaucratic behavior which he describes as is possible.

I believe that this requires that group processes should always be followed by experienced interpretation done by one individual who is thoroughly familiar with the group processes and with the difficulties inherent in making the results known to higher levels in the organization.

The preceding statement carries with it the assumption that the highest levels will not engage in open group processes and can benefit from group work done by subordinates only when it is expertly offered to them in formats which they can comprehend. Whether they will never, themselves, engage in such group processes is uncertain, but it seems that it almost never happens so one is justified in designing ways to help assure that the benefits of group processes, soundly designed and carefully planned and carried out, have the greatest opportunity for becoming understood by powerful executives; who are in a position to apply the results for the benefit of the organization and its surround.

Infrastructure

Infrastructure is a critical component of the quality control apparatus in organizations. The physical infrastructure that is known to be highly beneficial is the situation room in which group work is done to produce descriptions, diagnoses, designs, and plans for implementation. It is anticipated that another key part of the infrastructure will be the observatorium in which the products of group work are displayed and updated as a means of educating those whose understanding of work done by others will be applied in processes aimed at resolving problematic situations in organizations.

Physical infrastructure is designed with the known needs of the specialized staff who plan and carry out the processes that are required by the systems science. In a sense the staff are also part of the infrastructure, and if they cannot be marshaled to carry out the work that is indicated by systems science, the physical infrastructure may not be worth the investment required to make it available.

The Collective Apparatus

Interactive Management provides for overcoming the individual, group, and organizational behavioral pathologies except for those at the highest levels in the organizational that stem from unwillingness to accept ideas. When the collective processes are allowed to function with enabling infrastructure, very powerful means are available to gain quality control of modeling, which demonstrably yields very good results, as the various examples in **Part 4** will illustrate.

Chapter 7

The Situation Room

Yes, they sit around the table. Some think the table should be round, as though symmetry of behavior is dependent on the shape of the table, at the possible expense of making it difficult to hear the other who is speaking, or to be heard when speaking. To make the table round, while still accommodating 30 or 40 people, it has become so large in diameter that people directly across from each other cannot hear each other's comments. Moreover, effective processes require that the facilitator be able to demonstrate a voice of process authority and to sit at the head of the table.

Outside there is an occasional truck going by that obscures some of the dialog. Now and then a cell phone rings and a muted reply is given by the respondent while the discussion continues. Now and then a bird flies by one of the windows and attracts the attention of observers. Occasionally the air conditioner comes on with a kind of bang and its blowing noise provides a dull roar, working against the efforts of people to hear other people. A participant has a bad back, and is continually shifting his body in the inexpensive, squeaking chair to try to get comfortable. Participants type into computers now and then, with each one's keyboard noise disturbing the others, as they try to keep track of what is going on. Some try in vain to remember what was said some time ago that they found relevant.

Varying in computer skill and keyboard expertise, some participants have no problem in typing information into the computer that will be shared with the others; while some do not want to display their ineptness by complaining about the requirements they are asked to accept by the design of the processes and their surround.

No, that is not the kind of surround in which people can be highly communicative with one another and highly productive, either. The complexity in problematic situations is best dealt with by groups when the surround is not abusive, and when they are able to focus all of their attention upon the mini-topic that has been set before them in the form of a question.

Even under the best of conditions, some problematic situations are sufficiently challenging that every possible step should be taken to make it easier to work together. In recognition of this, the organization will invest significantly in a situation room, and in order to get the most benefit they will operate this room as a shared facility, open to scheduling for different parts of the organization as they strive to cope with complexity by working in groups.

The room design and the methods to be used in working with complexity are complementary. The room and its furnishings and equipment are tailored to match the requirements of the methods and the challenge of the problematic situation that is the subject of the work.

Organizational management recognizes that group time is both expensive and valuable. It is important that no time is wasted by unsuitable factors in the surround and by inadequate preparation of the participants. What could be done well by individual contacts, e-mail, or small lecture sessions is done before and after the group meets to work together. Intermediate products of group work are printed and made available periodically by the staff. Ideas generated in the course of group work are written on butcher paper, numbered sequentially, and posted on the wall where reference is readily made to previous contributions. The needed learning is facilitated by such readily available short-term histories. Ability to see what is desired is enhanced by the silent and readily moved casters on the comfortable chairs; which facilitate rotating the body without disturbing adjacent people.

The table is chosen to provide work space for between 10 and 20 people, including one or two staff members, one of whom will be a group facilitator, experienced in the methods to be used. Heating and/or cooling equipment will be engineered to be virtually silent in operation. Lighting is designed to eliminate possible eyestrain as a factor during long work days. Essential computer equipment is physically separated from the working group at the table, where its keyboard noise is not troublesome. Staff who work at the computer are distinctly separated from the working group at the table.

Copying equipment, readily available, is in an adjacent room where the noise from the copier will not be heard in the situation room, enabling intermediate results to be copied and made available.

Material to be posted is typed in very large and upper-case font on stationery-size paper. Walls are free of windows, and designed to accommodate a large amount of posting, whether by using magnetic walls with small rubberized magnets, or stationery-size post-its that can be held in place and not fall on the floor.

The table, while large enough to provide ample working space for participants seated at the table, is also small enough that traffic around the table has abundant space in which to move, so that the staff who are posting items on the wall do not interfere with the individuals seated at the table.

Rooms of this type have been put in place in several organizations. The first one that met rigid specifications was built at the University of Virginia in the early 1980s. Lessons learned from that room were used to amend the design for future applications.

Some of the rules applied in connection with the situation room are:

- **No Abuse.** No one should be abused by the process or the surround
- **Participant Symmetry.** Every participant has the same amenities (symmetry principle)
- **Facilitator Authority.** The facilitator is at the head of the table (authority principle)
- **Low-Profile Staff.** The staff work does not interfere with the work of the participants
- **Low-Profile Equipment.** Equipment is separated from participants, permitting them to focus on one thing at a time
- **Comfort.** Comfort is important
- **Rotation.** Rotation in chairs for visibility is important
- **High-Quality Chairs.** Chairs should provide lumbar support and sufficient width to be accommodative to all shapes

- **No Extraneous Noise.** All forms of extraneous noise are prohibited
- **High-Quality Lighting.** Excellent lighting design accommodates the need to see a lot of text at the same time
- **Well-Positioned Microphones** (if the session is to be recorded).

Figure 7-1 in **Appendix 1**, The Gallery, is illustrative of a floor plan of a situation room that is suitable to support group work based in systems science.

Part 2

Discovery: The Chapters

I have set forth in Part 1 the two basic processes of systems science, Nominal Group Technique (NGT) and Interpretive Structural Modeling (ISM). Each of them has the necessary property of being neutral; i.e., each can be applied in any problematic situation as long as a group of people can be found that share two properties: (a) none of them imagines that he or she understands fully the situation that is to be explored—exploration is not for people who already know all the territory and (b) each of them believes that he or she has some beliefs to contribute to well-defined group processes aimed at organizing complexity. Complexity, organized, is weakened complexity, or may no longer be complexity. Awareness of whatever specialized processes may be required to augment or reinforce established belief will be identified as consequences of the application of the system science, and not as *ad hoc* pronouncements of an advocate who has not delved deeply into the specific problematic situation.

Organizing begins with an individual activity to define context and scope. These definitions typically involve about two paragraphs each. The context is the broader of the two; the scope is to circumscribe what goes on in a particular group. Group members are never *told* to participate in discovery. They are shown the context statement and the scope statement and asked (a) if they believe these statements can be improved and (b) whether they wish to take part in a project aimed at organizing the diffuse problematic situation described broadly in the context statement and more specifically in the scope statement. When a sufficient number of people have agreed to take part, the project can be moved forward. The project typically involves a staff that is experienced with the processes emanating from the systems science, and the team of participants. There may also be observers who do not participate at the table, but may be invited from time to time to offer their views.

The group work is broadly categorized through the Work Program of Complexity in two parts: Discovery and Resolution. Discovery involves Description and Diagnosis.

Description of the problematic situation **(Chapter 8)** typically involves these parts:

- Generation of a problem set
- Choice of a problem subset obtained by "importance filtering"
- Definition of a problems field in which at the least the members of the subset are placed in categories
- Construction of a (Type 1) problematique (a structural model showing how the **problems** influence each other) and (occasionally)
- Construction of a second (Type 2) problematique showing how the **problem categories** influence one another. The latter is obtainable directly from the Type 1 problematique and the categories shown in the problems field.

A variety of *measures of complexity* ("metrics", **Chapter 9**) can be found from the products of work with NGT and ISM. The numerical values have three interpretation modes. They are:

- **Internal comparisons** (e.g., which problem(s) identified as occurring within the same problematic situation have the greatest or least influence on other problems in that same situation?)
- **Comparisons with theory** (e.g., by how much does this problematic situation deviate from what would be thought of as a normal situation, as interpreted through the behavioral pathologies?)
- **Empirical comparisons** (e.g., where does this particular problematic situation lie on a scale of the class of comparable

problematic situations for which previously-found metrics are available?)

After all the products have been produced through facilitated group work, a specialist who has extensive experience in interpreting the graphical products studies them and, following completion of the study, conducts an "interpretation session" for *diagnosis* **(Chapter 10)**, where he or she presents to the group what their work has produced and what it means. This is strictly a technical pursuit, where the interpreter is not to add personal beliefs about the topic, but merely to recite what the interpreter believes the structures imply. This gives the team an opportunity to review and interpret their product and, if need be, to propose amendments. Such proposals rarely surface, because of the painstaking nature of the group processes that produced the results, and the interpretive expertise of the supporting staff.

Chapter 8

Describing Problematic Situations

"It seemed to me that there was one element that was capable of describing the history of thought; this was what one could call the elements of problems or, more exactly problemizations."

Michel Foucault quoted, page 388 of Paul Rabinow (1984): *The Foucault Reader*, New York: Pantheon.

The term "problematic situation" is widely believed to have originated with John Dewey. It can be fruitfully contrasted with the term "problem". Many who toil in the systems gardens are heard to say "the first step is to define the problem". If one admits "the problem", then where does one look for refuge if the problematic situation involves more than one problem? Is it systematic to allow "the problem" and "more than one problem" in the same space of thought and discourse? When complexity is involved, how courageous must one be to insist on a language that demands one definition per term? Oh, you say, it's just a semantic issue. And how many such issues are required in a language before coherent communication becomes impossible? **Appendix 4 elaborates at length on this issue.**

The Problem Set. In my studies of complexity, I have finally decided that it always essential to discover the problematic situation first by pooling the view of an alert group as to what problems they perceive in that situation. NGT is ideally suited to this discovery. Once that discovery is made, then it is necessary to discover, through dialog, how to interpret each of those problem statements that describe the problems as seen by individuals in the group. I call the collection of statements the "problem set".

The Selected Subset.   Once the problem set is discovered using NGT, it can be safely assumed that the set can be refined. One way to refine the set is to divide it into two parts. The first part, the "selected subset" consists of all the members of the problem set such that at least one of the group members placed it in the "most important" five during the NGT voting.   No matter how many problems appeared in the problem set, it should be clear that if all members perceived the same subset of five to be the most important, the selected subset would contain only five members. But in light of the Spreadthink phenomenon, we are able to estimate ahead of time with considerable confidence that the number of problem statements in the selected subset will be between 25 and 40. We can call the selection process "filtering" of the problem set.

If we assume there are 10 members in the group and 50 problems; in one extreme case where everyone agreed on the members of the selected subset, the cardinality (number of members) of that subset would be 5. If in the other extreme where no two members voted for the same problem, the cardinality of the selected subset would be 50. In this extreme, all of the problems would be in somebody's selected subset.   In extensive practice, I have never seen either of these extremes even approached.

Developing and Interpreting The Problematique

Constrained Discovery.   The selected subset is loaded into the computer, and the ISM session begins. The purpose of this session is to discover how the problems are related to one another. In the first ISM session, the group members collectively determine, for each problem, whether it makes other problems worse. At the conclusion of this work, Foucault's idea of problemization can be said to have taken place. By showing the structure on the wall, the members of the group can be invited to study the product of their work.

Should it happen that the structure was totally linear; each problem except the last in the sequence having exactly one succedent, and each problem except the first in the sequence having one antecedent; it would be possible to reconstruct the structure in prose in the deadly dull form as follows:

Problem 1 (in the sequence) aggravates Problem 2, which aggravates Problem 3, which aggravates Problem 4, and so on, until at last Problem ($n–1$) aggravates Problem n.

In practice, linearity in a problematique has not been seen. Instead, all the problematiques could be described as non-linear, meaning that the result cannot be transcribed as just shown. Moreover in about 98% of the problematiques, cycles appear. A cycle of three could be expressed as follows:

Problem 1 (in the cycle) aggravates and is aggravated by Problem 2.
Problem 2 aggravates and is aggravated by Problem 3.
Problem 3 in the cycle aggravates and is aggravated by Problem 1

Still other sentences could be formed from the cycle, but these would be redundant, because of the nature of the relationship.

Every member of a cycle aggravates every other member in the cycle.

The discovery is constrained because of the use of a subset. If time permits, all remaining members of the problem set can be added to the structure.

Interpreting the Problematique. Even though the participants have produced the problematique correctly, there is no guarantee that they will be able to "read" it. Since institutions of higher learning systematically ignore formal concepts of relationships and the reading of digraph-like structures and cyclic structures, while spending more than a decade on language instruction; it cannot be assumed that reading such structures is automatic. To explore the ability to read such structures, G. S. Perino administered questionnaires to several dozen managers to see how well they could choose from multiple-choice questions what a structure portrayed. Not only did the managers lack the skills, but they misread the structure in ways suggestive that they were basing their responses on their prior experience with a problematic situation involving their own disciplinary backgrounds—one which happened to be inappropriate for that situation.

Since other instances support Perino's findings, it should always be assumed that a person who is skilled in interpreting such structures should meet with the group that developed the structure, and explain what can be learned from the structure.

It is rather dangerous to suppose that there exists any way to read a structure other than by stating the sentences that can be derived from exploring the structure itself and taking advantage of the fact that the relationship propagates along the direction of the arrows. But having said that, three points may often be worth emphasizing:

- **Working With Cycles.** Whenever a subset of problems lies in a cycle, a team formed to help resolve the problematic situation should always include at least one member who is knowledgeable of each (though not every) problem that lies in the cycle.

- **More Troublesome Problems.** Some problems lying at the extreme left of the structure (arrows directed from left to right) are among those that are most responsible for the problematic situation, because many problems to the right are made worse by those on the left.

- **Postponing Work.** Work on problems that lie toward the right of the problematique, (those being aggravated by problems on the left), may often be deferred until later while the problems lying to their left are dealt with since the latter, if left alone, will likely continue to work against efforts to resolve those on the right.

Developing the Problem Categories

It is very helpful to develop categories of problems for at least three reasons:

- **Ease of Discussion.** The availability of categories enables at least a two-level language to be used. This enables a discussion to speak of both the totality and of the components of the totality; a category and the elements in that category.

- **Developing a Category (Type 2) Problematique.** When both a problematique as described previously and a set of problem categories are available, it is possible to superimpose on the problematique a set of symbols representing the categories. Once this is done, it is possible to derive by inspection a second or Type 2 problematique: a problematique showing only the categories. This Type 2 problematique often yields insights that are not readily apparent from the Type 1 problematique. At other times, the pressure of time has forced Interactive Management staff to seek a Type 2 problematique directly, rather than do no structuring at all.

- **Matching Action Options With Problem Categories.** Once the descriptive work on problems has been completed, it will often be desired to move to a design posture, where it is very convenient from an informational-organization standpoint, and to satisfy Ashby's Law of Requisite Variety, to use NGT for each Problem Category as a way of stimulating the generation of options for the design. Further discussion of this condition and its successor conditions will be given in Part 3, Resolution.

Chapter 9

Metrics of Complexity

The system designer often wishes to compare several different designs before making a choice. The number of ways to compare designs is often quite limited, cost being a prominent consideration. But significant insight into the relative merits of different designs can be gained if metrics (i.e., numerical measures) of the different designs can be found.

Few metrics of complexity have been proposed. The most common is the number of elements in the system. This metric is not very useful. Compare the situation where System A has 1,000 elements, but no interactions among them; and System B has only 100 elements, but all of its elements are mutually interdependent. For System A, only 1,000 instances of concern are present, but for System B, if one adds the number of elements to the number of interactions, one gets 10,000; or ten times the number of instances of concern compared to System A.

Many researchers believe that complexity is in the system being observed, or in the system being imagined as a potential design. Whatever metrics might be chosen to reflect those beliefs, they may have a common property: they ignore the cognitive aspects of the problematic situation.

If, on the other hand, complexity is supposed to be a characteristic of the limited mental capability of the human being (who, if possessed with unlimited capacity would seldom find any system to be "complex"), several complementary metrics can be developed, based upon the synergistic connections between

- The empirical results coming from the behavioral scientists in the second half of the 20th century.

- The products from the use of NGT and ISM already mentioned.

In offering the several metrics to follow, the connections between these empirical results and the products from the use of NGT and ISM will be the focus of attention. All of these metrics are a consequence of group work. Why does group work take such a prominent place in systems science? There are many reasons, but one that influenced me considerably in my early research came from a study carried out by B. W. Tuckman.

B. W. Tuckman (1938-   ). (For a picture of B. W. Tuckman, please see Appendix 1: Gallery.) **Four Stages in Unregulated Group Work.** Tuckman studied many instances of group work, and identified a set of four stages that could describe most unregulated group work. These stages were "forming, storming, norming, and performing". No estimates of the amount of time for each of these stages has been given. Neither can it be assumed that all four stages occur in all group work. For example, it is quite possible that people who will be part of a group can come together, spend some time in getting to know each other, begin to argue about the topic (or some other subject altogether, unrelated to the purpose set for the group), and never arrive at any mutual understanding as to procedures which will allow the group to produce any constructive results. More generally, many groups may never reach the performance stage. Even if they reach the performance stage, they may not be able to produce any useful results.

In beginning my study of group work, I felt quite confident that it would be possible to develop processes that would bypass almost completely the first three stages discovered by Tuckman, moving directly into a performance posture.

Bypassing the Forming Stage. I felt that the forming stage could be bypassed if some individual would do enough preparatory work with the individual members of the group so that all that would be needed when the group convened were brief self-introductions of the members. With sufficient advance planning, no group time would be required for the forming stage.

Bypassing the Storming Stage. The vagaries and ambiguities of language imply that virtually all discussions of difficult situations will suffer from very low quality discussion. Moreover old animosities and previously ill-formed viewpoints help assure that a substantial amount of time is used in arguing. In addition, there will be factual information that ought to be shared by all, but instead may have to be discovered during the group process. Again, if careful planning is carried out that emphasizes providing the group with non-controversial common factual bases, and if the discussion itself is eliminated in the group process until such time as it can be dealt with totally in a clarification mode whereby the linguistic barriers are broken down, it should be possible to bypass the storming stage.

Bypassing the Norming Stage. Group facilitators may frequently ask the group how they should proceed. Almost all groups come together because of some special expertise gained from experience and specialized beliefs; but not from expertise in group work. Norming usually resolves itself into agreeing on a procedure (or even on facilities, as in international arguments about the shape of the table). There is no reason why groups should be asked to deal with any of these matters. If an adequate physical facility, a "situation room" as discussed in Chapter 7, is prepared ahead of time, the group can convene and begin immediately at the performing stage.

Social Overhead. The first three stages described by Tuckman can collectively be called "social overhead". As I have just discussed, sufficient advance preparation can eliminate virtually all of this social overhead which, of course, also represents financial overhead and may, often, consume all of the time that had been reserved for performing. If there be readers who think that what I have said here is unsubstantiated theory, let me assure you that these remarks have been verified hundreds of times in groups all around the world, by using Interactive Management.

Using NGT and ISM. The plan for NGT eliminates the storming stage by eliminating group discussion when ideas are being generated and by separating idea generation (done silently) from idea clarification.

Joint use of NGT and ISM eliminates the norming stage, because the processes have already been chosen based on scientific content and long experience.

The forming stage is virtually eliminated by adequate individual interaction from a member of the planning activity, whose special role is to assure that each participant comes to the group action expecting there will be no abuse, no surprises, no group asymmetry, and with well-defined and accepted roles.

Given these conditions, attention can be focused upon the complexity that typically accompanies the kind of problematic situation that requires group work.

Two Types of Metrics. The metrics to be discussed fall into two categories: situation metrics and problem metrics. All of the metrics are determined from group products emanating from the use of NGT and ISM. As I proceed, I will relate the metrics to the scholars who developed the underlying conceptual base.

Metrics for Which Data are Found from the NGT Products.

Two significant metrics can be computed easily from the products of applying NGT as described in Chapter 8. I have named these the "Miller Index" and the "Spreadthink Index". I named the former after George A. Miller.

George A. Miller (1920-   ). The "Magical Number Seven–Plus or Minus Two". Miller's publication in which he outlined experiments carried out to help determine the limits of human mental activities stemming from physiological limitations is among the most frequently referenced subjects in psychology. The idea is that the human being can call into mind at any given time only about 7 items. At the same time, it appears that the implications of these results for human behavior, individually, or in groups, is regularly ignored. How many times has a meeting been planned that takes into account the limitation discovered by Miller? What special planning is done which reflects this discovery?

Some time later, H. A. Simon (1916-2001) carried out similar experiments, the results of which supported Miller's views, and suggested that the "magical number" might be closer to five than seven.

Still later, I noted that if the number seven (made up from three elements and their four possible interactions) were thought to be those elements in the "magical number", perhaps the magical number ought to be thought of as three, because with four elements there are 11 possible types of interactions, giving a total of 15, which is well beyond seven.

In any case, Miller's work makes clear that the human mind can call into its working arena, its "scratch pad memory", only a few items. This being the case, why should anyone suppose that the many interactions involved in a system with more than a few variables could be dealt with by an individual manager or researcher without any frame for analysis that took Miller's findings into account?

With this in mind, I have chosen to name a metric of complexity The "Miller Index" after Miller.

The Miller Index (a Situation Index). The Miller Index is easily computed from the results obtained from NGT. Simply take the number of elements in the problem set and divide by 7. This gives a very conservative estimate of how remote is the possibility that, for many elements, all of the elements in the problem set could be considered simultaneously. At the same time if there are just 7 elements, then the value of the Miller Index would be 1. This gives a useful way to distinguish complexity from its counterpart. A Miller Index value of 1 is the border value between the Domain of Complexity and the Domain of Normality; the latter being the Domain where virtually all work in higher education is carried out.

Values of this index computed from 43 cases in the 1980s showed a minimum of 5.1, a maximum of 18.1, and an average of 9.2. These values are representative of what has been seen in intervening years. No value has ever been seen that is as low as 3, for example, hence in every instance the presence of complexity has been indicated. It can be reasonably inferred from this that people do not attempt to apply the systems science unless other methods have failed them, for otherwise it might be expected that now and then a value of less than 3 would have been seen.

The Spreadthink Index (a Situation Index). As mentioned earlier, spreadthink refers to the differences of viewpoint among individuals when voting on the five most important elements in the NGT selected subset. If each chose the same subset, the value of this index would also be 1. The value of this Index is found by counting the number of elements in the selected problems subset and dividing that number by 5. If everyone were in agreement on the most important elements, the value of the Spreadthink Index would be 1. Values of the Spreadthink Index coming from 43 instances of 1980's data are as follows: minimum value 3.8, maximum value 13.8, average value 6.8. These values should help understand why this index is so named.

Metrics for Which Data are Found from the ISM Products.

The problematique enables the computation of three problem metrics and two situation metrics. The problem metrics will be discussed first, since an understanding of them will help to understand the situation metrics.

Problem Metrics. For **each problem** shown on the Problematique, it is possible to count the number of *antecedents* (i.e., the number of problems that aggravate that particular problem). This number can range from zero to (one less than the total number of problems shown on the Problematique).

For **each problem** shown on the Problematique, it is possible to count the number of *succedents* (i.e., the number of problems that are aggravated by that particular problem). This number can also range from zero to (one less than the total number of problems shown on the Problematique).

Influence Score (a Problem Index). The number of succedents for a given problem is called the *Influence Score* for that problem. The higher the *Influence Score*, the more that problem aggravates other Problems. An initial hypothesis would be that the problems with high *Influence Scores* should be worked on first.

Activity Score (a Problem Index). The sum of the succedents and antecedents for a given problem is called the *Activity Score* for that problem. The higher the *Activity Score*, the more the given problem interacts with other problems. A problem may have a high *Activity Score* even with a modest *Influence Score*.

Net Score (a Problem Index). Subtract the *Antecedent Score* from the *Succedent Score*. If the result is positive, the particular problem tends to aggravate more than to be aggravated, but if the result is negative, the particular problem tends to be aggravated by others more than to aggravate others. This *Net Score* is helpful in interpreting the problematique, and in determining a strategy for future actions.

Situation Metrics. Two situation metrics are computed from data taken directly from the problematique. These are the De Morgan Index and the Aristotle Index.

De Morgan Index (a Situation Index). Let X and Y represent any two problems on the Problematique. If it is possible to get from X to Y by following the arrows, it is said that X and Y are "in the relationship" represented by the problematique (which is "significantly aggravates") and that there is a "path" from X to Y on the problematique. The *De Morgan* Index is found by counting all the unique paths on the problematique and dividing by 10. A value of 1 for this Index is the borderline between the Domain of Normality and the Domain of Complexity. [This definition is explained in my 2002 book *Understanding Complexity: Thought and Behavior*]

The *De Morgan Index* was evaluated by Dr. Scott M. Staley of the Ford Motor Company following twelve Interactive Management Workshops held at Ford. The values ranged from 11 to 51, with an average value of 26. For this set of workshops, the *Miller Index* ranged from 8.4 to 18.7, with an average value of 12.

Aristotle Index (a Situation Metric). This metric combines the syllogism of Aristotle with its one-sentence phrasing by Abelard, and the corresponding graphical construct showing an element, its antecedent, and its succedent as the three components of the syllogism, as reconstructed by Abelard. With this formulation, the number of "graphical syllogisms" in the problematique can be counted, and their number divided by 10 is what I have called the *Aristotle Index*. It measures the number of syllogisms in the problematique; and interpreting the number in this way helps explain why the problematique represents a very tight logic formulation that is seldom found to require any changes in the weeks and months following its development. Inevitably some changes could occur over time due to the introduction of new elements or to the removal of old elements as a result of successful implementation of a design.

The syllogism, discovered by Aristotle, is widely recognized among scholars as a fundamental breakthrough in comprehending formal human reasoning. In graphical terms, it corresponds to paths on a digraph of the form (X,Y), (Y,Z). Counting all such paths on the problematique one arrives at a count of the number of syllogisms contained there. Dividing that count by 10 yields a number that is called the *Aristotle Index*. For a single syllogism, the Aristotle Index is 0.1.

It is commonplace to find several hundred syllogisms on a problematique. Can you believe that managers think they can intuit ways to resolve such situations without applying the kinds of processes that have been constructed to assist people in working with problematic situations that involve such attributes? Believe it!!

Chapter 10

Diagnosing

Complexity is understood to arise when **no one** understands a problematic situation that is of concern to many. The context for such situations is invariably in some kind of organization (whether formal or not) in which some resources are available and in which some individuals are able to share information which, properly organized, will enable a diagnosis of the problematic situation to be made that is founded in the best available perceptions of the situation. There are many such situations around the world. When I speak of one of them, I use the term "local", although this does not rule out geographic spread. Each local situation requires the development of a local language with which to describe it, as stated in Chapter 3.

Empirical evidence gained in using Interactive Management over more than two decades has shown clearly that following any single individual's perspective on the local situation offers no optimism for success in resolving the situation. This is a very important conclusion to make because in today's world that is precisely what appears to be happening in many locations. Even when there is an appearance of representative government, there seems to be little enhancement of conditions because, as our work has demonstrated, the possibilities for more rapid learning and the possibilities for benefitting from the study of interactions among component problems invariably yield to political power–to power that does not benefit from in-depth study of interactions because the sole computer-assisted process that offers the learning opportunities that are needed is rarely used–namely, Interpretive Structural Modeling.

There is no other method available that assures the following combination of attributes:

- Consistency in model structure
- Facilitated dialog on component interactions, carried out in a way that assures the consistency
- Metrics of complexity that yield insights into different aspects of the problematic situation
- A track record of worldwide application in different cultures
- A track record of application in a wide variety of problematic situations
- Full documentation of scientific basis and of methodology, including role definitions
- Placement in the ongoing stream of scientific discovery extending through more than two thousand years of study on the efficacy of thought
- Simultaneous placement in the ongoing stream of scientific discovery of human behavioral pathologies emanating from the last half of the 20th century, supported by empirical evidence that they have been overcome by sound process design
- Facility designs that enable effective group work to be carried out, and a strategy for making those results available to persons who could not be present for the group work

In place of proposals for processes that incorporate this combination of attributes, what is found is a group of small organizations who offer membership in a network with opportunity to gain "brownie points" by giving papers in meetings, usually held in resort areas. In place of educational programs that offer instruction in the foregoing, it is found that most (not quite all) programs of higher education are restricted to "disciplines"; i.e., aggregates of unstructured, undisciplined information that is not embedded in a broad enough context to be readily applicable to local problematic situations.

One finds a few academic journals that have gained some respect by publishing contributions that lie in narrow areas, often supported by prior work developed in those narrow areas.

Diagnosis as a Specialty

Upon completion of the discovery activity, as described in Chapters 8 and 9, in a facility of the type described in Chapter 7, a large compendium of well-organized documentation has become available. It will often be possible to move ahead to carry out a design process that will take maximum advantage of this compendium. This compendium typically includes at minimum the following:

- A clarified problem set representing all of the problems that lie ahead which could be perceived by a dedicated group of individuals with complementary insights into a problematic situation
- A clarified, selected subset of the problem set
- A problems field in which the problem set has been placed in categories
- A problematique; a structure showing how problems significantly aggravate and/or are aggravated by other problems

Extensive empirical evidence shows that this compendium is best diagnosed by a specialist; an individual who has seen quite a few compendia, and has mastered the methods of diagnosis that have been devised. This individual may be identified as the "Interpreter". The individual who fills this role understands that nothing is to be inserted in the diagnosis that cannot be shown clearly to be a derivative of material developed by the group. The interpreter is not there to add new substance to the group's product, but only to carry out analyses and proposals that come directly from the materials developed, in the light of the basis provided by systems science.

The Interpreter. Using data only from the group products, the interpreter is assigned the following duties:

- Develop the Type 2 problematique
- Compute the values of the metrics of complexity from the data offered

- Apply the experience from the past to propose a strategy for design which incorporates the problem metrics, and develop a discussion paper that relates this strategy to the problematique
- Through study of the Type 2 problematique and, especially of any cycles contained there, develop a discussion paper that proposes membership assignments for teams where any cycles are found in the Type 2 problematique
- Prepare a slide presentation which presents all of this information to the group that produced the compendium. This presentation will first explain how the problematique is interpreted, proceed to explain and interpret the various metrics, explain the strategy as founded in the preceding material, and discuss team assignments
- Ask that those who attend the interpretation session consider the presentation from three perspectives: (a) whether the interpretation offered appears to be faithful to the material presented in the compendium, (b) whether any amendments appear to be appropriate to the compendium material, and c) whether the diagnostics as offered in the slide presentation seem to be appropriate as a basis for proceeding further toward resolution of the problematic situation

Following the conclusion of the diagnostic work, which could include iteration of the interpretation meeting if it seems to be required, a report of the discovery work (i.e., the description and diagnosis) will be prepared and disseminated as widely as appropriate, in preparation for a followup to resolve the problematic situation, if it should be concluded that a followup is appropriate. This will normally require a budget appropriation, which will often be made as a consequence of weighing the value of proceeding along the established lines against the value of carrying out other projects, all funded from a finite budget.

Part 3

Resolution: The Chapters

The Work Program of Complexity consists of Discovery and Resolution. Discovery was the subject of Part 2. At the completion of the Discovery component, all the products of that work are available as resources for use in resolving complexity. The Resolution component consists of two parts: Design and Implementation.

The task of producing a system design **(Chapter 11)** is informed by what was learned from the interpretation of the problematique and the problems field. The categories in the problems field become categories for action options in an options field. Starting with one of the categories, action options for resolving the problems in that category are generated and clarified using NGT. Once that category is completed, another category is chosen and action options are generated and clarified for that category. Continue until action options have been generated and clarified for all the categories.

At this point, the group is split into two or three sub-groups. Each sub-group takes the options **field** that was just produced and discusses among themselves which options they believe should be chosen for implementation. After at least one option is chosen from each category, the sub-group prepares a presentation in which the choices are to be explained to the other sub-group(s). To facilitate the presentation, each sub-group constructs an options *profile*. (The options profile is also called a "design alternative".) The options profile shows clearly which options were chosen and which were not chosen in each category. The options profiles are posted on the walls, and a representative of each sub-group explains their choices for the IM staff and the entire group. In the process, each sub-group notes the points of agreement with the other(s).

Whatever differences may appear are reconciled with the help of the facilitator from the staff **(Chapter 12).**

In past experience, there is a great deal of similarity among the alternatives, which is readily explained by the fact that a lot of prior work has gone into clarifying all of the problems and options. Because of this, the differences are few, and are usually readily resolved. Once the set of options to be carried out has been agreed on, the group now uses ISM to examine and organize the support relationship among the options. This type of relationship is responsive to the question: "Will achievement of option x help achieve option y?" Repeated use of this generic question using ISM leads to the development of a "support structure" or "optionatique". The latter word is coined to represent the parallel status of the options structure with the problems structure called a "problematique", the latter being a legitimate French word, no doubt created to represent the common focus on problems; while the absence of the other word from the language is no doubt representative of the lack of focus in education on design. Once again, the staff individual who is highly experienced in reading the structures will interpret the optionatique for the group.

At that point, they are ready to construct the detailed action chart that shows the chosen sequences for implementation **(Chapter 13)**, and a workbook that will explain each of the elements on the action chart in great detail. The chosen format for the action chart is that of the DELTA chart[1], which shows decisions, events, logic, time, and action. The chart and the workbook show who is expected to do what, beginning and ending at what estimated times, and the estimated costs. This material becomes the detailed plan of action which, as time proceeds, will be modified if necessary, as new information comes into view.

In carrying out the Discovery and Resolution activities, large amounts of structured information are generated. Usually quite a few people will be involved in implementation, who were NOT involved in the work that produced the work plan. It becomes essential for these people to learn

---

[1] The DELTA Chart is explained and illustrated in John N. Warfield (1994), *A Science of Generic Design*, 2nd Ed. Ames, IA: The Iowa State University Press.

some or all of what went on. For this purpose, a corporate observatorium **(Chaper 14)** is used, in which the products of prior work are laid out in the development sequence along the walls of a large room. Supplementary material (e.g., videotapes of the prior work, documents explaining the results) is laid out in the same sequence. Depending on the complexities and volume of material, an individual from the original group may be assigned to help people who pass through the observatorium with any questions they may have and to incorporate any amendments that may be required. Availability of this facility throughout the implementation time helps greatly to avoid confusion and to prevent mistakes before they can occur.

Chapter 11

System Design

Some enthusiasts believe that system design should be governed by a set of "requirements" drawn by the elite to focus and bring discipline to the unwashed minions who carry out design.

Others believe that system designers should inevitably be creative people who, if relentlessly urged to follow a large compendium of "requirements" in some design area, will leave that area in disgust and go to a field where their creative powers can be unleashed.

I suppose we can imagine some satrap handing requirements over to Da Vinci or to Michelangelo or to Beethoven or other creative people.

Insights from Spreadthink. We have already stressed the interpretation of Spreadthink to the effect that no one understands a problematic situation. When the developments described in Part 2 are carried out, we can expect that insight rather than requirements will govern the design situation. Those developments will unearth and provide the best-informed rationale and well-justified analytical aspects for future resolution of complexity and easing or eliminating the problematic situation.

Generic Design and Specific Design. The process of system design can be subdivided into generic design and specific design. The former is carried out as far as possible with generic methods; i.e., those already described, which are founded in systems science. The specific parts of the design are carried out using established methods or such innovation as is possible within the spectrum of insight that has been gained using the developments described in Part 2, which are the primary sources of insights to be used in carrying out the generic portion of the system design.

The generic portion is intended to yield responses to questions such as these:

- **Design Options.** What designable action options are possible to help resolve each problem category in the Problems Field? (These options, assigned to the appropriate problem categories, now make up the Options Field.)
- **Design Alternatives (Combinations of Options).** What combination of design actionable options (at least one from each options category) should make up a design alternative? (A design alternative is also called an Options Profile.)
- **Implementation Responsibility.** What organizational component should bear the responsibility for carrying out each option in a particular alternative?
- **Time and Costs.** What are the approximate work hours and costs associated with carrying out each design option?
- **Interdependence of Options.** Supposing that a particular design option x is carried out, would that help in carrying out another design option y, answered for all x and y in the Options Profile?

A system design reveals the set of actions to be taken, their interdependence, their locations in an Options Field, their place in an Options Profile, and the time program for carrying out the options contained in a particular Options Profile. The development of this time program is best done after the options have been generated, clarified, and structured; and then aggregated into a few Options Profiles (design alternatives). All of this activity is carried out by groups. The interpretation, once again, is a task for a specialist who is expert at reading and interpreting the group products in the same manner described in Chapter 10.

The Specialist at Work. The specialist now has another task, which is to prepare a work plan for resolving the problematic situation. The specialist cannot rely on old means of presenting the work program for a problematic situation. The PERT (Program Evaluation and Review Technique) Chart and line diagrams (Gantt Charts) have been used for many years to portray time programs for implementing system designs. Their wide acceptance does not mean that they are adequate for the purpose of structuring a time program for problematic situations.

Older methods of presenting work programs suffer from several serious flaws, largely related to assumptions that lie behind the presentations. Here are assumptions that lie behind these presentations which are not useful:

- **Defective Assumption.** Work programs are at best only moderately dynamic, so only a very few intermediate decisions will be made as the program proceeds, so a graphic that shows only events and actions will be adequate to portray program progress. A few changes may be made, but the diagrams can be easily updated to reflect the progress.
- **Defective Assumption.** Large amounts of information should be compressed into small pages, otherwise they will not fit in the required reports; but if this proves to be completely impossible supplemental slide presentations and videos or compact disks can be provided to portray the work program and its progress, along with percentage of completion and percentage of expenditure.

This Chapter is deliberately short to emphasize the key concepts in system design. The generic design science, a component of systems science, is presented in a book of about 600 pages.

Chapter 12

Choosing From The Alternatives

There exist in some of the several systems communities established sets of algorithms that are recommended in those communities for choosing among a set of alternatives. While these algorithms differ in some details, they typically have in common that they are numerical in character and rely on numerical computations to prioritize the alternatives. The preferred situation often is one in which the numbers arise out of physical or economic data, but the use of data from social "instruments" such as questionnaires is not precluded. It is also common to suppose that one analyst, supplied with the data and the algorithm, can carry out the computations and arrive at the recommended choice.

On the other hand, powerful executives are known often to override results obtained analytically, preferring to reach conclusions based on their own intuitive judgments, stemming from their personal experiences.

Occasionally legislation is passed that requires the use of certain procedures to arrive at choices, when excessive public pressure is brought to bear and the threat of immobilizing litigation seems to be too much to tolerate.

Often none of these ways of reaching a choice seems to be very satisfying to those involved, and many times outcomes seem to occur that are not what anyone desired.

In the light of what has been said in this book, one ought to be prepared for the possibility that the processes that have historically been used to arrive at choices of system designs have been limited in the first instance by the inadequacy of the design alternatives themselves, so that none of the processes thought to be appropriate could have found a satisfactory design.

If the systems science described in this book were used in the manner set forth to create sound design alternatives, it is conceivable that the various methods used in the past to make a choice among those sound alternatives may well have been suitable in instances where they otherwise would have failed. In any event, it is certainly true that the first prerequisite to making a good choice is to have sound alternatives from which to make a choice.

If that condition can be presumed, then a beginning point at making a choice can be made with the assumption of the following starting conditions. (The willingness to accept these conditions does not rule out the use of one or more of the algorithms referred to previously in this chapter; but it does delay their application at minimum until much greater insight has been gained into the problematic situation.)

- The problems field for the problematic situation has been found, and the dimensions of the situation have been identified, named, and used as categories in the problems field.
- The options field for the problematic situation has been generated, using the named dimensions from the problems field.
- Small groups, acting separately, have constructed at least two alternative designs, and have compared them to see how they overlap and differ.
- If possible, the two have been integrated into a single alternative through facilitated group discussion.
- If it is not readily possible to integrate the two designs, each design can be analyzed and, if possible, complexity metrics may be found and compared for the designs.
- Design criteria may be generated, using NGT.
- The designs may be compared based on the outcome of the application of the design criteria, as indicated in the Tradeoff Analysis Methodology[1] .

---

[1] The Tradeoff Analysis Methodology refers to a process that is described in detail in the author's 1994 book *A Science of Generic Design* (full citation, page 81). It allows objective and subjective measurements to be combined in making and portraying choices. It has been used with citizen groups concerned with public resource allocations.

- Still more sophisticated methods may be called on when required.

Choices of alternatives often involve iteration. Preliminary choices are often made on the basis of the best available information. Such choices then become the basis for allocation of funds to deepen the available information base. Whatever methods were used for the preliminary choice may be invoked a second time when the information base has been deepened. If this philosophy is invoked, one should recognize that the choice is not one of the final design, but rather one of the strategy for reaching the final design. Dr. Scott M. Staley's contribution in Chapter 15 is illustrative of the use of Interactive Management to develop a design strategy for developing the fuel-cell vehicle of the Ford Motor Company. The design problem is, then, the design of the strategy, and it would be well to recognize this at the outset of the work. Later the design of the proposed system can be called up as the task when enough insight has been gained by applying an appropriate design strategy.

Sometimes a well-chosen design strategy will reveal that the original intent of a program was, itself, ill-chosen.

Chapter 13

Implementing the Design

Systems science can be applied at small scale and at large scale, but one supposes that its principal application will be at large scale. Applied at large scale, one supposes that large sums and large numbers of people will be involved ultimately in implementing a design.

Not many people design systems from a beginning in a scientific base all the way through continuously to a finished and documented design. The pool of documented design experience with stories of success and failure from which to draw lessons is relatively small. The extensive effort and considerable difficulty involved in documenting all the steps from beginning to end in a large system project is foreboding. A major challenge in implementing a system design lies in conveying what was conceptualized from those who conceived the design to those who will implement the design. So we arrive at the issue of how the work of a small number of creative people who have **collaborated in achieving a design of substantial intricacy, with considerable difficulty, can be communicated to a larger group of people who will often play a variety of roles in implementing the work of the small group.** This challenge is to be met in the face of what we have already seen to be a number of behavioral pathologies that will be found in every part of human endeavor which, if left unattended to, will be working constantly against success.

Hence it is no surprise that George J. Friedman, from his post as chief technical officer of Northrop Corporation, found that the most prevalent reason for the failure of large systems lay in the cognitive aspects lying between design and implementation; and that experience with the small numbers of variables in the equations of physics proved to be poor background for working with large numbers of variables in systems of high complexity.

The pioneering spirit that drives human beings to take chances in designing systems with high values of complexity metrics is in line with that of Columbus when he chose to cross the Atlantic. But the time is near at hand when a kind of sea change is now possible in the way large systems can be designed and implemented. It is time to appreciate that a scientific basis is now available and that, while it can be still be very exciting to take part in large-scale systems projects, the nature of the excitement can turn from that arising out of surprises that guesses turn out to be successful to a kind of excitement that group achievements turn out to be even more successful than those which the early rugged individualists could achieve with limited resources.

Chapter 14

The Corporate Observatorium: Sustaining Management Communication and Continuity In an Age of Complexity[1]

The prevalence of complexity is a fact of life in virtually all large organizations. However the ways in which organizations try to manage that complexity are largely out of touch with relevant scholarly results. Instead management actions are still overly-governed by fads. This phenomenon has been described by Russell Ackoff as "panacea overload".

The late Harold Lasswell recognized a critical aspect of the management of complexity (essentially ignored in academia and in the political scene), when he proposed the development of the "social planetarium", and (later) the "urban planetarium" back in the days when cities were in turmoil through the United States of America.

That proposal, with some modifications, is the basis for the concept of the "corporate observatorium". It is a piece of real estate, whose building interior can be loosely compared with that of the Louvre, in that it contains a variety of rooms, and facilitates rapid familiarization with their contents by the persons who walk through that property. Further analogy comes from the recognition of the importance of wall displays (with complementary explanatory electronic adjuncts), large enough in size to preclude any necessity to truncate communications; and tailored

---

[1] This Chapter draws heavily on my article "The Corporate Observatorium: Sustaining Management Communication and Continuity in an Age of Complexity", in Tanik, M. M., et al (Eds.), Integrated Design and Process Technology, IDPT-Vol. 2, 1996. (*Proc. Society for Design and Process Science*, Austin, TX), 169-172.

to help eradicate or minimize complexity in understanding, both broadly and in depth, the nature of the large organization, its problems, its vision, and its ongoing efforts to resolve its difficulties. Comparison with the planetarium for envisaging a broad swatch of the sky is self-evident.

Seven critical forms of representation of complexity will be described briefly. Their significance in sustaining communication and organizational continuity via the corporate observatorium will be indicated. Potential application in higher education will also be briefly described.

In June of 1988, Professor Henry Alberts of the Defense Systems Management College, Fort Belvoir, Virginia, conducted an "Interactive Management Workshop" (Warfield and Cárdenas, 1994) on the subject "What do Technical Managers Do?" The participants in this activity were experienced program managers who oversee very large and expensive military systems development. (More on Professor Alberts' work is included in Chapter 16.]

A little over eight years later, Professor Alberts walked down the aisle in London to receive his Ph. D. degree, majoring in systems science. This degree was awarded as a result of an extensive period of intermediate work that began in 1988, as indicated above, and culminated in 1994 with the passage of U. S. Public Law 103-355, the "Federal Acquisition Streamlining Act of 1994." A large number of Interactive Management Workshops managed by Professor Alberts provided the intermediate outcomes required.

There was little or no expectation in 1988 that the entire U. S. defense acquisition system could be systematically redesigned nor, if it could be, that such a design could find its way through the political establishment and replace mountains of prior U. S. code under which military acquisition had become the subject of intense distrust and large waste of resources.

Still, this work had answered "yes" to the following question:

"Is it possible to redesign a very large, expensive, significant public system, systematically, relatively remote from the normal political processes that produced the existing unsatisfactory system, and then get that old system replaced through the standard political mechanism?"

Having observed what had to be produced to comprehend and design such a large system, inevitably serious questions ensued, of which the following is of great present interest:

"How can people learn in depth what is involved in the design, operation, and amendment of very large, expensive systems, once such a design has been completed?"

This question may, also, have a positive answer. It may well be possible for many people to learn what is involved in designing, operating, and amending such a large system and, actually to understand in depth how it works. If so, there is every reason to believe that the means of achieving this can be adapted, with minimal conceptual change, to many other systems of importance to society. It is with this belief in mind, that the concept of "corporate observatorium" is set forth here.

THE LASSWELL TRIAD

The possibility of broad-based learning about very large systems becomes more realistic when what is called here "The Lasswell Triad" is understood.

Harold Lasswell (1902-1978) was a political scientist, one of the foremost authorities in that field. As a faculty member, he taught law and political science at the University of Chicago, Yale, and elsewhere. Author of many books and papers, he originated key ideas relevant to the effective design and understanding of public policy, which remain essentially dormant today.

One of his key views he expressed as follows:

"Our traditional patterns of problem-solving are flagrantly defective in presenting the future in ways that contribute insight and understanding"

The Lasswell Triad is responsive, in part, to this view. It consists of these three concepts:

- The decision seminar (taking place in a specially-designed facility) (Lasswell, 1960, 1971)
- The social planetarium (Lasswell, 1963)
- The pre-legislature, or pre-congress (Lasswell, 1963)

In brief, here are the key ideas involved in this Triad, adapted to correlate with the latter part of this paper:

The Situation Room. First, a special facility needs to be put in place, where people can work together on design of policy (or other) issues, and where the display facilities have been carefully designed into the facility, so that they provide prominent ways for the participants to work with the future "in ways that contribute insight and understanding".

The Pre-legislature. Second, this special facility should be used extensively to develop high-quality designs long before legislatures or corporate bodies ever meet to try to resolve some issue facing them by designing a new system (e.g., this is a sensible way to go about designing a health-care system to which the political establishment can repair for insights and such modifications as seem essential).

The Observatorium. Once a system design has been accepted, the observatorium layout is designed and established so that people can walk through a sequential learning experience, in which they gain both an overview and an in-depth understanding of the system that has been designed and which, most likely, will be prominent in their own lives.

The description of the observatorium represents only modest deviations from the situation room component of the Lasswell Triad, but slight changes in nomenclature have been adopted for purposes of this paper.

Given that relatively little has been done with the Lasswell Triad, two questions might arise. The first might be: "Why?". Another might be, "Are there additions that have to be made that, when integrated with the Lasswell Triad, provide a practical means for enhancing greatly the design, management, amendment, and understanding of large systems? This last question will now be answered: "Yes".

Preparing For The Observatorium

No one would expect that the observatorium would be brought into place unless the "art" required to fill it were available, and if the topic were of vital social importance.

It would, therefore, be important to have conceived and created the situation room required for effective group work, and to have conducted the necessary pre-legislative activity to provide the raw display information for the observatorium.

A situation room of the type desired was developed in 1980, and has since been put into place in a variety of locations (Warfield, 1994). Rooms of this type provided the environment for the Alberts work, and for many other applications of Interactive Management (Warfield and Cárdenas, 1994). Thus the first essential preparation for the observatorium is complete.

The Alberts application, and other ongoing applications are providing the second essential raw display information.

What kinds of displays are required for the observatorium? These displays must meet stringent communication requirements. In brief, they must meet the demands of complexity for effective representation. This means, among other things, that they must be large, and they must cater to human visual requirements.

Representation Of Complexity

The Lasswell Triad clearly relies for its adoption and use, upon the availability of ways of representing complexity that place it within the realm of human comprehension.

There is a long-established penchant among scientists of all varieties to place everything possible in mathematical or numerical terms. Depending on the specific mathematics chosen, and the numerical forms adopted, the potential learner group for such representations is greatly reduced. Does this mean that only the mathematically-educated or the numerically adept can fill effective citizenship roles in a democracy, where public understanding is necessary for good decisions?

A prolonged study of complexity (Warfield, 1994) establishes that it is high-quality, graphical communication means which must be used if large, complex systems of the type studied by Alberts can be brought within the grasp of ordinary mortals.

Literally dozens of such defense-acquisition-specific representations were developed by Alberts and they provide the raw material which, if introduced appropriately into a "defense acquisition system observatorium", could provide the sequenced pattern of learning that even the Congress would require in order to understand the system beyond the confines of a few of their committees.

Prose alone is inadequate to portray complexity. Mathematics is often unavailable because mathematical language is restricted to a small percent of the population. For this reason, language components comprised of integrated prose-graphics representations enjoy unique potential for representing complexity.

Because of the desirability of taking advantage of computers to facilitate the development and production of such integrated representations, it is best if the prose-graphics representations are readily representable in computer algorithms, even if their utility for general communication is limited. Mappings from mathematical formats to graphical formats can often be readily done, although manual modification of graphics for readability may be necessary.

The following specific graphical representations have proved useful in representing complexity:

- **Arrow-Bullet Diagrams** (which are mappable from square binary matrices, and which correspond to digraphs)
- **Element-Relation Diagrams** (which are mappable from incidence matrices, and which correspond to bipartite relations)
- **Fields** (which are mappable from multiple, square binary matrices, and which correspond to multiple digraphs)
- **Profiles** (which correspond to multiple binary vectors, and also correspond to Boolean spaces)
- **Total Inclusion Structures** (which correspond to distributive lattices and to   power sets of a given base set)
- **Partition Structures** (which correspond to the non-distributive lattices of all partitions of a base set)
- **DELTA Charts** (which are restricted to use with temporal relationships, and which sacrifice direct mathematical connections to versatility in applications)

Virtually no instruction is given in higher education even simply on how to read these high-quality, scientifically-based representations. On the other hand, it is very common to see low-quality instances of graphics types in use, where they communicate very little except, possibly, to their originators. These low-quality graphics are frequently adjuncts to a wide variety of proposed management strategies for dealing with complex situations. Over 20 of these have been discussed as "alleged panaceas" (Ackoff, 1995), who concludes that "very few of these panaceas have delivered all they promised to those who adopted them".

All of the scientifically-based representational types have been thoroughly explained, and many examples of their use in a wide variety of applications are available (Warfield, 1994). Most of these types were used in the Alberts dissertation (Alberts, 1995), and can be seen there as they related specifically to defense system acquisition. The same types were used to explore in a student design course, the redesign of a large systems curriculum (Cárdenas and Rivas, 1995), and to explore high-level design activities at Ford Motor Company, where aspects of the graphics representations facilitate computation of numerical indexes of complexity (Staley, 1995).

The exploration of the large systems curriculum can, itself, be a prototype for exploitation in academia, to open up curricula (e.g., public policy curricula currently heavily oriented to "policy analysis") to activities such as large-system design.

Summary

A significant step in resolving issues related to large systems, is to provide a well-designed situation room, equipped to enable groups to work together effectively. A further step is to carry out whatever prolonged design work is required, using processes proven to be effective, yielding visual displays of the system patterns that hold understanding of the logic underlying the system. The results of the further step can be shown in the corporate observatorium, where insight into the large system comes both at overview and detailed levels, according to the efforts put forth to comprehend what is seen in the sequenced displays.

References

Ackoff, R. L. (1995), "'Whole-ing' the Parts and Righting the Wrongs", *Systems Research* 12(1), 43-46.

Alberts, H. C. (1995), "Redesigning the United States Defense Acquisition System", Ph. D. Dissertation, Department of Systems Science, City University, London, United Kingdom.

Cárdenas, A. R. and Rivas, J. C. (1995), "Teaching Design and Designing Teaching", in *Integrated Design and Process Technology*, (A. Ertas, C. V. Ramamoorthy, M. M. Tanik, I. I. Esat, F. Veniali, and Taleb-Bendiab, Editors), IDPT-Vol. 1, 111-116.

Lasswell, H. D., (1960). "The Techniques of Decision Seminars", *Midwest Journal of Political Science* 4, 213-236.

Lasswell, H. D., (1963). *The Future of Political Science*, New York: Atherton Press.

Lasswell, H. D., (1971). *A Pre-View of the Policy Sciences*, New York: American Elsevier.

Staley, S.M. (1995), "Complexity Measurements of Systems Design", *in Integrated Design and Process Technology*, (A. Ertas, C. V. Ramamoorthy, M. M. Tanik, I. I. Esat, F. Veniali, and Taleb-Bendiab, Editors), IDPT-Vol. 1, 153-161.

U. S. House of Representatives Report 103-712 (1994), Public Law 103-355, "Federal Acquisition Streamlining Act of 1994"; August 21, 1994.

Warfield, J. N., (1976). *Societal Systems: Planning, Policy, and Complexity.* New York: Wiley.

Warfield, J. N., (1994). *A Science of Generic Design: Managing Complexity Through Systems Design*, 2nd Edition. Ames, IA: The Iowa State University Press.

Warfield, J. N. and Cárdenas, A. Roxana (1994), *A Handbook of Interactive Management*, Ames, IA: The Iowa State University Press.

Part 4

The Practitioners ("Systemists"):
The Chapters

Part 4 represents the encapsulation of empirical evidence of systems science as it is represented in action. The action normally is of two types: teaching parts of the subject matter in universities, or applying the action component in some problematic situation. In the second form, it will normally be discussed by indicating how "Interactive Management" (which is the action component of the science) has been used.

This Part consists mostly of contributions of individuals from different parts of the world who have found the systems science useful in some way in their own careers. They were invited to describe in their own language how they saw the work as contributory to their careers, being made aware that what was sought was some evidence that the systems science had been tested in use and not found wanting.

I felt that there were two ways that could have been most useful to organize this Part. One would have been to organize it by **the geography of the applications**, to emphasize that the work has demonstrated the absence of geographical boundaries. The other would have been to emphasize **the type of organizational setting in which the applications took place**. I felt that this second way would be more beneficial to readers, since they would be more likely to find a way to envisage themselves in the same type of organizational setting where a particular kind of application took place. In order for this to be valid, I had to try to choose application types such that most readers could identify with at least one type. I hope that I have been successful in this respect. I have organized the chapters by the types that I have chosen. Although I am showing in Appendix 1 (the Gallery) pictures of the principals corresponding to each Chapter, several of them have been involved with more than one of the types, and I apologize for appearing to restrict the domain in which they have been active. Professor Broome, for example, is employed in the education sector. He provides educational services related to the systems science in his employment in that sector; but provides services in the social arena on the island of Cyprus, where he has been working with Greek and Turkish Cypriots for quite a few years. Roy Smith was employed in the private sector, and some of his applications took place there, but most of his recent work has been in the social arena. Others of those listed are retired from their regular employment and may be working across sectors as consultants. The sector designation just means that the actor provided the services described here to the identified local sector.

I thank those who are represented here, and apologize to those who may feel that they have been slighted by not appearing here. Some whose work deserved to be represented here are not represented for various reasons unrelated to the quality or nature of their work. I especially regret the absence of contributions from Carol Jeffrey and Alexander Christakis.

There are four local "sectors" represented here:
- The private sector
- The government sector
- The social sector
- The education sector

These sectors often overlap, this being one reason why several of the practitioners have been involved with more than one sector.

The reader will note that the level of specificity concerning applications varies from one contributor to the next. This is an inevitable consequence of my desire to avoid constraining the contributors, since I felt the greatest value would be found if they were to write what they felt was most appropriate for a book of this type. Readers who would have preferred more detail on the part of some contributors should not hesitate to contact them directly, since I feel that any of them would be pleased to provide more information in all instances other than those which may involve proprietary information.

In addition, substantially more information is available on many of the applications mentioned here in the "Warfield Special Collection" at the George Mason University Fenwick Library in Northern Virginia. Appendix 2 provides details on this body of information, including computer links.

Chapter 15

The Private Sector
The Practitioners ("Systemists")

G. S. Chandy
Photo: Appendix 1 Gallery Fig. P15-1
Rediscovering The World: The Structure In The System
(organizational management)

G. S. Chandy is a mathematician and entrepreneur in India, who is also known across India for his political writings in striving to enhance democratic government. As he describes in his article, he seeks to improve management at various levels, including the self-level of the individual, and higher organizational levels.

Koichi Haruna
Photo: Appendix 1 Gallery Fig. P15-1
Ontologically-Based Systems Engineering
(systems engineering strategy and leadership)

Koichi Haruna is Corporate Chief Engineer, Research & Development Group, Hitachi Corporation. Formerly, he was Director of all three of Hitachi's Systems Engineering Laboratories, before attaining his present position at the Corporate level.

Wan Jiangping and Yang Jianmei
Photo: Appendix 1 Gallery Fig. P15-1 Fig. P15-2
Research On Software Production Support Structure
(software design)

Wan Jiangping and his faculty colleague and adviser **Yang Jianmei** are working to enhance software development in China through the South China University of Technology. Choosing to bypass conventional practice, they are applying the "Work Program of Complexity" to software design and development.

Jorge Rodriguez
Photo: Appendix 1 Gallery Fig. P15-2
Warfield Methodologies In Mexico's City Arena
(project management)

Jorge Rodriguez is a faculty member in one of the three Mexico City branch campuses of the Instituto Tecnologico y de Estudios Superiores de Monterrey (ITESM) and consultant to local industry and governmental institutions. In Mexico City he has found numerous applications in his teaching, working with the project method where present or former ITESM students find projects in their organizations and apply the action component of the systems science to resolve the complexity.

Scott M. Staley
Photo: Appendix 1 Gallery Fig. P15-2
Application Of Interactive Management
In Ford Motor Company, 1990-2005
(corporate strategy design, software system design)

Scott M. Staley is Chief Engineer for Fuel Cell Systems and Vehicles in Ford Motor Company, where he has been providing the principal leadership in the introduction and application of systems science and Interactive Management at Ford for about 15 years.

G. S. Chandy (India)
Rediscovering The World:
The Structure In The System

"General Systems Theory"–a way to understand the world?

I first came across subject matter described as "general systems theory" in 1974-75. This material seemed, at first sight, to offer real answers to a couple of questions that were seriously troubling me: why do our human-made systems – individual, organisational and societal – so often go wrong (to contrast with the spare elegance and *rightness*, so to speak, of "nature's systems")? And further: what, if anything, can we do to set our human-made systems right?

I'd had a fair bit of experience with my own 'personal systems' going very wrong – and I could see, all around me, innumerable examples of individual, organisational and societal systems also going wrong or at least performing sub-optimally. There are literally millions of human-made systems, and the great majority of them (I feel) are performing sub-optimally; a quite sizable number of them are even failing catastrophically. Nature's systems do seem to perform much better. If so, it should be worth a lot to humankind to work towards improving the effectiveness of our systems.

Therefore I embarked on a study of the available systems theory quite intensively for several years, but found that I was quite unable to *do anything practical at all* with this seemingly very exciting concept of 'systems'. Then, In 1979, I read that John N. Warfield (JNW) was visiting several cities in India on an invitation from Tata Consultancy Services through the Institute of Electrical and Electronic Engineers, courtesy of Dr. Robert W. House and Mr. Faqir Kohli, to present his view of systems, with specific reference to applications. I visited JNW at his hotel at Bangalore to proffer him my conundrum of being hugely excited about the concept of systems but simultaneously being quite unable to do absolutely anything with this exciting concept.

A Practical Way to Look at Systems: A Whole New World

JNW suggested that I might like to attend a workshop he was conducting where he would be explaining his view of systems, which should show a way of doing things practically in systems. I attended the 3-day workshop (with some little skepticism in my mind, I must confess, as I had read a great many books and papers on systems that had promised just that and failed to show me anything practical that I could do with a system). But I went away at the end quite convinced that I really had to explore, in much more depth, the fundamental idea that JNW was putting forth: "understand the structure of the system in order to understand the system". (Reverse the idea, and its validity is possibly even higher: **If you do not understand the system structure, you just *cannot* understand the system!**)

After the workshop, on getting hold of the book *Societal Systems: Planning, Policy and Complexity* (J.N. Warfield, Wiley, 1976) and then a whole lot of other papers discussing Warfield's views, I found a whole new world opening up before me. This is a world where the previously mysterious working of systems could, just possibly, become clear to the people involved, at each and every level of the system. Looking at systems in terms of their structure was certainly helping to make things clearer to me.

But 'Pure Technology' is Not Enough!

My own background is engineering, followed by studies in pure mathematics – and it does happen that we technical types often fail to realise that technical ideas that have become locked into our thought and our natural language, so to speak, may not be natural at all to non-technical people. We will not succeed in applying systems science in the world till we enable people to think of and work in systems using their natural language (or something very close to it). It took me quite a while (and considerable internal struggle) to understand the enormous implications, in terms of the way we work, of what JNW has identified as **'The Foundations': the human being; language; and second-order thought.** These implications include:

One: The people involved in any problem or issue have to be seen as integral to the design, maintenance and operation of the system that's designed to resolve the problem, handle the issue (whatever it may be). If this is not done, you can simply bid goodbye to the hopes of creating an effective system for any purpose.

Two: The people involved need a language that is appropriate to the needs of communicating about systems – if an appropriate, sufficiently rigorous language is not used, then communication about and in the system will suffer and again it will be goodbye to effectiveness of the system.

Three: People at every level do need to possess some basic understanding about how to work with 'ideas' (their own ideas and as well as those belonging to others), because those ideas are the 'elements' that go into creating the systems within which we work and play and live. This may be a major hurdle for IM people in working to implement the structural view of systems – but it has to be overcome in order for it to be propagated widely.

It's All So Obvious – When You Know All About It!

Today - to anyone who has properly 'seen' a system in terms of its structure, and has worked with a system on these terms - most of these ideas seem to so very obvious as to be almost self-evident. **But it evidently could not have been all that obvious to begin with,** as it took many centuries, first, to develop the ideas that culminated in Interpretive Structural Modeling (ISM), the first practical tool that enables us to work with high effectiveness and efficiency towards understanding system structure. And then again, the benefits of this process are - even to this day - not obvious at all: to the world at large outside the relatively small community of people involved in "Interactive Management". We practitioners do need to do much more to enable the world to understand the extraordinary power and clarity that can develop, for the people involved through the fundamental idea of 'system structure'.

Integration: Creating "Models of Models"

Now here's a simple idea that has many implications: **If there are benefits in constructing 'structural models of *elements*' to describe a system, then those benefits would be multiplied manifold if we create 'structural models of *models*' to describe the system.**

What is a "model of models" – and how does one create such a thing? It turns out that the modeling process in "Field Representation" (FR) is perfectly designed to help us create a model of models. Consider, for example, the natural process we use to work towards a Mission – *any* Mission. Any individual or group would go through more or less the following multi-step process → think a bit about what needs to be done in order to accomplish the Mission, and then start doing that (perhaps making notes about various things to do). On doing various things to accomplish the Mission, the problem-solver(s) may come across barriers, difficulties, weaknesses and threats (BDWT) that may hinder accomplishment of the Mission. As we come to understand these, we try to create strengths or properly use the strengths we may already possess that would help us overcome BDWT. All the while, we try to keep our mind open to the opportunities that may arise, and we do various things to avail or capitalise on the opportunities.

Now, if we happen to be using the structural view of systems for our work, we would be making various lists of elements and structural models from those elements, to represent various aspects of the Mission. It turns out that we can create a very useful model of models to enable Mission accomplishment by using the categorisation process of Field Representation. We then obtain a model of models involving various natural dimensions of the complex of issues that arises while working towards the Mission – and these dimensions remain broadly the same regardless of the complexity or size of the Mission, whether it belongs to an individual or to a group (e.g. an organisation or even a nation). This particular 'model of models' is at this time called the "One Page Management System" (*OPMS*). [This name is likely to change in due course].

Paid Workshops for Organizations.

About 100 workshops were conducted for companies ranging in size from small to large. These received very favourable responses from almost all participants. The Missions taken up at those organisations are not listed here, as most are confidential. Some specific successful Missions with which I became engaged included the following:

- A student (Paul Coelho): "To understand my mathematics syllabus and thereby to improve significantly my results in my mathematics examinations"
- A student: "To get myself a satisfying and well-paying job". The student used a manual form of the process to develop and prepare herself to get a job, with exceptional success. This type of application can become a powerful human resources development tool
- Myself: "To write a non-fiction article". This is another prototypical application in which structuring enhances greatly the power of an author of prose.
- Software Design Team: "To create software up to an alpha test level". This was done in creating the OPMS software, with significant success.

Koichi Haruna (Japan)
Ontologically-Based Systems Engineering

Through his life of system scientist, John Warfield found that system science should go back to Greece.

Since 19th century, human beings have been only engaged in so-called linear model approach, that is the method of problem solving where human being should focus on finding what God made and on inventing how to use it efficiently. It also meant unnecessary fear about transcendental power in the field of science and engineering. However, it completely contradicts against our real experiences in system engineering field. His way is not the linear model approach, but a complex model approach, that is an ontological approach.

His technology does not belong to the modern technology but to technique as defined in Greece, and it is more scientific than the modern technology because it is more truthful.

He loves the works of Harary, Lasswell and Foucault.

He studied from Harary that group method is scientifically (mathematically) possible. Thereafter he recognized the importance of the concept of process while he attacked real system engineering problems. And he studied Lasswell and found what Lasswell had found, that is the fact that the problematique includes structure of problem solvers and process of problem solving as well as problems themselves and interactions among them. Then John tried to solve the problem with a hierarchical arrangement of four sciences because he felt sympathy with Foucault's philosophy of ontology.

Probably he is the first research scientist in the field of system science and engineering who found that integration of problematique-resolving activities should be ontological, but not recognition with methodologies. It was so deep findings that so few people could understand what he has been doing.

He taught such names as Harary, Lasswell and Foucault to me as soon as he felt those are important. I have to say that he always has been afraid if he could be appreciated by peoples of systems scientist and engineers of our ages and that he has always wished to have companions in the field. He has been a true innovator of our field in the point that he found the importance of the ontological approach in the field of science and engineering.

In the early ages of his research activities of Interpretive Structural Modeling, I knew it with my Stanford University teacher, Prof. Bill Linvill in 1973, and started the application project in Hitachi Corp. The following sentences show how and what it was.

In the initial stage of developing a complex system, each interest group sees the system according to its own requirement that is a reflection of its missions, experience, standpoint, and so forth. The fragmental pieces of the system's picture, so to speak, held by the interest groups must be brought together to yield a harmonized comprehensive view to be commonly owned by the whole interest groups of the system through mutual enlightenment, cooperation, and discussion in order to resolve the system problems. My papers firstly analyze such activities of the system requirement analysis for clarifying the necessary methodological conditions, next propose a method named PPDS (Planning Procedure to Develop Systems) for developing an objectives tree with its human-computer interactive system, and finally report the results of its applications in industries.

The PPDS consists of a problem finding method by using I-F (Interest groups vs Functions) matrix, a structuring algorithm named HSA (Hierarchical Structural Analysis) developed by the authors, and a group session procedure.

The problem finding method by using I-F matrix is effective in terms of (1) enabling about ten members to identify several hundred (200-300) pieces of requirements in a couple of hours, (2) allowing each participant to present his/her concrete requirement in a lively thought-provoking atmosphere, (3) giving a means both for observing whether problems have been identified sufficiently and for deciding a problem domain within which an objectives tree should be developed.

The structuring algorithm HSA is capable of making one to visualize an objectives tree in a style easy for him to see. It is a crucial capability of the system which supports improving a large scale complex objectives graph.

The human computer interactive system enhances the capability to develop a large scale objectives graph including more than two hundred items by facilitating a set of functions such as correcting, decomposing, merging, filing and retrieving of objectives graphs.

The results of more than fifty practical applications of the method show that one method for problem identification and structuring has passed the field tests and qualified itself to be of use in industry group activities including those of high-level managers.

John Warfield further has developed his technology as his other companions tell in this book. In those ten years, I have tried to design collaborative creating process(*) in organization while still continuing to keep contact with John, because his recent research results are also very interesting as well as suggestive.

(*)Haruna, K., (2002) "Technology Policy Process to Cope with the Complexity of Enterprize Technology Strategies" *Proceedings of the 46th meeting of the ISSS* in Shanghai, China.

Haruna, K., (2003) "Integrating Function for Managing Complexities in Organizational Co-creation", *Proceeding of the 2003 SICE Annual Conference*, Fukui, Japan.

Haruna, K., (2004) "Judging Function of Enterprise R&D Process to Adapt Information Technology Innovation", *Proceedings of the 48th meeting of the ISSS*, Asilomar, California.

Wan Jiangping and Yang Jianmei (China) Research On Software Production Support Structure

Software and Software Production

Recall the title of Brooks' famous and influential article is "No Silver Bullet". Brooks' theme is that the very nature of software makes it highly unlikely that a "silver bullet" will be discovered that will magically solve all the problems of software production, let alone help to achieve software breakthroughs comparable to those that have occurred with unfailing regularity in hardware. He divides software difficulties into two Aristotelian categories: **essence**, difficulties inherent in the intrinsic nature of software; and **accidents**, difficulties that are encountered today but are not inherent in the software product. He lists four of the latter which he calls complexity, conformity, changeability, and invisibility. In the context of his article, he uses the word "complex" in the sense of "complicated" or "intricate". The names of all four aspects are used in their non-technical sense. Brooks considers the three major breakthroughs in software technology to be high-level language, time sharing, and software-development environment, but stresses that they solved only accidental and not essential difficulties. For him, the greatest hope of a major breakthrough in improving software production lies in training and encouraging great designers. This idea is illustrated in Figure 15-1.

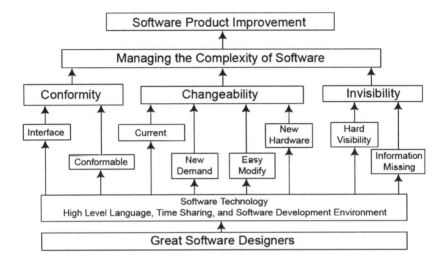

Figure 15-1. Illustrating Brooks' Concept of Software
Product Improvement Research Methodology

Since software is a kind of logic product, its quality improvement is related to complexity. Many researches are carried out to reduce the difficulty and the cost. The focus is on **software process** (SP) for software product. SP is the set of tools, methods, and practices we use to produce a software product. The objectives of **software process improvement** (SPI) are to produce software products according to plan while simultaneously improving the organization's capability to produce better products. A fully effective SP must consider the relationships among all the required tasks; the tools and methods used; and the skill, training and motivation of the people involved.

It is found that SPI involves complexity issues through literature reading and empirical investigation on the spot. **The study issue reduces to that of how to apply the Work Program of Complexity**

(WPOC) by Warfield to SPI. There are three problems in the following: (a) What is the theoretical foundation of WPOC being applied to SPI? (B) How to design the WPOC for SPI? And c) How to combine the WPOC of SPI with the business goals of the software enterprise?

The concept framework of study is formed from learning Warfield's complexity science, software engineering, and quality management. The hypothesis put forward is that the WPOC can be applied to SPI. The propositions of complexity of SP are set forth. The propositions are the theoretical foundations of WPOC of SPI. The WPOC of SPI is designed based on Warfield's WPOC, and the software enterprise model is also designed based on Microsoft's enterprise model and Infosys' knowledge management. Finally the software product support structure is established and its rationality and validity are illustrated by demonstration.

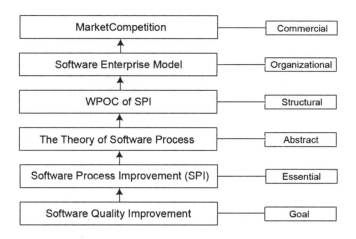

Fig.15-2 Diagram of Research Concept Framework Software Product Support Structure

The research concept is illustrated in Figure 15-2. It is established according to generating ideas, clarifying ideas, structuring ideas, interpreting the structure of ideas, and amending ideas. In the first, the goal of software quality improvement is essential to SPI, and SPI is abstract to the theory of SPI. The theory of SPI is structural to WPOC of SPI, and WPOC of SPI is organizational to software enterprise model and software enterprise model is commercial to market competition by business operation.

Based on the systems science support structure by Warfield, as it relates to Interactive Management, the software product support structure we provide is shown in Fig 15-3.

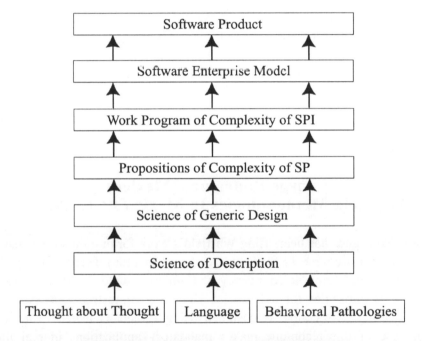

Figure 15-3. Software Production Support Structure

Software engineering, which is also a sociotechnical system activity, can be applied as an instance of the science of generic design, as conceived by Warfield. The propositions of SP are taken as theoretical foundations of SPI. This theory can guide the design of the WPOC of SPI (the structural presentation). When working in a software project, software engineers apply principles based on foundations of the software development process and product, through forming specific and pragmatic methods and tools. It requires interactive cognition processes that recognize the impact of complexity, making necessary that SPI be combined with software product management which, in turn, should conform with enterprise business goals. Software enterprise model also can be considered as an application model for software enterprise.

In our understanding, managing the complexity of software production can be abstracted through essence (i.e., the complexity propositions), and abstract problems can be made concrete through interactive cognition processes (i.e., the Work Program of Complexity of Software Process Improvement), and the concrete problems can be structured through continuous learning processes (i.e., knowledge management of SPI), with structural problems to realize business goals through the project management process (i.e., the software enterprise model).

Jorge Rodriguez (Mexico)
Warfield Methodologies In Mexico's City Arena

Jorge Rodriguez has been using Warfield's work for more than ten years. He lectures a course in Systems Design in Instituto Tecnológico y de Estudios Superiores de Monterrey at Campus Estado de México. This course is curricular for a Bachelor Degree in Industrial and Systems Engineering. His course is designed using Project Oriented Learning. The use of this technique makes mandatory applications in real life projects run by students. He has offered consulting services both by himself and leading students' teams.

The purpose of this paper is to present some empirical evidence of the utility of Systems Science and insights based on services provided for more than ten years to a considerable number of clients, including both Mexican Government Agencies, Institutes or Departments and private enterprises.

A Typical Case

Clients usually come from one of three different sources:
a.Referred from former students who understand application and benefits of Warfield's methodologies.
b.Referred from other satisfied clients.
c.Contacted by current students who happen to know client's situation and believed Warfield's methodological approach would be suitable.

First Meeting. On a first meeting, information is gathered in order to fully understand client's situation. The goal for this meeting is to get enough information for a proposal draft.

Second Meeting. On a second meeting, proposal draft is reviewed with decision makers in order to clarify any question and define necessary changes to achieve proposal approval. The main part to define in such a proposal consists on procedures and products. Typically Diagnosis (An analyzed and validated *problematique)* and Option Fields are offered and dates, number of sessions, sites, schedules, name of participants, materials and equipment needed are established as well as responsible for logistic issues. In this manner, a proposal summarizes the planning phase for Interactive Management.

Project Steps. Next step consists on the workshop phase. Proposal planning is implemented and results obtained. Normally, each workshop session represents a unique learning opportunity. Participants highly evaluate these sessions because they commonly find out different points of view from other colleagues involved in the problematic situation. These findings empower decision makers with better insights so they become able to solve problems effective and efficiently. All this is possible because proper use of diverse methodologies. First session include Nominal Group Technique to get a list of problems. Then, usually in the same session, ISM software is run to structure a *Problematique*. Next session begins validating the *Problematique* obtained. In order to do it, results from NGT are contrasted with the *Problematique* using some Metrics of Complexity to get critical, overrated and underrated problems and confronting participants with this evidence to determine if previous perceptions of problems importance or structural model are right. Once *Problematique* is validated an NGT session is run to get a list of solutions. Usually it is possible to structure solutions in an Option Field in the same session.

For Profiles determination it is normally necessary to prepare some feasible design concepts. Since development of design concepts requires strategic thinking, it is difficult for participants to develop such concepts by themselves. Once a design concept is defined, it is easy to determine if a specific option is part of the associated Profile.

Trade-off Analysis Methodology is used if a set of profiles become alternatives. In such cases, it is necessary to program an additional session to run it.

Typically, projects scope covers up to this point, but in some instances it becomes necessary to continue for a more specified design.

Satisfied Clients

Government Clients. Some satisfied clients that can be mentioned from Mexican Government Agencies, Institutes and Departments are: FIDE (Fideicomiso para el Ahorro de Energía) devoted to promote energy savings, INEA (Instituto Nacional de Educación para Adultos) dedicated to reduce educational gap in Adults, Secretaría de Desarrollo Social, Secretaría de Energía, Subsecretaría del Medio Ambiente del Gobierno del Distrito Federal.

Private Enterprise Clients. Also, it is possible to mention some satisfied clients from private enterprises: 3M, Procter and Gamble, Cemex, J.LYMYL, Exxon Mobil, Viajes Gerpa, Smurfit, Sara Lee, GE, Aseguradora Hidalgo.

As it may be observed, Warfield's work can be applied in both big and small enterprises and also in public or private sector. It should be mention that Dr. Warfield's geniality consisted on taking a series of powerful systems concepts who no one really knew how to use and created useful methodologies in order to make possible for people to understand and face complexity.

Scott M. Staley, Ph.D., P.E. (USA)
Application Of Interactive Management In
Ford Motor Company, 1990-2005

Introduction

It is my pleasure to respond to a request from Professor Warfield to summarize the activities, and the impact of those activities, that have taken place over the last 15 years concerning the application of his scientifically-conceived design process called Interactive Management (IM). In late 1989, as a member of the technical staff of the Ford Research Laboratory, I was involved in work to improve design and analysis processes in support of product developers in Ford Motor Company. Earlier, I believe sometime in 1987, I had read a paper from an NSF workshop on design theory and methodology that I thought would be of some help in my work. Returning to that article, I realized that Prof. Warfield and his team at George Mason University were well along in the process of developing the foundations of a science of design that could be applied in Ford. I contacted Prof. Warfield and that began a 15 year collaboration that included working together on applications of Interactive Management in key strategic areas for Ford, continued theoretical work on the scientific foundations of complexity and design, and the complete technology transfer of Interactive Management to Ford.

The Research Plan

The plan was simple. First, learn all that we could about the work that Prof. Warfield had completed on the science of generic design over the prior 20 years, starting from his work at Battelle Labs in the late 1960s. Second, apply Interactive Management to a key design problem in Ford to test its suitability for industrial use. And third, if the pilot project was successful, transfer the technology into Ford and develop the infrastructure to support widespread use.

The first application of IM in Ford was on the design of a large software system for the design and analysis of new vehicle powertrains. The project was called Analytical Powertrain, and the Ford Chief Engineer for the project, Robert DeLosh, sponsored this first IM workshop in Ford. Mr. DeLosh went on to become a key executive champion for the use of IM in other projects on the basis of the success of this first application. This first IM workshop in Ford took place in April, 1991. Over the next 13 years hundreds of Ford personnel would participate in IM workshops on topics ranging from the design of engineering software to create and optimize vehicle sub-systems, to the development of corporate strategies that would set the technical direction of Ford Motor Company product development for the next decade. The most recent Ford IM workshop was held in October, 2004, on the topic of a strategy for future powertrain technologies for Ford vehicles.

The Transfer Of IM Technology

The pilot application of Interactive Management was very successful, and a multi-year process was undertaken to bring IM into Ford Motor Company. Interactive Management was designed to be used intermittently in organizations for the purpose of enabling the organization to resolve those issues that could not be dealt with by normal processes. When nothing else worked, because of the complexity of the situation being dealt with, Interactive Management was to be available to help resolve the difficulties. In order to make this possible, a gradual progression in internal competency was anticipated which proceeded as follows:

a. **Year One**: All projects were planned jointly between Prof. Warfield and me, and all projects were carried out by external personnel (non-Ford) who were experts in conducting IM projects; with Ford providing the participants and the site for the work. The site was prepared according to the specifications of Prof. Warfield.

b. **Year Two**: All projects were planned jointly between Prof. Warfield and me, and all projects were carried out by Ford personnel who were closely supervised by IM personnel who were experts in conducting IM projects; with Ford providing the participants and the site for the work. The site was prepared according to the specifications of Prof. Warfield. During this period, with the support of Robert DeLosh, Ford built a specially designed room for the conduct of IM work. This facility was used for many years.

c.Year Three: Outside personnel were called on only when absolutely necessary; with well-trained Ford personnel planning and carrying out most of the work. When necessary, the Ford IM planners (normally me) consulted informally with Prof. Warfield on unusual matters arising in the course of work. During these years over 30 IM workshops were conducted, and hundreds of Ford people were exposed to IM as participants, observers, sponsors and benefactors of the work.

By the year 1995, Ford had become virtually self-sufficient in the application of IM. Workshops were routinely held to work on key strategic issues for Ford, and Prof. Warfield prepared a final report summarizing what had been achieved in the transfer of IM technology to Ford. All of this was done as part of his Ford-sponsored academic research assignment at George Mason University.

Key Applications

To give some flavor for the breadth of applications that have been carried out at Ford, the following list of select examples is provided. This is a very short sample from the topics of the 75 to 100 workshops that have been held over the last 15 years at Ford sites in the US as well as in Europe.

a.**Computer design of air-conditioning hose layouts for automobiles**. This application was one of several IM projects in vehicle subsystem design.

b.**Comparing rapid-response manufacturing concepts of four corporate giants**. This work was part of a multi-year, multi-million dollar government contract involving development of new CAD/CAM system concepts. IM was used on multiple work streams in this large project.

c.**Designing a corporate-wide product information management**

system. This was the first of many IM projects in the area of engineering information management and engineering software systems.

d.**Developing a Computer-Aided-Design (CAD) system strategy**. This work was the first to use Warfield complexity measures in reaching a consensus design for a CAD strategy for Ford. This work set a direction for the company which has been held now for over 10 years. In fact the name of the project, which would be easily recognizable by most Ford employees, was invented in the IM workshops conducted to develop this key corporate strategy.

e.**Designing a new corporate IT organization focusing on systems integration**. This organization is nearly a decade old, has over 400 employees, and has been a key enabler for Ford IT processes.

f.**Improving vehicle fuel economy**. IM has been used several times in developing improvements to fuel economy across the corporation.

g.**Improving and extending the Ford design process**. The Ford Product Development Process (FPDS) has been the focus of several IM projects to upgrade and revise its operating strategies over time.

h.**Deciding whether to strive for world-wide leadership in a new vehicle technology**. This is a relatively recent application of IM that gets into key strategic decision processes at the highest levels of the company.

As can be seen from the list, IM has been broadly applied in Ford. From designing car parts, to designing organizations, to redesigning processes, the domain of application is very broad. IM has been used for designing strategies probably more than anything else. And given the power of clearly reasoned strategies to a company, it is no wonder that IM has had such an impact on Ford.

Applications Feed Back Data to the Science

While IM was being first piloted, and then implemented in Ford, Prof. Warfield continued his development of the theoretical underpinning of the IM processes in the Science of Generic Design. Through a process of continually evaluating the results of applying the science to design in an industrial setting the developed science was verified or amended as needed. It was this aspect of working with Prof. Warfield over the years that was the most satisfying to me. Seeing, in a practical setting, the connections between the foundations of his design science and their impact on the tangible products of design work at Ford has convinced me that his is the only scientific theory of design.

The continuing association of the close link between real-world experience and the honing of the scientific treatment is very difficult to achieve, yet is essential to achieving the historical connection between theory and experiment that is required of scientific integrity.

As it has turned out, the work at Ford also lent new insights into the application of Interactive Management which have found their way back into the earlier stages of systems science. Among some of the developments that were made possible partly by Ford sponsorship and partly by the experiences gained while working on Ford projects were the Interpretation Session, the metrics of complexity, the direct application of Ashby's Law of Requisite Variety in matching problem fields with option fields, and the concept of the observatorium as a training vehicle for persons who were not involved in the system design, but who would have to be involved in the application of the system designs in various aspects of production and maintenance.

Conclusions

Much has been accomplished at Ford Motor Company in the application of Prof. Warfield's theories and techniques. However much remains to be done. The scale-up of the technology transfer of IM to Ford has yet to receive the infrastructure support that is necessary for enlarged, widespread and routine application. There is infrastructure required to support the conduct of IM work on a day-to-day basis, and there is infrastructure required to support the implementation of designs produced as the product of IM work. Neither of these infrastructures has been developed to the level required to implement the Work Program of Complexity (WPOC). It would seem that, at a minimum, the observatorium concept and the notion of interactions budgeting would be required for successful implementation of designs.

However, some of the key benefits of IM have been achieved over and over again in the Ford work:

a.Designs with clear strategic power are consistently produced.

b.Plans with broad consensus develop from a strategy.

c.Team building as a by-product of group work facilitates implementation.

d.Transparency of logic linking situation description to actions and budgets is well documented.

e.Complexity is managed by a set of tools specifically designed for the purpose.

The power of science is often forgotten in the process-driven world of engineering. I once read an article where the author said that design processes are not something that one could have a science of. With such thinking, which is not uncommon, unsupported theory is often substituted for science and this has been the state of design until Warfield. But in today's world, when the chips are down and technical progress must be made in designing complex systems in the face of worldwide competition, resort to science offers benefits that cannot be found from any other source. The Interactive Management system, based soundly in science, supports strongly the framework of systems science set forth in this book; at least from the perspective gained in its application in Ford Motor Company over the past fifteen years.

Chapter 16

The Government Sector
The Practitioners ("Systemists")

Henry C. Alberts
Photo: Appendix 1 Gallery Fig. P16-1
**Reminiscences of My Experience With
Interactive Management (IM)**
(systems engineering leadership)

Henry Alberts, Ph. D., retired from more than a decade of service at the Defense Systems Management College, following a distinguished career in industry and government, took on the task of leading the redesign of the defense acquisition system–a task that extended over more than five years. As he reports, this culminated in a legislative act that, on paper at least, revised the acquisition system.

At this writing, Henry teaches graduate students at the University of Maryland from his heavily-computerized basement in McLean, Virginia, for which he was rewarded with a distinguished teaching honor by the University.

Moses N. B. Ayiku,
Photo: Appendix 1 Gallery Fig. P16-1
**Introducing Interactive Management to
Ghanaian Scientists and Managers**
(national science and technology leadership)

Moses Ayiku, Ph. D., is a remarkable Ghanian patriot who is retired from a post at the Ghana Centre for Scientific and Industrial Research (CSIR). Degrees in Electrical Engineering. Doctorate in Systems Engineering. Studied law at the Inns of Court. Qualified to practice law in England. Heads his own law practice in Accra now that he has retired from government service.

Surinder K. Batra
Photo: Appendix 1 Gallery Fig. P16-1
My Experiences With Interactive Management
(contract research for clients)

Surinder K. Batra, Ph. D., gained experience in contract research with Tata Corporation. After spending a research period at George Mason University Center for Interactive Management he eventually obtained his doctorate in New Delhi and later left Tata to start his own consulting organization: CIMI, Center for Interactive Management, India.

Robert McDonald
Photo: Appendix 1 Gallery Fig. P16-2
The National Forum on Non-Industrial
Private Forest Lands
(natural resource strategy)

Robert McDonald, presently a private consultant, retired from a long and honorable career with the U. S. Forest Service and the Florida Forestry Service, where he pioneered the use of Interactive Management in a variety of projects, and continues to do so today in various settings. He has traveled to India (to work with Chandy), to Puerto Rico, and to other sites where his expertise is highly valued. His good humor is one of his greatest assets.

Reynaldo Treviño
Photo: Appendix 1 Gallery Fig. P16-2
Application to Prospective of Interactive Management
(national education strategy and long-range planning)

Reynaldo Treviño, at this writing, is a part of the Mexican federal government. He attended a short course in ITESM Campus Monterrey, on the subject of The Mathematics of Modeling. Shortly after that Roxana Cárdenas and Carmen Moreno did a followup course in the state of Leon, where Reynaldo was on the faculty of ITESM. Then Reynaldo and other ITESM faculty collaborated on an extensive program to enhance government in Mexico through strategic planning, with heavy public involvement. He had a leadership role in the First Interloquium during the Guanajuato Siglo XXI project, responsible for Scenario Building. Later, because of his outstanding work in assisting groups from various sectors of Mexican society in the vicinity of Leon, Guanajuato, he was invited to join the government of Guanajuato. There he had heavy responsibility for the enhancement of education. The 3-volume strategic plan for Guanajuato was produced by Reynaldo and other ITESM faculty associates from the Leon community.

Henry C. Alberts (United States)
Reminiscences of My Experience With
Interactive Management (IM)

First Experience with IM

My first experience with the Interactive Management process left me with doubts about the utility of the methodology and unhappy about having wasted my time. I had been asked by the Commandant of the Defense Systems Management College (DSMC) to participate in the attempt to surface and understand problems that were burdening the Defense Acquisition System (DAS). A number of members of the College faculty were invited to participate, among whom were the Provost, Academic Dean, Dean of Research, Heads of Departments, and a few Senior Professors. In total, there were 15 of us at the table. Additional faculty members were seated behind the active participants as observers who were only able to contribute through those seated at the table. The location was the George Mason University Center for Interactive Management (GMU-CIM).

On the first day, we participants went through the first steps in the specially equipped room that GMU had established for such purposes. We thought of and listed a large number of issues (problems) we thought were important, and had provided them in rotation around the table. All our issues were written down on paper and hung on the walls of the room. After more than one hundred issues had been listed and we were able to look at all of them on the walls of the room, the group was asked whether everyone understood what was meant by each stated issue. In many cases, the issues had to be much more carefully defined to ensure that everyone did comprehend the issue and the reasons for its existence and why it had been raised at the session. Since not all of us were familiar with the Nominal Group Technique (NGT) process, to some of us it was a mystery as to why all of this was necessary. By the time the day ended, I was tired, and unhappy.

Discussion with My Wife

When I returned home at dinner, I spoke about my day with my wife, a Clinical Mental Health Therapist. She immediately recognized the process and provided me with a well thought through statement about its utility and why it was necessary to be sure that all participants were "speaking from the same paper". Afterward, I began looking forward to the rest of the process hoping it would provide a basis for making suggestions about how to improve Defense Acquisition.

Continuing the IM Experience

The following day and the three days thereafter, I was an eager participant who was learning more each day about the problems of Defense Acquisition and the power of IM. When we began to construct relational models that showed how each of the various individual problems we had presented might affect all of the other problems raised, I saw the great utility of the directed graphics (which we called Problematiques, but whose mathematical nominative was "directed graphs – digraphs").

By the time the session ended, all of the participants were convinced that much learning had taken place, that each of us understood both the problems and their ramifications and we even thought we might be able to suggest acquisition system changes that would improve the DAS. In fact, some actions were suggested at the session and the Commandant indicated he both understood and would favor adopting some of them.

A Course Initiative

A few weeks after the session, I went to the Provost and the Commandant and asked for permission to adapt the Interactive Management Process to one of DSMC's special courses of which I was Course Director. The Technical Managers Advanced Workshop (TMAW) was suited for such a process since it was specifically aimed at developing better understanding of the way in which the DAS affected application of technology in developing new systems. The Provost and the Commandant agreed that I could experiment with the TMAW and inaugurate an extensive change in the methodology of its instruction. We also changed the process of selection of participants in the TMAW to ensure that those who came to spend a week with us exploring DAS in detail were qualified to help each other (and the DSMC faculty and staff) to understand how problems arose, the probable causes of those problems, and potential actions that might ameliorate them. We limited attendance to Project Managers (Military and Civilian Government Employees and Contractors) and exercised the right of participant selection. Not everyone who wanted to come was able to do so. Over the course of two and one half years, we held 15 sessions of TMAW and a wide spectrum of participants agreed on the most fundamental problems involved with the DAS. We then held a session among DSMC Faculty and Management to consolidate those problems and create a visual display of "hierarchy of difficulties".

A Timely Opportunity

Fortunately, at that time, the U. S. Congress was debating making change to the legal structure that governed Federal acquisition activities and the Senate Armed Services Committee (SASC) was the primary advocate for doing that. I spoke with both the Minority and Majority Counsels to the Committee and made them aware of the work we had done. I also made some suggestions about how to continue that exploration of potential changes to the DAS - this time under the auspices of the SASC. Both majority and minority counsel thought the idea had merit and the Committee Chairman wrote to the Commandant requesting him to devote the necessary resources to that work.

During the succeeding two years, many more Interactive Management Sessions were held to develop suggestions for change to the DAS and to pre-evaluate their potential assistance in making the system more effective and efficient. The SASC counsels participated in those sessions to help provide a product that might be suitable for putting into legislative action.

Passage of Legislation

At the end of 6 years of work, the SASC members introduced the legislation that would implement ideas for change that had been developed in DSMC's Interactive Management activities into the legislative process. The bill was passed by both houses of Congress and became the law governing the DAS process. It was the first time that such extensive research had been applied to a National issue and the mix of talented people participating in that research produced what has, over the years, proven to be a very useful product.

My Conclusions

My own belief after having used Warfield's Interactive Management Process extensively for over 15 years to focus on many diverse processes and problems is that it represents a most powerful tool that can, when properly applied, offer opportunities to craft change that has great potential to improve situations that create difficulties. I have helped in its application to such widely diverse areas as design of new aircraft, ships, and ordnance systems as well as production in both continuous process and batch process industries. I have also participated in IM discussions of management systems and how to improve those processes under conditions of almost continuous change in the environment within which they operate.

I am convinced that Warfield's IM process is the preferred approach to understanding complexity and devising mechanisms to improve operating systems involved with it.

Henry C. Alberts
McLean, Virginia, April 29, 2004

Moses N. B. Ayiku (Ghana)
Introducing Interactive Management to
Ghanaian Scientists and Managers

Introduction

In the early 1990s, the Ghana Council for Scientific and Industrial Research (CSIR) embarked upon a programme of commercialising its research results. At the same time, the CSIR was undergoing restructuring of its ten research Institutes and management structures. It was therefore welcome when a UNDP funded programme on **Capacity Development and Utilization Programme (CDUP)** included a project component on **Commercialisation of Science and Technology Information**. The Social Sciences Sector of the CSIR was then implementing this component of the CDUP. The other components of the UNDP programme implemented by other public and private institutions in Ghana are:

a. **Employment generation, job creation and career guidance**
b. **Training of entrepreneurs and operatives**
c. **Credit sourcing, and**
d. **Establishment of business bureau**

The programme was under the general supervision of a Programme Coordinator. The Coordinator felt that there was the need for a scientific approach to the problem of collaboration among the five implementing agencies of the programme. This essentially depends on efficient exchange of information among the components of the programme to enhance overall integration of the programme components. Since the CSIR itself was at that time undergoing structural changes, it was felt that these changes would make the CSIR more responsive to the needs of society. The CSIR management was therefore also interested in simplifying the problems associated with the need for attitudinal changes in the CSIR and also strengthening the linkages between producers and users of technology. The stage was then set for an invitation to Dr. John Warfield then a distinguished professor in George Mason University, Virginia, USA, to design and oversee the workshops.

Objectives of the Workshops

Dr. John N. Warfield, the originator of the Interactive Management System, designed three separate workshops. They were on:

a. Linkages between producers and users of technology in Ghana,
b. Attitudinal changes in the CSIR, and
c. Collaboration among the implementing agencies of the CDUP

The objectives of the workshops were generally similar. They were:

1. To introduce participants (CSIR top management and CDUP implementing agencies) to the science and utility of Interactive Management.
2. To generate ideas, classify/prioritise them and generate action plans to assist in solving problems appropriate to particular cases.

The Three Workshops

The first IM workshop conducted by Dr. Warfield (assisted by Ms. Roxana Cárdenas and Mrs. Carol Jeffrey) was on **Linkages between Producers and Users Of Technology in Ghana**. In answer to the triggering question "**what problems do you see in trying to strengthen the linkages between producers and users of technology in Ghana**", participants identified over 50 problems. Sixteen of the problems were prioritised and used to develop a 'problematique'. This problematique illustrated the extent to which a problem aggravated the others or was aggravated by others. Participants were pleasantly surprised to note that the problem of getting the two parties to meet and the problem of lack of enabling environment to adopt technologies generated in Ghana aggravated many problems. None of the others, however, aggravated these two problems. It was therefore clear that the solution to the linkage problem should first begin by tackling these two problems.

The second workshop dealt with **Attitudinal Changes in the CSIR**. Participants generated ideas that could support the development of a positive mind set in the CSIR, determined and classified the actions, which should be taken to foster the identified positive attitudes and also to develop action plans for enabling the CSIR to strengthen the identified positive attitudes. The action plans generated were prioritised. The result as seen from the priority chart was that there was the need **to re-engineer the CSIR** followed by solving the perennial problem of providing well-designed service conditions for the staff.

Finally, Dr. Warfield and his team also conducted a workshop, of great interest to the CDUP project, on **Collaboration among the Implementing Agencies of the CDUP**. This workshop was designed to assist in the integration of the five components of the CDUP. The immediate objectives were therefore to identify the main inputs that each implementing agency required from the other implementing agencies and to determine the priorities of the identified inputs for each agency. The priority structure of the inputs needed by each implementing agency was produced and discussed. It was found by the participants that there might be the need to reorder some of the priorities generated by the computer. Participants, however, found this workshop useful in detailing what was expected of each implementing agency in terms of collaboration within the CDUP.

Conclusions and Lessons Learnt

The workshops achieved their objectives. Participants were introduced to the science and practice of Interactive Management. Participants were introduced to various forms of idea generation and development of action plans. These workshops clearly demonstrated to participants the need to work together and to exchange information appropriate to the needs of others. The results of the workshops established clearly the utility of Interactive Management in simplifying complexity and showing the way to possible solutions to complex problems. In this connection, it was noted that re-engineering the CSIR was identified as priority action to be taken to ensure effective reorganisation of the CSIR. It is, however, regretted that this action was not taken because of lack of commitment – political and administrative. As Dr. Warfield has noted in his presentation of systems science, no science is known that can override the determination of the top level of a power structure to pursue a chosen course, no matter on what basis that course may be chosen.

Surinder K. Batra (India)
My Experiences With Interactive Management

To begin with, I give a brief about myself and my first exposures to the systems sciences, way back in 1988. I then share my experiences in using the Interactive Management (IM) approach to real life problem solving, particularly with regard to government and public systems. In the process, I highlight the strengths of this approach as experienced by me through these applications. I also mention some variants of the rigorous IM approach and share some examples of this approach being combined with other system approaches to good effect.

Induction to Systems Sciences

I joined Tata Consultancy Services (TCS), New Delhi, India, in 1984 as a management consultant, after having worked with industry and a prestigious management institute (Administrative Staff College of India) as a faculty, for about eleven years. There, I came in contact with Prof. P. N. Murthy, Head Systems Engineering & Cybernetics Centre (SECC) of TCS at Hyderabad. He along with his team was supporting the TCS management consultancy division in applying systems sciences to client problem solving. Through him I learnt about IM, and was fascinated by its intrinsic merits in management consultancy applications as compared to the conventional approaches hitherto being adopted. I also familiarized myself with Stafford Beer's Viable System Model and James Miller's Living Systems and India's own holistic thinking seen through its ancient scriptures. In 1988, I was nominated for a six weeks information exchange programme with the Institute for Advanced Studies in Integrative Sciences (IASIS) at George Mason University (GMU), USA, of which Prof. Warfield was the then Director. I fully dedicated this period to understand Prof. Warfield's invaluable contributions to systems sciences. After returning from GMU, I was formally inducted into the SECC for about a year, which gave me yet another prolonged opportunity to grasp the subtleties of systems sciences and "cope with the variety" of various strands of this discipline.

I remained in TCS till 1994, having moved to the Management Consultancy Division at New Delhi in 1990. The sabbatical at SECC had apparently equipped me with the "arsenal" of systems techniques and enriched my conceptual understanding of the subject to be a "viable" systems engineer and management consultant at the same time. I established my own "Centre for Interactive Management India" (CIMI) in 1994, which is actively engaged in using IM approach in problem solving till date. I have a multi-disciplinary background, and my current fields of professional work include consultancy and applied research in environment, education, training and technology sectors. In addition to IM, I have been adopting other approaches for diagnostics, situation analysis and strategy development, which are some of the key functions of a management consultant.

IM Applications

I have used IM approach in a number of application areas spanning the social sector, technology sector and general management. Some of these applications have been during my tenure with TCS, while several other applications have been in my independent capacity as the Principal Consultant of CIMI. Some of the key applications are listed below:

- Strengthening India's national capabilities to cope with ecological refrigeration capabilities

- Strengthening linkages between producers and users of Technology, Ghana

- Developing a quality policy for the health care division of a medium size corporate sector enterprise in India

- Impact of information technology on organizational effectiveness: a diagnostic study in the Indian environment

- A Study on effectiveness of apprenticeship training in India, Sri Lanka, Bangladesh and Malaysia

- Vocational training for advanced technology in India

- Diagnostic Study on energy sector of Ghana, as part of the UNDP project titled, Strengthening the National Capabilities for the Transfer, Utilization and Development of Technology

- Study on enhancing passenger satisfaction for Indian Airlines

- Review of the mission and objectives of Doordarshan, the then only TV broadcasting company of India

- Training programmes/ workshops on innovative approaches to problem solving, for many Government and public sector institutions in India

Strengths of IM

As a management consultant, what I find most fascinating about IM is its insistence on knowing all perspectives of a problem from the point of view of different stakeholders. It recognizes that every human being possesses an unshakable cognitive burden with which he necessarily approaches every problem situation. It also recognizes that there exists wide variability amongst members of a problem solving team in their assessment of the relative saliency of the factors pertaining to a complex problem situation; and that, the problem solving process should aim at diminishing this variability by incorporating specific provisions for human learning. It provides an antidote to the phenomenon of "groupthink", and ensures non-threatening full participation of all stakeholders.

The development of a hierarchical structure of elements according to a pre-defined contextual relationship is at the core of typical IM applications. This is greatly aided by the Interpretive Structural Modeling (ISM), which essentially uses the transitivity relationship amongst various elements of the problem situation to minimize the time and steps required in establishing the structure amongst elements. ISM also helps control the rate of presenting information to the team of participants by seeking pair-wise comparisons.

In essence, IM can be seen as an approach aiming to synthesize individual models of a complex system limited by the virtual world and bounded rationality of the individual stakeholders into a group model, which can then be "played with" to derive strategies for problem resolution. This starts without any pre-conceived notion of what the solutions and designs should be. Each individual furnisher of an idea is completely autonomous in expressing his/her idea. IM rightly emphasizes sigma five conditions for a successful generation and structuring of ideas through collective enquiry. In this, the role of a process manager is crucial, as he/she has to steer the group through the process, without himself/herself providing the content. A great deal of importance is attached to the environment enhancing processes such as physical comfort and ample and flexible working space.

How IM Was Applied

In this brief contribution, it is not possible to give a detailed account of how IM was applied in the various applications listed above. But the insights gained from these applications were really valuable. For example, in most of these applications, a combination of NGT and ISM techniques was used to first generate a set of ideas from a diverse group of stakeholders, and then structure those ideas (redefined as elements) with reference to a pre-defined contextual relationship. This structuring was extremely useful in bringing out a route map of the emerging strategy for problem solving in each case. The clients (of the management consultancy) could associate themselves with the structure, offer amendments, and then agree to an enhanced structure, which could be a blueprint for action.

In some cases, we combined IM applications with other system models. For example, the Viable System Model (VSM) Framework was used in combination with IM in some of these applications to carry out mapping of the existing organizational structure on a normative structure emanating from VSM, to identify the organizational lacunae and suggest measures to enhance the organization. In some other applications such as the first one above, the "moderation" approach, commonly used by German and Swiss International Development Aid Agencies, was also used as a method for idea generation. The Cybernetic Influence Diagram approach developed by the Systems Engineering & Cybernetics Centre of TCS was used in several cases to good effect, in combination with IM, to more deeply understand and represent the client problem system and develop a framework for possible solutions.

Some other variants of the IM approach were also used in some of the applications. For example, some early applications of ISM were made without computer support (no ISM software available then). Of course, it was very tedious and cumbersome to do so, but it was successfully accomplished, nevertheless. (In retrospective, use of IM without computer support could have been avoided, as it does not prove any point. On the other hand, successful application with computer support gives more credibility). In some applications, individual rather than group model was first developed (by the consultant) to get a feel of the relationship between various elements, before plunging into a group based ISM. A key difference from the rigorous IM approach was that the "management consultant" having been given the brief about a problem, has to find solutions with the help of the group of stakeholders in the client system, and be equally responsible for ownership of the final product that emerges from IM application.

Robert McDonald (USA)
The National Forum on Non-Industrial
Private Forest Lands

Abstract. From October 31st to November 3, 1983, a National Forum for Non-Industrial Private Forest Landowners was convened by the Secretary of Agriculture of the United States Department of Agriculture (USDA) in St. Louis, Missouri. Interactive Management (IM) was used to conduct the Forum with the specific intent to achieve consensus on a wide variety of issues and to ensure ample opportunity for the participants to make their views heard. There were 180 participants of whom 20 were designated as "active" and 160 were part of a supportive caucus group. The active participants were engaged directly in identifying, structuring, and resolving public policy issues confronting the forestry community. The supportive participants were able to observe the facilitated discourse by means of TV monitors dispersed throughout the large hotel ballroom. Numerous caucuses were held at frequent intervals to enable the supportive participants to contribute their views to the active participants for incorporation in the products of the work. The products had and continue to have far-reaching consequences for forestry in the USA.

Problem Situation. Interactive Management (IM) is particularly relevant to organizational situations of substantial complexity. A situation facing the USDA in 1983 can be described in terms of the following four major dimensions:

- **Supply Dimension.** There exists a widespread concern about long-term wood supplies and prices. Inventories of both soft wood and hard wood are expected to increase until about year 2010. Thereafter, harvest levels are expected to exceed softwood growth.
- **Divisiveness Dimension.** There is a continuing and probably growing divisiveness among the forestry community over the role of non-industrial private forest lands in meeting future demands for wood. The role of the federal and state governments in this situation remains undetermined.
- **New Information Dimension.** New information has become available to the community on the nature and characteristics of non-industrial private forest lands and the owners, regarding economic opportunities for timber production, and effectiveness of programs and policies designed to improve production from private lands.
- **Shared Convictions on Opportunities.** There is a shared conviction in much of the forestry community that there are opportunities for everyone in the forestry production and processing arena to contribute towards improving the efficiency and productivity of non-industrial private forests and U. S. forests in general.

Because of previous experiences of the U. S. Forest Service with IM, the Steering Committee for the Forum appointed by Assistant Secretary Crowell to organize the Forum recommended the use of IM. This Committee represented all major segments of the forestry community, consisting of federal employees, state employees, consultants, industry representatives, and non-industrial private land owners. The Committee met several times to design the Forum, to determine the extent and composition of the participation, to agree on the plan for conducting the

Forum, and to set the agenda. All planning was coordinated with the Center for Interactive Management at the University of Virginia, represented by Dr. Alexander Christakis.

Design Of The Forum. The Forum focused on gaining consensus on three major questions:

- **Problems and Opportunities:** What are the problems and opportunities for managing non-industrial private forest lands?
- **Action Options:** What can be done to work on the problems and realize the opportunities?
- **Roles and Responsibilities:** What should be the roles and responsibilities of the various segments of the forestry communities (who should do what, and how should they interact among themselves in moving forward?)

The Steering Committee appointed by Assistant Secretary Crowell ensured that the spectrum of the forestry community was well-represented. The Committee asked organizations in each segment to select three representatives and alternates to attend the Forum. The Steering Committee recommended 20 participants be invited as active participants and approximately 160 as supportive participants.

The final distribution of active participants among the segments of the community was as follows:

Consulting foresters	3	Private landowners	8
Commercial forestry industry	3	Federal agencies	3
State foresters	3		

Once participants agreed to participate in the Forum, briefing and background papers ("white papers") concerning the status of forestry were mailed to them well ahead of time, so that all could share the same information. Other preparatory events included DELPHI questionnaires. The first solicited participant definition of issues that might be considered at the Forum as being significant. Participants generated about 160 issues. Clustering and merging of these enabled the number to be reduced slightly to 140, which were then mailed in a second questionnaire. This time participants were asked to select the 5 they considered most important. This time a list of about 40 most important issues emerged, these being issues that received at least one vote from at least one participant. This list defined the initial content of the discussion to be carried out among the participants at the Forum when it convened.

The overall plan for the Forum called for early participant clarification of the 40 issues, with facilitator guidance of the process. Next, with facilitator and computer assistance, prioritization of discussion was carried out to get a sequence for discussion to maximize time and information processing efficiency.

Once a sequence was developed, active participants would consider the first few issues in plenary followed by caucusing, and then consensus would be explored. Later issues would be considered in small groups, and reports would be made to the plenary sessions.

Still later small groups would be asked to develop options for dealing with each of the main issues in accordance with the sequence structure developed earlier. Each small group would assist in developing and ranking these options with facilitator help, using the IM consensus methodologies.

Then the groups would be reconfigured in accordance with the various stakeholder perspectives. Each group would be asked to decide and display which of the stakeholder groups should take responsibility for achieving some of the options. All of this work culminated in wall displays using colored circular stickers with different colors for each stakeholder group. This enabled rapid scanning, efficient discussion and tradeoffs, and rapid consensus building.

Participants were then asked to suggest in writing what should be done to implement the Forum results. They were also asked to express in writing their reactions to the Forum.

Brief closing speeches were made by some of the principals including Assistant Secretary Crowell.

Products Of The Forum

The Forum yielded both tangible and intangible products.

Tangible Forum Products

- The pre-Forum list of over 140 issues related to Non-Industrial Private Forest Lands (NIFP).
- A smaller list of about 40 issues chosen as of greatest importance by participants.
- A still smaller list of 16 issues clarified and discussed by active participants during the Forum, which winnowed down the broad subject for greater focus.
- A structural map showing logic relationships among the members of the smaller list, with two key "first statements".
- Consensus on two key first statements contained in the smaller list.
- Based on the consensus, a large options field showing options that might be pursued in striving to resolve the remaining issues in the group of 16, identifying which stakeholders might pursue which options; furnishing the primary basis for future implementation of the Forum results.
- Five pages of participant suggestions for ways to implement the Forum results. A principal suggestion was to prepare a report showing the products and to distribute this report to a wide audience with all due haste.
- Ten pages of participant comments showing their reactions to the Forum.

Intangible Forum Products

- Improved appreciation of the diversity of perspectives and their relevance in defining and resolving a many-faceted problematic situation.
- Significant learning among the participants by encouraging them to generate, clarify, and organize their ideas in a variety of

structural representations. The visual displays which they produced enabled each participant to observe an audit trail of progress as it advanced during the Forum.

- Efficient and productive use of limited participant time spent together in a national Forum.

Conclusions

The Interactive Management (IM) system of processes provides unique opportunities to leaders of organizations who are interested in resolving difficult issues by making best use of individual capabilities and awareness in organizations. As illustrated in this paper, a national forum designed and conducted in accordance with the principles of IM enabled very significant results to be achieved in about 3 days by effective involvement of the variety of stakeholders.

The significance of the results is not only captured by the comments and reactions of the Forum participants, but also by numerous state and federal government policymakers who have repeatedly mentioned to the Forum leadership that the Forum report has become a road map for their daily decisions and actions in the forestry community.

It is very encouraging to demonstrate, through the design and conduct of the national forum reported in this article, that a conscientiously managed application of IM is sufficient to overcome what could otherwise have been very counterproductive behavior, in group work dealing with the resolution of a difficult public policy issue.

Reynaldo Treviño Cisneros (Mexico)
Application to Prospective of Interactive Management

In 1994, in the State of Guanajuato, Mexico, there was conducted a pioneering experience named the First Interloquium, in which the Interactive Management methodology was applied to achieve a prospective analysis of the world and of Mexico to the year 2010.

The enormously difficult field of future studies was addressed by a first segmentation of phenomena in four areas of interaction between the world and our country: politics, economics, socio-demographics and techno-scientific issues foreseen for the following 17 years.

A set of four different international questionnaires, each one related to one of the four areas of analysis, was designed by myself, revised by experts in prospective matters, and sent to many different foreign scientists and opinion leaders, to achieve as a result the first list of relevant international trends, factors and events foreseen to impact the Mexican development during the seventeen years ahead. The same was replicated with a set of specific national questionnaires that were sent to Mexican scientists and leaders of opinion to get the Mexican list of relevant trends, factors and events foreseen as highly plausible for the following seventeen years. A further selection of the most relevant issues was made by the active participants before entering the Interloquium, and this selection became the prime materials for it.

This whole endeavor was immersed in the Regional Development research that ITESM, campus Leon, was leading for the State of Guanajuato. The complete study was sponsored by Carlos Medina Plascencia, then Governor of the State, and partnered by ITESM itself and by the Guanajuato, Siglo XXI Foundation. Prospective analysis was a key piece for understanding which decisions had to be taken in order to improve the living conditions of the inhabitants of Guanajuato, as well as the competitiveness of the particular predominant economic sectors in the State in the context of sustainable development (normative approach), and also for looking at the real interactions within the country and within a world experiencing globalization (exploratory approach).

This application of the general methodology of Interactive Management was for the first time conducted facing a big audience that participated in voting steps, with a Mexican facilitator for the national public meeting, and with Dr. Alexander Christakis as facilitator for the international meeting and for the cross-fertilization meeting between Mexican and international experts.

We achieved relevant results of this application: a very profound rationale around each selected issue, a map for each level of resolution, and a cross-fertilization map of various international trends, factors and events impacting Mexico during the following 17 years. Their interpretation became a solid base for designing the first family of scenarios described in Chapter 9 of the general regional development study titled Guanajuato, Siglo XXI.

Again, for the first time, methodology was applied having as relevant active participants fourteen international experts and eleven national experts, in very different branches of life and science, to assure the inclusion of multidisciplinary perspectives and approaches to the complex field implied. Besides, this was also the first time that IM was applied to link three different kinds of ideas encountered in prospective studies: trends, factors and events. This specific feature introduced as a transitive linking relation the concept of "plausibility".

I just have to add that the most salient consequence of this great endeavor was to serve as a major guidance for Vicente Fox as president of Mexico, when he was the Governor of the State of Guanajuato during the administration term 1995-2000, as well as an inspiration for many politicians, economic agents and leaders of opinion, who have read the text regarding the four families of plausible scenarios depicted in Chapter 9 of the above mentioned study.

Chapter 17

The Social Arena
The Practitioners ("Systemists")

Benjamin Broome
Photo: Appendix 1 Gallery Fig. P17-1
Design of Peacebuilding Efforts in Cyprus
(conflict resolution and local leadership development)

Benjamin Broome is Professor in the Hugh Downs School of Human Communication at Arizona State University (ASU). Much of his academic career was at George Mason University (GMU), where he met John Warfield in 1984. While at GMU, he worked closely with Warfield's colleague Aleco Christakis and the Center for Interactive Management (CIM) on a variety of projects. After CIM left GMU, he continued to work with Warfield, primarily on projects with Ford Motor Company and the Defense Systems Management College (DSMC), and he helped develop a Windows-based version of Interpretive Structural Modeling (ISM). From 1994-1996, Broome held the position of Senior Fulbright Scholar in Cyprus, where he applied Interactive Management (IM) with members of the local Greek-Cypriot and Turkish-Cypriot communities in an effort to promote citizen peace-building on the island. In addition to work with Ford, DSMC, and Cyprus, Broome has worked with Native American Tribes, educational institutions, professional organizations, and non-profit groups. At ASU, he teaches courses in facilitation, conflict management, and intercultural communication. He has a number of publications in international academic journals about the practice of IM. For more information, see
http://www.public.asu.edu/~bbroome/

Carmen Moreno
Photo: Appendix 1 Gallery Fig.P17-2
Involving Citizens In Planning Communities
(citizen involvement in local planning)

Carmen A. Moreno has been working at ITESM (Technological Institute of Monterrey) for 19 years. During the first ten she was full-time professor in the Systems Engineering Department teaching subjects related with Systems Sciences. Later she was at the Centro de Estudios Estratégicos (Center for Strategic Studies, also at ITESM) as Planning Director. Now she is teaching partially at the Industrial and Systems Department and contributing as external consultant in several entities at the Institute.

She first got in contact with Warfield's work in 1991 when he gave a seminar in Monterrey, and from then on she has been a constant and enthusiastic practitioner.

Although she has been involved in projects directed to several areas, her special interest is focused in the social field, where she has participated in development of strategic plans for indigenous groups; countries, states, cities and communities; non-governmental associations, etc., in USA, Mexico and Latin America.

She is convinced that structured participation of people is one of the most relevant challenges for development, especially in the complex environment in which we are living nowadays. That is why the practice of Interactive Management has been a powerful tool in her work.

Roy Smith
Photo: Appendix 1 Gallery Fig. P17-2
Some Experiences In The Social Arena
(assisting varied clientele in resolving local situations)

Roy Smith worked for Ford Motor Company in England for many years until his recent retirement. In the latter part of his employment he served as a group facilitator, both inside and outside of the company, taking advantage of the Ford policy that encourages employees to be active in community life. He visited Dearborn, Michigan, where he took part in several Interactive Management Workshops arranged by Dr. Scott M. Staley, and there learned the processes described earlier in this book. Returning to England he began to use these processes, both inside and outside of Ford.

Because of his special interest in the Catholic Church, he began to find opportunities to use what he had learned both in that Church and in social settings of the type which are normally engaged in by church members. In addition his work attracted the attention of F. Ross Janes, an early practitioner of IM and long-time faculty member at City University, who brought him to City University to lecture once a year to students in the business school who were interested in matters relevant to resolving complexity.

Benjamin J. Broome (USA)
Design Of Peace-Building Efforts In Cyprus

I've been involved with Interactive Management (IM) for nearly 20 years, since John Warfield and Alexander Christakis moved to George Mason University in 1984. During that time, I've been associated with more than 50 IM projects with a variety of groups, including large corporations, defense agencies, professional groups, non-profit organizations, faculty and student groups, and Native-American tribes.

Ethnic Divisions in Cyprus. During the past ten years I've been deeply involved with the work of Greek Cypriot and Turkish Cypriot peace-builders in the small eastern Mediterranean island of Cyprus. Members of the two ethnic communities have been physically separated for decades, speak different native languages (Greek and Turkish), follow different religious traditions (Christian Orthodox and Muslim), hold drastically different views of history, and are schooled from an early age to view the other community as the enemy.

Ethnic division began to occur following skirmishes in 1963, when the Turkish Cypriots withdrew into enclaves. In 1974 a full-scale war broke out, resulting in the ethnic division of the island, creating several hundred thousand refugees and resulting in the loss of homes and businesses by nearly one-third of the population. Today there stands between the two communities a buffer zone guarded by United Nations peacekeeping forces separating heavily armed Turkish and Turkish-Cypriot forces in the north and Greek-Cypriot forces in the south.

Slow Early Progress in Efforts to Resolve Conflict in Cyprus. Since the cease-fire that was arranged in 1974, political negotiations have made little progress toward resolving the conflict, and Cyprus recently entered the European Union as a divided island. Despite the lack of progress at the political level, ordinary citizens of the two communities have made contact with one another, primarily through workshops they attended abroad, and started working toward ways to promote peace in Cyprus. Because it was very difficult for them to communicate directly with one another (there were no telephone or mail links between the two sides of the buffer zone), and because authorities would not grant them permission to hold bi-communal meetings, progress has been slow and the participants have experienced many frustrations.

A Senior Fulbright Scholar. In the early 1990s, members of both communities convinced the U. S. Cyprus Fulbright Commission to bring a conflict resolution scholar from the United States to work with them on a full-time basis. In September 1994 I took on this newly created position as Senior Fulbright Scholar in Cyprus, which I held through 1996. My primary goal in Cyprus as Fulbright Scholar was to assist the peace-building group in developing ways to work together productively across the physical, historical, cultural, and conflict divide that separated them.

My responsibilities as Fulbright Scholar included offering seminars, workshops, and training in communication, problem solving, inter-group relations, and conflict resolution. In fulfilling these responsibilities, I made extensive use of Interactive Management (IM).

Applying IM in Cyprus. The applications of IM in Cyprus provide an instructive example of how practical knowledge based in the study of human communication and systems design can be applied with a protracted conflict situation. During the first nine months of my Fulbright residency, I met weekly with 15 Greek Cypriots and 15 Turkish Cypriots for discussions that utilized IM methodologies to develop a strategic plan for peace-building activities on the island. Each group consisted of men and women from various sectors of society (education, business, politics, NGOs), a range of ages (approximately 25 to 55), and across the political spectrum (left-leaning to right of center). Participants spoke English as their second language, and although the group sometimes used Turkish or Greek in the mono-communal meetings, English was used in the joint meetings.

In the beginning stages, most of our meetings were held in separate communal groups, because we could not obtain permission from the authorities to meet jointly. Later, we were able to come together on a regular basis over several months in bi-communal meetings. Discussions (in both the mono-communal and bi-communal settings) were often intense and emotional, at times inspiring and at other times extremely frustrating for everyone. The group nearly broke apart on several occasions, but the commitment and dedication of participants kept us together.

Moving into Joint Design Activity. We progressed through several phases of group work, including: (1) conducting an in-depth examination of the barriers facing peace-builders and the peace-building process in each community in Cyprus, (2) developing a collective vision for these efforts, and (3) designing a collaborative action agenda to make their vision a reality (see Broome, 1997, for an overview of both the process and the results). The group bonded in a special way through these meetings, and they became the core group of peace builders in Cyprus, forming the nucleus around which most of the developing inter-communal activities were centered.

As part of the implementation of the core group's collaborative action agenda, IM workshops were offered to several targeted groups. During the two-year period following the sessions with the core group (1995-

1996), design workshops were conducted with: (1) young business leaders, (2) young political leaders, and (3) a women leaders forum. These groups were targeted because of the critical role they will play in the future of Cyprus and because no previous rapprochement work had been conducted in these specific contexts. In addition, we believed that the IM process would be the most appropriate tool to help them move forward.

Building Local Capacity. The workshops that were conducted with the young business leaders, young political leaders, and the bi-communal women's forum not only helped create forward movement and momentum within the specific groups, but they also served as a training platform for the practice of IM in Cyprus. By the time I returned to the United States in early 1997, several individuals had gained experience both as participants in an extended series of IM sessions and as part of the facilitation team for various IM applications with other groups. In order to continue the capacity-building process, I returned to the island in December 1997 to offer a two-week training program focused on the specifics of the consensus-building methodologies we had been using, as well as behavioral and process concerns in working with groups in a conflict setting.

This training served as the impetus for a number of projects that were launched by various local teams, including design workshops with various citizen groups, educators, university students (see Broome, 1999), and workshops involving individuals from several middle-eastern countries. Additionally, since my return to the United States in 1997, I have organized a number of workshops, seminars, and other meetings outside Cyprus, in Switzerland, Sweden, Brussels, Athens, and Istanbul.

Achivements. The IM sessions in Cyprus came at a crucial time in the development of a citizens' movement for peace on the island, contributing in several ways to its growth. First, they helped the early participants gain a deeper understanding of the situation they faced and the obstacles they must overcome. Second, within each community and across community lines the IM sessions promoted the development of teamwork, helping a diverse group of individuals work together in spite of different motivations and different ideas about peace. Third, they led to the creation of a collective vision statement that provided a crucial framework for the group's work, helping them to move forward with a single voice. Fourth, the IM sessions left the peace builders in Cyprus with a collaborative action agenda that served as a structure for action, helping them direct their energies in a more integrative manner.

Keeping Hope Alive. At the time of this writing, Cyprus is still a divided island, with no settlement in sight. However, ordinary citizens are finding ways to work together, and although the peace movement has not led to a political solution, it has helped keep alive the possibility for peace. There have been many actors involved in the development of the peace movement, and it is impossible to know the specific role played by the IM sessions. But based on my personal experience in working with a variety of groups over the past ten years, I believe the IM process and its products helped the group members sustain their motivation over time, overcome numerous obstacles to their work, and act with a more unified voice during periods of crisis. If the bi-communal movement will someday be judged as an important factor in bringing peace to Cyprus, perhaps the IM design sessions will be viewed as having played an important role in their evolution.

List of Publications about Cyprus Peace-building Efforts

Broome, B. J. (2005, in press). *Building Bridges Across the Green Line: A Guide to Intercultural Communication in Cyprus.* Prepared for the United Nations Office of Project Services (UNOPS).

Broome, B. J. (2005, in press). Applications of Interactive Design Methodologies in Protracted Conflict Situations, in Lawrence Frey (Ed.), *Innovations in Group Facilitation,* MacMillan.

Broome, B. J. (2005, in press). The Role of Bi-communal Activities in Building Peace in Cyprus, in Anastasios Tamis and Michalis Michael (Eds.), *Cyprus in the Modern World,* La Trobe University Press.

Broome, B. J. (2004). Reaching Across the Dividing Line: Building a Collective Vision for Peace in Cyprus, *International Journal of Peace Research, 41* (2), 191-209.

Broome, B. J. (2004). Building a Shared Future Across the Divide: Identity and Conflict in Cyprus. In Mary Fong and Rueyling Chuang (Eds), *Communicating Ethnic and Cultural Identity,* pp., 275-294, Rowman and Littlefield, Publishers.

Broome, B. J. (2003). Responding to the challenges of third-party facilitation: Reflections of a scholar-practitioner in the Cyprus conflict, *Journal of Intergroup Relations, 26* (4), 24-43.

Broome, B. J. and Murray, J. S. (2002). Improving Third-Party Decisions at Choice Points: A Cyprus Case Study. *Negotiation Journal, 18* (1), 75-98.

Broome, B. J. (2001). Participatory Planning and Design in a Protracted Conflict Situation: Applications with Citizen Peace-Building Groups in Cyprus. *Systems Research and Behavioral Science, 18,* 1-9.

Broome, B. J. (1999). Inter-Communal Contacts Help Build Links for the Future of Cyprus. *Washington Report on Middle East Affairs,* 18(6), 69-71.

Broome, B. J. (1999). Greek and Turkish Cypriot University Students Have More in Common Than Expected. *Washington Report on Middle East Affairs,* 18(6), 82-83.

Broome, B. J. (1998). Designing Citizen-Based Peace-Building Efforts in Cyprus: Interactive Management Workshops with Greek Cypriots and Turkish Cypriots. In A.E.R. Woodcock (Ed.), *Cornwallis III: Analysis for Peace Operations,* Cornwallis Park, pp. 33-58. Nova Scotia, Canadian Peacekeeping Press.

Broome, B. J. (1998). Overview of Conflict Resolution Activities in Cyprus: Their Contribution to the Peace Process. *The Cyprus Review,* 10(1), 47-66) [reprinted in A. Ioannou, Andreas Theophanous, and Nicos Peristianis (Eds.), *The Cyprus Problem: Its Solution and the Day After,* pp. 43-58. Intercollege Press, Nicosia, Cyprus.]

Broome, B. J. (1998). Views from the other side: Perspectives on the Cyprus Conflict. In Judith Martin, Thomas Nakayama, and Lisa Flores (Eds.), *Readings in Cultural Contexts,* pp. 422-433. Mayfield Publishing Company.

Broome, B. J. (1997). Designing a Collective Approach to Peace: Interactive Design and Problem-Solving Workshops with Greek-Cypriot and Turkish-Cypriot Communities in Cyprus. *International Negotiation,* 2(3), 381-407.

Carmen Moreno
Involving Citizens In Planning Communities
(an English version will follow)

En la historia de México y de América Latina, ha sido siempre práctica común la realización de planes de desarrollo de ciudades, regiones y comunidades intervinendo solamente las entidades gubernamentales. Especialmente en comunidades rurales o comunidades que no representan grandes centros urbanos, la práctica de la planificación participativa no se ha generalizado.

Desde hace algunas décadas, se han incrementado los esfuerzos para que los ciudadanos intervengan en la realización de planes de desarrollo, con resultados altamente positivos como lo demuestran algunos proyectos exitosos en Brasil, Colombia, Argentina y México, entre otros países latinoamericanos.

Cuando se habla de la participación masiva de ciudadanos en proyectos que requieren conceptualizar de manera grupal problemáticas actuales en la comunidad, o proyectar imágenes compartidas de la comunidad a futuro, se está hablando de un grado muy alto de complejidad, que debe ser administrado con metodologías sistémicas que aseguren la presencia de tres elementos fundamentales planteados por Warfield para el manejo de la complejidad: variedad, importancia y parsimonia (Warfield 1990). "Variedad" para garantizar la inclusiónde todos los enfoques y puntos de vista necesarios para tratar la situación, "importancia" para centrar el análisis en las variables de mayor relevancia relativa y "parsimonia" para evitar la sobre exposición de los participantes a cantidades de información que no puedan procesar de manera eficiente. También es importante contar con herramientas que ayuden a la gente a estructurar y visualizar de manera clara el "modelo de comunidad", que van creando de manera conjunta a medida que avanzan en el proyecto.

En mi experiencia la utilización de la Administración Interactiva ha sido de gran utilidad en lo que respecta al involucramiento de los habitantes de comunidades en la planeación de su propio destino, principalmente por las siguientes razones:

1. Permite al facilitador y/o dise ador del proyecto de planeación ofrecer una metodología ordenada mediante la cual lleva a los particpantes paso a paso por el trabajo a realizar, es decir, permite al facilitador aplicar el principio de parsimonia al análisis de la situación. Esto a su vez permite entender cómo va evolucionando el grupo en el análisis de la problemática analizada y facilita el introducir cambios imprevistos de manera lógica, sin que estas improvisaciones caucen desestabilización en la continuidad de la sesión.

2. Promueve un diálogo productivo entre todos los participantes, asegurando la exposición de todos los puntos de vista que representan las diversas dimensiones de la situación (variedad).

3. Gracias también al diálogo y a sus herramientas para priorización y selección de elementos, facilita la exploración de las variables relevantes de la situación a un nivel satisfactorio de profundidad, evitando en el grupo la pérdida de enfoque en las discusiones (importancia).

4. Permite construir de manera gráfica los modelos mentales que se van creando de la situación, y discutirlos de manera focalizada para hacer ajustes en caso necesario.

Entre los proyectos en los que he intervenido aplicando la Administración Interactiva, se pueden destacar los siguientes:

a. "Plan Integral De Desarrollo Para La Población De Colombia N.L."

Proyecto realizado en la comunidad rural de Colombia, en la frontera Noreste del Estado mexicano de Nuevo León y el Estado de Texas. El proyecto se realizó en el marco de la construcción del Puente Internacional Colombia; el cual se realizó para incrementar la captación de recursos económicos derivados del cruce de mercancías entre USA y México.

El objetivo del proyecto fue la realización de un plan de desarrollo para la población marginada de la comunidad, con el fin de evitar que el impulso económico dado a la zona generara mayor marginación de la población de escasos recursos y por el contrario, plantear oportunidades de desarrollo de este núcleo poblacional.

En las sesiones de trabajo intervinieron pobladores de la comunidad, la mayoría de los cuales no sabían leer y escribir, sin embargo tenían un profundo conocimiento de la problemática de la zona. Se realizaron TGNs (Técnicas de grupo nominal), donde se apoyó a los participantes analfabetos en las votaciones de elementos mediante la lectura y recapitulación de las listas de ideas. Así mismo se construyeron las estructuras o modelos estructurales mediante símbolos y dibujos, aunados a las ideas escritas.

El grupo participante se constituyó posteriormente en una asociación vecinal para dar seguimiento al plan.

b. Plan De Desarrollo Para El Estado De Tabasco, Mexico.

Este proyecto fue realizado en el Centro Internacional de Agronegocios del ITESM, bajo la coordinación del Dr. Ernesto Lozano y de la Ing. Celina Torres. Consistió en definir una serie de iniciativas para impulsar el desarrollo del Estado de Tabasco, entidad localizada en la costa del Golfo de México, con la particiáción de representantes del gobierno estatal y municipal, así como representantes de los principales sectores económicos del Estado.

En este proyecto la utilización de una "ESTRUCTURA DE APOYO ENTRE PROYECTOS" fue de gran utilidad en la última fase, haciendo posible visualizar la importancia de algunas de las iniciativas del plan, dado el apoyo que prestarían a la realización de todo el conjunto.

c. Plan Estratégico Mendoza 2010, Mendoza, Argentina.

Este proyecto fue realizado en la Provincia de Mendoza en el oeste de Argentina para el Consejo Empresario Mendocino. Su objetivo fue la realización de un plan de desarrollo para la Provincia con la participación y representación de todos los sectores de la comunidad.

La utilidad de la Administración Interactiva en este proyecto en el que intervinieron más de 1200 personas, quedó manifestada básicamente en la aplicación de los lineamientos de Warfield para el diseño de sesiones e identificación clara de roles; y en la aplicación minuciosa de las reglas de los procesos de técnica de grupo nominal.

Esto ayudó a que los participantes entendieran claramente su rol, el de los patrocinadores y el de los facilitadores, pudieran separar y manejar adecuadamente los elementos del proceso, del contexto y del contenido (Warfield 1990). Así mismo, en las Técnicas de Grupo Nominal utilizadas, los participantes tuvieron clara la necesidad de comprender el significado de cada una de las ideas, sin juzgar a priori su acuerdo o desacuerdo con las mismas para posteriormente ser capaces de realizar una votación por aquellas que consideraran de mayor importancia relativa y así poder seleccionar un conjunto de ideas representativo de todo el grupo.

En general, la utilización de los procesos que Warfield propone en la Administración Interactiva proporcionan un ORDEN y ESTRUCTURA muy importante para cualquier tipo de proyecto, siendo esto más valioso y apreciado en aquellos proyectos de participación masiva de personas.

Reference

Warfield John N. *A science of generic design. Managing complexity through systems design.* Volume I. Intersystems Publications. Salinas, Ca. USA 1990

Carmen Moreno
Involving Citizens In Planning Communities

In the history of Mexico and Latin America, there has always been a common practice that development plans for cities, regions, and communities would only involve government entities. Especially in rural communities, or communities that do not represent large urban centers, the planning process has not become standardized.

For several decades, there has been an increase in efforts on behalf of citizens to become involved in the realization of development plans, with highly positive results, as has been demonstrated by several successful projects in Brazil, Colombia, Argentina, and Mexico, among other Latin American countries.

When one speaks of the widespread participation of citizens in projects that require group conceptualization, real problems in the community, or projecting shared visions of the future of a community, it involves a very high degree of complexity, which must be managed using systematic methodologies that will assure the presence of three fundamental elements proposed by Warfield for managing complexity: variety, importance, and conciseness [brevity?] (Warfield 1990). "Variety", to guarantee that all necessary approaches and points of view to manage the situation are included, "importance" to focus the analysis on the variables having the most relative relevance, and "conciseness" to avoid the over-exposition to the participants of quantities of information that cannot be processed efficiently.

In my experience, Interactive Management has been very useful with respect to the involvement of community members in the planning of their own destiny, principally for the following reasons:

1. It allows the facilitator and/or project manager ["designer of project planning"] to offer a structured methodology which leads the participants step by step through the work plan; in other words, it allows the facilitator to apply the principle of conciseness to the analysis of the situation. This does two things: it allows the understanding of how the group evolves during the analysis of the problem, and it facilitates the introduction of unforeseen changes in a logical way, without which these improvisations would destabilize the continuity of the session.
2. It promotes a productive dialog between all of the participants, assuring the exposition of all points of view that represent different dimensions of the situation (variety).
3. Thanks also to the dialog and tools for prioritization and selection of elements, it facilitates the exploration of variables that are relevant to the situation at a satisfactory level of depth, preventing the loss of focus in group discussions (importance).
4. It allows graphic construction of mental models that evolve with the situation, and focused discussion of them so that adjustments can be made if necessary.

Among the projects where I have applied Interactive Management, let me emphasize these:

I. Integrated Development Plan For The People Of Colombia N.L.

A project realized in the rural community of Colombia, on the border between the northeastern Mexican state of Nuevo Leon and the state of Texas. The project took place during the construction of the International Colombia Bridge, built to increase the capacity of economic resources arising from the interaction of business between the USA and Mexico. The objective of the project was the realization of a development plan for marginalized people in the community, with the goal of preventing the economic growth of the area from causing greater marginalization of people having scarce resources, and instead, creating opportunities for development of this population center.

In the work sessions, members of the community participated, the majority of whom did not know how to read and write; nevertheless, they had a profound knowledge of the area's problems. During the process of voting for elements, there were a number of NGT's (Nominal Group Techniques)-employed, where the illiterate participants had the support of reading and recapitulating lists of ideas. Likewise, structures or structural models were constructed using symbols and drawings, along with written ideas.

The group of participants later formed a neighborhood association in order to follow up with the plan.

II. Development Plan For The State Of Tabasco, Mexico.

This project took place at the International Agri-business Center of the ITESM, under the coordination of Dr. Ernesto Lozano and Ing. Celina Torres [Ing., short for "ingeniero" or engineer, would probably be equivalent to Dr.] It consisted of defining a series of initiatives to promote development in the state of Tabasco, located on the coast of the Gulf of Mexico, with the participation of representatives of state and municipal governments, as well as representatives of the principal economic sectors of the state.

In this project, the use of a STRUCTURE OF SUPPORT AMONG PROJECTS was very useful in the final phase, making it possible to visualize the importance of some of the initiatives of the plan, with the support of the entire group.

III. Mendoza 2010 Strategic Plan, Mendoza, Argentina.

This project took place in the province of Mendoza in western Argentina for the Mendocino Business Council [Chamber of Commerce?]. The objective was the realization of a development plan for the province with the participation and representation of all sectors of the community.

The use of Interactive Management for this project, in which more than 1200 people took part, stuck to the application of Warfield's guidelines for the design of sessions and the clear identification of roles; and the meticulous application of the rules of the Nominal Group Technique process. This helped the participants to clearly understand their role, and the roles of the sponsors and facilitators. They were able to adequately separate and manage the elements of process, context, and content (Warfield 1990).

Also, while using Nominal Group Techniques, the participants clearly needed to comprehend the significance of each one of the ideas, without prejudging their agreement or disagreement, so that later they would be able to vote for the ones they considered most important, and thus to be able to select a set of ideas that would represent the entire group.

In general, using the Interactive Management processes proposed by Warfield lends ORDER and STRUCTURE, which is very important for any type of project, and is most valued and appreciated in projects where many people participate.

Reference

Warfield John N. *A science of generic design. Managing complexity through systems design.* Volume I. Intersystems Publications. Salinas, Ca. USA 1990

Roy Smith (England)[1]
Some Experiences In The Social Arena

Opening Reflections

"For every complex problem there is an answer that is clear, simple, and wrong".

H. L. Mencken[2]

"Sponsors are rarely willing to invest adequate time in building firm foundations for their teams at the start of a project. But they are often willing to start over when the project fails."

Traditional[3].

"Search every land, from Cadiz to the dawn-streaked shores Of Ganges, and you'll find few men who can distinguish A false from a worthwhile objective, or slash their way through The fogs of deception, Since when were our fears or desires Ever dictated by reason? What project goes so smoothly That you never regret the idea, let alone its realisation?"

Juvenal[4]

---

[1] Retired internal consultant, Ford Process Leadership Office. Roy took advantage of Ford's liberal policy of allowing employees to engage in community activities as part of their Ford service. Roy ran several sessions, including one to explore declining attendance in the Catholic Church in England. He also lectured on Interactive Management at City University. Now retired from Ford, Roy continues to apply Interactive Management from time to time. *International Journal of General Systems*, December 2003 Vol. 32 (6), P548

[2] H. L. Mencken Political Commentator,
http//www.montgomerycollege.org/Departments/hpolscrv/tdolfi.html
http://www.brainyquote.com/quotes/authors/h/h_l_mencken.html

[3] Common expression among facilitators

[4] (Juvenal, The Sixteen Satires, Satir X – Roman satirist Juvenal AD 55 – 140) Capital letters in middle of sentences are as shown in original publication.

Social Arena Experience Grounded in Industry

While this chapter focuses on the Social Arena, my experience is grounded in industry, and was helped enormously by Ford's liberal policy of allowing employees to engage in community activities as part of their Ford service.

Many Ordinary Processes Are Inadequate

There are many processes open to practitioners in collaborative group work. After fourteen years working in workshop design and facilitation, I now use only two methods. One is the Nominal Group Technique (NGT)[5] (a very well-designed process that incorporates key behavioral concepts, unlike most group processes which fail even to emphasize the critical importance of dedicating a significant percentage of group effort to clarification of statements, guided by a skilled facilitator).   Many group leaders seemingly are unable to distinguish "brainstorming" from NGT, but the latter is far superior.   The other method that I use is Interpretive Structural Modeling (ISM)[6].

I had worked as an engineer in industry for some forty years before suddenly transferring to "people-work". For the first five years in this new discipline, I worked with wise colleagues learning facilitation, brainstorming, and Nominal Group Technique. To my surprise, I discovered that I had a natural flair for facilitating groups.

---

[5] Delbecq, A.L., Van de Ven, A.H., and Gustafson, D.H. (1975) *Group Techniques for Program Planning: A Guide to Nominal Group and DELPHI Processes* (Scott Foresman, Glenview, IL).

[6] This matches an assertion of Dr John Warfield: the two processes taken together (NGT & ISM) are the only methods that are needed to enable a group to move from a point of no integration of their ideas to the point where they have reached a preliminary structural design of a system for resolving the complexity inherent in the problematic situation.- *International Journal of General Systems*, December 2003 Vol. 32 (6), "Autobiographical Retrospectives" John N. Warfield. P538

However, I felt uneasy. While many methods were far superior to just sitting in a room discussing and arguing, participants seemed to need something more. Some comments were:

- "Hang on Roy, you are rushing us into voting, and we don't understand the items we are voting on".
- "Hang on Roy, you are asking us to vote, and we are overloaded with a huge number of ideas – and many are similar to others. We can't cope".

I have learned that NGT and ISM together significantly reduce these concerns.

Interpretive Structural Modeling (ISM)

Since then I have run some 150 workshops involving about 1,400 participants. Ninety-five workshops have been in Industry and Commerce, and fifty-five in the Social Arena. Fifty-one have been with ISM preceded by NGT, and about ninety-nine[7] have been with NGT alone. Table 1 shows information on the types. About 30% of workshops have been with low numbers, for example five or fewer participants. Table 2 responds to the question "When do I use NGT alone, and when do I use NGT followed by ISM?"

---

[7] Half the NGT workshops are estimated from a period of a couple of years when I typically ran a couple of NGT workshops a month.

Table 1. Workshop Types I Conducted Since Learning of IM in January, 1995

METHOD	QUANTITY OF WORKSHOPS			QUANTITY OF PARTICIPANTS		
	Industry and Commerce	Social Arena	TOTAL	Industry and Commerce	Social Arena	TOTAL
NGT Alone	67	32	99	572	563	1135
NGT, then ISM	28	23	51	176	89	265
TOTAL	95	55	150	748	652	1400

Table 2. NGT Alone, or NGT and Then ISM?

Expected number of participants	Anticipated insights of participants into key issues	Quality of decision will have profound consequences	Intuitively feel that ISM will give helpful insights	Sponsor willing to invest adequate group time to understand issues thoroughly	Situation where I use NGT alone	Situation where I use NGT and then ISM
Large (e.g. 10 or more)	Diverse	Yes	Yes	Yes	Yes	
Small (e.g., 5 or less)	Not relevant	Not relevant	Yes	Yes	Yes	
Me alone	Not relevant	Not relevant	Yes	Yes	Yes	
Large (e.g., 10 or more)	Diverse	Yes	Yes	No	Decline workshop	
Large (e.g., 10 or more)	Diverse	No	No	No		Yes
Any number	Not relevant	No	No	Not relevant		Yes

Example of Excellent Results from an ISM Workshop in the Private Sector

1. Thirty people from Ford across North America and Europe. From multiple divisions: Body & Assembly, Engine, Estates management, Systems etc. Two workshops totalling five days: three days Dearborn USA, then interim work, then two days Dagenham UK.

   "ISM is the best method for many people with wide differences of opinion handling complex issues. The right choice of methods for each workshop task. Team of experienced facilitators (four in Dearborn, three in Dagenham).

   THIRTY PEOPLE achieved UNANIMOUS AGREEMENT on their major policy decision for a world-wide computer platform".

Examples of excellent results from ISM workshops in the Social Arena

2. Order of Redemptorist priests. Two linked workshops of eight days over two separate weeks. Twenty participants at first workshop and thirty-four participants at follow-up workshop. The leader said: "Roy enabled us to clarify issues and reach good decisions".

3. Chairman of the charity 'To Romania with Love'. "We ran this workshop because we feared we would have to close our charity. With the help of Roy and his ISM processes, we are now confident of our way forward."

4. Chairman of mediawatch-uk, an organisation concerned with standards in the media, particularly campaigning against TV programmes that promote violence and pornography. "We have been struggling with declining membership, and apathy of the public. We could not see a clear strategy ahead. With Roy and his remarkable ISM process, we can now see a clear (though tough) strategy ahead".

5.	Curriculum[8] St Thomas's church, Grays. In 1996, five leaders from the RCIA[9] team spent a day using ISM to develop a curriculum. The curriculum has been very sound, and has survived virtually intact for eight years. One wise observer pointed out a pattern in the results: "that the topics progress from the concrete (for example history and tour of our local church) to the more abstract (for example scripture)".

A typical example of workshops declined

1.	A senior Ford manager asked me to help thirty people from all over Europe to design a solution to a complex situation in three days (where participants travelled in on day one, and travelled out on day three). When I offered to help them understand the situation in three whole days, he replied, "You must be (expletive deleted) joking. If you think I am going to waste my team's time wallowing around, you are mistaken!"[10]

A personal mantra when contemplating the design of a workshop
I remind myself three times: "Always do a problematique" . This was learned from my friend and long time Ford guru, Dr. Scott M. Staley.

A personal view
"ISM preceded by NGT is the best method I know for dealing with the most troublesome situations that you might ever encounter." When planning or pondering, I often run the ISM process by myself.

---

[8] A curriculum structure is described in *A Handbook of Interactive Management* by J. N. Warfield and A. R. Cárdenas, Ames, IA: Iowa State University Press, 2nd Edition, 1994 (p 69).

[9] RCIA refers to "Rite of Christian Initiation" for adults: a 36-week programme for adults joining the Catholic Church.

[10] Dr John Warfield refers to a similar situation in *A Handbook of Interactive Management*. op . cit. footnote 9, (p 28).

Chapter 18

Education Sector
The Practitioners ("Systemists")

Graciela Caffarel
Photo: Appendix 1 Gallery Fig. P18-1
Projects of Students Using Interactive Management
(teaching project management to university students)

Graciela Caffarel is a faculty member in the Instituto Tecnologico y de Estudios Superiores de Monterrey (ITESM). She is one of several faculty members at ITESM who have learned and have begun to teach and practice Interactive Management, through the leadership of Dr. A. Roxana Cárdenas, who has been involved with Dr. Warfield's work for about a decade and a half. In the government sector of Mexico, one finds Reynaldo Treviño who previously was a member of the faculty of ITESM in Campus Léon (one of more than 30 branch campuses of ITESM).

A. Roxana Cárdenas
Photo: Appendix 1 Gallery Fig. P18-1
Assessing Systems Science
(embedding design practice into higher education)

A. Roxana Cárdenas directs a project in strategic planning for the ITESM system that consists of more than 30 campuses across Mexico, with an emphasis on development and innovation. She has been a leader in developing systems design activity and in strategic and participative planning, and in high-level faculty development activity during her career in ITESM. She has collaborated for more than decade with Dr. Warfield in the development and application of systems science, with emphasis on Interactive Management in which she has provided strong leadership in Mexico.

Xuefeng Song
Photo: Appendix 1 Gallery Fig. P18-2
Structure-Based Science of Complexity in China
(embedding complexity studies in business education)

Xuefeng Song is Dean of the School of Business at the Chinese University of Mining and Technology in Xuzhou, China. He spent a sabbatical period studying complexity with Dr. Warfield at George Mason University, and returned to China to initiate further research on complexity. His sabbatical and later research was sponsored in part through the offices of Cheng Si Wei, Vice Chairman of the People's Congress, who headed the Management Department of the National Science Foundation of China. Some of the students of Dr. Song have translated the Warfield book titled *A Science of Generic Design* into Chinese which may be published in China.

Li Da Xu
Photo: Appendix 1 Gallery Fig. P18-2
Contributions to Information Systems
(high-level information system design)

Li Da Xu is Professor of Information Systems at Old Dominion University in Virginia.

He has used Warfield's books in his classes, and his analysis to follow is based on his experience in teaching and research based upon those materials and also on his knowledge of Warfield's presentations to audiences in China.

Graciela Caffarel (Mexico)
Proyectos de Alumnos usando Administración Interactiva

Uno de los retos más significativos que como profesor se nos presenta, es cómo dar respuesta a las necesidades que demanda el mercado laboral en nuestros alumnos y futuros profesionistas. Una realidad, es la tendencia a trabajos mucho más interdisciplinarios, con mayor nivel de participación, y de mayor complejidad en la toma decisiones; así como la búsqueda de respuestas más efectivas en menor tiempo.

En el ITESM, un alumno de la carrera de Ingeniería Industrial y de Sistemas(IIS), es un ingeniero con una formación altamente diversificada que logra desarrollarse a niveles de mandos intermedios en el corto y mediano plazo, y en diferentes sectores productivos como lo son: la industria, el sector servicio, financiero y gubernamental, entre otros.

Considerando este contexto, se ha venido haciendo un esfuerzo formal en un curso terminal llamado "Diseño de Sistemas"; en el cuál, se utiliza la metodología de Administración Interactiva (IM) como una respuesta a las necesidades planteadas anteriormente; y soportado por la estrategia didáctica de Aprendizaje orientado a Proyectos (POL). De tal manera, que el alumno experimenta el ser responsable de un proceso de intervención en una empresa de la localidad.

Este tipo de proyectos aborda problemáticas de naturaleza "suave", que requiera un enfoque participativo. Se plantea como un proyecto de tres fases: (a) Diagnóstico, (b) Generación y evaluación de alternativas de solución y (c) Diseño a detalle. IM se aplica especialmente en la fase dos.

Este esfuerzo de alrededor de 5 años, ha redituado en la realización de aproximadamente 28 sesiones de IM por semestre; las cuáles son planeadas y realizadas por alumnos de IIS; y donde se han visto beneficiadas, igual número de empresas de la localidad. El tipo de resultados en estos proyectos abarcan el diseño de sistemas como: planes de capacitación, programas de mejora en calidad en el servicio, programas de motivación, y planes de acción para el arranque de cambios organizacionales y en control administrativo, entre otros.

Las intenciones educativas planteadas para este curso reflejan la necesidad de usar una metodología como lo es IM:

- Fomentar el compromiso profesional para llevar a cabo cambios organizacionales que incrementen el bienestar humano y la efectividad económica de la sociedad.
- Fomentar el uso del Pensamiento Sistémico como característica esencial para la comprensión de situaciones problemáticas y para el diseño de sistemas.
- Apreciar las restricciones y características culturales y sociales existentes al realizar un Proceso de Intervención con base en el Enfoque de Sistemas.
- Contribuir al desarrollo de un alto sentido de responsabilidad del IIS, en relación a lasdecisiones, resultados e implicaciones que se deriven de su quehacer profesional.
- Concienciar sobre la importancia de involucrar a los grupos e individuos relacionados con una situación problemática en sus procesos de solución y/o diseño.

La forma en que opera este curso se puede expresar en un esquema cuya columna vertebral es la realización de un proyecto, y en donde la interacción entre el profesor y el alumno se establece a través de tres elementos: (a) una clase enfocada ver los aspectos metodológicos en el proceso de intervención; un taller de entrenamiento en la facilitación de una sesión con IM , y un espacio de asesoría periódica como apoyo y retroalimentación a los avances y resultados del proyecto. Cabe señalar que en un curso previo a éste, llamado Modelación Estructural de Sistemas, el alumno tiene su primer contacto formal con IM, tanto en las metodologías asociadas, como en la posibilidad de uso de diferentes estructuras y el concepto de Sigma Cinco.

A diferencia de otros cursos, en éste, el énfasis de la aplicación de IM es en la Fase de Diseño, abarcando la generación, estructuración y evaluación de alternativas de solución. Se aplican de manera formal NGT e ISM (utilizando el software de Windows) principalmente para la generación de estructuras como: Apoyo, Soporte y Campo de Opciones; así mismo, se enseña y aplica el Perfil de Opciones. La experiencia resultante de este esfuerzo conjunto entre profesores, alumnos y gente de empresas ha sido realmente satisfactoria a través de estos años. Los alumnos son capaces de:

Valorar la importancia y el alcance de la Tarea de Diseño, considerando la necesidad de aplicar enfoques participativos. Ellos perciben que en el ámbito laboral la empresa está esperando recibir respuestas integrales a sus problemáticas, donde se logre el involucramiento de la gente de la organización. Aquí la aplicación de IM les ha sido muy útil como enfoque metodológico.

Si bien es un esfuerzo didáctico a nivel de alumnos de profesional; esta experiencia ha significado el uso de una metodología que apoya y sensibiliza al alumno y la gente de empresa, sobre la necesidad de contar con esfuerzos planeados y sólidos en los procesos que requieren una toma de decisiones participativa que promueva tanto resultados significativos como un aprendizaje de la interacción.

Graciela Caffarel (Mexico)
Projects of Students using Interactive Management

One of the most significant challenges a professor faces is how to respond to the needs that labor market demands in our students and future professionals. A fact is the tendency to have more interdisciplinary work, participation level, and complexity in making decisions; as well as the search for more effective answers in less time.

In the ITESM, a student of Industrial and Systems Engineering (IIS) is a person with a highly diversified formation who is able to carry out tasks at intermediate controls levels in the short and medium term. Besides he can be found in different productive sectors as: industrial, service, financial and government, among others.

By considering this context, the ending course called "Systems Design" has incorporated a formal effort to respond to the previous mentioned needs. This course is based on the methodology Interactive

174 An Introduction to Systems Science

Management (IM) and it is supported by the didactic strategy of Learning Oriented Projects (POL). In such a way the students are responsible for an intervention process in a local company.

This kind of projects considers "soft problematic" that requires a participative approach. The project is comprised by three phases: (a) diagnostic, (b) generation and evaluation of solution alternatives, and (c) detailed design of selected systems. IM is particularly applied in the phase two.

This effort has been implemented for the last five years. It has implied the development of 28 IM sessions per semester with the same number of local companies receiving benefits of them. These sessions are planned and carried out by students of IIS. The type of results in these projects embraces the design of systems like: training plans, programs of improvement in quality service, motivation programs, action plans for the start up of organizational changes and administrative control, among others.

The outlined educational intentions for this course reflect the necessity to use a methodology like IM, they are:

- To promote the professional commitment to carry out organizational changes, which increase the human well-being and the economic effectiveness of the society.
- To promote the use of the Systemic Thinking as essential characteristic for the understanding of problematic situations and designing of systems.
- To appreciate the restrictions and cultural and social characteristics existing in any intervention process based in a systems approach.
- To contribute to the development of a high sense of responsibility of the IIS, in relation to the decisions, results and implications that are derived of their professional exercise.
- To be aware about the importance of involving the groups and individuals related with a problematic situation in their solution processes and/or design.

The core of this course is the development of a project, and where the interaction between professor and student settles down the following three elements: (a) a centered class in methodological aspects of intervention processes; (b) a special training in the facilitation of a session with IM, and (c) periodic sessions to advise and feedback advances and results of the project. It is necessary to point out that in a previous course, called "Structural Modeling of Systems," the student has his first formal contact with IM. In this course, they learn associate methodologies, the possible usages of different structures and the Sigma Five concept (participants, facilitator team, demosophia, consensus methodologies, and technological support.)

Unlike to other courses, in this one, the emphasis of IM application is in the phase of design, which embracing the generation, structuring and evaluation of solution alternatives. NGT and ISM (using the software of Windows™) are formally applied mainly to generate structures of: Support, Enhancement and Options Field. During this process, the students become trained to apply the Option Profile method as well.

The results of this experience that has joined efforts between professors, students and people of companies have been really satisfactory through these years. At the end of the course, the students are capable of valuating the importance and enrichment of the of design task, considering the necessity to apply participative approaches.

The students perceive two main issues: the company expectations for integral answers and the commitment of the people of the organization. In these projects the application of IM has been very useful and successful as methodological approach to tackle complex problems.

If well this is a didactic effort at professional's students' level; this experience has meant the use of a methodology that supports and sensitizes both the student and company people. They recognize the necessity of having planned and supported efforts based on structured processes for participative decision making. IM has been promoted significant results and learning during these intervention projects.

A. Roxana Cárdenas (Mexico)
Assessing Systems Science

Fifteen years of association with the concepts involved in systems science as presented in this book have placed me in a position to relate my experiences to help add insights about this science.

My experiences have been of several types:

- Teaching the generic design science in a systems engineering masters degree program, both in the classroom and by satellite to branch campuses of ITESM
- Teaching short courses in Interactive Management both in Mexico and in the United States
- Leading application projects in Mexico
- Carrying out research studies to compare Interactive Management with other application systems, such as the Tavistock system and systems dynamics, to compare the scientific bases
- Serving as co-author with John Warfield of the *Handbook of Interactive Management* (1994)

The systems science, as presented in this book, comes relatively late to the group of studies normally thought of as systems studies; hence it has had to compete with the more entrenched studies in order to enter the curriculum. At least in Mexico, this new material has been well accepted by faculty and students. The accompanying articles by Caffarel, Moreno, and Rodriguez are illustrative of this.

Over the years I have invited John Warfield, Alexander Christakis (CWA Limited) and Ross Janes (City University) to Mexico to make presentations to students and faculty in person and via satellite. These have always been well accepted.

In my personal research, comparisons of the systems science with other systems subjects from a scientific perspective has been difficult. There are several reasons for this difficulty. One reason is that only the systems science, as presented in this book, has adhered in its organization to the ideals of the scientific method as carried forward in time from the days of Aristotle and honored by such names as Bacon, Popper, and C. S. Peirce. Typically, most systems material consists either of theory with little or no attached empirical evidence or methods with little or no stated foundational hypotheses and theory to circumscribe the domain of application. Notably Warfield emphasizes the necessity for "neutrality" of systems science in order for it to be widely applicable.

Another reason is that many of the systems methods do not incorporate in their methodological designs the results of the empirical behaviorists of the second half of the twentieth century, hence do not take advantage of what has been learned about human behavior in a way that has now been incorporated in Interactive Management.

Still another reason is that it is very difficult to follow any of the systems methods all the way through into implementation. In my own research program in the late 1990s, I found that it was difficult to assess the merits of Interactive Management in terms of implementation. Since that work was completed, significant advances have been made in that respect, through incorporation of the direct connection of Ashby's Law to tighten the relationship between the problems field and the options field; through the computation of the metrics of complexity which provide excellent insights into priority setting for actions; and through the contemplated and briefly tested use of the observatorium as a means of maintaining continuity throughout the life of an implementation project. All of these practices have evolved out of the ongoing relationship between John Warfield and Scott Staley at the Ford Motor Company, their most recent application being to the development of the accepted four-year strategic plan for the design and rollout of Ford's fuel-cell vehicles.

Another way to assess the systems science as presented here, is to note the achievements of those individuals who learned one or more of the components sciences fairly early in their careers, and to observe the progress in their careers. In this respect, a sampling of some of the notable individuals includes:

- **G. S. Chandy**, who is developing a software system for high-level management overview in India, called the "One-Page

Management System" (OPMS), based on the methods of the systems science described in this book, OPMS being field-tested at this writing

- **Dr. Alexander Christakis**, who carried out many successful projects using Interactive Management in his own organization, CWA Limited.
- **Dr. Raymond Fitz**, S. M., recently retired from his position as President of the University of Dayton, who pioneered the use of Interpretive Structural Modeling in the early 1970s.
- **Dr. Koichi Haruna**, who studied Interpretive Structural Modeling at Battelle with Warfield in the early 1970s, and later became the Director of Hitachi's three Systems Engineering Laboratories, and is presently Corporate Chief Engineer of Hitachi Corporation
- **Dr. Xuefeng Song**, who spent a sabbatical with Warfield in the late 1990s and is now Dean of the School of Business at the China University of Mining and Technology, where he leads research on complexity and on safety in the mines in China
- **Dr. Scott M. Staley**, who introduced Interactive Management to Ford Motor Company in 1990, and who has advanced to become Chief Engineer in charge of Ford's fuel cell vehicle development
- **Dr. Robert James Waller**, who was the first to use Interpretive Structural Modeling in an urban application, and who later became world-famous with his best selling *The Bridges of Madison County* and other novels and essays

Perhaps the most significant aspect of the systems science reported here lies in the unique marriage of formal logic (as made available through facilitated group process to the every-day citizen) with the human problems of people, through the use of Interpretive Structural Modeling. This marriage has taken this systems science a long way toward achieving the ideals advanced by Sir Geoffrey Vickers in his path-breaking book *Human Systems are Different*.

Xuefeng Song (China)
Structure-Based Science of Complexity in China

Dr. Xuefeng Song, as a visiting scholar, visited George Mason University from September, 1999 to April, 2000 to study Structure Based Science of Complexity (SBSC) with Dr. John Warfield. As soon as he came back from GMU, he set up an Institute for Economic and Management Complexity at China University of Mining & Technology (CUMT) in 2000. Meanwhile, he organized a small group of people to research Complexity of Economic and Management Systems. Under the financial support by National Natural Science Foundation of China, the first workshop on complexity was held in CUMT in June, 2001. And the second workshop on complexity was held in Shanghai, in August, 2002. From 2003, Dr. Song began to have a course of the Theory and Application of Complexity Science for his postgraduate students at CUMT, to teach the ISM and other theory of complexity science.

An ISM lab will be set up in the new campus of CUMT in 2005. In 2004, Dr. Song and his Ph. D. students have finished the translation of John Warfield book of *A Science of Generic Design: Managing Complexity through Systems Design*, which it is planned to be published in Chinese soon.

Beside, Dr. Song and his group are researching the safety management problems in the coal mines of China with SBSC, in which, there are thousands of workers die of safety accidents every year. They are trying to solve the problems in safety management of coal mines of China in order to do best to decrease the accidents and to save workers' lives.

Li Da Xu (Old Dominion University, USA)
Contributions to Information Systems

John Warfield has made major contributions to the area of systems sciences that are foundational to information systems research. He was one of the founders of the field of systems sciences. His work had a major impact on information systems analysis, design, implementation, decision support systems, and information systems research methods.

Systems theory has been considered as the basis for information systems, and has been applied to or proposed to be applied to information systems research. Systems concepts have direct relevance to the field of information systems. Based on the work by Warfield, Ackoff, Churchman, Checkland, Jackson, Xu, and other scholars, a wealth of research in information systems in the framework of systems sciences has produced an astonishing array of theoretical results and empirical insights. Several of Warfield's major publications are related to the field of information systems, and his contribution to the field of information systems is unique.

Studies have systematically identified decision support systems reference disciplines and traced how concepts and findings by systems researchers have been picked up by information systems researchers to be applied, extended and refined in developing decision support systems. According to the studies, in the early stage of decision support systems development it was systems sciences that provided an essential concept for defining the concept of decision support systems and justifying the need for such systems in organizations. In the early 1970s, at the same time when the concept of decision support systems was initially proposed, Warfield discovered algorithms for constructing digraphs as part of a group decision process which he called "Interpretive Structural Modeling".

Warfield's ideas were first presented in a 1974 monograph from the Battelle Memorial Institute, and later enhanced in his 1976 Wiley Interscience book titled *Societal Systems: Planning, Policy and Complexity*. The mathematical portion was republished in 2003 in *The Mathematics of Structure*. The Interpretive Structural Modeling algorithm was one of the earliest group decision support models and the Interpretive Structural Modeling software was one of the earliest group decision support systems. Research indicates that Interpretive Structural Modeling has made important contributions to the development of group decision support systems in the areas of foundational concepts, systematic group decision making process, modeling, model management, user interface, and implementation.

To some extent, information systems development (ISD) has been developed as science in the images of the established natural science, with the belief that the success of the natural sciences can be repeated in information systems if ISD emulates the methods of the natural sciences. Proponents of this view assume that ISD problems can be largely resolved by sophisticated technical tools, models, methods, and principles. Systems sciences indicate that an information system involves a variety of well-structured sub-systems that are clearly found in natural sciences, as well as ill-structured subsystems that involve behavioral factors. Warfield's work portrays information systems as social-technical systems and criticizes the traditional model of information systems because it leads to a narrow view of the role of information systems in organizations. From a system point of view, Warfield's work clarifies that ISD is to be treated as a technical process, as well as an ill-structured behavioral process.

Warfield's concept of dimensionality is an exemplary piece of work in this regard. Dimensionality is a fundamental concept in physical science. It has intuitively been introduced into information systems feasibility studies, information retrieval, information systems planning, software development, and information systems development process. However no such application had been conducted with sound theoretical basis until Warfield's theory on dimensionality was formally put forth. Warfield made it clear that if we assume that a system includes identifiable subsystems, there is reason to suppose that there might be collections of dimensions, some of which would apply to particular subsystems, some of which would apply and have meaning only when the total system is assessed.

Warfield's statement of Ashby's law of requisite variety provides a theoretical guide to further treat the complex dimensions involved with information systems development. The law requires a match between the dimensionality implicitly represented in an information system and the dimensionality encompassed in information systems development methods. In this law, an information systems implicitly represents an integer dimensionality K_s, and a system designer defines an integer dimensionality K_m. In current information systems development practice, information systems are usually under-specified in dimensions due to poor system conceptualization. In fact, an information systems development process should exhibit requisite variety, i.e., $K_m = K_s$.

For any rigorous scholastic research in the field of information systems, one cannot argue more about the importance of choosing right inquiring systems and appropriate accompanying research methods. There are two distinct types of paradigms described in the literature: the science paradigm and the system paradigm. More and more information systems researchers have realized the importance of choosing appropriate research methods for information systems research. Warfield has been the first proposing the concept of macro-mathematics. He pointed out that micro-mathematics is the primary tool of engineering and systems analysis. Macro-mathematics potentially is the primary tool of synthesis and overview   Traditional information systems research relies primarily on micro-mathematics rather than macro-mathematics. It can be expected that the impact of emerging macro-mathematics on information systems research will be tremendous and long-lasting.

The second half of the twentieth century ushered in the age of systems sciences. Many terms have been developed since the 1940s, such as systems science, systems engineering, systems theory, cybernetics, systems analysis, systems methodology, systems approach, and systems thinking. Today we can consider these terms under the common umbrella provided by systems science. For over three decades, Warfield has studied systems science. The product of his intense efforts is the creation of a new version of systems science. His research concludes that systems science is a hierarchy of sub-sciences, all of which incorporates the fundamental triangle of all science. Warfield's version of systems science and the ideas behind it have penetrated and/or will penetrate not only the field of information systems but also many other disciplines. John Warfield has probably been the most influential thinker of the systems movement thus far.

Part 5

Systems Science: The Chapters

I can now explore in depth why systems science is successful as a base of applications in many problematic situations, some of which have been described in Chapters 15-18 inclusive. It has already been mentioned that systems science, like all sciences, has foundations in the fundamental triangle consisting of the human being, thought, and language.

Because of the extensive preparatory material given previously in this book, I am able to present the essence of systems science in **Chapter 19**. Then, in **Chapter 20**, I offer reflections and speculations on where systems science is headed in the future, with emphasis on its potential for applications.

I take a guess at extrapolating what is going on now, as indicated to some extent by the contributions in Part 4. Perhaps these ideas will be suggestive to budding scholars who may find in them some spark of opportunity for future action.

Chapter 19

Systems Science

Systems Science is Not Merely a *Single* Science. An understanding of systems science requires an understanding of its four sub-sciences and how they are interrelated. These sub-sciences are: a science of description, a science of design, a science of complexity, and a science of action. I will describe each of these in turn, and indicate how they are interrelated.

- **A Science of Description** forms the basis whereby a group of well-informed people pool their beliefs in a highly-disciplined process, in order to construct a description of part of a problematic situation. It is most useful to imagine that each individual has been an observer of part of that situation while engaged in pursuing a personal life trajectory and, in that pursuit, has acquired certain key experiences that have been transformed into relevant beliefs, which can be articulated to help form a description of the situation. A similar activity will serve well at design time, when a description of the problematic situation furnishes a basis for a description of an imagined new situation. The latter is intended to provide the basis for evolution from the problematic situation to a brighter situation that replaces its predecessor.

- **A Science of Design**, provides the insights whereby a group of people collaborate in constructing a design for resolving a problematic situation, taking advantage of the products achieved by using the Science of Description. *The Science of Design* *includes the Science of Description as a subset*, but now the description is one of an imagined situation generally aimed at resolving the problematic situation that has already been described.

- **A Science of Complexity**, erects defenses against those human frailties that might otherwise induce us stealthily to ignore the findings about human fallibility and the necessity of accounting for these in describing and resolving problematic situations. The Science of Complexity draws upon the Science of Description and the Science of Design and the products obtainable from application of those sciences; and provides measures of complexity in problematic situations that add insights beyond those available in other ways, and against which other proposed ways of trying to resolve problematic situations can be compared. *The Science of Complexity includes the Science of Description and the Science of Design as subsets.* One may readily imagine that without the sciences of description and design it would not be feasible to carry out the steps required to gain necessary insights into situations characterized by complexity; hence the first two sciences described must be stretched to their imaginable limits in order to serve the aim of helping resolve complexity.

- **A Science of Action**, offers a very detailed description of processes for resolving complexity, showing the infrastructure and roles that are required to apply the three component sciences just named. *This Science includes the three components mentioned previously.*

We may draw on these four sub-sciences of Systems Science (which are explained in great detail in various references) to help explain why Systems Science is successful as a base of applications in many problematic situations.

Interactive Management (IM). Interactive Management (IM) is the methodological component of the Science of Action, and the processes that are part of IM incorporate many of the practices that are essential to promote and achieve success in working with problematic situations that involve complexity.

Interactive Management is the principal component that has been used by the practitioners whose work is discussed in Part 4 of this book. As mentioned earlier, the *Handbook of Interactive Management* is available free as a download from the Internet. This book, of approximately 340 pages, has served to educate a generation of practitioners who have applied IM to a variety of diverse situations on several continents, and have now offered examples of their work in Part 4 of this book.

Success often requires that a complete set of possibilities is achieved. If one of them is not achieved, failure may result from that omission. Hence in discussing these practices, one should keep in mind that they are part of a larger array and are not offered as singly adequate. While Interactive Management is believed to be very robust (i.e., not sensitive to failure to apply each of its components perfectly), there is no reason deliberately to omit components that are known to add to its effectiveness.

Some practices that are quite common in group work are to be avoided (even though commonly used in other practitioner venues), and some are to be included in Interactive Management. I will call those that are to be avoided "negative practices" and those that are to be included "positive practices". Negative practices work **against** success. Positive practices work **for** success.

Context Confusion (Negative). Three factors are defining for group work. These are context, content, and process. It is strongly negative to bring a group together without prior understanding of context. Since context can usually be stated in one or two carefully-prepared paragraphs, it should always be part of preparation for group work to display for each potential participant the Context Statement to see if the individual feels comfortable in being placed in a role of contributor to a group activity founded in that context. Conversely, the individual who is tossed into an unfamiliar context, or who is not given an opportunity to prepare, is abused unnecessarily, and often is not as ready to contribute as would otherwise be anticipated.

Perhaps the potential contributor can suggest changes that would strengthen the Context Statement and make it more readily understandable. Time spent in honing the Context Statement and in promoting participant self-assurance in working cooperatively on the themes in that statement will save valuable group time later. Moreover it is likely that a higher-quality product will ensue from dispelling confusion about context before the group comes together. **Group time is a rare and valuable asset, not to be squandered through poor advance work!**

Process Confusion (Negative). Process confusion is a negative practice which often occurs in group work, and often occurs at the initiative of a group facilitator. As an example, a facilitator may ask the group this question: *"Now how should we proceed to work on this issue?"*

When people come together to work in a group because of some commonality of interest and complementary backgrounds and belief, to help each other unravel a problematic situation, asking this question of the group is a major mistake. Here are some of the factors involved:

➢ **Misplaced Knowledge.** The group is seldom, maybe never, present because its members are expert in group methodology. By asking this question the facilitator is conveying a message like this: "I am not a process expert; it is your role to select process. You cannot count on me to have prepared processes suitable for enabling you to work on a problematic situation. We will have to delay getting down to work on your problematic situation while you have a discussion about what process to use."

➢ **Cued Intellectual Dis-symmetry.** Often there will be one or two people in the group who have some experience leading processes; especially if they are middle managers. Others may have little or no experience. Hence the facilitator has immediately created a potential conflict situation in the group, where those who have group process knowledge stand out over those who have none, and those who have such knowledge may disagree on what is best; hence a protracted period of team dissonance may result, simply because of asking this wrong question.

➢ **Intermittent Distraction.** By cueing the group that the facilitator is dependent on them for process ideas, intermittent distraction from the stated purpose of bringing the group together is likely to occur, adding to the inefficient use of valuable group time, and angering those who feel that their time is not respected, being diverted by discussions about process.

Content Confusion (Negative). Sometimes facilitators believe that their role is to aggregate the results of group discussion on the spot and render these results, adding the facilitator's own opinions and conclusions about the problematic situation. This places the facilitator in the role of being a participant. This type of behavior may be fairly common in lower-level management practice. It may be justified when the topic is one like "where shall we have lunch today?" or "have you all received the notification from the President's Office?". It is not suitable behavior when a problematic situation warrants group work of the type described in the Science of Action. The Spreadthink phenomenon is always present in those circumstances, meaning that the views of the facilitator (or manager) are no more to be taken as gospel than those of any other member of the group.

Indifference to Stopping Rule (Negative). Members of groups are asked to contribute to help resolve a problematic situation. The stopping rule that is indicated for Interactive Management is to stop a process or some sub-process only when it has been determined that no one has any further contribution to make. (Even then, participants should be encouraged to contribute further at a later time if some new thought comes into mind.)

This stopping rule can be disregarded in several ways, all undesirable.

Group Work Termination by the Clock (Negative). Group work necessarily follows a schedule. The schedule serves two purposes: a) to give a gross overview of what is expected and b) to enable members of the group to understand why it will be necessary to reconvene at some future time; whether it be to review and consolidate what has been learned, or to complete processes that had to be temporarily abandoned because of failure to allow enough time in planning.

The quantity and quality of what is generated using IM depends on many factors, including how many contributions members of the group make, and how much discussion is required to clarify the elements of the discussion. Termination by the Clock should almost never be allowed, except as an interim measure until such future time as work can be reconvened. The principle at work here is this: **The clock does not determine quality**. When it is used to terminate work the management that supports that mode of termination clearly misunderstands what is required to help resolve the problematic situation, and thus loses esteem in the opinion of the participants.

Moreover the processes become suspect, if they do not incorporate a recognition of this condition, and efforts to get members to take part in future processes of the same type will be compromised for those with a sense of quality work; though perhaps will be unaffected by those who just "go through the motions".

Group Work Interrupted in Deference to Higher-Level Management Interests (Negative). Group work on problematic situations should be enjoyed as a special commitment by higher-level management, with reinforcement of importance at the beginning, and expressed appreciation at the end of the work. If leaders arrange group time and then indiscriminately allow it to be abruptly interrupted or terminated, i.e., if they allow aborted group work, they deservedly lose face in the eyes of their employees.

Abusive Infrastructure (Negative). Group work on problematic situations is very difficult and requires prolonged activity and dedication. If the infrastructure is abusive to members of the group, it is a signal of lack of comprehension and lack of respect on the part of clients for the products of the group to ask them to carry out such work in abusive infrastructure; e.g., noisy facilities where conversations are fragmented by spurts of noise or excessive separating spaces among participants (of the type often seen on television when forty or fifty people take part in government meetings).

A question that should always be considered in preparation for a meeting is: "What does a participant in this meeting require to maximize the individual's ease of contributing to the results?" Chairs should be comfortable and mounted on high-quality casters, so that no squeaking occurs when participants rotate chairs to review previously-generated information that appears on the walls of the room. Participants with back trouble (many people have back trouble) should have lumbar support from the chair backs.

Support Staff That Lack Extended Training in Interactive Management (Negative). Many organizations may have several problematic situations to resolve in a year's time. Others, such as universities, have accumulated many over the years without ever working to resolve any (such as organizing the social sciences). Either type should have access to support staff with extending training in IM. Experience with one large organization testifies that an excellent way to attain this state is to have outside staff run processes within the organization during the first year; have in-house staff run processes within the organization during the second year, while being supervised by the outside staff; with the in-house staff running the processes themselves during the third year and thereafter.

In-house staff can be relatively small, keeping in mind that outside staff can be contracted for some of the routine work, if necessary because of internal overload.

If staff attempt to carry out IM without such training, the first casualty will typically be all of the behavioral aspects of IM, since they fall outside the scope of education of people who tend to get involved in managing group work. The results are twofold: a) internal failure and b) giving IM an undeserved bad name, thereby making it unlikely to be called on when needed.

The Work Program of Complexity (WPOC). Systems Science can be described not only by its four sub-sciences, but also by its process nature. In its application it is representative of what may be called the Work Program of Complexity (WPOC). To envisage this, suppose that a scientist begins with a desire to comprehend a poorly understood problematic situation. Suppose the scientist realizes that the foundational components must be honored; that the centuries of thought about thought must be recognized and the implications taken into account; that both the creativity and the fallibility of the investigators must be recognized; and that whatever language may be available is almost certainly inadequate. Then the scientist may choose to play a lead role in bringing into existence the Work Program of Complexity, based in the Systems Science as described in this book. How would this evolve?

First of all, some form of Context Statement would be prepared that would describe in general terms the problematic situation that is to be explored. A group of people would be identified who are willing to work together and who have some relevant insights to contribute to a process of discovery. A small staff of people who are familiar with the IM process would be found, and a Workshop Plan would be produced. A suitable situation room for carrying out the processes would be found, and at least three days of continuous time would be dedicated to the first portion of the Discovery phase of the Work Program of Complexity: Description.

The Description provides the material that the experienced IM staffer needs to render a dispassionate interpretation (free of personal bias or distortion) to the group for possible amendment. This interpretation, when complete, is considered to be the group's Diagnosis, completing the Discovery phase of the Work Program of Complexity.

The next phase of group work consist of Design activity, following the concepts set forth in the design sub-science. The complexity sub-science allows computation of indexes of complexity, which help in priority setting and choice of an alternative from the design possibilities. The action plan is developed, whereupon the finishing touches occur, as the integrating work of Systems Science involves assessing which, if any, non-neutral sciences or methods are required to add more specifics to what has to be done to resolve the complexity inherent in the problematic situation.

Certain positive practices are followed throughout this work.

Group Symmetry (positive). Individuals in the group should always be treated as equals, whatever their roles may be in life or in organizations. This behavioral aspect is greatly aided if every individual in the group understands his or her role before coming to the meeting.

No Surprises (positive). There should never be a reason for anyone who attends as a participant or an observer to be surprised by what happens. This condition is heavily dependent on proper playing of role by the IM Planner and the IM Broker. Both of these roles are defined in detail in the *Handbook of Interactive Management* (1994). There has **never** been a problem with any group for which these roles have been properly carried out ahead of time. When these roles are properly carried out, certain conditions that may arise in group work are precluded. One of these is the emergence of an individual participant who decides to take over the conduct of the meeting by claiming to understand the situation and what has to be done. This has occurred in perhaps 1% of all IM Workshops, always when the IM Broker role has not been properly carried out. It occurs when the offender does not understand his or her role in the meeting and has not given and then honored a verbal contract to the IM Broker to play that role.

No (or few) Multiple Roles (positive). While on rare occasions the client or sponsor may also be a participant at the table, normally this is not permitted. Exceptions may occur after that individual has already witnessed IM Workshops and understands how they proceed, provided the individual is known to have an appropriate personality, and to have experience that seems to be essential to the conduct of the activity.

The client or sponsor may, however, play a very valuable role in two respects. First, that person may initiate the Workshop activity by explaining clearly the importance of the work in a very positive way, and making it clear that the participants should feel free of any other responsibilities for the duration of the activity. At the end of the Workshop, that person should commend the participants on the extent and quality of what they have accomplished—something that will be readily apparent to anyone who observes what has been produced.

Valuing Group Time (positive). Even long-experienced IM Staff have been known to forget, on occasion, the value of group time. It can be seen from at least three different perspectives.

- **The Direct Cost of Group Work.** From one perspective, the cost of bringing a group together can be seen in terms of the composite salaries of the participants and the IM staff, and the costs of the working environment, etc.

- **The Difficulty in Preparation.** From another perspective, there is difficulty involved in the preparatory work of identifying the people, developing the plan, etc., all of which pays off through the products of the group.

- **Potential Opportunity Cost.** From a third perspective, the group produces products that only the group can produce; hence any time that is lost may have a very large opportunity cost associated with it. For this reason, every minute of time that is available to a group should be planned most carefully, based on the double criteria of (a) facilitating creativity and (b) circumventing fallibility that comes from the discovered behavioral pathologies.

Since the systems science has been formulated specifically to satisfy this pair of criteria, it is important that those who choose to use it try very hard to discipline themselves not to infringe on the time of the group by doing such things as short lectures, giving extra instructions that are not really needed, etc., etc. Unless activities are specifically spelled out as part of the two methodologies (NGT) and (ISM), it is very desirable not to insert them if they use time that otherwise could be dedicated to the group. It is worth noting that both NGT and ISM are group learning processes, that both of them have built in corrective procedures, and that it is not necessary for IM staff to protect the group members from possible errors by rendering instructions beyond those contained in the descriptions of the two processes.

Providing Skills Not Normally Available (positive). The graphical structures that are developed in the course of the application of systems science are the most unique and essential products that groups create because they establish the interrelationships among system components (whether observed, or potential in new designs) that cannot be developed in any other known way. In the earlier work, IM staff made the incorrect assumption that participants could read and interpret these structures. Later research by Perino and others has shown unequivocally that they cannot, even though they may think that they can. Hence it is very desirable for IM staff to provide interpretation of the graphic structures that are developed in a very thorough way, in order to make certain that the groups understand their collective products. Ample time must be provided for this, and it will often be desirable to videotape the discussion for later reference.

Providing the Situation Room (Positive). It is very clear now that the relatively high cost of group work, the often very significant problematic situations, and the potentially high payoffs of viable outcomes, all merit the use of a dedicated situation room in which to carry out the work. Typically a period of up to a day in preparation of the room and its various facilities (flip-charts, computers, etc.) is warranted, to make sure that no time is wasted when the group arrives.

Providing an Observatorium (Positive). It has been typical in observing the evolution of Interactive Management that most projects have involved the early part of the Work Program of Complexity. Once groups have been able to describe the problematic situation, the tendency is to fall back into the standard behavioral mode, instead of proceeding to continue the process into its design phase. However, when it is clear that no one understands how to proceed, Interactive Management has been continued into the design phase. Even after the design phase has been successful, and the results applied, the concept of Observatorium has not been recognized. Yet these matters seem abundantly clear:

- **Followup Requires Further Insightful Experiences.** People who will implement the design often were not involved in the extensive period of communication that produced the design.
- **Prior Investment Should be Capitalized Upon.** Opportunities for misunderstanding and mis-communication remain great during the Implementation portion of the Work Program of Complexity.

Because of these two factors, it seems clear that sensible management will provide a facility which we call the "corporate observatorium". This facility will house the products of the group(s) that produced all of the work leading up to the implementation. It will serve as a kind of living educational facility where people who will be involved in implementation can go to learn what happened or just to refresh themselves on specific points. This facility can also be used to provide a record showing an update of progress as time passes.

Systems science provides an opportunity for action to be founded in the fundamentals of scientific thought. A pathway from the origins to the conclusions of pragmatically generated activity can be made clear. The alternative is to rely on *ad hoc* decisions, on authority without sufficient awareness of complexity, and on abuse of those who rely upon good judgment and effective use of human experience for their satisfaction and livelihood.

Chapter 20

Reflections And Speculations

What is likely to be the future of systems science, as set forth in this book? That is the question that I wish to respond to in this Chapter. I choose to discuss it in terms of the four "local sectors" introduced in Part 4:

- The private sector
- The education sector
- The government sector
- The social sector

I follow the conservative practice of supposing that what will be favorable to systems science in the future is not going to be significantly different from what has been evidenced in the past. I hope that there will be an expansion, but I suspect that the expansion will not be too different from what has been seen. The metaphor of trying to turn the Queen Mary in the ocean is probably representative of what is involved in trying to establish systems science in society.

The Future of Systems Science in the Private Sector

Without doubt, the most salient success of the application of systems science in the private sector, as measured in terms of the use of its action component, Interactive Management, has been in Ford Motor Company. As indicated in Chapter 15, this success involved these key factors:

- **An Individual Initiative.** A highly-motivated, dedicated individual (Scott M. Staley), who pursued the incorporation of IM in Ford over more than a decade.
- **An Early Entrepreneurial Sponsor.** An early sponsor who was willing to risk his personal reputation by allocating funds and staff time to the use of what was at the time an untried system.
- **A Suitable Physical Infrastructure.** Willingness to provide suitably equipped infrastructure in which to carry out repeated applications.
- **Receptiveness to Informed Outside Advice.** Willingness to follow expert advice from persons that were highly knowledgeable of systems science and IM over significant time periods.
- **Participant Enthusiastic Acceptance.** Enthusiastic acceptance of IM on the part of hundreds of participants from within the Company.
- **Comprehensive Documentation of Products.** Continuing documentation of results by reports and videotapes, applied to educate personnel involved in implementing results.
- **Visible Success Correlated with Future Prospects.** Measurable success stories arising out of the work that could be seen to have significantly valuable results upon the future of the organization.

In addition to these factors, it is significant that "spillover effects" occurred from this work in Ford in three respects.

- **Export Into Surrounding Communities.** Ford encourages its employees to be active in its surrounding communities. Because of this, Roy Smith, an employee in England, began to apply IM in church work and related matters with considerable success, which helped Ford in its local community relations.

- **Consulting Opportunities for Retirees.** In a second respect, two retirees from Ford who had taken part in IM work at Ford, found it to be so effective that, upon retirement, they began to do IM consulting work in various sectors. One of these was Roy Smith himself, who reported on his post-retirement work in Chapter 17, and the other was Philip Ernzen who returned to Ford after retirement to facilitate IM workshops from time to time and also facilitated other IM work along with a close relative.

- **Software Enhancement.** A third spillover effect occurred when Ford provided partial support to develop an upgraded version of software to support the IM process. This software later served numerous applications in universities and elsewhere.

Will the success at Ford stimulate similar success in other large organizations? It is impossible to be certain, but since a pattern is now apparent, it seems reasonable to suppose that some organizations will begin to observe the merits of the work and ultimately adopt it to resolve those lingering problematic situations that continue to haunt their organizations. It is known, for example, that several individuals who are highly placed in large corporations are presently studying the systems science in depth, and this suggests that at some point when the time is ripe they will be able to introduce IM into their organizations. One humorist has described this possibility with the term "guerilla cybernetics".

The Future of Systems Science in the Education Sector

Just as the most salient success of the application of systems science is readily identifiable in the private sector, as measured in terms of the prolonged use of its action component, Interactive Management, it is also readily identifiable in the education sector, and for some of the same reasons. It is in the Instituto Tecnologico y de Estudios Superiores de Monterrey, i.e., ITESM, or as it is known locally, "the Tec".

With over 30 locations in Mexico, the Tec is recognized as an outstanding private institution of higher education, offering leadership throughout Latin America, with its influence now extending throughout the world, with its virtual university and its satellite facilities. From its beginnings in the mid 1940s, this institution has developed outstanding leaders in a variety of areas. It now offers courses in Interactive Management, and it supervises project work both on and off its campuses in a variety of its locations. Several of these are illustrated in Part 4 of this book. Moreover, several of those who now are involved in the national government have previously applied Interactive Management to help in local planning activities. At least six faculty are known to be active in teaching aspects of the subject.

Some of the factors involved in the success of this material in higher education in Mexico are:

- **An Individual Initiative.** A highly-motivated, dedicated individual (A. Roxana Cárdenas), who pursued the incorporation of IM in Mexico for more than a decade, with the close assistance of a strong faculty friend (Carmen Moreno).
- **Institutional Openness.** Willingness to allocate staff time to the use of what was at the time a relatively new and untried system.
- **Appropriate Technological Infrastructure.** Willingness to provide computer-equipped infrastructure to carry out repeated applications.
- **Receptiveness to Informed Outside Advice.** Willingness to follow expert advice from persons that were highly knowledgeable of systems science and IM over significant time periods.
- **Enthusiastic Internal Acceptance.** Enthusiastic acceptance of IM on the part of colleagues and students from within the institution.
- **Willingness to Compare With Other Methods.** Research to compare IM with other methods that purported to seek to achieve similar results.

- **Large-Scale Testing, With Very Significant Visible Consequences.** A large project in the state of Guanajuato, in which IM was used to establish scenarios for the future of the state and of Mexico, with wide public participation and wide publicity, as well as strong political implications.
- **Accumulation of External Empirical Evidence.** Invitations, frequently accepted, for outsiders to come to Mexico to speak about systems science, IM, and related subjects, by such speakers as Broome (USA), Christakis (USA), Janes (England) and Warfield (USA), to faculty, students, and on the satellite to branch campuses across the country; including to campuses as part of the ITESM Virtual University.
- **Use of Short Courses in Faculty Development Programs.** One-week short courses offered as part of the ITESM faculty development programs.

In addition to the foregoing, as in the Ford instances, there were spillover effects, as material learned in the classrooms and on the satellites, spill over into Mexican industries, and into off-campus projects which are part of the educational programs offered by the Tec.

Not long ago I offered a short course at the University of Hull in England to over 40 Mexican students who were there for a summer program in the School of Business.

Aside from the Mexican success story, which is now about 15 years old, newer programs are moving ahead in China. One that is progressing significantly is being led by Dr. Xuefeng Song at the China University of Mining and Technology in the School of Business, with an emphasis on complexity; and still another is continuing at the South China University of Technology with an emphasis on the design of software (as discussed in Part 4). These programs, while young, have solid footing, and there is every reason to think that they will advance.

Whether programs can take root in the United States is another question altogether.

Systems programs in the USA have a habit of beginning, living for a brief time, and dying. A similar fate often befalls them in Europe. And of those that have survived, they tend not to be able to sustain an original intent, but rather to be forced to change their focus to accommodate to shifting academic winds. Whether the force of a sound systems science footing can be sufficient to give the necessary academic credential for stability, only time will tell. In my personal experience, a program began as a Center for Interactive Management at the University of Virginia and survived for about 3 years, then resumed at George Mason University (GMU) as a Center for Interactive Management and survived for about 5 years. Both of these programs generated significant sponsorship through the outstanding work of Dr. Alexander Christakis and his associates, and produced excellent educational values and spillover, but both of them were terminated for reasons having nothing to do with the programs themselves, but as a consequence of decisions coming down from the rarefied levels of the academic hierarchy involving decision-makers that were not in their decision-making roles at the time the programs were initiated. While the GMU Center was terminated, my Institute continued there with another name, and produced significant spillovers, including continuing activity in several countries and organizations, which are described in some of my other books and also elsewhere in this book.

The Wandwaver Solution. In the western world, the term "panacea overload" coined by Dr. Russell Ackoff to describe what happens in the business schools and engineering schools, and consequently in their ultimate client organizations, is an accurate representation of a continuing shift in what is taught, always looking for a new set of theories or methodologies and turning a blind eye to the scientific basis that has served so well for centuries in many areas of society.

To overcome the shifting sands in academia which seem always to be responding to the latest fad associated with systems, I have proposed what I consider to be a kind of ultimate solution for the university of the future. It recognizes several severe weaknesses in ongoing programs. Specifically, it recognizes the absence of historical perspective in the technical programs, and the absence of graphical communication skills in most of the literature and arts programs. Moreover it recognizes the absence of design skills and forward-thinking skills on a scale commensurate with the future of societies. Rather than attempt to force all of these into the same time frame, it has been proposed to sort these three kinds of things into a sequence.

The arts and sciences are learned first in the College. The contemporary contributions are learned next as a sort of social maintenance program. And finally a horizon curriculum prepares a subset of individuals to design for the future. This very brief summary replaces the 100-plus page description on the web site where this concept was delineated some years ago, and where it still resides and can readily be found with the modern search engines under the title "The Wandwaver Solution".

The Future of Systems Science in the Government Sector

Two major successes stand out in the government sector, these being associated with the names of Henry C. Alberts via the Department of Defense and Robert McDonald via the U. S. Forestry Service. As before success begins with a single, dedicated individual, willing to persevere with a focused goal in mind until success is achieved.

Since that has proved to be the factor that has been found in each of the three sectors discussed so far, I think it is safe to say that **it is the one ingredient that must be present if success is to be had.**

Both the Alberts and the McDonald programs have been discussed in their papers in Part 4. Their two programs are unique, with unique features, attesting to their drive and originality.

It is my belief that it is only when individuals such as them decide to undertake programs with the kind of drive and intensity they exhibited that we will see results of the type that they achieved. On the other hand, I believe that many such possibilities are there for the taking.

Just as with Ford and the Tec, spillover occurred. The short courses that were given to the Defense Systems Management College (DSMC) were taken by Carol Jeffrey who was employed there. After she left the College, she and her husband moved to Liberia, where her husband became president of a bank in the capital city.

Carol Jeffrey ran IM sessions with Liberian women on the subject of the status of women in Liberia (and particularly, as they were affected by the civil war) and, later, with warlords and warriors on disarmament (with help from the European Commission), which helped greatly to cause a significant decrease in hostilities in that country.

Later, two faculty members at DSMC received doctorates for their studies related to systems science and to Interactive Management. The work of George Perino related to the ability (or rather inability) of highly trained technical people to read structured graphics, which gave new insights into severe deficiencies in education in communication that remain unsatisfied in higher education.

The Future of Systems Science in the Social Arena

Remarkable things have been done by individuals in the social arena. It is impossible for me to document these, but the actors have often documented their work in part, and I can at least call attention to some of the more remarkable work that has been done. I have done this in several of my books. Included in this book are discussions of the work of Professor Ben Broome, which has to be seen as one of the more remarkable forays into a very difficult social arena; the work of Carmen Moreno, which extends across the Western Hemisphere; and the work of Roy Smith, which is truly notable for both its volume and its impact in the church in England.

The work of Dr. Alexander Christakis extends across the various categories, but I mention it here to highlight especially his work with the Native American community, which spilled over also into the work of Ben Broome. Christakis has also worked a lot with a variety of health care communities both nationally and internationally, and with natural resource communities. His work involves a mix of private and public work, confidential and open, which makes it impossible for me to sort out, and may account for the absence of a contribution from him to this volume. Notably, he is mentioned in this book in the contribution by Reynaldo Treviño concerning the success of the First Interloquium held in Guanajuato, where I had arranged with Dr. Carlos Flores to bring Christakis there to facilitate much of the on-stage programmatic work.

All of the work described so far has had spillover effects, mostly describable as spawning a set of private consultants who go forth to work in a variety of social arenas, using IM to work on a variety of issues, often with less than ideal infrastructure. Were it not for the robustness of the methods used, it would be unlikely to find that such activities would meet the kind of acclaim that has been found. Nonetheless, a substantial amount of success has been reported by the consultants, so consulting does work. It is not possible to maintain any kind of oversight as to how much of this is going on, because of the industrial competitiveness of the work. Not all practitioners are motivated by a desire to help enhance the science.

From time to time surprising reports reach me as to how much occurs, and how much it is appreciated. Because of this, I am optimistic that from time to time some of this consulting will cause roots to be put down in institutions, and what begins as small consulting activity will flower into larger institutional components.

All in All

There is abundant reason to be pessimistic about the future of systems science. It is easy to see the powerful behaving smugly with arrogant posturing, while striving to manage problematic situations whose cognitive demands far exceed the cognitive limitations of the managers who have boldly taken on the task of managing the situations. On the other hand, enough success stories at the level of middle management have been reported to engender optimism. The power of science, when considered, has to be seen as very substantial, yet it is often ignored or replaced with something less. I often recall Charles S. Peirce's comment: "Truth, crushed to earth, shall rise again." This sustains me in a moment of weakness, as does Sir Geoffrey Vickers' comment, following his visit to a well-known US institution: "In the beginning was the Word–not the equation."

If patience is a virtue, as is sometimes said, the forward movement of systems science as a force to be reckoned with in improving the human condition will test the virtuous wherever they may be. Let us together hope that patience will be rewarded.

Appendix 1

Gallery

The Gallery shows a mixture of photographs and sketches of people whose work has influenced in some way the development of systems science as presented in this work. The sketches have kindly been contributed by Mr. Greg Thomas of Vanderbilt University. The pictures are organized by first appearance of the individual, to be compatible with Chapters and Appendices, as appropriate. Several scholars are shown in more than one location, since their work cuts across categories. The letter P is used to precede a figure number to represent "picture". Figure P2-1, for example, indicates that Chapter 2 mentions George A. Miller, Alexander Pope, and Herbert A. Simon as scholars of individual behavioral pathologies.

Chapter 2. The Human Being

Scholars of Individual Behavioral Pathologies
Miller, George A. (1920-   )   Fig. P2-1
Pope, Alexander (1688-1744)   Fig. P2-1
Simon, Herbert A. (1916-2001)   Fig. P2-1

Scholars of Group Behavioral Pathologies
Allison, Graham (1940 -   )   Fig. P2-2
Delbecq, Andre (1936-   )   Fig. P2-2
Janis, Irving (1918-1990)   Fig. P2-2

Scholars of Group Behavioral Pathologies
Kapelouzos, John (Iannis) (1949-   ) Fig. P2-3
Lasswell, Harold (1902-1978)   Fig. P2-3
Tuckman, Bruce W. (1938-   )   Fig. P2-3

Scholars of Organization Behavioral Pathologies
Argyris, Chris (1923 -   )   Fig. P2-4

Rabinow, Paul (1944-   )   Fig. P8-1

Chapter 9. Metrics of Complexity

Aristotle (385-322 BC)   Fig. P9-1
De Morgan, Augustus (1806-1871)   Fig. P9-1
Miller, George A. (1920-   )   Fig. P9-1

Chapter 10. Diagnosing

None.

Chapter 11. System Design

Banathy, Bela H. (1919-2003)   Fig. P11-1
Cárdenas, A. Roxana (1959-   )   Fig. P11-1
Hall, Arthur D. III   Fig. P11-1

Chapter 12. Choosing an Alternative

McDonald, Robert   Fig. P12-1

Chapter 13. Implementing the Alternative

Alberts, Henry C.   Fig. P13-1
Staley, Scott M.   Fig. P13-1

Chapter 14. The Observatorium

None.

Chapter 15. Practitioners Active in the Private Sector

Chandy, G. S.   Fig. P15-1
Haruna, Koichi   Fig. P15-1
Jiangping, Wan   Fig. P15-1
Jianmei, Yang   Fig. P15-2
Rodriguez, Jorge   Fig. P15-2
Staley, Scott M.   Fig. P15-2

Chapter 16. Practitioners Active in the Government Sector

Alberts, Henry C.   Fig. P16-1

Chapter 17. Practitioners Active in the Social Arena

Chapter 18. Practitioners Active in the Education Sector

Name, Chapter, Figure Number(s), Position or Status at Time of Writing

Alberts, Henry C. *P13-1, P16-1* Adjunct Prof., Univ. Of MD, Retired from US
   Government
Allison, Graham *P2-2* Professor Harvard University
Argyris, Chris *P2-4* Professor Harvard University
Ayiku, Moses N. B. *P16-1* Retired from Gov't. of Ghana, Attorney in Accra

Batra, Surinder *P16-1* Consultant Entrepreneur in New Delhi
Broome, Benjamin P17-1 Arizona State University Professor

Caffarel, Graciela *P18-1* Monterrey Tech Mexico Professor
Cárdenas, A. Roxana *P11-1,P18-1* Monterrey Tech Mexico Professor and
   Director
Christakis, Alexander *P17-1* Consultant, Paoli Pennsylvania

Delbecq, Andre *P2-2* Professor, Santa Clara University
Downs, Anthony *P2-4* Staff Member, Brookings Institution, Washington, DC

Friedman, George J. *P6-1* Retired from Northrop Corp, Adjunct Prof, USC

Hall, Arthur D. III *P11-1* Retired from Bell Laboratories, Private Investor
Harary, Frank *P5-2* Retired Professor of Mathematics
Haruna, Koichi *P15-1* Corporate Chief Engineer, Hitachi Corp, Japan

Janes, F. Ross *P18-1* Retired Faculty Member, City University, London
Jeffrey, Carol *P17-1* Retired Consultant
Jiangping, Wan *P15-1* Faculty Member, South China Univ of Technology
Jianmei, Yang *P15-1* Faculty Member, South China Univ of Technology

Kapelouzos, John (Iannis) *P2-3* Ret'd. from Supreme Court of Greece,
   Consultant

March, James G. *P2-5* Adjunct Professor, Stanford University
McDonald, Robert *P12-1, P16-2* Retired from Federal and State Govt,
   Consultant
Miller, George A. *P2-1* Faculty, Princeton University
Moreno, Carmen *P17-2* Consultant, Monterrey Tech Mexico

Rabinow, Paul *P8-1* Professor, University of California Berkeley
Rodriguez, Jorge *P15-2* Faculty, Monterrey Tech Mexico

Smith, Roy *P17-2* Retired from Ford Motor Co, England, Consultant

Song, Xuefeng *P18-2* Dean of Business, China Univ of Mining & Tech.
Staley, Scott M. *P13-1, P15- 2* Chief Engineer, Ford Motor Co.

Temblador, Mary Carmen *P18-2* Professor, Monterrey Tech Mexico
Treviño, Reynaldo *P16-2* Member, central government Mexico
Tuckman, Bruce W. *P2-3* Professor, The Ohio State University

Xu, Li Da *P18-2* Professor, Old Dominion University

Situation Room *P7-1* Design developed by the author

George A. Miller (1920-)

Discovered "the magical number seven–plus or minus two"

Alexander Pope (1688-1744)

Penned "A little learning is a dang'rous Thing:: Drink deep, or taste not the *Pierian* Spring: There *shallow Draughts* Intoxicate the Brain, And drinking *largely* sobers us again."

Herbert A. Simon (1916-2001)

Repeated George A. Miller's experiments and found very similar results

Figure P2-1. Scholars of *Individual* Behavioral Pathologies

Graham Allison (1940-   )

Illustrated in great detail the impact of Groupthink at the highest levels of the U. S. Government, in actions leading up to the Bay of Pigs incident

Andre Delbecq (1936-   )

With colleagues, developed the Nominal Group Technique (NGT) to help overcome group behavioral pathologies

Irving Janis (1918-1990)

Sharply defined the numerous facets of "Groupthink", explaining the pathological behavior of individuals acting in groups

Figure P2-2 Scholars of *Group* Behavioral Pathologies

Iannis (John) Kapelouzos (1949-   )

Discovered the extensive learning that takes place during the use of Interpretive Structural Modeling in groups

Harold Lasswell (1902-1978)

Recognized the propensity of people to develop policy in group setting without access to physical infrastructure sufficient to overcome cognitive burden

Bruce Tuckman (1938-   )

Described a regular pattern of unregulated group work as a sequence of stages: "forming, norming, storming, and performing", by studying numerous instances—with no guarantee that the last two stages would ever be attained

Figure P2-3 Scholars of *Group* Behavioral Pathologies

Chris Argyris (1923-   )

Clarified the unwillingness of executives to discuss "undiscussables" and their "undiscussability" in organizations

Kenneth Boulding (1910-1994)

Explained the importance of systems thinking and, by example, the genius of willingness to work cooperatively

Anthony Downs (1930-   )

Explained the predictability of bureaucratic behavior in organizations

Figure P2-4 Scholars of *Organization* Behavior

Friedrich Hayek (1899-1992)

Showed in great detail what evils can occur when pseudo-science (scientism) is substituted for science in administering organizations

James G. March

Pioneered the study of organizations and organizational behavior

Sir Geoffrey Vickers (1894-1982)

Went into great depth (both philosophical and from strong management experience) to emphasize that human systems differ greatly from physical systems, hence should involve different ways of exploration and modeling

Figure P2-5 Scholars of *Organization* Behavior II

George Boole (1815-1864)

Showed how to represent propositions by symbols and how to engage these with one another

Georg Cantor (1845-1918)

Showed how to operate with sets of symbols, constructing set theory which would be the basis of the theory of relations

Arthur Cayley (1821-1895)

Developed the theory of matrices, after giving up a lucrative law practice to pursue a university teaching and research career

Figure P3-1 Scholars Who Contributed to Precision and Expansion in Linguistic Representation

David Hilbert (1862-1943)

Understood the necessity of a small set of interacting, mutually supporting languages with complementary purposes (metalanguage)

Antoine Lavoisier (1743-1794)

Sensitive to language from his education in law, he reconstructed chemistry by reconstructing its faulty language

Bertrand Russell (1872-1970)

(Grudgingly?) introduced a directed graph as the lone drawing in his book on the mathematics of philosophy, in which he refined symbolic representations in linguistic constructions

Figure P3-2. Scholars Who Shows Clear Sensitivity to the Criticality of Language

Aristotle (385 BC - 322 BC)

Dedicated to thought about how to think soundly, and how to articulate thought and the relationships among components of thought, Aristotle conceived and applied the idea of science. He developed the syllogism, the basic pattern of deductive reasoning, from which patterns of belief can grow into larger patterns. His views animated many later scholars, including Abelard, Galileo, De Morgan, and Charles Sanders Peirce, to name a few. Today his ideas have finally been significantly amplified by using the digital computer to help groups construct structural hypotheses and test programs that can be used to guide efforts to resolve complexities on significant scales.

Pierre Abelard (1079 AD -1142 AD)

Recognizing that Aristotle's syllogism need not be expressed in three separate statements, but could be stated in one integrated expression (as noted by Bochenski), Abelard laid a basis around 1100 AD for processes that would come to fruition a millennium later. As a great logician his views played a major role in the thinking of nineteenth-century philosophers, and in the development of American pragmatism through the work of Charles Sanders Peirce.

His expressions laid the foundation for Interpretive Structural Modeling.

**Figure P4-1 Early Thought Leaders Concerning
Thought About Thought**

I M. Bochenski (1902-1995)

A Polish priest–philosopher–logician–I. M. Bochenski displayed a true love of scholarship in his book *A History of Formal Logic*. Alternately quoting from and interpreting logicians from the earliest recorded days up until the early 1930's, he provided a genuine overview of the flow of development of thought about thought, thereby undergirding the work reported here.

Augustus De Morgan (1806-1871)

Augustus De Morgan made a clear and strong contribution to the structure-based science of complexity (SBSOC) which underlies Interactive Management. He produced the theory of relations in 1847, and recognized the importance of transitivity to the validity of Aristotle's syllogism. He became head of the Dept. of mathematics at the University of London at age 22.

Gottfried Leibniz (1646-1716)

Educated as a lawyer, career as librarian, inventor of calculus, he restored logic to its state before the Dark Ages, and then added to its history. In one of his research notebooks, he showed the use of circles to represent set intersection, etc., even before sets were invented and long before Venn. Many of his works weren't published until long after Newton, but he is seen at least as on a par with Newton in terms of the invention of calculus.

**Figure P5-1 More Thought Leaders
Concerning Thought About Thought**

Frank Harary (1921-   )

Frank Harary, one of the world's great graph theorists, integrated logic with graph theory to produce digraph theory, which provided the analytic basis for the synthesis that constitutes Interpretive Structural Modeling (ISM): a foundational component of systems science.

Charles Sanders Peirce (1839-1914)

Karl-Otto Apel described Peirce as "America's greatest thinker". Popper described him as one of the greatest philosophers who ever lived. Peirce's insights provided the philosophical basis for the developments of the science of generic design and the structure-based science of complexity. Peirce met De Morgan and later lauded his work with great praise---something that Peirce was not in the habit of doing. Who else has read the works of all the great philosophers of his day and discovered where they were wrong--then integrated their best thinking into his "architectonic"?

**Figure P5-2 Recent Thought Leaders Concerning
Thought About Thought**

W. Ross Ashby (1903-1972)

Ross Ashby contributed to an understanding of cybernetics and to the understanding of the role of the theory of relations. His understanding of the linkages between real systems and design to correct poor systems performance produced his Law or Theorem of Requisite Variety.

George J. Friedman (1928-   )

George Friedman brought a combination of mathematical sophistication and engineering sensibility to the modeling of such systems as reflected in his Constraint Theory. He applied these insights to examine why such systems fail, and concluded that cognitive burden was inadequately faced in engineering and manufacture of such systems

Frank Harary (1921-   )

Please see Figure P5-2 for a picture and comments concerning Frank Harary

**Figure P6-1 Authors of Theorems for Quality
Control in Model Construction**

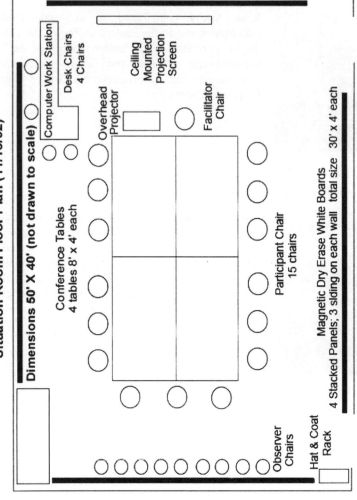

CENTER FOR INTERACTIVE SYSTEM DESIGN: FORD MOTOR COMPANY
Situation Room Floor Plan (11/15/92)

Dimensions 50' X 40' (not drawn to scale)

Computer Work Station

Desk Chairs
4 Chairs

Ceiling Mounted Projection Screen

Overhead Projector

Facilitator Chair

Conference Tables
4 tables 8' x 4' each

Participant Chair
15 chairs

Magnetic Dry Erase White Boards
4 Stacked Panels; 3 sliding on each wall   total size   30' x 4' each

Observer Chairs

Hat & Coat Rack

Figure P7-1. Example of Situation Room to Support Group Work

Michel Foucault (1926-1984)

Three people were especially important to me in focusing me on the importance of history and the evolution of thought, with special emphasis on the philosophy of science. These were C. S. Peirce, Michael Foucault, and Friedrich A. von Hayek. Foucault emphasized the criticality of social power, as well as the importance of trying to sustain high quality as ideas evolved from the originator. He convinced me that there is high opportunity to warp and pollute great ideas. And what a magnificent writer! Even the English translations of his prose are superb. Recently I am inspired by two of his ideas: founder of discursivity and the psychology of the "leader" who risks countless lives, who destroys countless others, and yet is accepted by his underlings. What leads to the self-image of these people?

Paul Rabinow (1944-   )

The anthropologist, Paul Rabinow, has provided a fine academic and public service by publishing *The Foucault Reader* in which he mixed a selection of Foucault's works with transcripts of several excellent interviews of Foucault that took place shortly before Foucault's death; and added to the foregoing his own insightful interpretation of the materials, which help the reader to absorb and further understand the ideas of Michel Foucault.

Figure P8-1 On How to Write History—How to Describe Situations

Aristotle (385 BC- 322 BC)

He moved the world with his ideas and he is honored by the concept of the Aristotle Index, representing the number of syllogisms embedded in the problematique that represents some problematic situation---as derived with the use of Interactive Management.

Augustus De Morgan (1806-1871)

Augustus De Morgan made a clear and strong contribution to the structure-based science of complexity (SBSOC) which underlies Interactive Management. De Morgan produced the theory of relations in 1847, and recognized the importance of transitivity to the validity of Aristotle's syllogism.

George A. Miller (1920-   )

George Miller studied the capacity of the human mind to work with and retain quantities of information in various ways and, in doing so, produced a manuscript that is referred to over and over again whenever a discussion turns to the finite capability of the human mind. The famous "magical number seven" is well-known in many circles, not merely in the behavioral sciences.

Figure P9-1 Providers of Constructs Related to Metrics of Complexity, Which I Have Named After Them

Bela H. Banathy (1919-2003)

Bela H. Banathy provided leadership to the systems community with emphasis on systems design and systems education for many years

A. Roxana Cárdenas (1959-   )

Formerly Head of Systems Engineering at ITESM, Monterrey, Mexico. Diplome in Economic Systems from Aix-en-Provence, and Doctorate from City University of London; she is a scholar, researcher, author, and supreme teacher using the best of today's technology. She leads strategic planning for the ITESM system of more than 30 campuses across Mexico.

Arthur D. Hall III

Arthur D. Hall III taught systems engineering to graduates at the Bell Telephone Laboratories and wrote a definitive early textbook on Systems Engineering Methodology. He introduced behavioral concepts such as creativity into his teaching when they were strongly frowned on by positivists in his organization.

Figure P11-1 Scholars With an Emphasis on Systems Design in Their Research and Teaching

Robert McDonald

Robert McDonald made Significant Contributions to Public Participation in the Management of Forestry and Other Natural Resources in the United States and Elsewhere with the U. S. Forest Service and the Florida Division of Forestry

Figure P12-1. A Contributor Who Made Significant Contributions to Public Participation

Henry C. Alberts

Henry C. Alberts provided leadership for more than 5 years to more than 300 program managers in the US Department of Defense to redesign the Acquisition System. Only 6 months after this herculean task was completed, the US Congress passed a law known as the "Federal Acquisition Streamlining Act of 1994". In retirement, he teaches systems engineering electronically for the University of Maryland.

Scott M. Staley

Scott M. Staley provided leadership for more than a decade within Ford Motor Company to several hundred engineers and managers. Among the accomplishments were the design and implementation of Ford's system-wide shared data base for product design and strategies for various vehicle designs including the fuel-cell vehicle.

**Figure P13-1 Two Who Enabled System Designs
From Beginning Through To Implementation**

G. S. Chandy (1938-   )

G. S. Chandy is a mathematician and entrepreneur in India, who is also known across India for his political activity in striving to enhance democratic government. As he describes in his article, he seeks to improve management at various levels, including the personal level of the individual, and higher organizational levels.

Koichi Haruna (1941-   ) and grandson

Koichi Haruna learned ISM in 1972 while visiting Battelle, applied it in Japan, later became leader of Hitachi's three systems laboratories, and now works at the Hitachi corporate level to enhance the quality of human settlements in Japan.

Wan Jiangping

Wan Jiangping is a researcher on software design and production at the South China University of Technology who has won prizes for his research results

Figure P15-1. Practitioners Acting for the Private Sector

Prof. Yang Jianmei

Yang Jianmei is the faculty adviser of Wan Jiangping who received his doctorate under her supervision, and who has written papers jointly with him, including the contribution in this book.

Jorge Rodriguez

Jorge is a faculty member and businessman in the Mexico City area on the faculty of ITESM del Norte. He works with young, aspiring entrepreneurs. Jorge led a group studying energy options for the Mexico City area, and teaches in the business school program at ITESM, Mexico's outstanding technical institute (which has branches all over Mexico, tied together through satellite connections).

Scott M. Staley

Scott Staley is a mechanical engineer with Ford Motor Company. His doctorate is from Purdue University. He spent nearly a decade in the Ford Research Laboratory. He pioneered the use of Interactive Management in Ford Motor Company. At this writing he is Chief Engineer for fuel-cell powered vehicle developments.

Figure P15-2. Practitioners Acting for the Private Sector

Henry C. Alberts

Adjunct Professor at U. of Maryland; Emeritus from the Defense Systems Management College, Fort Belvoir, VA He described the largest IM project ever run by anyone--in which he led over 300 Defense Program Managers in redesigning the defense acquisition system.

Moses N. B. Ayiku

A remarkable Ghanian patriot. Retired from a post at the Centre for Scientific and Industrial Research (CSIR). Degrees in Electrical Engineering. D.Sc. in Systems Engineering. Studied law at the Inns of Court. Qualified to practice law in England. Heads his own law practice in Accra now that he has retired from government service.

Surinder K. Batra

Doctorate from Indian Institute of Technology, New Delhi. Experienced in contract research with Tata Company. Left Tata to start his own consulting organization: CIMI, Center for Interactive Management, India

Figure P16-1 Practitioners Acting for the Government Sector

Robert McDonald

Robert McDonald, presently a private consultant, retired from a long and honorable career with the U. S. Forest Service and the Florida Division of Forestry, where he pioneered the use of Interactive Management in a variety of projects, and continues to do so today in various settings. He has traveled to India (to work with Chandy), to Puerto Rico, and to other sites where his expertise is highly valued. His good humor is one of his greatest assets.

Reynaldo Treviño

Reynaldo Treviño in his office in the Mexican government. He had a leadership role in the First Interloquium during the Guanajuato Siglo XXI project, responsible for Scenario Building stage and Chapter 9 which referred to the World, Mexico and Guanajuato Scenarios to 2010. He was an ITESM faculty member. Later he was invited to join the government of Guanajuato where he had heavy responsibilty for the enhancement of education. He has applied Interactive Management in many settings, mostly inside Mexico.

Figure P16-2 Practitioners Acting for the Government Sector-II

Benjamin Broome

Benjamin Broome is a Professor, Arizona State University. Ben has used Interactive Management in many settings. Some of them are: with the Americans for Indian Opportunity, the Tarahumari Tribe in Mexico, Greeks and Turks in Cyprus (where he was a Fulbright Fellow), and Ford Motor Company.

Alexander Christakis

Dr. Alexander Christakis is President and CEO of CWA Ltd. He is a world leader in applying Interactive Management using his trade-marked Cogniscope™ software. His company is headquartered in Paoli, PA. He served as President of the International Society for Systems Science, which held its annual meeting on the island of Crete in the year 2,002.

Carol Jeffrey

Carol Jeffrey had to have the courage of a lion to run Interactive Management with warlords and warriors in Liberia (where they developed a disarmament and demobilization plan, and with the capital city where she worked with water and sewer people. Then she worked with me in Accra, Ghana. More recently she worked in the former Yugoslavia and in Peru.

Figure P17-1 Practitioners Acting for a Social Sector

Carmen Moreno

Carmen Moreno, a close friend of Roxana Cárdenas, took part in early Interactive Management work, both in Mexico and in the United States. As a faculty member at ITESM, she provided leadership for groups sessions both inside and outside the institution. Her work in strategic planning with localities is becoming well-known both inside and outside Mexico.

Roy Smith

Roy Smith is now a private consultant in England. Retired from Ford Motor Company, he has had substantial and long-term experience in working with groups on complexity. He speaks annually at City University School of Management, where he attracts a large crowd of students. He is very active in church and community.

Figure P17-2 Practitioners Acting for a Social Sector-II

Graciela Caffarel and two children

Graciela Caffarel teaches Interactive Management in ITESM, and leads groups in carrying out projects of sufficient size to demonstrate the merits of the processes.

A. Roxana Cárdenas

Roxana Cárdenas introduced Interactive Management to ITESM, and educated a group of young faculty who are continuing to educate others in Mexico in this practice.

F. Ross Janes

Here we see a Welshman, Ross Janes, on graduation day at the Guildhall. Ross pioneered the use of Interpretive Structural Modeling (ISM). He first used it at the University of Virginia (while a Fulbright Scholar) to explore the future of engineering education, and later in England at City University (London). He completed his Ph D on the subject of ISM and its applications, and later served as dissertation adviser to Henry Alberts and Roxana Cardenas.

Figure P18-1 Practitioners Acting for the Education Sector

Xuefeng Song

Dr. Song has held two key posts at the China University of Mining and Technology. He was Dean of the Graduate School, but is now Dean of the School of Management. He is doing research on complexity, and is helping Chinese people learn more about how to master complexity and how to improve mine safety.

Maria Carmen del Temblador and son

Maria Carmen del Temblador and her son Sergio. "Mary Carmen" is an industrial engineer, professor, mother, and friend. She is one of possibly a total of 10 people in the world who have studied and mastered the mathematics of structure, as I presented it in my 1976 book titled *Societal Systems: Planning, Policy, and Complexity.*

Li Da Xu

Li was one of the first to start teaching students of information systems using SOCIETAL SYSTEMS as a text (John's 1976 book, which introduced Interpretive Structural Modeling). He has been very active in interchange with Chinese universities, and in systems societies. His leadership in these activities has been very noticeable, as have his research contributions.

Figure P18-2 Practitioners Acting for the Education Sector-II

The "Warfield Special Collection" at the George Mason University Fenwick Library

This Appendix is a partial description of the contents of the "Warfield Special Collection" contained in the George Mason University Fenwick Library. Located in Fairfax, Virginia, this collection is further described on the Internet at

http://www.gmu.edu/library/specialcollections/warfield.htm

The material in this Appendix is excerpted from the following publication which is available in the Special Collections division of the Fenwick Library:

John N. Warfield and Rosamond Warfield, *A Guide to the John N. Warfield Collection: Special Collections and Archives*, George Mason University, 2nd Edition, (2005), Ajar Publishing Company, Palm Harbor, FL., 106 pp.

Philosophy Behind this Collection

This collection of research work is all founded on these basic ideas:

- **Uniqueness of Science**. The most wonderful discovery in human history is that humans can discover things by a disciplined process which is called "science"; producing archival material also called "science," enabling those who follow to take advantage of the archival material to upgrade and expand the resource for the benefit of humanity[1].

- **Pollution of the Archival Woods.** The archival woods contain vast amounts of material that were not produced using this disciplined process, but which nonetheless apply the trappings of science, thereby causing untold difficulty to the serious scholar who is striving to determine what is sound and what is unsound from the masses of material.

- **Growth of Complexity.** As time passes, the complexity of societies grows rapidly along with the interdependence of people, and the importance of collaborative work also grows rapidly, outdistancing individual human cognitive apparatus. Hence the importance of adapting the computer to help human beings work together first to describe, then to diagnose, then to design, then to implement, and finally to enjoy the fruits of their collaboration.

- **Replacement of Obsolete Systems and Practices.** Many of the systems that are in place have become obsolete, but there is a relentless momentum that tends to keep them in place. Dislodging them is not a simple task, and for those pioneers who intend to take on this challenge, the very least that archival material can do is to provide the highest quality evidence possible that what they are proposing has been found empirically to be very functional under highly variable conditions in many different cultures. That is why I have put so much emphasis on gathering and displaying evidence from countries around the world. Names and pictures of individuals have been collected to emphasize the role that people in various countries have played

---

1 As far as I have been able to determine, there has been relatively little change in the idea of science since its articulation by Aristotle. I feel that the best relatively modern articulation is that given by Charles Sanders Peirce. Popper, whose work is often cited nowadays, has given a very strong endorsement to Peirce's work.

in demonstrating the utility and viability of the work described in the Warfield Special Collection.

- **Neutral Science.** Neutrality of the science is essential for widespread utility. Regrettably much of what has been advanced in the so-called "systems" field and "complexity science" is quite specific to particular domains, and is not portable from one domain to another. My work emphasizes the neutrality of the systems science, and its applicability across problematic situations. Moreover, it makes minimal demands on variety in methodology. It does, however require sound learning of foundations. It is expected that, when properly applied, indications of whatever special methods are required will bubble up from the interactions among the actors who are guided in local applications by the process experts who have mastered the work described in this Collection.

Options for Exploring the Collection

Understanding the Evolution of the Content. I write this while imagining that I am a person coming to the Fenwick Library with some interest in the "Warfield Special Collection" only to find that it occupies more than 90 linear feet, and wondering how to gain quickly some kind of perspective on this collection. I have read now the "Philosophy Behind the Collection," but that offers relatively little guidance on how to plan to use this Collection.

It seems to me that it would help the person approaching this Collection to understand how it evolved. It is generally known that, as researchers age, their views on subjects change. If they continue to study areas for long periods of time, their views might change significantly. Should someone study the more than 35 years of publications here a year at a time, beginning in the first year and proceeding month by month, perhaps following the list given in the Warfield Vita? Or would it be better to start in the last year and work backwards? Or should some topic be selected? And if so, how? Are search engines appropriate for this kind of search? As I write this, search engines are not very likely to be helpful. So I am going to talk about how you can learn with an investment of about an hour how this work evolved, and why it evolved as it did.

Two Overview Publications. Late in my career (2003 and 2004), I published two overview publications, intended to give interested persons a feeling for the history and motivation of my work. These are available for review in the Fenwick Library. It is suggested that they be the first documents to be read before looking into other aspects of the Warfield Special Collection. The first one I will mention next is also available as an Appendix in this book.

In this way, you can walk with me through more than three decades and, in the process, probably make some notes about things that you might like to look into. This ought to make it somewhat easier for you, at least, to set some time markers as you approach the "Warfield Special Collection." The citations for these publications are as follows:

- John N. Warfield (2003), "Systems Movement. Autobiographical Retrospectives: Discovering Systems Science," *International Journal of General Systems* 32 (6), 525-563, (a publication of Taylor and Francis Group, edited by Professor George J. Klir, University of Binghamton, New York.)This is a paper invited by the Editor, invitations extended to persons who have made significant contributions to the study of systems.

The reader of this article will note that it refers to "Exhibits" that are integral parts of the article. These Exhibits contain pictures of individuals who are related in some way to the content of the paper. Also, one of the Exhibits contains titles of presentations that have been offered over the years under the heading "Managing the Unmanageable," listing the number of slides associated with each presentation. It is intended that ultimately these presentations will be available in the "Warfield Special Collection," if they are not present now. These Exhibits were accepted in two different places (the same in each): http://policy.gmu.edu/res/jwarfield and http://www.ijgs.org/ar/warfield

- John N. Warfield (2005), "Systems Profile: 1925 to Now," *Systems Research and Behavioral Science 22, 249-259,* a Wiley Journal, edited by M. C. Jackson, Dean of the School of Business, University of Hull, Hull, United Kingdom. This is a biographical sketch that is intended to fit a standard type of article published by this journal.

Internet Finding Aid. A complete list of everything in the collection is on the internet at URL –
http://ead.lib.virginia.edu/vivaead/published/gmu/vivadoc.pl?file=vifgm0 0008.xml. This web page will display a blank field for typing in search terms and document titles. In this web page, the CONTENTS LIST for the collection is arranged numerically by BOX NUMBER. If requesting a manuscript or video, researchers should give the BOX number just as it is shown in the CONTENTS LIST. and also if the item is a DOCUMENT, the request should include the FOLDER number.

Types and Origins of Media Included in the Collection[2]

Video Tapes. The collection contains over 200 video tape cassettes, many of which are minute-by-minute tape recordings of Interactive Management (IM) Workshop sessions in progress. Also there are tapes of some of John Warfield's class lectures as well as lectures by several of his colleagues, On two occasions his students made formal video taped interviews of Warfield, in which he discussed his work and ideas.

Workshop Reports. John developed a specific pattern to be followed in writing up the results of every IM Workshop, and providing a printed report to the Workshop client. We have saved as many of these reports as possible, including not only those done by his own office staff at GMU but also those done by colleagues at other institutions and in other countries.

---

2 This section was contributed by Rosamond Warfield.

Audio Tapes. No less significant, though fewer in number, are the audio tapes of some of his class lectures. On audio, just listening to him talk, ideas frequently become clearer than when one is viewing the same lecture on video tapes.

Teaching Transparencies. There is a large collection of transparencies and slides used in teaching and lectures. In addition to the hard copy transparencies stored in a box in a library shelf, there is also a disk holding digitized versions of the same slides, plus many more. On the CD-Rom his teaching transparencies are numbered, the total exceeds 300.

Papers by Others. For the Fenwick Library collection, he selected a number of papers which he intended for use by scholars in the future. John called these papers his "Comparison Papers" because his intent was that students would use them to compare with Warfield's works, and to then draw their own conclusions. He has stated that his Comparison Papers are of three types (but he leaves it to the student to decide which type is which).

These are the three types included in Warfield's Comparison Papers collection:

- **Supportive Work**. Papers not written by Warfield which are descriptive of or otherwise useful in understanding and using Warfield's Interactive Management system; e.g., writings by C. S. Peirce, H. Lasswell, and others identified by Warfield as "Thought Leaders." (Additional references to works by the "Thought Leaders" can be found Warfield's "CELLS" database, and in Chapters 2 and 3 of his 2002 book "UNDERSTANDING COMPLEXITY.")

- **Topically-Relevant Work**. Papers by other authors which are not about Warfield's work, but are highly relevant to Warfield's own research progress; e.g., articles with photographs & floor plans for Interactive Management facilities such as observatoriums and situation rooms.

- **Linguistic Pollution**. Papers which are neither relevant to Warfield's research program nor useful in understanding it, but which illustrate, by their content, subjects that Warfield feels were poorly treated, and which required correction in the literature. He often spoke of this type of work as "linguistic pollution." Much of the "systems" literature is of this type, as is much of the "operations research" literature. However Warfield took pains to mention that his discussions were always about complexity, and his critiques are to be seen within that context; and are not intended to apply outside that context. (He made this clear in a paper dealing with what he calls "Killer Assumptions" and "The Demands of Complexity.")

Book Manuscripts. There are probably too many drafts of the books he was writing. I tried to save them to track changes and development of the manuscripts.

Battelle Years. There is a lot of miscellaneous material not very well sorted, of the time he spent at Battelle Memorial Institute in Columbus, Ohio, when he was first developing ISM. The Battelle years were 1966 - 1974 .

Papers by Warfield. There are manuscript copies of almost everything he ever wrote, as far as could be managed. All of the publications are there, plus miscellaneous unpublished items of varying quality and quantity. He has now digitized many of his unpublished articles and put them on disk. The Special Collections has been given a copy of the disk and the plan is that eventually these will be uploaded to the Internet.

Early Teaching Career. Warfield taught Electrical Engineering at Penn State, Univ of Illinois, Purdue, Univ of Kansas, Ohio State and Univ of Virginia. Documents and teaching materials can be found relative to these universities.

Situation Rooms. There are photographs of the facilities and spaces needed for Interactive Management to function properly, also some floor plans and articles about good situation rooms written by Warfield and others.

Origins of the Media. "Oh my God, I could write a book.............how could I begin?" There was the time when Christakis left and the office was being disbanded and moved to a hut in the back part of the campus. John cleaned out his files and left lots of papers in boxes out in the hall for the janitors to pick up. I saw the boxes and went out in the hall and carried them back in and put them away again as much as I could, although I am sure much of it was lost. By then I had come over to help out in the office and answer the phone for a short while, because the secretary had left for a better job and the University was in a hiring freeze. (In the end I was an office volunteer over there for years and years) Meanwhile Ben had carried off all the videotapes because it seemed no one was going to claim them. He took them to the Communications Department to be recycled by students as they were needing new tapes for class work. I found out about these tapes by accident when looking around the office, and went down to the communication department and got them back. Some of them were gone forever but I saved most of them.

Later I collected all the old tapes that I could find and took them over to one of the GMU Library departments which was in charge of library videos. I got many of them copied from big old heavy 3/4 inch tape onto VCR cassettes, and also wrote notes on lots of them. Here again there were some that were lost and never found again. When the Ford contract was in force there were some good complete videotaping of IM workshops, and these were sent to John's office. There was no room in the office so I rigged up a big closet in the basement and lugged all the videos to our house and kept them in that closet for about ten years, along with bunches of file cabinets containing all the old documents and papers.

Occasionally I would make a stab at sorting and labeling some of the documents, and also I cataloged the videos as well as I knew how, but not as properly as should have been done. They will all have to be done over some time I am sure, if anyone wants them. Also I made quite a few transcriptions of video-tapes, simply because there was no one else around to do it and it seemed as if some of the stuff ought to be available to students. The Chinese students were very grateful for the transcripts, because they could read the English and understand what was being said on the videos.

After CIM crashed Christakis didn't have the nerve to ask John, but he sent Ben back instead and Ben went through our office and dug out nice published copies of every single one of the IM Workshop Reports and sent them to Christakis. When I found this out it was too late to get a complete set for John, but I collected up all that was left. John himself was too discouraged and demoralized to do anything but just watch the ravens pick at the leavings.

I finally got copies of most of the CIM Reports from David Keever, who had himself carried off every single manuscript printout of the Reports in a couple of brown banker's file boxes. I coaxed David into **lending me** his box of manuscript copies! And then I made copies from them and from those manuscripts eventually got nearly all the old CIM Reports back into report shape, nicely printed with good looking covers and everything, some of them even hard copy bound. Also of course I returned the manuscripts to David when finished with my project. I wonder if he ever realized that what he got back was not his originals but photocopies of what he had given me. I kept the originals and eventually got them bound into an eleven volume set and put into the Library of Congress.

I tried very hard to get the original computer software program which was on the big computer at the University. I knew David and Christakis had taken copies of it but I wasn't able to get a copy for John. If I knew as much about software as I do now I could have gone in and stamped my foot and demanded the executable files, but I didn't even know what an executable file was, and so I meekly accepted what the GMU computer office gave me, which was simply data and supporting files, not the source code. Later I tried to get David Keever to give me a printout of the software from the office computer and he finally did that for me but it was just a big bunch of garbagey paper and not worth much.

Meanwhile John had moved to the shack they gave him for an office and was holding his head, so I just kept stuffing stuff away as much as possible but there was no place to put it, really, and John's filing system which was never very good - made it almost impossible to keep track of anything. I tried to save Email correspondence but did very poorly at it. John just left his Email everywhere and also the computer was unforgiving if you were naive enough not to make backups. Much of his good Email correspondence was lost.

We can't thank Ben Broome enough for his contribution to creation of the tapes. Christakis drafted Ben early on to help out with the taping and editing of the first IM workshops. It seemed a natural thing to do since Ben was just down the hall from the Center for Interactive Management. Ben was at that time a young professor in the GMU Communications department where lots of youthful video productions were taking place with the students. Ben was the instigator for nearly all the interviews of John and Christakis, and he promoted the videotaping of John's Mathematics of Structure class, coaxing John into providing funding for student video work on the project. Another person to whom we owe a great deal is Scott Staley from Ford Motor Company who took to heart John's insistence on the importance of videotaping the workshops and while the GMU project at Ford was in operation he made sure that the taping was done in the detailed professional manner that had not been possible at GMU where we relied chiefly on student labor.

When time came to retire no word was heard concerning disposal of all the Warfield papers. So we packed all of John's office into brown stor-file boxes and stored it for a year in a United Van Lines storage warehouse in Quantico and later after we bought a house in Florida all the boxes were shipped to Palm Harbor. There we had thirteen filing cabinets sitting in the garage, plus dozens and dozens of brown banker's stor-file boxes stacked all over the dining room and bedrooms.

After we arrived in Florida an invitation came from GMU to consider archiving John's work. This was due to an outside influence, some of John's colleagues from systems societies in the U.S. learned of the collection and urged its preservation in letters which eventually reached Jim Finkelstein at GMU School of Public Policy and John Zenelis the GMU librarian. Meanwhile Ben Broome succeeded in getting parts of

John's materials into the Arizona State University library in Tempe, where Ben had a new job. We were grateful for the attention, but almost defeated at the prospect of organizing packing and shipping hundreds of items west to Arizona and back north to Virginia. I sorted and listed and cataloged as much as I could and packed and packed and packed and packed, day and night for over a year. The boxes all went away in trucks at last, and now the 13 filing cabinets are gone from our garage, to say nothing of the other boxes all over the dining room.

Fortunately Jim Finkelstein in the School of Public Policy found a spare room in the Public Policy building where we were able to consign the returned boxed documents and videos until Special Collections and Archives department got a look at them and decided to take the whole collection. It was quite a nervy thing to do, accepting that giant bunch of John's papers.. I do hope they can make good use of it in the future. Meanwhile Arizona has copies of important papers and videos as well as digitized documents.

We were quite amazed when a professional appraiser from the American Society of Appraisers evaluated the audio-visual portion alone of the charitable donation to the Fenwick Library to be worth $1.6 million dollars because of the scientific uniqueness of the collection!

List of Audio Tapes and Video Tapes in the Collection

Interactive Management (IM) Workshops and Center for Interactive Management (CIM) Short Demonstration Tapes

● Oldies. (Before 1984) BOX 69
Kent, Ohio City Council, 20 min. (1978 or 1979) One original 3/4" tape cassette
Genessee County, Michigan, 20 min. (1979) One original 3/4" tape cassette

● National Marine Fisheries Service (NMFS) (Sept 1985-Jan 1986)
Interactive Management sessions, 15 VHS cassettes BOX 63
Old heavy master tapes, Five 3/4 inch tape cassettes BOX 70 & 71
Edited 2nd ver. 20 minute video, 1 VHS cassette BOX 67
Edit master for old 1st ver. 20 minute video 1 3/4 inch tape cassette

● Nurses. Tapes from two workshops with GMU School of Nursing (1986-87)

Interactive Management sessions, lengthy.(May 1986) 5 VHS cassettes BOX 62
Edited 15 minute video (June 1987) 1 VHS cassette BOX 62

- National Science Foundation-Sponsored Computer Science Curriculum Workshop (1986-1987)
Excerpts from IM Workshop sessions, lengthy, 5 VHS cassettes BOX 65
Edited 15 minute video 1 VHS cassette Box 65
Note: Reports and paperwork on this workshop BOX 9, Folders 17 & 18
And in BOX 28, Folder 28

- DSMC-(Defense Systems Management College), 1st IM session (Dec 1986)
Excerpts from IM Workshop sessions, 125 min 1 VHS cassette BOX 66
Edited 15 minute video 1 VHS cassette BOX 66
Note: relevant documents in Folder 26 BOX 25

- AIO-(Americans for Indian Opportunity) Congressional committee hearing (June 1987)
Four hours of an IM demonstration session 2 VHS cassettes

- Defense Advanced Research Projects Agency (DARPA) - Wrap up Comments by DARPA group (July 17, 1987)1 VHS cassette BOX 66

- Winnebago (American Indian) Tribe in Nebraska (July 31, 1987)
Portions of IM sessions and Interviews with Indian leaders.
Lengthy, 8 VHS cassettes BOX 55
Edited 20 minute video, 1 VHS cassette BOX 55

- Niagara Mohawk Power Corporation Workshop (June 1989)
        12 VHS cassettes BOX 64

- Defense Systems Management College, Technical Managers Workshop
(TMAW 91/2, June 1991)
30 hours, filmed during 5-day session, 11 VHS cassettes BOX 66
19 min videotape, edited from tapes, by Mary Austin, 1 VHS Cassette BOX 66

- Analytical Power Train (APT) Workshops at Ford Motor Company
First APT Workshop, 19 hours. (April 14-16, 1992)
19 hours, filmed during 3-day session, 10 VHS cassettes BOX 56
Slow Speed version of 1st APT workshop, 19 hours, 4 VHS cassettes BOX 55
Note: Viewer's Guide to accompany slow speed version BOX 50, FOLDER 9
Second APT Workshop, approx 20 hours (July 7–10, 1992)
        10 VHS cassettes BOX 57

Third APT Workshop, approx 16 hours (August 18-19, 1992)
                    8 VHS cassettes BOX 57
Cultural Seminar , approx 2 hours (August 20,1992) 1 VHS cassette BOX 57
Fourth APT Workshop, approx 22 hours
(August 25-27, 1992) 11 VHS cassettes BOX 58
Fifth APT Workshop, approx 20 hours
(December 9-11, 1992) 10 VHS cassettes
NOTE: Recently (2005) some of these have been converted to DVD format.

• Rapid Response Manufacturing (RRM) Workshop at Ford Motor Company
Approx 18 hrs (May 19-21 1993) 9 VHS cassettes

• Product Information Management Systems (PIMS) Workshop at Ford Motor Company
(Jan 11-14,1994)
Approximately 26 hours, filmed during 4-day session, 13 VHS cassettes
Demo Tape I, Video Excerpts from PIM workshop, 1 VHS cassette
NOTE: Recently (2005) some of these have been converted to DVD format.

• System Integration Center Workshop at Ford Motor Company
Workshop approx 26 hours (Jan 24-26, 1995) 13 VHS cassettes BOX 59

Lectures, Classroom Sessions on Video and Audio Tape

• Warfield Class and Seminar Lectures at CIM (1986-1987)
Each seminar lecture is approx 1 ½ hours, 16 VHS cassettes BOX 60 or 61

• Lectures at Center for Interactive Management (1987-1988)
Elohim's talk, Warfield & Christakis giving seminars, and
Ben Broome's Communication 531 class.
                    A group of 12 VHS cassettes BOX 60 or 61

• Great University Seminar series (Warfield) (1990-91)
Six seminars, during academic year, 6 AUDIO tape cassettes BOX 52
Sixth & last seminar, Dr. George Johnson, GMU President, speaking
on Leadership & the Great University, 1 VHS cassette BOX 58.

• Mathematics of Modeling (January 1993)
Five day short course taught by Warfield, 10 VHS cassettes

• Video made in Monterrey Mexico
Ross Janes' lecture for Roxana Cárdenas' ITESM class and satellite connections

(April, 1996) 1 VHS cassette BOX 65

• Resolving Complexity in Organizations (nickname Complexity Lectures):
(Spring 1999) Semester Class at GMU BOX 62 and BOX 68
Lecture No. 1 (Jan 30, 1999) 2 VHS cassettes
Lecture No. 2 (Feb 6, 1999) 2 VHS cassettes
Lecture No. 3 (Feb 13, 1999)One is a slow-speed copy of original lecture,
combining tapes 1 and 2 on a single cassette, 3 VHS cassettes.
Lecture No. 4 (Feb 20, 1999) 2 VHS cassettes
Lecture No. 5 (Feb 27, 1999) Complete class lecture on one cassette
only. The second cassette is a copy of original lecture,2 VHS cassettes
Lecture No. 6 (Mar 6, 1999) 1 VHS cassette
Lecture No. 7 (Mar 13, 1999) 1 VHS cassette
Lecture No. 8 - (Mar 20, 1999) 2 VHS cassettes
Lecture No. 9 - (Mar 27, 1999) 1 VHS cassette
Lecture No. 10 - (Apr 3, 1999) 1 VHS cassette
Lecture No. 11 - (Apr 17, 1999) 2 VHS cassettes
Lecture No. 12 - (Apr 24, 1999) 2 VHS cassettes
Lecture No. 13 - (May 1, 1999) 1 VHS cassette
Lecture No. 14 - (May 14, 1999) 1 VHS cassette
Note: these same 14 class meetings which were also recorded on audiotape,
Total - approx 27 AUDIO cassettes BOX 53

• Johnson Center Lecture Series, Complexity Lectures (Fall 1998)
Complexity Lecture No. 1, Missing(student videotaping not off the ground)
Complexity Lecture No. 2, Missing (student videocamera operator failed to show)
Complexity Lecture No. 3, 1 VHS cassette
Complexity Lecture No. 4, 1 VHS cassette
Complexity Lecture No. 5, Missing (student videocamera equipment failure)
Complexity Lecture No. 6, 1 VHS cassette
Complexity Lecture No. 7, 1 VHS cassette
Complexity Lecture No. 8, 1 VHS cassette
Complexity Lecture No. 9, 1 VHS cassette
Complexity Lecture No. 10, 1 VHS cassette
Complexity Lecture No. 11, 1 VHS cassette
Complexity Lecture No. 12, 1 VHS cassette
   (Total - nine COMPLEXITY cassettes) BOX 67
Note: documents relating to this lecture series BOX 36

• Managing the Unmanageable: Process Leadership in Organizations
70 min. (Feb 2000) 1 VHS cassette BOX 62
Note: documents relating to this and other lectures in the same series BOX 21

Interviews and Miscellaneous Videos

● Christakis & Warfield on camera at GMU center (1985-1986)
Hilary Austin interviewing Warfield (Feb 26, 1986)1 VHS cassette BOX 66
Hilary Austin interviewing Warfield (Mar 20, 1986)1 VHS cassette BOX 66
Broome's 1st Video:"QUALITY DESIGN" 15 min (1986)1 VHS cassette BOX 65
Christakis in GMU forum interview 15 min (1987)1 VHS cassette BOX 65
Original masters, 2 different interviews of Christakis BOX 69

● Preguntas. Cárdenas interviews Warfield(Feb 1991)
Lengthy videotaped interview at GMU (Feb. 21, 1991)2 VHS cassettes BOX 55
Audiotape recordings of the video, 2 AUDIO cassettes BOX 52
Note: Typed transcript of this interview is in BOX 50 FOLDER 26

● American Institute for Interactive Management (AIIM)(Feb1989)2 VHS cassettes
      BOX 68

● Miscellaneous Videos
International Interactive Symposium, Austin Texas (June, 1993)
Videotapes given to us by William A. Smith of Austin, TX, 2 VHS cassettes
Interactive Management Workshop/CALS IMP(June 1992)
      Videotapes given to us by Stan Crognale, from DSMC, 2 VHS cassettes BOX 65

List of Works by John N. Warfield

Books

Knausenberger, G. E. and J. N. Warfield (1958) *Synthesis of Linear Communications Networks.* New York: McGraw-Hill. (Translation from German of the classic work Theorie der Linearen Wechselstromschaltungen by Wilhelm Cauer, originally publ. by Springer Verlag).

Warfield, J. N.(1959) *Introduction to Electronic Analog Computers.* Englewood Cliffs: Prentice-Hall

Warfield, J. N. (1963) *Principles of Logic Design.* Boston: Ginn and Company

Warfield, J. N. and J. D. Hill (1972) *A Unified Systems Engineering Concept.* Battelle Monograph #1, Columbus, OH: Battelle Memorial Institute

Warfield, J. N. (1973) *An Assault on Complexity.* Battelle Monograph #3, Columbus, OH: Battelle Memorial Institute

Warfield, J. N. (1974) *Structuring Complex Systems.* Battelle Monograph #4, Columbus, OH: Battelle Memorial Institute

Warfield, J. N. (1976, 1989, 1993, part in 2003) *Societal Systems: Planning, Policy, and Complexity.* New York: Wiley Interscience 1976 (reprinted as a paperback edition by Intersystems, Salinas, CA, 1989; Chinese translation directed by Professor Zhang Bihui, Chairman of the Wuhan Science and Technology Commission, and Director of The Administrative Office of Wuhan East Lake High Technology Development Zone, publisher is the Hubei Science and Technology Press, Wuhan, Hubei Province, China, 1993; Reprint of Chapters 8-14 by AJAR Publishing Co, Palm Harbor, FL, 2003).

Warfield, J. N. (1990, 1994) *A Science of Generic Design: Managing Complexity Through Systems Design.* Salinas, CA: Intersystems (two volume soft-cover set); Second Edition published by Iowa State University Press, Ames, IA, 1994 as a hard-cover single volume.

Warfield, J. N. and A. Roxana Cárdenas (1994) *A Handbook of Interactive Management.* Ames, IA: Iowa State University Press

Warfield, J. N. (2002) *Understanding Complexity: Thought and Behavior.* Palm Harbor, FL: AJAR Publishing Company

Warfield, J. N. (2003) *The Mathematics of Structure* [chapters 8-14 of *Societal Systems*]. Palm Harbor, FL: AJAR Publishing Company

Patents

"Double Bridge Network for Producing Signals Having a Modulation Envelope Phase Difference," U. S. Patent Number 3,328,798 dated June 27, 1967, with G. M. Gooch and J. R. Hogan, assigned to Wilcox Electric Company.

"Digital Squelch System," U. S. Patent Number 3,437,937, dated April 8, 1969, assigned to Wilcox Electric Company.

Papers and Research Reports
1953-1963

Warfield, J. N. and D. L. Waidelich. (1953) A Table of Steady-State Transforms. Engineering Research Reports, Research Report Number 1, Columbia, Missouri, *University of Missouri Bulletin* 54(29, August).

Truxal, J. G. and J. N. Warfield. (1953) Synthesis of a Dynamically-Variable Electronic Filter. *Proceedings of the National Electronics Conference* 8(January): 419-426.

Warfield, J. N. (1953) Little-Known Facts About Big Computer Developments. *Pennsylvania State University Engineering Review* (December) 68ff.

Warfield, J. N. (1955, 1956) *Systems Engineering.* Serial # NOrd 7958-307, Penn State University, Ordinance Research Laboratory, (August). Repr. NTIS, PB111801, United States Department of Commerce.

Warfield, J. N.(1957) Optimum Diagnostic Sequences for Systems With One Faulty Element. Report M-67 (February), *University of Illinois Control Systems Laboratory.*

Warfield, J. N.(1957) How to Improve Systems Engineering. *Aeronautical Engineering Review* 16(7, July): 50-51.

Warfield, J. N. (1958) A Note on the Reduction of Switching Functions. *Transactions of the IRE,* PGEC-7(2, June).

Warfield, J. N. (1958) Switching Circuits as Topological Models in the Discrete Probability Theory. *Transactions of the IRE* PGEC-7(3, September).

Butler, K. J. and J. N. Warfield. (1959)A Digital Computer Program for the Reduction of Logical Statements to Minimal Form. Chicago: *Proceedings of the National Electronics Conference* 15 (October 12-14): 456-466.

Warfield, J. N. and L. E. Weaver.(1959) Cut-Product Approximants for Time Delay in Electronic Analog Computers. *Proceedings of SWIRECO, the Southwest IRE Conference* (April) p16.

Warfield, J. N.(1963) *Solution Manual for 'Principles of Logic Design'.* Boston: Ginn and Company.

1965-1973

Warfield, J. N., and G. M. Gooch (1965) A Precision Electronic Goniometer. *Proceedings of the National Electronics Conference* 21:174-179.

Warfield, J. N. (1965) Corrective Systems for Minimizing TACAN-DME Spurious Radiation. *IEEE Transactions on Aerospace and Navigational Electronics* ANE-12(1, March): 89-90.

Warfield, J. N. (1965) Synthesis of Switching Circuits to Yield Prescribed Probability Relations. In *1965 IEEE Conference Record on Switching Circuit Theory and Logical Design* (Ann Arbor, MI, October): 303-309.

Warfield, J. N., and T. Channel. (1965) Spurious Signal Amplitudes in High-Frequency Transistor Mixers. In *Proceedings IEEE Mid-America Electronics Conference* (Kansas City, November): 91-95.

Warfield, J. N., and P. Lally (1966) Comment on 'Corrective System for Minimizing TACAN-DME Spurious Radiation'. *IEEE Transactions on Aerospace and Navigation Engineering* ES-2 (5, September): 616-618.

Warfield, J. N.(1968) Switching Networks as Models of Discrete Stochastic Processes. Chapter 4 in *Applied Automata Theory*, J. Tou,(Ed.). New York: Academic Press; 81-123.

House, R. W. and J. N. Warfield. (1968, 1969) What is System Planning? *Automatica* 5:151-157. Reprinted from *Proceedings of 1968 IFAC Symposium*, Cleveland, Ohio.

Warfield, J. N. (1969) Modulation Measurements--Theory and Technique. *IEEE Transactions on Instrumentation and Measurement* IM-18(2, June): 139-144.

Warfield, J. N. and J. D. Hill, et al. (1971, 1972) The DELTA Chart: A Method for R&D Project Portrayal. *IEEE Transactions on Engineering Management* EM-18(4, November 1971): 132-139. Reprinted in Battelle Monograph No. 1, Columbus: Battelle Memorial Institute.(June 1972):42-50.

Warfield, J. N. (1972, 1973) Participative Methodology for Public System Planning. In *Proceedings of an International Symposium on Systems Engineering and Analysis*, West Lafayette: Purdue University vl(Invited Lectures, October): 23-40. Reprinted in 1973 *Computers and Electrical Engineering* 1(1): 187-210, by invitation of the Editor.

Hill, J. D. and J. N. Warfield. (1972) Unified Program Planning. *IEEE Transactions on Systems, Man, and Cybernetics* SMC-2(5, November): 610-621.

Warfield, J. N. (1973) On Arranging Elements of a Hierarchy in Graphic Form. *IEEE Transactions on Systems, Man, and Cybernetics* SMC-3(2,March): 121-132.

1973-1975

Warfield, J. N. (1973) Intent Structures. *IEEE Transactions on Systems, Man, and Cybernetics* SMC-3(2, March): 133-140.

Warfield, J. N. (1973) Binary Matrices in Systems Modeling. *IEEE Transactions on Systems, Man, and Cybernetics* **SMC-5**: 441-449.

Warfield, J. N. (1973) Constructing Operational Value Systems for Proposed Two-Unit Coalitions. *In Proceedings 1973 IEEE Conference on Decision and Control*, San Diego (December); 204-213.

Warfield, J. N. (1974) Developing Subsystem Matrices in Structural Modeling. *IEEE Transactions on Systems, Man, and Cybernetics* SMC-4(1, January): 74-80.

Warfield, J. N. (1974) Developing Interconnection Matrices in Structural Modeling *IEEE Transactions on Systems, Man, and Cybernetics* SMC-4(1, January): 81-87.

Warfield, J. N. (1974) Toward Interpretation of Complex Structural Models *IEEE Transactions on Systems, Man, and Cybernetics*, SMC-4(5, September): 405-417.

Warfield, J. N. (1974) An Interim Look at Uses of Interpretive Structural Modeling. In *Research Futures*, Columbus: Battelle Memorial Institute (3rd Quarter); 32-34.

El Mokadem, Ahmed, J. N. Warfield, D. Pollick, and K. Kawamura (1974, 1975) Modularization of Large Econometric Models: An Application of Structural Modeling. In *Proceedings of the 1974 IEEE Conference on Decision and Control* (November): 683-692. Reprinted in *Portraits of Complexity*, M. Baldwin, (Ed.), Monograph No. 9, Columbus: Battelle Memorial Institute.

Warfield, J. N. (1975) Transitive Interconnection of Transitive Structures. In *Proceedings of the 6th Pittsburgh Conference on Modeling and Simulation*, Pittsburgh: Instrument Society of America (April): 791-794.

Warfield, J. N. (1975) *Improving Behavior in Policymaking.* Approaches to Problem Solving-No. 2, Columbus: Academy for Contemporary Problems, Battelle Memorial Institute (August).

1975-79

Warfield, J. N. (1975) *TOTOS: Improving Group Problem-Solving.* Approaches to Problem Solving-No. 3, Columbus: Academy for Contemporary Problems, Battelle Memorial Institute (August).

Warfield, J. N., H. Geschka, and R. Hamilton (1975) *Methods of Idea Management.* Approaches to Problem Solving-No. 4, Columbus: Academy for Contemporary Problems, Battelle Memorial Institute (August).

Warfield, J. N. (1975) Profiles of Metapolicy. In *Proceedings of the 1975 Conference on Cybernetics and Society,* San Francisco (September) 14ff.

Warfield, J. N. (1976) Implication Structures for System Interconnection Matrices. *IEEE Transactions on Systems, Man, and Cybernetics* SMC-6(1, January): 18-24.

Warfield, J. N. (1976) Extending Interpretive Structural Modeling. In *Proceedings of the Seventh Annual Pittsburgh Conference on Modeling and Simulation,* Pittsburgh: Instrument Society of America (April); 1163-1167.

Fertig, J.A., and J. N. Warfield. (1976) Relations and Decision Making In *Proceedings of the Seventh Annual Pittsburgh Conference on Modeling and Simulation,* Pittsburgh: Instrument Society of America (April); 1177-1181.

Warfield, J. N. (1977) Crossing Theory and Hierarchy Mapping. *IEEE Transactions on Systems, Man, and Cybernetics* SMC-7(7, July): 502-523.

Warfield, J. N. (1978) Notes on Conceptual Sciences. *IEEE Transactions on Systems, Man, and Cybernetics* SMC-8(10, October): 744-745.

Warfield, J. N. (1979) The Interface Between Models and Policymakers. *Journal of Policy Analysis and Information Systems* 3(1, June): 53-64.

Warfield, J. N. (1979) Some Principles of Knowledge Organization. *IEEE Transactions on Systems, Man, and Cybernetics* SMC-9(6, June): 317-325.

Warfield, J. N. (1979, 1983) Systems Oriented Environmental Education. In *Improving the Human Conition: Proc. Society for General Systems Research*, R. Ericson (Ed.), Society for General Systems Research Silver Anniversary International Mtg, London, England (August); 797-799. Reprinted in *Systems Education: Perspective, Programs, Methods,* B. H. Banathy, (ed). Intersystems Publications, Seaside, CA; 61-63.

Warfield, J. N. (1979) Systems Planning for Environmental Education. *IEEE Transactions on Systems, Man, and Cybernetics.* SMC-9(12, December): 816-823. (First appeared in *Proceedings IEEE-SMC International Conference on Cybernetics and Society,* October 8-9, Denver, Colorado; 901-907)

1980-1982

Warfield, J. N. (1980, 1990) *Annotated Bibliography: Interpretive Structural Modeling and Related Work.* Charlottesville: Department of Electrical Engineering, University of Virginia. (June 1980). Rev. ed. 1990 Fairfax, VA: George Mason University, IASIS (Institute for Advanced Study in the Integrative Sciences).

Warfield, J. N. (1980) Science and Systems Science: A Technology Perspective. In *Proceedings Society for General Systems Research,* 24th Annual Meeting, San Francisco (January): 212-218.

Warfield, J. N. (1980) Modeling Management. *IEEE Transactions on Systems, Man, and Cybernetics* SMC-10(4, April) page 197.

Warfield, J. N. (1980) Complementary Relations and Map Reading. *IEEE Transactions on Systems, Man, and Cybernetics* (June) 285-291.

Warfield, J. N.(1980) Priority Structures. *IEEE Transactions on Systems, Man, and Cybernetics* SMC-10 (10, October): 642-645.

Warfield, J. N. (1980) A Role for Values in Educational System Design. In *Proceedings 1980 IEEE-SMC Conference on Cybernetics and Society,* Boston, October 7-9, IEEE Number 03608913/80/0000-0234, New York: IEEE (October): 234-241.

Warfield, J. N. (1981) Learning Through Model Building. In *Computer-Assisted Analysis and Model Simplification,* H. J. Greenberg and J. Maybee (Eds.), New York: Academic Press; 69-78.

Warfield, J. N. (1981) Mapping Environmental Education. University of the District of Columbia *Graduate Journal* 1(1, Fall): 23-28.

Warfield, J. N. (1982) Interpretive Structural Modeling. In *Group Planning and Problem-Solving Methods in Engineering* Chapter 5, Shirley A. Olsen (Ed.), New York: Wiley; 155-201 and 408-411.

Warfield, J. N. (1982) Organizations and Systems Learning. *General Systems* 27:5-74.

1983-1986

Warfield, J. N. (1983) Comments on B. Golden and A. Assad: 'A Preliminary Framework for Urban Model Building'. In *Adequate Modeling of Systems,* H. Wedde (Ed.), WestGermany: Springer Verlag; 333-335.

Warfield, J. N. (1983) Principles of Interactive Management. In *Proceedings International Conference on Cybernetics and Society,* New York: SMC-IEEE (January); 746-750.

Warfield, J. N. (1983) Selecting Participation Methodologies for Systems Design. In *Proceedings International Conference on Cybernetics and Society,* New York: SMC-IEEE (January); 762-764.

Warfield, J. N. (1984) Progress in Interactive Management. In *Proceedings 6th International Congress of the World Organisation of General Systems and Cybernetics,* Paris: AFCET-WOGSC; 29-35.

Warfield, J. N.(1984) A Model of a Discipline. In *Proceedings of the IEEE International Conference on Systems, Man, and Cybernetics* Halifax, October 9-12, New York: SMC-IEEE; 78-84.

Warfield, J. N. (1985, 1987) Developing a Design Culture in Higher Education," In *Proceedings Society for General Systems Research, International Congress*, Los Angeles, May 27-31, Seaside, CA Intersystems; 2:725-729. Repr.1987 in *General Systems* 30:63-68.

Warfield, J. N. (1985) On the Choice of Frames for Systems Studies. In *Proceedings Society for General Systems Research, International Congress*, Los Angeles, May27-31, Seaside, CA: Intersystems; 1: 294-299.

Warfield, J. N. (1985) Structural Analysis of a Computer Language. In *Proceedings 17th Southeastern Symposium on Systems Theory* Auburn, AL, March 24-27, Silver Spring, MD: IEEE Computer Society; 229-234.

Warfield, J. N. (1985) Institutionalizing Environmental Education. *Environmental Education and Information*, Manchester, England: University of Salford; 4(3).

Warfield, J. N. (1986) Education in Generic Design. In *Proceedings Intnl Conf Mental Images, Values & Reality, Society for General Systems Research*, Philadelphia, May 26-30, Salinas, CA: Intersystems; 1:H22-H33.

Warfield, J. N. (1986) The Domain of Science Model: Evolution and Design. In *Proceedings Intnl Conf Mental Images, Values & Reality, Society for General Systems Research*, Philadelphia, May 26-30, Salinas, CA: Intersystems; 1: H46-H59.

Warfield, J. N. (1986) Dimensionality. *Proceedings 1986 International Conference on Systems, Man, and Cybernetics*, Atlanta, October 14-17, New York: IEEE; 2:1118-1121.

1986-1988

Warfield, J. N.(1986) Micromathematics and Macromathematics. In *Proceedings 1986 International Conference on Systems, Man, and Cybernetics*, Atlanta, October 14-17, New York: IEEE; 2:1127-1131.

Warfield, J. N.(1987) Interpretive Structural Modeling. In *Systems and Control Encyclopedia*, M. Singh (Ed.), Oxford, England: Pergamon Press; 2575-2580.

Warfield, J. N. (1987) Implications of Scale for System Design. In *Proceedings Society for General Systems Research*, Budapest, June 1-6, SGSR; 1205-1211.

Warfield, J. N., and A. N. Christakis. (1987) Dimensionality. *Systems Research* 4(2):127-137.

Warfield, J. N. (1987) What Disciplines Large-Scale Systems Design? In *Proceedings 1987 Conference on Planning and Design in Management of Business and Organizations*, Book No. 100240, P. C. Nutt (Ed.), New York: ASME (American Society of Mechanical Engineers); 1-8.

Warfield, J. N. (1987) A Complexity Metric for High-Level Software Languages. In *Proceedings IEEE 1987 International Conference on Systems, Man, and Cybernetics*, Alexandria, VA October 21-23, note -the published version has omitted appendices which were a part of the original conference paper manuscript; New York: IEEE; 438-442.

Warfield, J. N. (1987, 1988) The Magical Number Three--Plus or Minus Zero. In *Proceedings Society for General Systems Research*, Budapest, June 1-6, SGSR. Repr. in 1988 in *Cybernetics and Systems* 19:339-358.

Warfield, J. N. (1987, 1988) Thinking About Systems. Editorial in Systems Research 4(4): 227-234. Repr. in 1988 *General Systems* 31:77-82.

Warfield, J. N. (1988) On the Design of Language for System Design. In *Cybernetics and Systems '88, Proc. 9th European Meeting on Cybernetics and Systems Research*, Vienna, April 4-8, R. Trappl (Ed.), Dordrecht: Kluwer; 133-140.

Warfield, J. N. (1988) Criteria for a Science of Design. In *Proceedings 19th Annual Pittsburgh Conference on Modeling and Simulation*, Pittsburgh, May 5-6, Research Triangle Park North Carolina: Instrument Society of America; 643-646.

Warfield, J. N.(1988) Implicit Aspects of Much Systems Thinking. *Systems Research* 5(4): 333-342.

1988-1990

Warfield, J. N. (1988) Do As I Say: A Review Essay of John W. Burton, 'Resolving Deep-Rooted Conflict: A Handbook.' *International Journal of Group Tensions* 18(3): 200-208.

Ohuchi, A., I. Kaji, and J. N. Warfield. (1988) Structural Analysis and a Complexity Metric for High-Level Software Languages. In *1988 Proceedings of the Conference of the Japan Information Processing Society*, Kyoto, September 12-14 (in Japanese language); 646-647.

Warfield, J. N. and M. N. B. Ayiku. (1989) Sociotechnical Modeling for Developing Nations. *SCIMA-- Journal of Systems & Cybernetics in Management*, New Delhi; (January) 25-40.

Warfield, J. N.(1989, 1991) Underconceptualization. In *Proceedings, Part II, of the Conference on Support, Society, and Culture: Mutual Uses of Cybernetics and Science* Univ. of Amsterdam, March, G. De Zeeuw and R. Glanville (Eds.); pages 15-39.

Reprinted in *Mututal Uses of Cybernetics and Science, Special Issue of Systemica*, Journal of the Dutch Systems Group (R. Glanville and G. de Zeeuw, Eds.) Amsterdam: Thesis Publishers; 8(1-6, Part 2): 415-433. Note: There are typographical errors in the 1991 reprint. The 1989 version is correct.

Warfield, J. N. (1989) Design Science: Experience in Teaching Large System Design. In *Proceedings ASEE 1989 Annual Conference*, Lincoln, Nebraska, June 25-30; Washington, D.C.: American Society for Engineering Education; 39-41.

Warfield, J. N. (1989, 1992) Artificial Philosophy and the Decline of Technology. In *Simposio Internação de Communição, Significão e Conhecimento*, Seccão I, Set. 13/15, Lisbon, Portugal. Reprint 1992 in *Information Technology & Society, Simposia International de Lisboa/Lisbon International Simposium, [September]1989*, Joao Lopes-Alves (Ed.); Lisbon, Portugal: Associacao Portuguesa para o Desenvolvimento das Comunicaoes and Sociedad Portuguesa de Filosofia; 542-550.

Warfield, J. N. (1989, 1988) Simple System Models Based on Sophisticated Assumptions. Unpublished manuscript (in English Language) accepted for a February 1988 AAAS Annual meeting in Boston where it was never presented due to a bad snowstorm in Boston. A 1989 translation titled "Proste Modele Systemowe Oparte Na Skomplikowanych Zalozeniach: Klucz do Spojnosci w Zlozonym Uniwersum" was published (in Polish language) *Zagadnienia*

Naukoznawstwa (Science of Science), Warsaw: Polish Academy of Sciences; 3(4): 653-662.

Warfield, J. N. (1990) *Annotated Bibliography: Generic Systems Design and Interactive Management.* IASIS Research Report, Fairfax,VA, Institute for Advanced Study in the Integrative Sciences. 141 p

Warfield, J. N.(1990) Presuppositions. In *Cybernetics and Systems '90, Proceedings of EMCSR, Vienna, April 17-20.* R. Trappl, (Ed.), Singapore: World Scientific; 213-219.

Warfield, J. N. (1990) Cybernetics, Systems Science, and the Great University. *Systems Research* 7(4) 287-294.

Warfield, J. N. (1990, 1995) Projektowanie Ogolne Dla Inzynierow. Kursowy Wyklad Uniwerstecki ["A Course in Generic Design for Engineers,"-- translation into Polish edited by W. W. Gasparski.] *Projektowanie i Systemy* Warsaw, Poland 11:25-43. An English language 1995 version was published in *Design and Systems: General Applications of Methodology,* A. Collen and W. W. Gasparski (Eds.), New Brunswick, NJ: Transactions Publishers; 415-437.

Warfield, J. N. (1990) Generic Planning: Research Results and Applications. In *Managing Knowledge for Design, Planning, and Decision Making* W. F. Schut and C. W. W. van Lohuizen (Eds.), Delft: Delft University Press; 109-128. In *Knowledge in Society,* Special Issue, William Dunn (Ed.), School of Library & Information Science, Univ. Of Pittsburg, 3(4, Winter 1990-91): 91-113.

Warfield, J. N. (1990) Economics and Systems Science. *SCIMA--Journal of Systems & Cybernetics in Management,* New Delhi 19(3): 65-71.

1991-1993

Warfield, J. N. (1991, 1993) Complexity and Cognitive Equilibium: Experimental Results and Their Implications. *Human Systems Management* 10(3): 195-202. Repr. in *Conflict Resolution Theory and Practice: Integration and Application,* Dennis J. D. Sandole and Hugo van der Merwe (Eds.), New York: Manchester University Press; (Chapter 5): 65-77.

Warfield, J. N.(1992) *Annotated Mathematical Bibliography for Interpretive Structural Modeling.* IASIS Research Report, Fairfax,VA, Institute for Advanced Study in the Integrative Sciences. 10p

Warfield, J. N.(1992, 1994) *Design and Manufacturing Methodologies: A Comparison of American and Japanese Developments.* IASIS Research Report, Fairfax,VA, Institute for Advanced Study in the Integrative Sciences (January). Working Paper Number 92-9, The Institute of Public Policy, George Mason University (March). Repr.1994 as "Chapter 14: Comparing IM with Methods Widely Used in Japan" in *Handbook of Interactive Management* Ames, IA: Iowa State University Press 183-223.

Warfield, J. N. (1992) Dwie Podstawy Projektowania. ["Dual-Basis Design" -- translation into Polish edited by W. W. Gasparski.] *Prakseololgia* 1-2(114-115): 43-58. Published by Polska Akademia Nauk, Instytut Filozofii i Socjologii, Warszawa.

Warfield, J. N. (1992) Widely-Ignored Subtleties That Are Critical to Decision-Making. In *Multiple Criteria Decision Making [Proceedings of the Ninth Multicriteria*

Decision-Making Conference: Theory and Applications in Business, Industry, and Government, Fairfax, VA August 5-8,1990]   Ambrose Goicoechea, Lucien Duckstein, and Stanley Zionts (Eds), New York: Springer Verlag; 449-457.

Warfield, J. N. (1993) *Structural Thinking: Producing Effective Organizational Change*, a Silver Anniversary Paper commemorating 25 years of research on complexity by the author. IASIS Research Report, Fairfax,VA: Institute for Advanced Study in the Integrative Sciences. 65p

Warfield, J. N., and Carol Teigen.(1993) *Groupthink, Clanthink, Spreadthink, and Linkthink: Decision-Making on Complex Issues in Organizations*. IASIS Research Report, Fairfax,VA: Institute for Advanced Study in the Integrative Sciences. 68 pages.

1994-1996

Warfield, J. N. (1994) Cybernetics. In *Encyclopedia of Human Behavior*. V.S. Ramachandran (Ed.), San Diego, CA: Academic Press 2:63-72.

Warfield, J. N. (1994) Accelerating Productivity of Intellectual Organizations by Systems Methodologies. In *Proceedings, International Symposium on Intellectual Facilitation of Creative Activities*, Miel Parque, November 14-15, Tokyo: Science & Technology Agency of Japan; 34-39.

Warfield, J. N. (1994)*The IASIS File: A Bibliography of Books and Papers Relevant to Complexity, Organizations, and Design.* compiled by Rose Warfield.   IASIS Research Report, Fairfax, VA, Institute for Advanced Study in the Integrative Sciences. 180p

Warfield, J. N. (1995) SPREADTHINK: Explaining Ineffective Groups. *Systems Research* 12(1, March): 5-14.

Warfield, J. N.(1995,1988) A Course in Generic Design for Engineers. In *Design and Systems: General Applications of Methodology*, Arne Collen and Wojciech W. Gasparski (Eds.), New Brunswick, NJ: Transaction Publishers; 415-437. First published 1988 in Polish language as "Projektowanie Ogolne Dla Inzynierow" in *Projektowanie i Systemy* Warsaw, Poland 11:25-43. .

Warfield, J. N.(1995) Demands Imposed on Systems Science by Complexity. In *Proceedings of the United Kingdom Systems Society 4th International Conference: Critical Issues in Systems Theory and Practice*, Hull, United Kingdom, July9-13, Keith Ellis, Amanda Gregory, Bridget Mears-Young, and Gillian Ragsdell (Eds.) 81-88.

Warfield, J. N., and S. M. Staley. (1996) Structural Thinking: Organizing Complexity Through Disciplined Activity. *Systems Research* 13(1): 47-67. Reprinted as an IASIS Research Report, Fairfax, VA: Institute for Advanced Study in the Integrative Sciences. *Note:* The publisher (Wiley) modifed Table 2 after the page proof had been approved, in order to save space, and in doing so garbled the text in the Table. IASIS prepared and distributed a report that included both a reprint (with Table 2 garbled) and the version of Table 2 that was originally sent to the publisher. In *Systems Research* 13(2) a publisher-created correction appeared.

Warfield, J. N.(1996) *Annotated Bibliography on Complexity Research: Reports, Papers, Bibliographies, Cell Packets, and Indexes from IASIS 1993-1996.* IASIS Research Report, Fairfax, VA: Institute for Advanced Study in the Integrative Sciences. 37 p

Warfield, J. N. (1996) *Publications Related to Computers.* IASIS Research Report, Fairfax, VA: Institute for Advanced Study in the Integrative Sciences. 11p

Warfield, J. N. (1996) Executive Mindbugs and Panetics. *Panetics* 5(2, December): 4-10.

Warfield, J. N. (1996) The Corporate Observatorium: Sustaining Management Communication and Continuity in an Age of Complexity. In *Integrated Design and Process Technology, Proceedings Society for Design and Process Science,* Austin, TX, December 1-4, M. M. Tanik, et al (Eds.) IDPT- 2:169-172.

Warfield, J. N. (1996) Five Schools of Thought About Complexity: Implications for Design and Process Science. In *Integrated Design and Process Technology, Proceedings Society for Design and Process Science,* Austin, TX, December 1-4, M. M. Tanik, et al (Eds.) IDPT- 2:389-394.

1997-1999

Warfield, J. N. (1997) A Platform for Sociotechnical System Design. *Journal of Integrated Design and Process Science* Austin, TX: SDPS Society for Design and Process Science 1(1, September): 37-53.

Warfield, J. N. (1997) Condensed Patterns Relevant to the Science of Complexity (Structure-Based School), Generic Design Science, and Interactive Management. In *Proceedings, International Systems Thinking Conference and Workshops,* November 4-7, University of Cape Town, Program for Systems Management, School of Engineering Management; 93-99.

Warfield, J. N. (1997) *Inventory 1997.* IASIS Research Report, Fairfax, VA: Institute for Advanced Study in the Integrative Sciences. 147 p

Warfield, J. N. (1997) *Essays on Complexity.* IASIS Research Report, Fairfax,VA: Institute for Advanced Study in the Integrative Sciences. 529p. A collection of papers on complexity written during the period 1991-1997, including some already published, some under review, and some never submitted for publication.

Warfield, J. N. (1997) *The Mathematics of Structure.* IASIS Research Report, Fairfax,VA: Institute for Advanced Study in the Integrative Sciences. 82p. An edited compilation made available as an IASIS report, drawn from Warfield's 1976 book *Societal Systems,* long out of print, and needed for short courses planned for offerings in the future.

Warfield, J. N. (1998) Systems Profile of Charles François–Introduction. *Systems Research.* (publisher garbled this badly)

Warfield, J. N. (1998) *What Questions Have Been Formulated and Answered in a 30-Year Research Program to Study Complexity?* Topics in Engineering: Great Author Colloquium, August, 1998. A NASA Engineering Training Monograph. Washington, D.C.: TADCORPS. Pages 1-30.

Warfield, J. N. (1999) Twenty Laws of Complexity: Science Applicable in Organizations. *Systems Research and Behavioral Science* 16(1): 3-40.

Warfield, J. N. and George H. Perino, Jr. (1999) The Problematique: Evolution of an Idea. *Systems Research and Behavioral Science* 16:221-226.

Warfield, J. N. and Rosamond Warfield. (1999) A Role for Formalisms in Integrative Studies. *Issues in Integrative Studies* 17:21-54.

Warfield, J. N. (1999) Enhancing Understanding in the Domain of Complexity Through A Model Exchange Strategy. In *Proceedings of Design Structure Matrix (DSM) Research Workshop,* Cambridge, MA , Sept 27-28, MIT Sloan School. 33p

2000-2004

Song, Xuefeng and J. N. Warfield, (2000) The Comparison Among the Schools of Science of Complexity. In *Proceedings of the International Symposium on Knowledge and Systems Sciences : Changes to Complexity* (Kss2000), Japan Advanced Institute of Science and Technology (JAIST), 246-254.

Warfield, J. N. (2001) Can Panetics be a Science or Academic Discipline?: A Conversation and Interview with Michel Foucault, Friedrich Hayek, and Charles Sanders Peirce, Part 1. *Panetics* 10(1): 6-16.

Warfield, J. N. (2001) Can Panetics be a Science or Academic Discipline?: A Conversation and Interview with Michel Foucault, Friedrich Hayek, and Charles Sanders Peirce, Part 2. *Panetics* 10(2).

Warfield, J. N. (2001) Humanitarian Intervention: Pros and Cons. *Panetics* 10(3), 28-29

Warfield, J. N. (2001) Book Review of *The Crisis of Global Capitalism: Open Society Endangered* by George Soros (1998). *Systems Research and Behavioral Science* 18(6): 577-585.

Warfield, J. N. (2001), Three Domains of Complexity. *under review by Systems Research and Behavioral Science.*, mailed September 27, 2001; withdrew from consideration in 2002.

Warfield, John N. (2003) Charles François: Friendship, Dedication, and Wisdom. In *Ensayos Sobre Sistemica y Cibernetica,* Ernesto Grün and Eduardo del Caño, (Eds.) Impresiones Dunken, Ayacucho 357 (C1025AAG,) Buenos Aires; 49-51.

Warfield, John N. (2003) A Proposal for Systems Science. *Systems Research and Behavioral Science* 20(6): 507-520.

Warfield, John N. (2003) Autobiographical Retrospectives: Discovering Systems Science. *The International Journal of General Systems* 32(6, December): 525-563. [This essay was invited by the Editor, Dr. George J. Klir of the University of Binghamton, New York]

Warfield, J. N. (2004) Linguistic Adjustments: Precursors to Understanding Complexity. *Systems Research and Behavioral Science*, 21:123-145. DOI: 10.1002/sres.601/, www.interscience.wiley.com.

Appendix 3

Discovering Systems Science

Introduction. With modest editorial changes, this Appendix first appeared as an invited article in the Taylor and Francis *International Journal of General System*s 32(6), December, 2003, 525-563. Long edited by George J. Klir[1], he had invited me to contribute to that journal "information regarding...thought processes and individual motivations" that had animated my career in the systems movement. This article is reproduced here with permission of Taylor and Francis Publishers, whose diverse publications are represented on their web site at http://www.tandf.co.uk.

At the outset I will tell the reader that **my motivation in carrying out the work described in this article was to develop a systems science; a science that extended all the way from its foundations through a sufficient number of applications to provide empirical evidence that the science was properly constructed and was very functional; a science that could withstand the most aggressive challenge.** Part of my strategy was to discover any prior scientific work that had relevance

---

[1] George Klir has kindly allowed me to depart from his protocols for this type of article in two ways. First, Exhibits 1 to 12 inclusive would be made available on the Internet, instead of appearing in the text. To see the Exhibits, please go to: http://www.ijgs.org/ar/warfield/. These Exhibits contain 90 pictures which, if published in this paper, would set an unnecessary journal precedent. Second, references before year 2001 could be omitted, since many of my contributions are contained in the Fenwick Library of George Mason University, Fairfax, Virginia, USA; a long listing being available at http://www.gmu.edu/library/specialcollections/warfield.htm. Relevant references to my work in years following 2000 are included in the paper. George warned me that some readers might not like the use of the term "Axiom". We agreed to disagree on this, and I ask reader indulgence on this point.

and to show its place in the science. The motivation for developing such a science was founded in the belief that many problematic situations could readily be observed in the world, and that a properly constructed and documented systems science would provide the basis for resolving these situations.

I now believe that I have succeeded in accomplishing what I set out to do. I suspect that the responsible reader will find this to be a very dubious statement, and that my challenge in this paper is to convince the reader that what I have said is true. The reader may keep this in mind in going through the paper, and may write challenges as the reading progresses. It is my hope that whatever challenges arise in the reading will be met with responses as the reading proceeds. If I fail in this, I hope that the reader will challenge me to respond to doubts. Also, in order to lend credibility to my assertions, I have displayed on a web site Exhibits 1 to 12, which include numerous pictures of individuals whose work in some way has contributed to the satisfaction of my purpose. Some of them constitute living empirical evidence.

To Write History. The skills needed to write a high-quality article of this type include that of writing history (about myself). **Is there someone that I could turn to and learn more about writing history to try to make this article more accurate and more interesting?** The twentieth-century French author, Michel Foucault, was head of the department of the history of thought at the Collège de France for more than a decade, and wrote widely-acclaimed publications such as *The Archaeology of Knowledge*, *The Order of Things*, and *The Discourse on Language*. Why would I want to look to a historian for help in writing autobiographical reminiscences? Several philosophers, including the great American logician Charles Sanders Peirce, have taken pains to emphasize the fallibility of the human being.[2] Also there is an obvious hazard in writing about an area where there is every reason to be biased, to paint a favorable impression of ones' self. **Mix fallibility with personal bias and you have a formula for a bad story.**

---

[2] Peirce Edition Project (1998, Eds.), *The Essential Peirce: Selected Philosophical Writings* (1893-1913), Vol. 2, Indiana University Press, Bloomington and Indianapolis.

Foucault's View. Shortly before his death in 1984, Foucault was interviewed by Paul Rabinow whose edited *The Foucault Reader*[3] would include the interview records. In an interview reproduced in that book, Foucault stated his opinion of how history should be written. In effect, he partitioned writing of history into parts: the **recordables** consisting of the identification of key actors, events, and dates (those items familiar to the beginning history student); and **two synthesized parts** consisting of (a) the historian's reasoned concept of what **problems** those actors were trying to solve through the events that they brought about and (b) the historian's reasoned concept of what their **motivations** were in choosing those problems to attack. To do these syntheses, Foucault decided that **"problemization"** by the historian was necessary. Problemization requires that the historian construct the problems and motivations. The "thought processes" and "motivations" that George Klir proposed as the centerpiece of this series of articles would best be divined, according to Foucault, from the narrative of the recordables: the actions, the events, the chronology.

Mises' View. A similar perspective has been set forth by the great Austrian economist, Ludwig von Mises. While the style of today in economics is largely positivistic, along the lines set forth by the sociologist Auguste Comte in the eighteenth century in France[4], and reinforced by the work of the influential English economist William Stanley Jevons in the nineteenth century (both of these actors having enormous influence on what is going on today in academic economics), both Mises and Hayek were confirmed enemies of the narrowly-founded positivistic movement. Hayek amply illustrated his disposition in his book titled: *The Counter-Revolution of Science: Studies on the Abuse of Reason.*

What did Mises bring to the writing of history? Mises chose the term **"thymology"** to refer to a mode of behavior in writing economic history that is severely at odds with the positivistic philosophy that dominates

---

[3] Paul Rabinow (Ed., 1984), *The Foucault Reader,* Pantheon, New York.

[4] F. A. Hayek (1952, 1979), *The Counter-Revolution of Science: Studies on the Abuse of Reason,* first The Free Press 1952, Glencoe, IL; then Liberty Fund 1979; Indianapolis.

much current thought. (Some writers see thymology as a synonym for praxeology.) As described by Mises[5],

> *"Thymology is on the one hand an offshoot of introspection and on the other a precipitate of historical experience...[and] with historians, of a foreign milieu about which he has learned by studying special sources."*

Further, thymology encompasses "knowledge of human valuations and volitions". When writing the history of ones self, **credibility (even to ones self) demands that an effort be made to derive the assessment of valuations and volitions from a demonstrated sequence of environments and events within those environments.**

History in Four Time Phases. It seems likely that the reader will find my article most useful if the thought processes and motivations are made transparent by a report of those events that took place within certain environments, the nature of which inevitably influenced the thought processes and motivations. By reading in this way, the reader cannot help but discern changes in the thought processes and motivations. For ease of reading, the chronology requires some markers in the form of categories. I think it is fair to say that I proceeded in **four career phases (the last, thankfully, incomplete!).** These were marked by changes in thought processes and motivations. While each phase was distinctly different from its predecessor, each of the last three phases owed much to its predecessor and evolved with some continuity from the interface with the predecessor.

History from a Variety of Environments. Before beginning to discuss Phase 1, it seems well to describe the variety of professional environments involved in my career. The beliefs and motivations that arose in my career were strongly dependent on the variety of environments. I was employed in 9 universities for an aggregate period of about 41 years. I was also employed in 7 industrial research settings for an aggregate period of about 11 years. The latter employments ranged from a small electronics firm to a large computer company in the

---

[5] L. von Mises (1985), *Theory and History: An Interpretation of Social and Economic Evolution*, 2nd Edition, Auburn, Alabama; Mises Institute.

for-profit sector and from two government-sponsored research laboratories to one not-for-profit contract research organization. In retrospect, the question clearly arises as to whether I could not hold a job, or whether there was some force telling me to stay on the move. **My thought processes and motivation were strongly affected by this mix of experiences, which saw me bouncing around from university to university to industrial research to university. Among the strong interests produced by these movements was an interest in organizations and management of organizations, which became a key part of my work in Phase 3.**

- *Phase 1. The Seventeen-Year Electrical Engineering Faculty Phase (1948-1965).* I began my university student experience with little insight into what I might do with my life. In my first two years at the University of Missouri, I developed an interest in mathematics and chemistry within the College of Arts and Sciences. My initial college exposure was interrupted by World War II. After being drafted into the infantry, I was eventually placed in the Army Specialized Training Program where I was able to experience five quarters of education in electrical engineering. Upon returning to campus after the war, I completed both undergraduate degree programs, and continued with a masters' degree in electrical engineering.

The Penn State Connection. Then I took an appointment as a faculty member in electrical engineering at what then was called Pennsylvania State College. It appeared my career would be as an electrical engineering faculty member. Given that assumption, the motivation was to excel in the faculty environment. This clearly required a doctorate. I completed the doctorate at Purdue in 1952, working on the synthesis of slowly variable control systems under Dr. John G. Truxal. He was only one year older than me, and had just completed his doctorate under the famed Professor Ernst Guillemin at MIT.

Building a Digital Computer. Returning to Penn State in 1952, I accepted an assignment to manage the development of a digital computer for the campus. To help prepare me for this, I was sent to visit the Institute for Advanced Study (Princeton) to speak with John von

Neumann. Most of our conversation was about long-range weather forecasting. I was surprised to see, on a computer tour of the Johnniac, that the storage tubes had been positioned almost on the floor where every passerby posed the threat of destruction of information due to vibration. (Later, when the Johnniac became the model for the Illiac, the storage tubes were placed at the top of the computer cabinet where they would be more immune to vibration.) Then I was sent to the Harvard Computation Center to speak with Howard Aiken. There I had a tour of the Mark III (I believe, but I may have the Mark number wrong.)

The Ordnance Research Laboratory Connection. While at Penn State, I held a part- time appointment in the Theory Section at the Ordnance Research Laboratory, reporting to Mr. Arthur T. Thompson, who would later be the founding dean of the School of Engineering at Boston University, and one of my lifelong friends. There I wrote one of the first papers ever written on systems engineering, which was distributed through government channels[6], and gained an understanding of automatic control and of operations in the undersea environment.

The University of Illinois Connection. When the Penn State computer assignment was near completion, I left to take a position at the University of Illinois where I spent two years in the vicinity of (among others) Ross Ashby, Heinz von Foerster, and John Bardeen; names that surely must be known to many readers of this article. Then I was called to Purdue to direct the analog computer laboratory and to serve as associate director of the digital computer laboratory.

Unfortunately both of the people who had hired me for Purdue had gone elsewhere when I arrived, and what had been viewed as commitments had vanished like the wind. Accordingly I left Purdue after one year and moved to the University of Kansas.

---

[6] Warfield, J. N. (1956) *Systems Engineering*, United States Department of Commerce PB111801. This would soon be followed by two other related articles: Warfield, J. N. (1957), Optimum Diagnostic Sequences for Systems With One Faulty Element", *University of Illinois Control Systems Laboratory Report M-67*, February and Warfield, J. N. (1957), "How to Improve Systems Engineering", *Aeronautical Engineering Review*, 16(7), July, 50-51.

The Ramo-Wooldridge Connection. Before moving to Kansas, I was able to spend two summers working in Inglewood, California, in the vicinity of Simon Ramo, a name well-known in systems engineering. The Ramo-Wooldridge company had undertaken to manage the development of intercontinental ballistic missiles. I spent part of one summer there in a systems engineering study and the other summer in studying precision electronic oscillators for space applications. Some of the people that I worked with included Dr. James R. Burnett, whom I had known at Purdue, and who later became head of Aerospace Corporation, and Dr. Lewis Terman, a son of the creative, one-time President and intellectual builder of Stanford University. These experiences opened new worlds to me that impelled me to consider whether to return to academia or to build a career in working with large systems. At this time, I was not ready to leave academia. I decided that California was not as interesting to me as Kansas at the time (I was a native of Missouri, and my wife Rosamond grew up in Lexington, Missouri, not far from Kansas. We see here the interaction of family origins and career aspirations).

The Sylvania Data Systems Connection. During the Kansas appointment, I spent two summers in the Boston, Massachusetts vicinity, working at Sylvania Data Systems on the famous Route 128 that circles Boston. Through this experience, I gained a second exposure to the world of industry, and worked with people engaged in experimental electronics.

The Nanosecond Research Environment. At Kansas I taught electrical engineering for about eight years and had the experience of working closely with Norris Nahman and his graduate students. Norris invented, built, and tested (in a Quonset hut) the first superconducting coaxial cable for carrying nanosecond pulses. I had the honor of serving as his dissertation adviser. One of his graduate student associates whom I knew quite well, George Frye, later became a key player in the Tektronix company, and eventually started his own firm which became a big player in the hearing aid market. These experiences deepened my appreciation for design and for experimental studies based in hypotheses that drew on scientific foundations. I was being moved away from the strictly theoretical end of engineering that had been exemplified by

Claude Shannon and Norbert Wiener in his studies of non-linear systems and time series analysis.

The Wilcox Electric Connection. In my last year in Lawrence, Kansas, I commuted to Kansas City to work for one year for Wilcox Electric Company as Research Director engaged in airborne electronics and electronic ground navigation. We designed, manufactured, and sold the first electronically-tuned VHF transceiver (the "807") for the large jet marketplace (both military and civilian). This transceiver eventually became a part of a remote sensing operation, allowing remote tuning to traverse the electronic VHF spectrum in a programmed way, and transmit scanning information to a distant receiver. We patented the key component of the 10-watt VHF omnirange transmitter with no moving parts, using a combination of electronic tuning and function generators to replace rotating mechanical equipment. This equipment served the navigational needs of small airports, where low-power omniranges were functional.

A Change in Motivation. My work up to this point in Phase 1 had finally changed my motivation. Originally I had planned to be an engineering faculty member (and had served that way for about 17 years), as I felt that electrical engineers performed a valuable public service, and that it would be possible in this role to have a family and a satisfying life. **But the excitement of discovery had become more than I could control.** I decided to take a full-time research position in a "systems science section" under Dr. Robert W. House at the Battelle Memorial Institute in Columbus, Ohio. While I would return to academia in an electrical engineering department eight years later as head of the department at the University of Virginia, I would continue to carry out the research program started at Battelle, which began Phase 2 of my career.

While at Kansas I had been contacted by Harold Chestnut, a pioneer in the study of control systems and one-time president of IEEE, to serve with a small group to help establish a component of IEEE that would specialize in systems and cybernetics. Harold explained that while there were already components in IEEE that dealt with control systems and with systems and circuits, these were far too specialized to serve the audience who wished to help advance the systems movement into larger domains. Along with Harold came Hans Ostreicher from Wright-Patterson Air Force Base who represented cybernetics: a field just coming into view with writings from Norbert Wiener and Ross Ashby, but which was beginning to focus on the human side of systems. I will describe more IEEE activity in my discussion of Phase 2.

- *Phase 2. Fourteen Years in Starting a Research Career Path (1966-1980).* The Battelle Memorial Institute in Columbus, Ohio, owned almost 300 patents on xerography. The story of how they developed the process that founded the copier revolution is exciting, but cannot be told here (it has been told well in a variety of publications). Its relevance to my story comes about because Battelle owned 22% of the stock in the Xerox Corporation. In 1970 that stock was worth about a quarter of a billion dollars. As I learned after coming there, Battelle intended to use income from this property to start a four-part, in-house-funded research program. The specific goal of one of the four parts was to develop a science to manage large, diverse, difficult programs. At that time, Battelle's slogan was "to apply science for the benefit of mankind". This inspirational slogan resonated with my interests. So I was extremely happy when I was tapped by Battelle to head what was called the "Science Base" project in a larger program called "Science and Human Affairs".

The Battelle Connection: The Science and Human Affairs Program. Battelle had both a scientific aim and a business aim. The former was to develop a science to underpin large programs. The latter was to equip Battelle to contract for and lead a variety of large programs with a variety of sponsors. To understand this aim, it will help to know that, at the time, Battelle had four research laboratories, two in the USA and two in Europe. In the Columbus, Ohio, headquarters, about 1500 technical people were employed in its Columbus Laboratories, which had almost the same number of research contracts per year. Clearly this meant that a lot of time had to be spent doing project development and writing proposals. The advantage of being able to take on some larger programs was clear. While I was surprised by these numbers, the surprise was augmented when I saw the statistics of research projects at the General Motors Research Laboratory. The average number of researchers per project at the time was about 0.8. In other words, research programs carried out in professional research establishments could hardly be thought of as "systems" programs, when fractional people were involved in a very high percentage of projects.

My interest in developing the Science Base was also spurred by the turmoil going on in U. S. cities in the late 1960s and early 1970s. It was amazing how little was known about what to do to help cities constructively to cope with civil rights issues, Vietnam War issues, and other social dissonance all taking place at the same time! **A science base to support systems programs that was not limited to automatic control interests was an aspiration worthy of a researcher.**

Early Thoughts. Worthy, perhaps. But what to do? At the beginning, I reviewed what was going on in the systems movement. Who were the main actors? What had they contributed? How relevant was their work to the contemplated science base? Some of the principal actors are illustrated in **Exhibit 1** (Please see Footnote 1 to locate and retrieve **Exhibits 1-12**, which are posted on the Internet.)

Evidently my task could be limited to building material complementary to what they had already done. This simplified a task that was clearly in need of simplification, but still extraordinarily challenging. Also I reviewed papers that I had written in the early 1950s on Systems Engineering (Footnote 7). Some of the thoughts that came to mind from that perspective are as follows (and I express them as axioms, to indicate both their fundamental impact on my thought processes and the implicit use of mathematical thought as a basis for my self-discipline):

Axiom 1 (The Collaboration Axiom). Large programs require people working collaboratively. Naturally, if a lot were known about groups working together on large programs, one could merely aggregate that literature and incorporate it into the science base. Can you believe that little was known at the particular time of the beginning of my Phase 2? When I say little, please realize that I am interested in what can be called "actionable research results". It is little help to hear such words as "Of course much more research remains to be done before we can apply these results...". Mayors of burning cities are not very friendly to ambiguous propositions or incomplete constructions. Following the line of thought that urged aggregation of what was known that could be applied, matters related to human behavior seemed to be of considerable importance. (Fortunately the last half of the twentieth century produced much significant research on the behavior of people that relates strongly to their ability to work together effectively on large programs. I have discussed this research in many publications.)

Axiom 2 (The Behavior Axiom). Knowledge about human behavior in working effectively in teams will be critically important to the success of large programs. At Battelle I sat up and funded about 20 people part time known as the "Large City Design Team", comprised of a mix of Battelle people and outside people with reputations in urban environments (e.g., the sociologist who helped plan Columbia, Maryland, and the investor who represented John D. Rockefeller III in financing high-rises). This group met three days a month for a year and a half. **It was both a great success and a great failure.** It was a great failure in that it could not produce anything actionable that treated the city as a system. **It was a great success to learn that research was badly needed to find a process that would enable people who have something to contribute toward resolution of complexity through system design to pool their knowledge and arrive at actionable conclusions. This was a key finding that would animate all of the succeeding research activity.**

Axiom 3 (The Design Axiom). Teams working on difficult issues require collaborative support through strongly-disciplined science-based processes which enable a group of expert individuals to aggregate their individual (and often conflicting) beliefs into actionable designs. A further thought ensued. The scholars who had thought most about thinking were philosophers. Which philosophers could contribute to the ongoing research? It was by sheer accident that the work of the great

American philosopher, Charles Sanders Peirce[7], came into view. This was enabled by a book by the late Professor Goudge[8] of the University of Toronto that summarized and interpreted much of Peirce's work. Then a second book came into view: the amazing and dedicated work by Father I. M. "Joseph" Bochenski[9] on a history of formal logic. And a third book arrived at just the right time: Harary's book on structural models[10], which tied together Boolean algebra, Boolean matrices, and digraphs. These works collectively fortified belief in a fourth Axiom.

Axiom 4 (The Graphics Axiom). *Organized beliefs reflect structure. When numerous ideas are linked together, communication implies structural graphics, as engineers have long recognized intuitively.* Why not just transfer engineering graphics into the larger arena and declare victory? Yes, engineers have learned to apply structural graphics in problematic situations. Unfortunately they have not learned how to construct such graphics systematically and how to explain them to others in a clear way. Their "immune systems" exclude cognitive aspects of the structural graphics. In applications, they typically reflect the perceptions of one or two people who arrive at the graphics without any clearly-defined procedures that have scientific bases. They have also traditionally accepted the constraint of small spaces, not being able to reflect the intricacy of communication in the size of displays. Moreover the balance between explicit and implicit in such displays is strongly tilted in favor of the implicit by the constraints of limited space. Future research would establish just how poor communication that mixed structural graphics and prose had become, and how recognition of this had eluded people whose careers required that they produce and propagate such mixtures.

Axiom 5 (The Structure Axiom). *It is necessary to develop a systematic means of synthesizing structure of systems in order to gain*

---

[7] Charles Sanders Peirce has inspired much of my work.
[8] Goudge, T. A. (1969), *The Thought of C. S. Peirce*, Dover Publications, New York.
[9] Bochenski, I. M. ("Joseph") (1970), *A History of Formal Logic*, Chelsea, New York.
[10] Harary, F. R., Norman, V., and Cartwright, D. (1965) *Structural Models: An Introduction to the Theory of Directed Graphs*, John Wiley, New York.

understanding and shared comprehension. The work of a variety of other authors also contributed to the research in its early stages. In retrospect, it is somewhat remarkable that the annotated research bibliography compiled later (titled the "IASIS File") occupied 88 pages.[11] It became clear from the work of Peirce and others mentioned, and from consulting assistance from Frank Harary and George Klir that the theory of relations would be a critical asset in developing system structure. Following this, another Axiom could be stated.

Axiom 6 (The History Axiom). *There exists a historical chain of "thought leaders about thought" extending all the way back to Aristotle, whose work remains to be exploited in developing relational patterns in problematic situations.* The development of such patterns could now be seen as a key objective which, if it could be satisfied at all, would demand a mathematical basis.

Mathematics as a Model of Reasoning. Having been a mathematics major as an undergraduate, it is inevitable that I would reflect on what mathematics had to offer to systems thinking, beyond the well-established use of ordinary differential equations to model control systems and partial differential equations to model atmospheric diffusion. The Peirces, Benjamin and Charles, father and son, agreed on the definition of mathematics. It is **"the science of necessary conclusions."** This definition, given credibility in the light of Euclid's formulation of geometry, and of subsequent developments in mathematics, reflects these concepts:

- There is a **core body of axioms**, from which all else flows

---

[11] When I retired in the year 2000, George Mason University requested that my research materials be deposited in their Fenwick Library in what came to be known as the "Warfield Special Collection". As libraries measure such contributions, the collection occupied 93 linear feet, and is still growing. A report called the "IASIS File" can be found there which provides the bibliography mentioned. It was compiled with the help of my wife, Rosamond. This collection is cataloged at this URL: http://www.gmu.edu/library/specialcollections/warfield.htm

- There is a **foundational relationship (implication)** that animates the flow.
- The flow is **deductive** in nature, based in **Aristotle's syllogism**
- The flow evolves as theorems and proofs developed in **a pattern of antecedents and succedents**. (This language was set forth by Peter Abélard in the twelfth century, as Bochenski had discovered. It enabled a one-sentence statement to replace the three-sentence statement of the syllogism, as I would later describe in my 2002 book *Understanding Complexity.*)
- The pattern is almost never drawn out for inspection as a whole. It does not fit the standard formulations in the form of books and journals, because it is too large. So it is constrained to be learned sequentially, **even though the underlying pattern almost never takes the form of a linear flow**, necessitating a perpetual backing-and-filling by a reader, posing a significant **cognitive burden** to the learner

Second-Order Thought. What was being studied here could be described as "second-order thought", i.,e., thought about thought itself. Exhibits 2 and 3 illustrate some of those who were leaders in this area, extending from Aristotle in the early days to George Friedman[12] (who produced "constraint theory" and who studied and reported the principal reasons for failure of large systems) today.

It seems clear that little could be done to develop a branch of mathematics without a beginning that incorporated a set of axioms. Of course iteration could be done in developing such a set. (As the various forms of set theory and Kenneth Arrow's well-known "Impossibility Theorem for Aggregating Individual Preferences into Social Preferences" illustrate, it is not always easy to find a consistent set or the most suitable set to serve a given purpose). Inability to find a suitable set of axioms from which to develop what Foucault calls "les sciences humaine" might be construed as one of two major de-motivating influences affecting workers in the behavioral sciences; the other being

---

[12] George J. Friedman (1967), *Constraint Theory Applied to Mathematical Model Consistency and Computational Allowability*, UMI Dissertation Services, Ann Arbor, MI.

the presumed inability to replicate findings. Both of these influences, I have concluded are specious.

Replicability in Science. Even in the physical sciences, **replicability at the micro level** is clearly impossible, since the same set of molecules will never be present in any two physical or chemical experiments. **Replicability occurs only at the macro level**, hence we are disposed to identify a few key categories that will subsume the lesser concepts. Typically one would require that the methodology be replicated and that the form of analysis of results be replicated. These are macro attributes, and their replication in social systems is demonstrably feasible.

What seems not to have been recognized are the true obstacles to macro replication. The combined impact of a set of six obstacles makes the work difficult: (1) the difficulty in bringing together in the same space at the same time the quality human resources that collectively own the set of beliefs needed to construct structures of the problematic situation; (2) unawareness of the methods that will be replicated, (3) non-recognition of the experienced staff to carry out the methods, (4) absence of the physical infrastructure to support the group work; (5) shortage of talent experienced in analyzing and interpreting the structural results of group work and, finally, (6) absent incentives and passion from managers in organizations to implement what has been learned from a quality, science-based, collaborative research effort. [As I will indicate in this article, I now believe that I have already described fully the resources that are required, the methods to be replicated, the demands on the staff to carry out the processes, the kind of physical infrastructure that is required, and the forms of analysis that apply.]

Digraphs and the Theory of Relations. Once it became clear that Harary had linked Boole's algebra, DeMorgan's theory of relations, and an unknown author's invention of the digraph[13] (directed graph), it was clear to me that I could implement the requirement stated in Axiom 5 (foregoing) if I could find a process that would use the aggregated

---

[13] I have searched intermittently to try to find the origin of the digraph. The earliest one that I have seen appeared in Bertrand Russell's 1919 *Introduction to Mathematical Philosophy*. One can hardly accuse Russell of setting a trend, for he used only one drawing in the entire book, apparently out of necessity to clarify an explanation.

mathematics of Harary and would enable groups to work together to organize their collective thoughts. Harary had done the analysis. I would do the process synthesis.

As Harary showed, there is a one-to-one correspondence between a certain type of binary matrix and a digraph. It was clear from his work that it would be much easier to find a way for a group to fill a binary matrix through voting than to construct a digraph directly. Accordingly I set out to discover such a process. Harary had already clarified the concept that "reachability" on a digraph could be isomorphic to any member of the entire class of transitive relationships. This clarification was sufficient to tie Harary's work directly to De Morgan's. **(As Bochenski had noted, De Morgan recognized that the validity of the syllogism depended on whether the relationship involved was transitive. This seems to have escaped scholars of the syllogism for more than 2,000 years. After De Morgan, C. S. Peirce noted the importance of this insight.)** Hence a second condition that I had to satisfy was to determine relationships that groups could use to construct structural models. Harary had used the term "structural model" to correspond to a digraph. I appended the word "Interpretive" and named the process that I would develop "Interpretive Structural Modeling"[14], to mean that the structure created would be subject to interpretation based upon the elements, the relationship among the elements, and the digraph-like structure. The latter would be structurally like a digraph, but would have words in boxes in place of the circles, and the directed paths on a structure would represent the transitive relationship used to do the construction of the interpretive structural model..

Interpretive Structural Modeling (ISM). One of the necessary conditions to improve the state of the science of modeling (such as it was) was to enable large numbers of elements to be related systematically. How many elements might be involved? George J. Friedman (see Footnote 12) noted that the equations of physics seldom

---

[14] John N. Warfield (1974), *Structuring Complex Systems* (Battelle Monograph No. 4, Columbus, Ohio). I would not choose this title today, since I no longer like the terminology "complex system", for reasons that I have explained in (Warfield, 2002).

involve more than six elements. How about starting with an aspiration to involve at least 30 elements? With 30 elements, the binary relational matrix would have 900 entries. I could insert 1's along the main diagonal, but still had to allow 870 binary digits to complete the matrix. How much time would it take for a group to construct such a matrix? And how difficult would it be? Would management support the activity? Each entry in the matrix would correspond to a question that could be answered "yes" for 1. What if the group didn't know the answer? **I decided that 0 in the matrix could represent the belief that the relationship didn't exist or that the voter in the group didn't know the answer.** This would satisfy two conditions. First, individuals didn't have to say that they didn't know; they could just vote "no", leaving the meaning of the 0 in the matrix ambiguous. Second, every path on the digraph would indicate group majority belief that the relationship was in effect. This meant that the digraph wouldn't have to be cluttered with representations of "no". But even then, if it took 870 binary digits, and if each one required one minute to emerge from group deliberation, the time involved to fill the matrix would be 14 hours. I made a judgment that this would not be initially acceptable to managers of potential participants in the matrix-filling group process; maybe later, after some experience were gained, but not initially. A further difficulty involved in matrix filling was the requirement for consistency in the model. A model that is inconsistent is not likely to be very helpful. But Harary's reachability condition that showed the necessary conditions for transitivity also represented the necessary condition for consistency; a greatly underemphasized condition in modeling. Suppose each time an entry was made in the matrix, all possible inferences were drawn by a computer, and then entered. This would mean that any opportunity for the group to be intransitive in its voting process would have been eliminated by the program. And it also meant that perhaps **a significant shortening of the time to fill the matrix would be brought about by letting the computer share the work of filling the matrix.**

Still another saving of group time could be gained if the computer were allowed to determine the sequence of questions involved in filling a binary matrix. At any point in the matrix-filling process, Harary's equation could be used to compute the possible inference available from all possible unfilled entries in the matrix.   By carrying out this computation, the computer could be provided with a decision rule to determine which question to ask next.   Some questions, if given one of the two allowed answers, might enable a lot of inference while, if given the other answer, might provide little or no inference. I decided it would be possible to go too far in saving time. It was not necessary to minimize the time. What was desired was to maximize the learning that went on during the process, so that the product would be high in quality. Accordingly I decided to use a maxi-min rule, whereby the computer chose the next question to maximize the minimum inference.   This decision tended to offer frequent, but not excessive, inference, meaning that the computer "answered" for the group based on transitivity. With this scheme, the time required to fill a 30 x 30 matrix came down from, e.g., 14 hours to a typical value of 3 hours.   Later experience showed that, while the time to fill such a matrix could not be predicted with any accuracy, the matrix-filling time for ISM hardly ever posed any difficulties for groups, mainly because the computer algorithms were sufficiently fast that it appeared to the casual observer that the computer required no time to do the computations. The enthusiasm generated by the learning experienced typically prompted groups to insist on more time if the time allowed was insufficient. This was very satisfying, and lent credence to the philosophy used in the process design.

Axiom 7 (The ISM Software Axiom).   In order to carry out the operations needed to structure problematic situations, interactive computer software for developing structural models would be essential. At the present time, many versions and extensions of ISM software have been written.   The first version was written at Battelle in 1973 in a Fortran language, and installed on a Control Data Cyber machine. It was expected that it would be used remotely through a telephone connection. The first such computer-assisted, long-distance application that I observed was held in Dayton, Ohio.   It was led by Brother Raymond Fitz, a member of the Society of Mary, who had a Ph. D. in electrical engineering from Brooklyn Polytechnic, and who was on leave from the University of Dayton at the Kettering Foundation.   He arranged for a group of planners to meet and apply ISM to study the improvement of highway transportation in the Dayton area. Later he would lead other sessions, including one in Kent, Ohio, which was videotaped and stands as an example of the application of ISM to urban budget planning in a budget-deficit situation. Later Dr. Fitz's team would write a new version of the ISM software to be used on a Univac 1100-series mainframe under a subcontract with the University of Virginia, supported by a contract with the Office of Environmental Education through Mr. Walter J. Bogan. (Ultimately Mr. Bogan would be the principal intellectual leader in the new science high school being originated in Newark, New Jersey and Dr. Fitz would become President of the University of Dayton, a position which he held for many years, retiring only recently.)

The Cedar Falls Application. Even before the Dayton application, an application was carried out in Cedar Falls, Iowa. This application was led by Dr. Robert James Waller, then an associate professor in the Business School at the University of Northern Iowa[15]. This session, which was very successful, established priorities for urban projects in the Cedar Falls area. Later Dr. Waller would lead the development of a version of the ISM software. (Still later, he would become a famous author with the publication of his best-selling book *The Bridges of Madison County* and its release as a movie starring Clint Eastwood and Meryl Streep.)

The Nominal Group Technique (NGT). Once it was clear from empirical study that the ISM process met the expectations and conditions contained in the Axioms, it became clear also that the ISM process alone was not sufficient to enable groups to work together effectively in problematic situations.

Fortunately, the Nominal Group Technique (NGT) appeared in the literature from a group of authors[16] at Kent State University at almost the

---

[15] Details of this application appear in John N. Warfield (1976), *Societal Systems: Planning, Policy, and Complexity,* Wiley Interscience, New York.

[16] Delbecq, A. L.; Van de Ven, A. H.; and Gustafson, D. H. (1975), *Group Techniques for Program Planning: A Guide to Nominal Group and DELPHI Processes,* Scott Foresman, Glenview, IL. The Nominal Group Technique is a very well-designed process that incorporates key behavioral concepts, unlike most group processes which fail even to emphasize the critical importance of dedicating a significant percentage of group effort to clarification of statements, guided by a skilled facilitator. Many group leaders seemingly are unable to distinguish "brainstorming" from NGT, but the latter is far superior.

perfect time from the standpoint of serving as a partner of ISM. This process, with a very sound behavioral design, has since proved to be everything that was desired to complement ISM. **In fact, the two processes taken together are the only methods that are needed to enable a group to move from a point of no integration of their ideas to the point where they have reached a preliminary structural design of a system for resolving the complexity inherent in the problematic situation.**

The Role of Theoretical and Positivist Methods. The theoretical and positivist methods that are often set forth as part of systems science or systems engineering are both a blessing and a curse. They are a blessing in that they often provide the opportunity to develop needed numerical results to complete a structural design developed with the help of ISM and NGT. They are a curse in that they are not well-suited to structuring problematic situations, and are only helpful when the constraints that these methods represent happen to be compatible with the constraints of a particular (local) problematic situation. Such methods may often be appropriate to the *domain* of systems science[17], but not to systems science itself. When needed, they are called into play by what has been discovered in prior work with neutral methods. The bulk of the contributions of the systems pioneers[18] shown in **Exhibit 1** were typically theoretical or positivistic in nature or both, and were mostly not sufficiently fundamental to provide the kind of material needed for the science base. In retrospect, a principal shortcoming of those contributions lay in the failure to connect them to human behavior. My task was beginning to take recognizable form. Although I did not

---

[17] The *domain* of systems science includes the systems science along with what I have called the "Arena", the site of applications. Systems science is viewed as the means of arriving at the overview plan for resolving complexity through the Work Program of Complexity. In carrying out this program, it will often be necessary to import specific methods in order to perform tasks that require computations. The distinction between the generic and the specific is one that I have used for more than decade and I note that Michel Foucault makes the same distinction. The fundamental idea is that the systems science must be a neutral science that is applicable across the board, but which will usually have to be supplemented by experts from the specific sciences or from other areas where relevant experience is found.

[18] Please see an Appendix for a list of the persons whose pictures appear in Exhibits 1-11 inclusive and their organizations.

know it at the time, Phase 3 was about to begin, and would continue for two decades.

The India Connection. Through the work of Dr. Robert W. House, my supervisor at Battelle, acting in his role as an official in the Institute of Electrical and Electronics Engineers, a trip to India was arranged as a guest of the Tata Corporation, via Mr. Faqir Kohli, a graduate of MIT, and a member of the board of directors of Tata Corporation. At the time of this trip, Mr. Kohli was in charge of the Tata Consultancy Services (TCS), largely a computer-oriented company, with about 700 employees (at the present time, it is up to more than 20,000). I was invited to make presentations in Mumbai, Pune, New Delhi, and Bangalore, and was privileged to visit the Taj Mahal. One of the lectures was attended by a young Indian mathematician named G. S. Chandy. I will mention Mr. Chandy again later in this piece, as he is doing some excellent work now as director of a small software firm in India. This trip, along with other travels to other countries, enlarged my horizons, and contributed to my world-view.

The Japan Connection. While working on ISM at Battelle, two visitors came to Battelle and were accommodated in Dr. House's Systems Science Section. One was the late Professor William ("Bill") Linvill, founder of the Department of Engineering-Economic Systems Ph. D. program at Stanford University. He was taking his sabbatical and was financed in part by the Battelle Science and Human Affairs Program. The other was Koichi Haruna, a young employee of Hitachi, Ltd. Koichi was on leave from Hitachi to spend a year with Bill Linvill. Both of them became acquainted with the ISM system. When Koichi returned to Hitachi, he began to work on it right away, and developed applications for Hitachi. I will say more about him later in this piece.

The IEEE Connection. As part of the service on an IEEE systems science committee which I referred to in my description of Phase 1, I became acquainted with Arthur D. Hall III who had authored the first widely read book on systems methodology[19]. Because of this work,

---

[19]   A. D. Hall III (1962), *A Methodology for Systems Engineering*, Van Nostrand Reinhold, Princeton, NJ.

when the IEEE granted society status as a consequence of Harold Chestnut's leadership, Arthur was asked to be the first editor of the new society's transactions. Known as the *IEEE Transactions on Systems Science and Cybernetics*, Arthur undertook to get this publication off the ground. He invited me to serve in his editorial team as Review Editor. After a few early issues, I was invited to take over as Editor. Battelle kindly allowed me to do this work on "company time" and provided secretarial assistance. With the help of various paper referees, I was able to move this journal forward until it became a quarterly. When the much smaller IEEE group on human factors merged with the Systems Science and Cybernetics Society, it seemed appropriate to change the name to reflect the interests of both groups. The new name became the Systems, Man, and Cybernetics Society. This new name was reflected in a change in the name of the journal as well.

To make the transition go more smoothly, I resigned as Editor so that the new Society could choose its own Editor. Later I served this Society as its President, and received an award for innovation. The years of experience that I gained with this Society and its journal would help me a lot when I accepted an invitation from George Klir about a decade later to be the first Editor-in-Chief of a new systems journal to be published by Pergamon Press. I will say more about this assignment later.

- **Phase 3. Twenty Years Accruing Empirical Evidence and Developing Components of Systems Science (1980-2000).** At the close of Phase 2, seven Axioms had been identified, and some progress had been made in arriving at conclusions. All of the seven Axioms could be integrated as follows: **we can see from history (both ancient and recent) that relationships among elements are the basis for arriving at necessary structure. We recognize that the resolution of problematic situations requires a group design capability, and demands combined prose-graphics structures, arrived at through collaborative processes which will benefit if behavioral aspects of humans (especially those that are responsible for fallibility) are taken into account. Two methods (NGT and ISM) had been found (one in the literature, one developed in** the research program) that, properly facilitated, appeared to be sufficient to carry out the kind of work required. Complexity is a major enemy of progress. The mistaken belief that science which involves human beings as actors cannot be developed by replication, so that only theory should be discovered, was an obstacle that demanded verifiable evidence. Finally, the role of the computer in helping groups had come to the fore, and ISM software would provide a capability never before available to people working together collaboratively.

Axiom 8 (The Verifiability Axiom). To gain acceptance for the work, it would be necessary to verify the kinds of progress that had been made in the area of methodology, and to establish that the work could apply around the world in many different situations; not being limited to any particular disciplinary domain or to any cultural domain. This Axiom undoubtedly was formulated in the light of the nineteenth-century work of Charles Sanders Peirce. He had been given the assignment to enhance ocean navigation by establishing the variation of gravity. For this purpose, he began to "swing pendulums" at many different locations, gathering data from the pendulum motion to determine how well pendulum motion could be used to verify position data for ships at sea. (Even today there is a well-equipped, ocean-going vessel, which bears his name as a testimonial to his early work.) But he was able to carry out this work as one individual. To gain empirical evidence of the work that had been done, additional requirements could be posed.

Axiom 9 (The Process Leadership Axiom). To do the necessary testing, a cadre of staff at different locations around the world would be required. They would need to know what to do to provide the process leadership needed to involve groups in local designs. This axiom defined a huge challenge. How could individuals be found that would undertake the necessary learning processes? And how could these processes be defined? It turned out that this situation would be resolved by a combination of authorship, laboratory experience, and chance–authorship that produced materials suitable for training, laboratory experience in several settings where group work could be carried out, and chance where individuals identified themselves as being interested in the work and began to apply the materials in various settings and on various topics of their own choosing.

Axiom 10 (The Undiscovered Actors Axiom). There exist, throughout the world, people who want to resolve complexity and are willing to spend considerable time learning how to do so. These may be called the "undiscovered actors" because there is no apparent way to identify them, other than to wait until they surface with requests for information and, in some cases for training. In almost three decades, numerous undiscovered actors have surfaced, and have become involved in process leadership roles, either directly by leading projects, or indirectly by offering relevant course work, or both. **Exhibits 4, 5, 6, and 7** illustrate some of these leaders. They are called "action leaders in Interactive Management". The term action implies that they have become involved in work that yields empirical evidence of the type called for in Axiom 8. The term "Interactive Management" was chosen to represent the action component of the science base.

Axiom 11 (The Behavioral Pathologies Axiom). Human beings are victims of certain behavioral pathologies that limit or nullify their potential for working together to resolve complexity in situations where they have something to contribute. This Axiom became clear slowly as the second half of the twentieth century brought forth research findings concerning human limitations. It became clear that some limitations were individual, some were associated with small groups, and some were almost inevitable in large organizations. **Exhibit 8** shows thought leaders on **individual** behavioral pathologies. **Exhibit 9** shows thought leaders on **group** behavioral pathologies. And **Exhibit 10** shows thought leaders on **organizational** pathologies.

Axiom 12 (The Necessary Organization Axiom). For most problematic situations that demand a systems science as a basis, at least one organization will necessarily be involved that provides the resources that are seldom available to the individual process leader. This Axiom caused attention to be directed to a study of organizations. In a typical application, a group would be formed from a larger organization. As the group work proceeded, using NGT followed by ISM, it became very apparent that organizational communication was a severe difficulty. While scholars have often recognized the difficulty in communication, specific evidence has seldom been provided except, perhaps, when some kind of crisis or catastrophe occurred that could be traced directly to communication failures. Because of the insistence in the NGT process that a specific component of time be dedicated to clarification only, any participant or observer who watches the performance of participants could see how severe the communication problem was. A participant would often say, in effect, "this idea that I have produced is obvious to everyone", only to find that it had been completely misinterpreted. Sometimes a participant would produce an idea which he could not explain when asked to do so. It is not far from the truth to say that "people don't know what they are talking about until their statements have been honed through human interactions." Hence, Axiom 13.

Axiom 13 (The Language Axiom.)   Much attention must be given to the matter of gaining a common perspective in any local situation, hence the process that is being applied locally must allot significant time to the construction of local language (even though it will be a by-product of the learning process, and not advertised as a main goal). In effect, each small group is a "founder of discursivity" (a term set forth by Michel Foucault) in a local situation. This means that the concept of language-duality is critical to a scientific base for working with complexity. The processes used must have language neutrality as a major attribute while greatly facilitating the construction of local language that is specific to the problematic situation undergoing description and design. It is not reasonable to expect that sponsoring organizations will pay to construct local languages, in spite of the necessity to do so. Hence linguistic constructions must be a by-product of the work program aimed at resolving the complexity.

Thought Leaders on Language. The necessity and ability to speak precisely on matters of substantial difficulty have been illustrated or enhanced by thought leaders on language shown in **Exhibit 11**.

The ideas developed by these thought leaders reinforce my belief that NGT and ISM are sufficient processes to enable the necessary local work to be carried out preparatory to applying any positivist processes that may lie *within the domain* of a science of systems (but not be part of such a science).

The Center for Interactive Managements–1 and 2. Early in the 1970s, Dr. Alexander Christakis worked with Professor Hasan Ozbekhan of a University of Pennsylvania Wharton School program in Social Systems Science to develop a prospectus for the forthcoming Club of Rome. Both of them believed that the Club of Rome would apply broad-brush treatments to world problems. They were greatly disappointed when the Club sponsored a project with Dr. Jay Forrester to strive to apply systems dynamics to world problems, so they resigned from the Club.

At the time a representative of the Battelle Geneva Laboratory was a member of the Club. Through association with Christakis, Battelle became aware of his activity, and he was ultimately hired by Battelle, after serving as a consultant for a few years. Earlier Christakis had tried to develop a mathematical social science, under the sponsorship of the Greek architect, Dinos Doxiadis, who was in the business of urban planning and new-city design and construction. He had decided it could not be done, but when he observed the ISM work, he became quite excited. His interest grew, and he began to take part in applications in conjunction with Dr. Kazuhiko Kawamura, a control systems engineer at Battelle (who is now a professor at Vanderbilt University)..

The University of Virginia Connection. When Christakis joined the faculty of the University of Virginia, where I had migrated in 1974, Christakis and I planned a Center for Interactive Management. The Center would aim to provide evidence of efficacy of the research results that had been documented in my 1976 book titled *Societal Systems: Planning, Policy, and Complexity*. The late Dr. John E. Gibson, who was then Dean of the School of Engineering and Applied Science, approved the use of a large room and allowed the design and construction of a special facility, just to carry out the work program as it stood at the time, for sponsors that might be attracted. I had already concluded that a dedicated facility would be required to carry out the work. This viewpoint came from the experience in running several ISM sessions in the late 1970s. These sessions typically involved several television sets wired to a telephone which was wired to a remote computer via the lines of some telephone company. Large cables ran around the room, and participants were frequently likely to trip over them. Moreover the long-distance connection to a host computer was often lost, interrupting the process and wasting group time–a very valuable asset.

The Saudi-Arabian Connection. A most amazing workshop was held in Riyadh, Saudi Arabia, in 1980 in a conference room at the Riyadh Palace Hotel. The sponsor was the Saudi Arabian National Center for Science and Technology, represented by Dr. Hashim Yamani (a Ph. D. in physics from Harvard, who is now the Minister of Trade and Industry.) The computer connection was arranged by Dr. Kazuhiko Kawamura who was then employed at Battelle. A telephone line from the Riyadh Palace went down the street to the local offices of the U. S. Treasury. From there, a loaned satellite channel (of many used for transmitting oil and dollar statistics) went to the big dishes in West Virginia. From there another telephone line carried the messages to Washington, D. C., from which still another made the connection to Battelle in Columbus, Ohio, to their Control Data Cyber mainframe computer. We had been assured that the equipment would all be "locked in" for us, so that our work would not be interrupted. While we expected to have quite a few participants, only three Arabs came. This matched the staff of three consisting of Dr. Robert James Waller of the University of Northern Iowa who served as facilitator, Dr. Kazuhiko Kawamura (who operated the computer terminal and took advantage of the shopping experience to buy an Arab costume for himself), and me who helped with various duties, part of which was providing a short course.

The Designed Situation Room. The Center for Interactive Management facility, 1st version, was completed in the School of Engineering and Applied Science at the University of Virginia in 1981 using a room design that I had constructed, with very few departures from my design. The name was chosen to reflect the belief that high-quality management of information would be critical to resolve complexity. Its early clients came from U. S. state and federal forestry resource groups. Another group that became active was the U. S. marine fishery resource groups, which were part of the U. S. National Oceanic and Atmospheric Administration. (Some of the work carried out with these groups was videotaped, and can be seen today at the George Mason University Fenwick Library in Fairfax, Virginia.) This work helped to provide verification along the lines of Axiom 8. One of the things we found in using this facility was that air-conditioning equipment made too much noise, just from blowing air, and made it difficult for participants to hear one another. This was corrected to some extent in the design of later situation rooms. The Center fell victim to high-level institutional disagreements in 1983, and moved to George Mason University (GMU) in 1984, where it became the second Center for Interactive Management.

The University of Northern Iowa Connection. Having reached a greater concern about management, I was fortunate to be a visiting professor in the School of Business at the University of Northern Iowa, thanks to Dr. Robert James Waller, who was then the Dean of that School. During my one-year stay there, I taught several courses involving what is often termed "management science", and sometimes called "operations research". Previously I had only a limited acquaintance with this material. But in teaching topics such as decision analysis, linear programming and the traveling salesman problem, I could see where this type of education was leading. Business school graduates were being given the equivalent of a set of mathematical algorithms of predetermined nature and taught to apply them to resolve a variety of problems that were modest in scale. It was my opinion that the application of these methods might give the graduates an exaggerated view of their management skills. (The University of Northern Iowa was not unique in these offerings, which were standard fare in schools of business.)

Later I would benefit from this experience by recognizing that the use of all numerical methods could be held in abeyance for problematic situations until the structuring of such situations had been essentially completed, in which case the need for numerical algorithms of whatever type would be manifested to anyone who had an inclination to explore the literature of management science and operations research.

The Burroughs Corporation Connection.   Meanwhile, because of the mentioned institutional problems at the University of Virginia, I had taken a position with Burroughs Corporation in Detroit, where my assignment was to make "computers for education software" contracts between Burroughs and universities who would develop educational software for Burroughs microprocessors. I was able to get this program approved and to encumber the first year's budget at a portfolio of several universities, but was fortunate to learn of a position opening at George Mason University for a director of an Institute for Information Technology.   I was offered and accepted this position in 1984, terminating my one-year stay at the corporate headquarters of the Burroughs Corporation, which had added to my understanding of organizations and what they needed to work with complexity.   The second Center for Interactive Management would be part of the anticipated Institute for Information Technology.

The Society for General Systems Research (SGSR) Connection. As my interest had grown in systems, I joined the Society for General Systems Research in 1980. I was elected President of this Society for the year of 1982. There was a distinct difference of world view between the leaders of SGSR and those of the IEEE Society. (SGSR had been started at the University of Michigan in 1955 to reflect the views of a handful of pioneers in the systems movement.   Pictures of several of these appear in the Exhibits.) The manifesto of the SGSR defined a general system as **"any theoretical system of interest to more than one discipline".** That definition was far less ambitious than the earlier Bertalanffian vision of laws for systems in general, but Bertalanffy agreed to the compromise in the belief that even a thousand-mile journey must begin with one step. Ironically, later it was declared by an influential member of the SGSR that "there is no such thing as a general system".

Clearly there are quite a few "general systems" if one understands the definition as stated by the SGSR founders. The comment about 'no such thing" was used (and seemingly accepted) as one reason to change the name of the society twice. Its' successor is now called the "International Society for Systems Science (ISSS)". Notably the first title was not so presumptious as to suggest the existence of a systems science; but rather invited cross-disciplinary research. Fortunately George Klir has kept the "General Systems" language alive with the journal in which my article appears.

The manifesto stated also that the SGSR's major functions would be to

- Investigate the isomorphy of concepts, laws, and models in various fields, and to help in useful transfers from one field to another.
- Encourage the development of adequate theoretical models in the fields which lack them.
- Minimize the duplication of theoretical effort in different fields.
- Promote the unity of science [by] improving communication among specialists.

The International Federation for Systems Research (IFSR) Connection. George Klir has always been an effective torchbearer for the general systems movement. When an opportunity came to bring about a kind of "holding company" for systems societies, George and Bela H. Banathy, along with Gerard de Zeeuw of the Dutch Systems Society and Robert Trappl of the Austrian Society for Cybernetics collaborated to start the International Federation for Systems Research. It would be headquartered in Austria, as Trappl had been able to get Austrian government support for a headquarters with clerical assistance. Very likely this was made easier for him by the earlier housing of IIASA, the International Institute for Applied Systems Analysis, in Austria so that the Austrian government had already experienced benefits from the systems movement.

George Klir was born in Czechoslovakia. Robert Maxwell, who was head of Pergamon Press at the time IFSR began, had also been born in Czechoslovakia. These two one-time Czechs came to a very nice agreement to create a journal for the IFSR which was intended to be a flagship for the systems movement, and to help cement a very fragmented set of activities that lacked coherence. George asked me to be the first Editor-in-Chief for this journal and I accepted. The three founding member Societies that I have already mentioned signed an agreement whereby they would provide various kinds of support for the

IFSR. I accepted the editorship with just two conditions: (a) I would not have to become involved in the business affairs of the new journal, so I could devote my time to the advancement of the field and to quality assurance of the journal, and (b) all of the members of the three founder Societies would receive the journal as a part of their membership. I saw these two conditions as requisite to success.

From the beginning, only the Dutch Systems Society lived up to the agreement. The Austrian Society, being a "verein" was subject to an Austrian law which prohibited revealing the names of members of the Austrian Society. Pergamon Press noted that this made it quite difficult to send copies of the journal to the members. The leadership of the SGSR (soon to be ISSS) immediately began to undermine the IFSR and the new journal by asking Pergamon Press to start a journal only for the SGSR. Promised funding from the member societies never reached Pergamon in a manner and amount consistent with the original promises. As a result I spent quite a bit of time in the later years in business-related talks with a representative of Pergamon Press. Finally, after due notification to the founding members without a suitable response, Pergamon and I agreed that the journal, titled *Systems Research*, would no longer be published by Pergamon, and my association with this activity would cease.

Fortunately the journal did not die. De Zeeuw of the Dutch Systems Society managed to continue to publish it for several years. Then John Wiley and Sons took on the journal to be edited in England by M. C. Jackson of the University of Hull. Still later, the journal *Behavioral Science*, long published by the late James G. Miller, merged with *Systems Research* to become *Systems Research and Behavioral Science*, which is now published six times a year. At the request of M. C. Jackson, I continue to serve on the Editorial Board, and offer suggestions from time to time.

The George Mason University (GMU) Connection. Before inaugurating the second Center for Interactive Management at the George Mason University, a new facility was built to reflect my original design with a few improvements, and it was inaugurated in October of 1995 with Dr. Alexander Christakis as Director, and his associate Dr. David Keever, a Ph. D. in Systems Engineering from the University of

Virginia, as Associate Director. This new facility enabled sponsored Interactive Management work to be carried out for five years, which furnished many valuable insights into how to make groups successful. IASIS, the parent Institute, also provided opportunities for visiting scholars from several countries, including China, Greece, India, and Mexico. But most importantly, it gave us extensive confidence that the various Axioms described earlier were correct.

The Center for Interactive Management, 2nd version, was terminated in 1990, once again involving matters not related to its work, but rather to high-level institutional actions. The Institute for Information Technology, which had been the parent organization, had never materialized, due to institutional matters at the state level in Virginia. Hence, while I continued to direct an Institute, the name was changed to the Institute for Advanced Study in the Integrative Sciences (IASIS). This name was jointly chosen by the late Provost, Dr. David King, and myself. Regrettably he fell victim to cancer, and new institutional arrangements followed. As part of these arrangements, IASIS became a part of TIPP, The Institute for Public Policy, which later would evolve into the School of Public Policy. Directed by Dr. Kingsley Haynes, a compatible home was found for IASIS that would persist for the decade (1990-2000).

One of the visitors to the Center, Surinder K. Batra, who stayed six weeks as a representative of the Tata organization in India, returned to India, eventually obtained a doctorate, and started his own company known as the Centre for Interactive Management India.

Design Science and Interactive Management. Late in the 1980s I wrote a book titled *A Science of Generic Design: Managing Complexity Through System Design.* This was a heavy book with about 600 pages, sized 8½ by 11 in order to make possible the inclusion of readable graphics. The first edition of this book was published in 1990 by Axel Duwe's Intersystems publishing operation in California. Regrettably it became necessary to choose another publisher later, which enabled some modest additions, including study questions, to be added. The second edition was published in 1994 by the Iowa State University Press, thanks to the efforts of Dr. Robert James Waller, who had his earlier essays published there. In the same year, another book was published. I had been working on this book for several years. It was titled *A Handbook of Interactive Management*, and went into great detail concerning the processes, roles, and other factors required to carry out the group processes. Early informal editions of this work were published at George Mason University. However the version that finally reached the Iowa State University Press was a joint effort with my long-time colleague, Prof. Dr. Alda Roxana Cárdenas of the Mexican Instituto Tecnologico y de Estudios Superiores de Monterrey (ITESM) who came to George Mason University to spend her sabbatical period studying Interactive Management and Generic Design Science. Her stay was a key component of a Mexico connection which began in Budapest, and which continues to this day and has been very professionally rewarding.

Roxana had first encountered the ideas involved when she met Dr. Alexander Christakis at a systems society meeting in Budapest. My wife Rose and I were riding on a tour bus and noticed the two of them sitting on an outdoor bench having a conversation, and wondered what it was about. We would learn later that this was the beginning event in what would become a long-standing and very valuable interaction with quite a few Mexicans, arising out of Dr. Christakis' explanation to Roxana. Roxana was accomplished in both English and French, since she had studied economic systems at Aix-en-Provence some years earlier as part of a faculty development program of ITESM. She revised the manuscript of the *Handbook of Interactive Management* completely and made it much more readable. Accordingly, she was named as co-author—a title that she had not asked for, but richly deserved. She had already been teaching generic design science in Mexico by satellite to students and faculty in many of the 28 branch campuses of ITESM. Later she would gain her doctorate in systems science at City University, London, comparing Interactive Management with the Tavistock processes.

Windows™-Based Interactive Management (IM and ISM) Software. Professor Benjamin Broome, at the time a faculty member in the Communications Department at George Mason University, had become aware of the Center for Interactive Management. He established a connection with the GMU Center early in its existence, and began to learn how to facilitate using the two main processes, NGT and ISM.

Because he was quite knowledgeable of computers and software, he would eventually help oversee the writing (mainly by Mr Dangsheng ("Daniel") Ma) of a Windows™ version of software for ISM that incorporated the primary elements of NGT. While the original software had been written for a mainframe, due to the need for speedy computations, improved versions of the original mainframe software had been written since the first version appeared at Battelle. The improved versions used the "Bordering Algorithm" in which the binary matrix evolved from 2 x 2 to 3 x 3 to 4 x 4 , etc. This plan fit in comfortably with Harary's Algorithm. One of the locations where new software was written was the University of Dayton, where Dr. Raymond Fitz led the development. This project was sponsored as part of a multiple university team, with funds from the United States Department of Environmental Education, supplied with great insight by Mr. Walter J. Bogan, Jr., who was its Director. By the time 1984 rolled around, the time had come to do a PC version. Dr. David Keever developed this version as an extension of the mainframe version. For the first time, the Interactive Management work, using NGT and ISM, was divorced from a mainframe and telephone connections. This greatly increased the flexibility of the work.

The English (City University) Connection. With the Center just beginning at the University of Virginia, F. Ross Janes took a Fulbright sabbatical from his position with the Systems Science Department at City University in London, and spent a year at the new Center in order to learn the processes, which he intended to apply upon his return to City. Ross was very helpful in getting the Center started, and carried out some projects there. Later, following his receipt of his doctorate on the subject of ISM and application, he served as dissertation adviser to both Henry Alberts (see later) and Roxana Cárdenas. Regrettably that department was discontinued upon the retirement of its former head and the ascendency of a new Dean. The faculty were dispersed to other parts of City. This phenomenon of the "disappearing systems department" came to be very common, a similar fate befalling the very successful Social Systems Science Department at the University of Pennsylvania Wharton School, coinciding with the retirement of Dr. Russell Ackoff.

The Ford Motor Company Connection. In 1989, at about the time the Center at GMU was terminated, the Ford Motor Company Research Laboratory was beginning to look for a scientific base for system design. Dr. Scott Staley, who was a group leader there, contacted me at GMU to find out what was happening. By that time, the book on Generic Design was in the hands of the first publisher.

Quality Function Deployment (QFD). As it turned out, Ford had been using, for design purposes, something that had become known as "Quality Function Deployment". This process was described in the *Harvard Business Review* (HBR) in 1987 in a paper jointly authored by faculty in Cambridge, MA.[20] I was surprised when people pointed out to me that what was described there was essentially the same system that had been published by J. D. Hill of Battelle and myself in an IEEE journal 16 years earlier, under the heading "Unified Program Planning" (UPP)[21]. This system consisted of a set of matrices that were linked to each other. Some of these matrices were triangular, and others were rectangular. Collectively they formed a feedback system with many interrelationships. The IEEE paper that Hill and I had published had even showed an insert drawing of an extended set of such matrices linked together in a feedback loop and applied to U.S. Air Force planning for a VSTOL aircraft. The HBR paper attributed the QFD process to Mitsubishi Shipyards. Under the influence of the HBR paper, Ford had committed significant resources to program the QFD process, which required construction of large matrices by hand, using inputs from various engineering staff. I saw immediately and was able easily to convince Dr. Staley that the Interactive Management system was far superior to the QFD system. In fact, the early work on ISM as opposed to UPP was initiated in recognition that there was no obvious way to get consistency in filling large matrices without using Harary's key theorem that became the basis for ISM, and which I have credited in many papers written since that time.

---

[20] J. R. Hauser and D. Clausing (1988), "The House of Quality", *Harvard Business Review*, May-June, 63-75.
[21] Hill, J. D. and J. N. Warfield (1972), "Unified Program Planning", *IEEE Transactions on Systems, Man, and Cybernetics* SMC2(5), 610-621.

As the use of Interactive Management spread within Ford, members of Ford's international community began to take part in some of the sessions. Included in some of these were Owen Berkeley-Hill and Roy Smith from Ford's English operations. Both became supporters of Interactive Management. Roy took advantage of Ford's liberal policy of allowing employees to engage in community activities as part of their Ford service. Roy ran several sessions, including one to explore declining attendance in the Catholic Church in England[22]. He also lectured on Interactive Management at City University. Now retired from Ford, Roy continues to apply Interactive Management from time to time.

The Defense Systems Management College (DSMC) Connection. A gradual buildup of sponsored work for IASIS with Ford came about. This occurred with some overlap with another significant effort involving Interactive Management that went on at the Defense Systems Management College (DSMC). Located at Fort Belvoir, Virginia, this College had been established around 1960 at the request of Dr. David Packard, a co-founder of the Hewlett-Packard Company, who had accepted temporarily a high position in the US Department of Defense, where major shortcomings in understanding of systems had become apparent. One of the faculty at DSMC (among several) who became interested in Interactive Management and Generic Design Science was Professor Henry C. Alberts. At the beginning of this interest we had run one session at George Mason University involving Henry and his colleagues. About a year later, an agreement was signed where I would offer some short courses at DSMC to familiarize people there with my work. At about this time there was a major upheaval going on because of what had become to be symbolized as the "800-dollar toilet seats" bought by the Defense Department; namely very high-priced acquisitions. Henry took it upon himself to start working to change the acquisition system. In this activity, which ultimately required five years of work using Interactive Management with more than 300 program managers, Henry was supported by several of the leaders at DSMC, mostly at the level of Provost or the Commandant of the College. As a

---

[22] Results from this work are included in (Warfield, 2002).

result of that, Congress passed, in 1994, something called "The Federal Acquisition Streamlining Act of 1994, Public Law 103-355". There was no clear trail appearing between IASIS, Henry Alberts, DSMC, and the Congress. But nonetheless, this is the trail that actually produced that Act.

As part of ongoing contracts, DSMC and Ford provided some support to construct the Windows™ version of the Interactive Management software. The detailed work in software development was shared by several graduate students supported by the IASIS Contracts, but the outstanding User Guide was written by Professor Benjamin Broome, also supported by IASIS grants.

The Mexico Connection. In the meantime, developments were proceeding apace in Mexico. A contract was written with IASIS to support some training in Interactive Management. Broome and Christakis gave some short courses in Monterrey. Later I offered a short course in Monterrey on "The Mathematics of Modeling"; a topic I would later change to "The Mathematics of Structure". Attending this course were two from the USA, Dr. Scott M. Staley of the Ford Research Laboratories and Walter J. Bogan, Jr., who had been so instrumental in sponsoring my developmental work on ISM software and applications at the University of Virginia. Also attending were ITESM faculty from several campuses. From the Monterrey Campus there was Roxana Cárdenas, who had initiated my short course, and her friends and colleagues Carmen Moreno and Mary Carmen Temblador. From the Léon Campus (in the state of Guanajuato) there were Carlos Flores and Reynaldo Treviño. Shortly after this one-week course was finished, Roxana and Carmen gave a second course in Léon at the request of Carlos and Reynaldo and their associates.

Carlos, Reynaldo, and other colleagues at ITESM Campus Léon then began to run sessions with various sectors in the Mexican State of Guanajuato. Along with the Governor's office, they initiated a comprehensive planning activity for the State in particular, and Mexico in general. This extensive planning continued with what was dubbed the "First Interloquium" in which several hundred people gathered to listen to speakers talk about the future of the world, and to observe Interactive Management sessions on the stage of the State Auditorium of

Guanajuato[23]. This remarkable event was followed some years later with a still more remarkable event. The former Governor of Guanajuato (Vicente Fox) was elected President of Mexico. Earlier Carlos and Reynaldo had left ITESM to become part of the State government. At this writing, they are both prominent members of the federal government of Mexico. From their location in Mexico City, they continue to carry out Interactive Management work involving democratization of Mexico through participative processes. Their photographs are among those in the Exhibits, along with those of others who have applied Interactive Management in numerous settings..

The African Connections. Interactive Management sessions were held in three African nations: Ghana, Liberia, and South Africa. Two were held in Liberia, both being conducted by Carol Jeffrey. Carol learned the subject at the Defense Systems Management College. When her husband accepted a position as president of a bank in Monrovia, Carol chose to become active there in local situations. She conducted an Interactive Management session with Liberian women on the topic of the status of women in Liberia, in preparation for the international meeting of women in Beijing. Later she conducted a session on disarmament and demobilization with warlords and warriors, which culminated in a respite from the hostilities that had plagued the country for years. Later one was held in Ghana which I planned in collaboration with Dr. Moses N. B. Ayiku, and which was facilitated by Carol Jeffrey, Roxana Cárdenas, and Ghanains who were being trained to carry out this work. This session had to do with the reorganization of the Centre for Scientific and Industrial Research (CSIR) in Ghana. It seems that researchers in the universities in Ghana had been supported 100% (though not lavishly) by the Government, which had grown tired of the failure to see any payoff for the nation. Accordingly the Government warned that within three years only 70% subsidy would be available, and researchers would have to find clients to serve to earn the remaining 30% of their income.

---

[23] Details are included in the Fenwick Library "Warfield Special Collection", courtesy of Reynaldo Treviño.

The application in South Africa was held at the university in Cape Town on the subject of how to organize the publishing industry in South Africa. This particular application suffered from poor facilities planning, being held in a hotel room with abundant vehicular traffic just outside the window, and with a very long table so participants couldn't hear each other. The insensitivity of planners to the requirements for effective communication was never more clear than in this application which, fortunately, was able to move to a better room for the second and final day.

The Verifiability Axiom (Axiom 8) Revisited. The reader may have noted the importance attached to Axiom 8, and to the documentation above of a variety of connections that ultimately provided excellent evidence of what Axiom 8 described as essential. With all of the activity that had grown up (much of which has not been mentioned here, but is documented elsewhere), I confidently assumed that the work would be recognized and become a part of curricula in higher education. It did so in Mexico, and to some extent in other countries and has footholds in both India and China. But in the United States it is best described as neglected. Universities in the USA have their own tracks and are generally determined to follow them. These tracks have been found to be functional in terms of tenure and promotion, where they rely almost entirely on individual activity as opposed to group activity. Even in a few US universities where group activity got a foothold in educational programs, the extensive documentation hopefully foreseen in Axiom 8 drew little or no attention. Cognitive burden is almost uniformly neglected and the importance of software for structuring goes largely unrecognized.

A great deal of emphasis had been placed on the resolution of complexity in the numerous publications that my colleagues and I produced. But complexity, as a subject of research and writing, started to mushroom in the late 1980s. My computerized search on "complexity" in 1972 (at the Ohio State University) had generated a grand total of two articles, both by John Kemeny[24]. But now, people who were well-connected at high levels or who were independently wealthy and looking for something to do were able to gain support and following. A recent search on "complexity" via the Google™ system produced 279,334 articles on complexity and 4,900,001 on systems. My work was generally not acknowledged by those engaged in these activities. This was very disappointing, and it showed that my Axiom set was hardly complete, and severely overlooked some important considerations. But as C. S. Peirce remarked "truth, crushed to earth, will rise again".

I felt that I had failed significantly to gain acceptance of ideas and methods that were very sorely needed in society. There could be no doubt that there were many local situations that would benefit greatly from the use of Interactive Management. Even in Ford Motor Company, where a whole series of successes had been achieved (and which continue to this day), acceptance has been very strong among middle managers, but formally absent in top management. This does not mean that top management did not become aware of what was happening with Interactive Management. On the contrary, a certain pattern began to manifest itself. Whenever an issue arose at corporate level that could not be dealt with, a request came down the bureaucracy to carry out Interactive Management work. While Ford had constructed and furnished its own situation room along the lines designed first for the Center at the University of Virginia, it would not provide corporate funding on anything but a piecemeal basis to staff Interactive Management. This was all the more troublesome, since Ford established a vice presidency for process leadership, whose office ignored the process that was demonstrably providing great benefits to the company.

Even the US Congress, which had passed legislation in 1994 to correct defects in acquisition management was now backtracking in ways that showed that it did not understand the problems of acquisition

---

[24] John Kemeny spent time at the Princeton Institute for Advanced Study, became a professor of mathematics at Dartmouth College, later became President of Dartmouth College, and chaired a very successful federal commission to investigate and report on the Three Mile Island nuclear disaster.

management, and was ready to respond to lobbyists whose firms did not enjoy the changes that had been made in acquisition practices. Attendees at congressional hearings reported to me that Senators Roth and Thurmond had made particularly unresponsive comments in relation to the changes that had been worked out over a five-year period involving more than 300 program managers in redesigning the system.

A New Challenge. A new challenge faced me. Where had I overlooked important matters, and what could I do to correct this situation? At this point in my career, I felt that the axiomatic base represented by the twelve Axioms stated to this point in this paper could now be taken not merely as assumptions upon which further actions would be based, but rather as proved ideas, founded in excellent science, that warranted broad acceptance. But clearly that set was not adequate. It was now time to reconsider.

The China Connection. In the late 1990s, China became very interested in the subject of complexity. As part of my thinking on organizational issues, I developed what I called "Killer Assumptions". These Assumptions had two key properties: (1) they were often **valid** in normal circumstances and (2) they were usually **invalid** when complexity was involved. When I was invited to China to give a plenary address, I chose the subject of the Killer Assumptions for the talk. Also speaking at the talk was Cheng Siwei, director of the management department of the Chinese National Science Foundation. This remarkable man apparently liked the talk, because he and Dean M. C. Jackson of the University of Hull jointly invited me to present again in Shanghai at the ISSS Conference in 2002. But before that took place, I had a guest at IASIS in George Mason University. He was Dr. Xuefeng Song, who at the time was the Dean of the Graduate School at the Chinese University of Mining and Technology (CUMT). His six-month stay was sponsored through Cheng Siwei. Xuefeng had already become familiar with the positivist trend in the study of complexity, and must have found the behavioral side somewhat disconcerting at first. Anyway this very bright and personable young man returned to China after his 6-month sabbatical and became Dean of the School of Business at CUMT. Some of his students are now translating my book on Generic Design Science. By working with him I was able to gain additional insight into the organizational nature of complexity. And soon another opportunity arose.

The India Connection Revisited. For some years, Mr. G. S. Chandy (mentioned earlier) had been considering the possible use of ISM in managing large companies. In the late 1990s, he started a small company to create what he called the "One-Page Management System", "an operating system for the human mind". This concept used an extensive set of "options fields" for different parts of an organization, all reachable from a central point, the "one page". It is now in the final stages of its testing, and may soon be evaluated in a large-scale test in India.

The Japan Connection Revisited. I was pleased to learn that my friend of several decades from HItachi, Koichi Haruna, had risen through the ranks to become the head of Hitachi's three systems laboratories. After giving up that position, he is now engaged in a research program in Hitachi having to do with a subject that had come to the fore in the early 1970s when Bill Linvill and Koichi visited Battelle: namely "community creative process...for resolving the community problematique".

The Mexico Connection Revisited. Many of the Mexicans who learned and applied Interactive Management are either in high-level positions in the government of Mexico, or have been promoted into the higher echelons of their universities, or have started their own consulting businesses.

The Study of Management Beliefs in the Killer Assumptions. Until the late 1990s, the idea that managers believed the Killer Assumptions lacked empirical evidence. Now an opportunity arose to gather empirical evidence. Professor George H. "Tony" Perino at DSMC became interested in collecting data on two aspects of my work. We had already come to suspect that people lacked the skills to read the graphics that they developed.

Testing Structural Reading Skills. Tony tested structural reading skills with more than a hundred managers or aspiring managers to see how well they could gain insights by examining a structure related to the manufacturing of pumps. He made the startling discovery that the managers' performance was poorer than what would be expected from a random respondent. In retrospect, this was explained by the fact that many of the managers were educated as mechanical engineers, and responded to the questions based on their experience instead of on what the structure revealed. (Tony chose part of a structure that appeared in *The Science of Generic Design*. In the situation represented there, a group of engineers used the results of ISM structuring to study a five-factor influence group on pump manufacturing. This work with a set of five, instead of an individual cause, produced excellent results. But alas, the managers who were tested behaved more like the engineers working fruitlessly with the pump manufacture until they applied the ISM process with the help of Dr. Robert James Waller!!!). After those results were obtained, Tony tested the beliefs of a sizeable group of individual managers and also of faculty colleagues at DSMC concerning the Killer Assumptions versus what I had identified as the "Demands of Complexity". The results were reported in his doctoral dissertation in the School of Public Policy at GMU and, later, in part, in the *Acquisition Review*[25] (from the Defense Acquisition University).

Manager and Faculty Beliefs in the Killer Assumptions. A great deal of data was reported by Professor Perino. It is not appropriate here to repeat all the data or even a significant amount. But suffice it to say that several of the key Killer Assumptions enjoyed considerable currency among both groups tested. On the other hand, it was encouraging to note that, for every one of the Killer Assumptions, the faculty group's support was less than that of the managers.

- **Phase 4. Three Years of Aggregation and Reorganization: The Emergence of Systems Science.** The applications work done in Phase 3 furnished significant insights into human behavior when faced with complexity. Data had been accumulated showing what I called "Spreadthink" (Warfield, 1995). This readily reproducible phenomenon could be seen, for example, in voting results obtained each time the Nominal Group

---

[25] For details, see G. H. Perino (1999), *Complexity: A Cognitive Barrier to Defense Systems Acquisition* (Ph. D. Dissertation, School of Public Policy, George Mason University, Fairfax, VA).

Technique was used. As the published article explained, it is a mark of the presence of complexity that every individual who knows something about a problematic situation sees it quite differently. The correlation between what any two individuals believes to be most important is extremely small. This finding is of great importance to managers for two reasons. First, the manager is also a victim of this particular behavioral pathology, and should not anticipate ready acceptance of the manager's point of view in any problematic situation. Second, the manager should realize that a major challenge to be faced is that of bringing any measure of consensus to a group of partially-informed individuals who might be expected to form a work team. Spreadthink assumed a place in the panoply of other pathologies such as Janis' groupthink and Miller's "magical number seven".

The Greece Connection. The Spreadthink (group) pathology needs to be seen in the light of another discovery that was made. Through the connection with Dr. Alexander Christakis, one of the visitors to the GMU Center for Interactive Management was Iannis Kapelouzos, a social scientist. He spent a sabbatical leave there from his position on a supreme court in Greece. He undertook to study the correlation between points of view held by participant groups before and after the application of ISM. Much to my amazement, and I suppose the amazement of everyone who had been associated with Interactive Management, **he found zero correlation between beliefs before and after application of ISM**. Since ISM had been developed as a group learning tool, this finding was not only amazing but also very gratifying. Kapelouzos concluded that there could only be one explanation of this effect: the ISM process enabled the participants to learn from one another, and their views changed as a result of this learning.

Please recall that whenever a relationship appears graphically on a structure, it is a result of voting in the ISM process as to whether a relationship exists. This means that any structure developed by a group with ISM necessarily portrays the majority viewpoint in every detail. No relationship among elements is shown there unless it has received at least a majority vote from the participants. All of the elements being related have been subjected to an extensive period of clarification by group discussion.

Laws of Complexity. This situation and others that had been observed along the way led me to construct and publish **"20 Laws of Complexity"** along with rationale and background for each law (Warfield, 2002). Seen in aggregate, these furnished a kind of composite that an individual could use to assess the merits of what had been discovered. I viewed them as critical components of a science of complexity, and trusted again that their statement would help gain acceptance of the work.

Metrics of Complexity. Those who write about systems tend, for the most part, to be mathematically and numerically inclined. I felt that this group would be more likely to study and accept the work if it were possible to define and obtain numerical values for metrics of complexity. I developed two types of metric. One type assigned numerical measures to each of the problems that had been defined by the group as among the most important during the NGT process. The other type assigned numerical measures to the structures developed during the use of ISM. My colleague, Dr. Scott Staley of Ford, computed numerical values for quite a few of the sessions run there, published the results[26], and later noted that by comparing alternative designs for a product information management system, Ford had decided to choose a system architecture with the minimum "Situational Complexity Index" for its corporate-wide use. As far as is known, other application groups have taken little note of these metrics, probably because they had already determined that the processes were successful and needed no numerical reinforcement. On the other hand, those who had not tried the processes apparently had either not become aware of the metrics, or had not valued them significantly.

Organizational Factors. Participative processes must be threatening to powerful executives. They are not accustomed to accepting

---

[26] Staley, S. M. (1995), "Complexity Measurements of Systems Design" in *Integrated Design and Process Technology* (Ertas, A; Ramamoorthy C. V., Tanik, M. M.; Esat, I; Feniali, F; and Taleb-Bendiab, Eds.), IDPT-Vol 1, 153-161 (Society for Design and Process Science, Austin, TX).

painstakingly worked out plans for resolving complexity. This view is most sharply seen in the actions of a certain manager. He had already decided upon a course of action. When the IM participant group proposed a different course of action he asked to know how they had arrived at their conclusion. After some discussion, he made this classic remark: "I disagree with and will not accept your conclusion, but I admire the way in which you reached it." A year later he asked the group to review their work and come in with a new recommendation. They made the same recommendation.

While I recognized early in the work, thanks to writings of scholars like Argyris and Downs, that organizational factors would be very important in getting acceptance of my work, I constantly underestimated and did not plan for the negative aspects of the great strength of the higher levels of power structures in organizations. When I see what appear to be very poor, self-serving, or illegal decisions being made, I often remember a remark by my one-time-research sponsor, Walter J. Bogan. Walter said "there is no law against stupidity". In many situations, it is virtually impossible to make a distinction between stupidity and an illegal intent as the motivating force in a particularly bad decision. I had always felt that if a well-documented, successful process could become the source of key decisions, it would become much easier to determine whether managers were not very bright, or whether they were operating on personal agendas which negated the results of quality group work.

Any high-level organizational decision often has impacts extending outward in the organization or even beyond it into other organizations. Once this situation is taken seriously, there is a virtual torrent of possible explanations for bad decisions, recognizing that no one has the insight required to determine all of the ramifications and consequences of a particular decision. Whether it would help to have an organizational model is debatable. But I have concluded that the tried-and-true organizational model known as the "organization chart" has been extended far beyond its useful range. For many purposes, a virtual chart will be much better than the actual chart and, if it is not adequate, one can always supplement it with the actual chart.

The Coherent (Virtual) Organization. The chosen virtual organization is a three-level organization. It becomes coherent when people in the three levels of the organization are, as the saying now goes, "on the same page".

In the Vertically-Coherent (VC) Organization, everyone in the organization shares a certain awareness of what is going on, to the extent that decisions are not made blindly, but with substantial insight into the likely effects of the decisions. Since the concept of VC Organization is fundamental to the resolution of complexity it will be helpful, when discussing it, to have a model of the organization in mind. For this purpose it will be assumed that the organization has three levels: the **strategic- or topmost level**, with the fewest membership of any of the levels; the **tactical- or middle level**, with a larger membership; and the **producing- or lowest level**, with much larger membership than either of the other two levels. For convenience in discussing this three-level organization, it will be assumed that everyone is a manager.   There are first-level (strategic) managers; second-level (tactical) managers, and third-level (operational) managers. These distinctions enable us to discuss responsibility for taking actions, and to suggest an allocation of authority, hence responsibility among the three levels. It will be assumed also that there is some oversight body to which the first-level managers report, called the "Board".

The Alberts Pattern (Alberts, 1995). In his work using the Interactive Management system to lead the redesign of the U. S. Defense Acquisition System, **Henry Alberts**' groups identified 678 problems (intermittently, over a five-year period). These were placed into 20 categories. The categories were placed into 6 areas. If we call the lowest level in the hierarchy the Producing Level, the middle level the Tactical Level, and the top level the Strategic Level, we see that the existence of this 3-level structure provides the basis for vertical coherence in the organization. This structure is called the "**Alberts** Vertical Coherence Pattern". It is illustrated in **Figure A3-1.**

The **first-level managers**, with six areas to deal with, can see from the details contained in that pattern how the 20 categories of problems reside within the six areas, and which categories are part of more than one area. This enables effective communication among the first-level managers, and between the first-level and second-level managers. The **second-level managers**, in turn, can see which of the 678 problems lie within their unique oversight and which lie in more than one category. As problems are solved, the descriptive structures are modified, enabling a constant up-to-date portrait of what progress is being made in enhancing the ability of the organization to perform its duties effectively and efficiently. The **third-level managers**, who are intimately involved at any one time in resolving some of the 678 problems, are able to convey to the higher levels what they perceive as essential to resolving those problems; and the higher levels are able to perceive the potential impacts of high-level decisions that might be made, or the potential impacts of decisions that might be promoted or made by their Board[27]. An organization so equipped is in a position to be a VC-Organization.

The Cárdenas-Rivas Pattern (1995). Working independently, but using the same Interactive Management system, researchers found a similar pattern to represent redesign options for a systems engineering curriculum at ITESM (The "Monterrey Institute of Technology") in Monterrey, Mexico (**Cárdenas and Rivas, 1995**). That pattern is structurally very similar to the **Alberts** Pattern. The **Cárdenas-Rivas** Pattern is shown in **Figure A3-2.**

The lowest level in the 3-level hierarchy consists of 270 design options. These appear in 20 categories (the same number as in the **Alberts** Pattern!). The categories appear in four areas.

The work cited shows that these "coherence patterns" can be developed with the support of the IM system. The development of the **Alberts** pattern took place over an elapsed five year period. The development of the **Cárdenas-Rivas** pattern required less than an elapsed year. I speak of "elapsed" time, because all of this work was intermittent with a sequence of Interactive Management activity interspersed with regular work assignments of all the actors that were involved.

---

[27] One should not suppose that what has just been described was only an academic study. The work described here became the basis for legislation by the U. S. Congress, known as "The Federal Acquisition Streamlining Act of 1994".

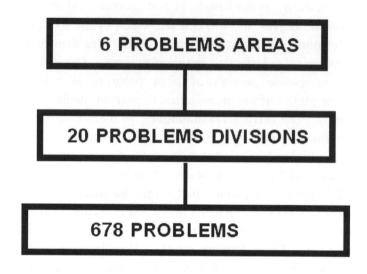

Fig. A3-1 The Alberts Pattern (Of Problems)

As in many instances, these empirical discoveries stimulated the development of a generic idea; in this instance, the Vertically-Coherent Organization. The principal benefit of this probably is that it provided a discursivity component that enabled the work of groups to be discussed in organizational settings without worrying about or incorporating specific organizational details unless and until they were needed as part of a broader action perspective. Unfortunately this addition did not necessarily resolve what I had come to view as a top-level negative in an organization: namely the agenda of an executive who was not prepared to be moved by careful work done at lower levels in the organization. This particular situation could benefit from a small number of observations that arose from the many instances of empirical evidence available to me. This observation was that whenever the individual who had the power to make a final decision on a major program had been involved in the detailed work using Interactive Management, individual made the decision according to what was learned from that experience. To use a common expression, he "owned" the thinking that came from that experience. If, however, the person who held the final decision-making power had not been involved, the decision tended to emerge from the prior agenda, and everything else was window-dressing. (This generalization awaits further experience, where it may be reinforced, amended, or discarded.) It is likely that much of the behavior of top-level executives arises from their interaction with management gurus, consultants described in a book using the language "witch doctors" by two editors from *The Economist*[28].

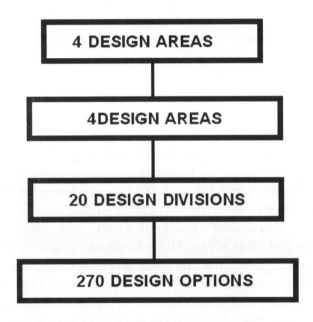

Fig. A3-2 The Cardenas-Rivas Pattern (of Options)

---

[28] Micklethwait, J., and Wooldridge, A. (1996), *The Witch Doctors: Making Sense of the Management Gurus,* Times Books, New York.

One can readily determine by a survey of what is happening that many consultants are taking advantage of the complexities envisaged by top managements of organizations to offer services aimed at helping them resolve the complexities. But scientific evidence of the efficacy of the methods that are offered is inevitably obscure.

External Factors for the Coherent Organization. I have shown that two independent practitioners worked with quite different groups on quite different issues, using Interactive Management, and both found that results of their work could be represented by *three-level inclusion structures*. One practitioner found a problems field. The other discovered an options field., It is only a small step to imagine that the organizations can be viewed as virtual three-level entities. Still this does not mean that the power structure is fully represented by the three-level structures. Alberts' teams discovered that about 10% of the problems that they identified could not be resolved by their acquisition system design. Upon investigation, they discovered that the power to correct those problems lay outside the Department of Defense, in the administrative branch of government (The "Board"). A similar recognition was found in the work in Mexico, where a modest part of the problematic situation involved factors lying above the Systems Engineering Department, where the work took place. A similar observation was made at Ford Motor Company, as mentioned earlier. To add to that description, the first group that used Interactive Management at Ford discovered that about 75% of the problems that emerged from group work had a "cultural component". The participants were surprised to discover that about 70% of those problems lay within the prerogative of the sponsoring management, and only 30% were the responsibility of higher-level groups. But one must be aware of the fact that the top level exerts continuing long-term effects on lower levels, hence can actually undo advances made at the lower levels. These insights are all relevant to the way in which Interactive Management is applied in organizations. There is no proof to validate the next Axiom, but it should be taken as a working Axiom until reasons to do otherwise are found.

Axiom 14 (The Ownership and Commitment Axiom). Whenever a group expends great energy and applies scientifically tested processes to a problematic situation, with strong process leadership, the participants and observers (if any) can be expected to "own" the results, because they all reflect majority points of view. But since evidence exists to show that such results are readily bypassed by top-level executives, an important part of the plan of action to develop the results will include participation of a "champion" from the strategic level in the Virtual Organization. This means that the top-level management of the organization should be represented, and should make a commitment to deliver a strong endorsement of the results to those who have the power to make the final decision.

Even if that power lies outside the host organization (as Alberts understood to be true in part in his work) it will be desirable to have links to that power represented in the work. In Alberts' case, he kept the attorneys who served the relevant House and Senate committees appraised of the work throughout the five year period, so when the time came to press for a legislative act, the 1994 law was passed in near-record time. Axiom 14 is a special case of a broader Axiom that will provide general guidance unless or until it shall be demonstrated to be faulty.

Axiom 15 (The Coherent Virtual Organization). The Three-Level Model of the Coherent Organization should be formally recognized in developing a plan for any program of work on a problematic situation. (If more than one organization is involved, the Axiom should be adapted to that circumstance.) Specific components of the plan of action should incorporate actors from all three levels, with articulated commitments for followup to the program of work.

Along with Axiom 15, it became clear that the early thoughts about working environments deserved more attention, which is now given in Axiom 16.

Axiom 16. (The Infrastructure Axiom). Because of the extreme challenge associated with complexity, all possible factors should be brought to bear on its resolution, and the establishment, budgeting, and operation of two physical facilities is vital to this purpose: the situation room and the observatorium. The former is equipped and staffed to provide the working space for group activity, including space for both participants and observers. The latter is a facility organized to hold the products of group work for later observation, study, discussion, and amendment (if required).

The Organization of Systems Science. With the foregoing concepts as resources, it gradually became clear that it would be possible to organize systems science. The epiphany related to this occurred, through the idea that a systems science could, and necessarily should, have sub-sciences. This idea came about by recognizing that systems science should be an over-arching science that is competent to serve all kinds of problematic situations.

Because of this, it had to be a **topically-neutral science**, not constrained to work with a restricted class of problematic situations. These thoughts posed two main challenges:

- How to reconcile the neutral nature of systems science with the existence of many methods that have been proposed for working with systems, some of which are probably presumed by their advocates to be a part of systems science
- How to decide which sub-sciences would be a part of systems science, given that there are already in existence a variety of areas called "science" that might make claims to be part of systems science

Resolving the First Challenge. The groundwork for resolving the first challenge had already been laid by distinguishing between a science and the domain of a science. The **domain of a science** has been described to consist of the science itself and another component that involves **the collection of problematic situations in which the science could be applied**. All of the non-neutral methods could be thought of as available in this larger component which might be called the "Arena". From this Arena they could be called into play whenever it is determined from the application of systems science that they are needed. The products of application of systems science include the determination of what specialized or biased methods are needed to complete work that has begun by applying systems science.

Resolving the Second Challenge: Sciences Within Systems Science. The experiences gained from several hundred applications of Interactive Management offered significant empirical evidence of which sub-sciences should be thought of as component sciences of systems science. The diversity of these applications, linked together through the common methodology of Interactive Management, provided ample opportunity to respond to the second challenge.

Science of Description. It is commonplace in practice to strive to move too soon and too directly to a resolution of complexity, before the problematic situation is well understood. Following Foucault's conclusion, a science of description supports the description of a problematic situation by problematization. Using NGT to generate problems, and using ISM to form a problematique and a problems field, the problematic situation is described in ways that are highly responsive to local concerns. Quality control is obtained by using Harary's Theorem of Assured Model Consistency, and the problem field makes the description suitable for later application of Ashby's Law of Requisite Variety at design time.

Science of Design. In applying the science of design, NGT is used to generate sets of options, one set for each category in the problems field. Then applying Ashby's famous Law of Requisite Variety, one or more options is chosen from each category in the problems field. The latter are referred to as dimensions of the problematic situation.

Science of Complexity. The science of complexity draws on what is known about behavior and the products of prior work to enable computation of metrics of complexity. These numbers along with the structures generated previously provide significant and interpretable inputs to the next science. From this science comes the **"Work Program of Complexity"** (Warfield, 2002) detailing what has to be done, in what sequence, to resolve the complexity in the problematic situation.

Science of Action. The established system of Interactive Management forms the science of action. It is quite sufficient to carry out most of the Work Program of Complexity, carrying it to the point where methods are drawn from the Arena, and where major decisions are made at the Strategic Level of the Coherent Organization.

Figure A3-3 summarizes the foregoing comments, with respect to the sub-science components of systems science.

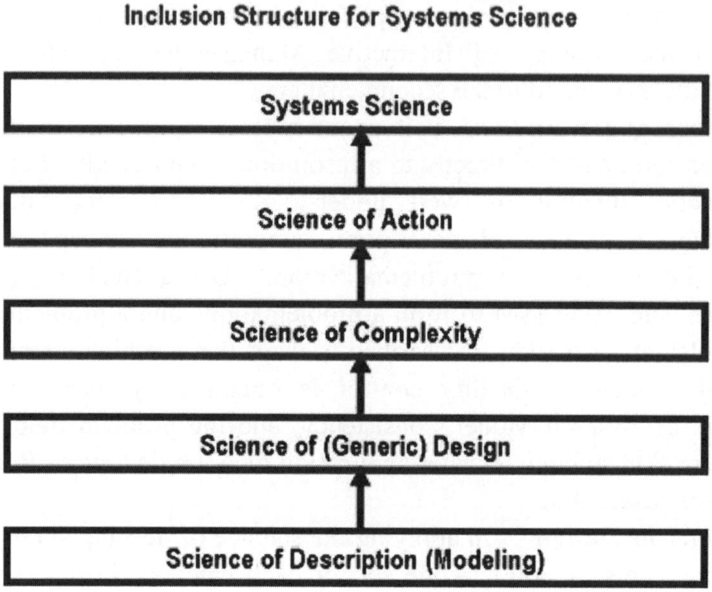

Inclusion Structure for Systems Science

Fig. A3-3 Summary of the Complexicon

The Complexicon. Because what has been described here constitutes a unique body of discovery and aggregation, a unique name is needed to describe it. A name chosen for this purpose is "Complexicon". **Figure A3-4** summarizes the Complexicon.

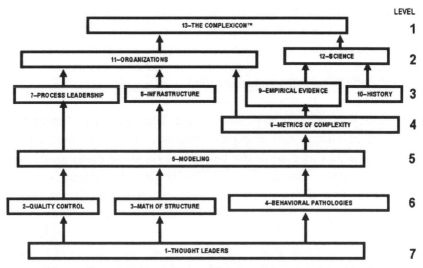

Figure A3-4. Organizing the Complexicon™: Transforming Complexity Into Understanding. The arrows represent the flow of understanding and the box contents represent what is to be understood. The Levels and Box Numbers are presentation aids.

Notes on Fig A3-4 - At **Level 7, Box 1**, we find thought leaders. These people provide leadership in three key areas: language, thought about thought, and human behavioral pathologies. At **Level 6, Box 2** (on the left), we find quality control leaders on language. The mathematics of structure **Box 3** is the key to applying the work of thought leaders on thought itself. The empirical work of behavioral scientists enable us to understand those human pathologies **Box 4** that frustrate working individually or together to resolve complexity. The integration of the components at **Level 6** are found in **Level 5** in modeling **Box 5**, whatever the type of modeling we are considering, but especially in modeling structure of problematic situations. Requirements for modeling help us learn (at **Levels 4 and 3**) the nature of Process Leadership **Box 7**, the kind of infrastructure required to carry out high-quality modeling **Box 8**, and the metrics that we can use to measure complexity **Box 6**. The metrics offer empirical evidence **Box 9** to support all of the thought that has gone on before. In organizations (**Level 2**) process leadership is carried out in the ambience of appropriate infrastructure, with a clear understanding of the nature of complexity (as evidenced through the metrics, with values obtained in numerous problematic situations). Empirical evidence **Box 9** is found in all of the preceding (lower) elements. Taken together with what can be learned from history **Box 10** about science **Box 11**, the ingredients of a sound science for working with problematic situations is found **Box 12**. This science, together with what is learned about organizations **Box 11** is integrated to form the Complexicon: a system for transforming complexity into understanding **Box 13**.

Managing the Unmanageable. I chose the phrase "managing the unmanageable" as an overview term for a series of slide presentations. These presentations are identified by numbers in the various boxes in **Figure A3-4**. The titles of the slide presentations, and the headings under which they have been placed, are offered in **Exhibit 12** (web site, Footnote 1). These titles illustrate the variety encountered in the research, and the central topics identified.

Conclusions. In retrospect and hindsight, my central goal was to create and document a systems science complete with foundations, theory, methodology, and empirical evidence from the domain of the science. I chose this goal in the belief that there are many problematic situations on earth that can benefit greatly from collaborative work—collaboration that is not likely to take place productively without the benefit of the sciences described here that make up systems science.

Whether this goal is the one that I started with is debatable; but it seems that I can make it believable to myself in light of the various environments, events, dates, and empirical evidence that have accumulated over the years.

References (to supplement the footnotes and contents of the web site identified in Footnote 1).

Warfield, J. N. (1995), "Spreadthink: Explaining Ineffective Groups", *Systems Research* 12(1), 5-14.

Warfield, J. N. (2002), *Understanding Complexity: Thought and Behavior*, Ajar Publishing Company, Palm Harbor, Florida

Warfield, J. N. (2003a), *The Mathematics of Structure,* Ajar Publishing Company, Palm Harbor, Florida.

Warfield, J. N. (2003b), "A Proposal for Systems Science", *Systems Research and Behavioral Science* 20(6), 507-520.

Warfield, J. N. (2004), "Linguistic Adjustments: Precursors to Understanding Complexity", *Systems Research and Behavioral Science* 21(2), 123-145.

Appendix A. Persons Pictured in Exhibits 1 to 11
(http://policy.gmu.edu/res/jwarfield/)

Exhibit 1. Persons Well-Known in the Systems Movement: Ackoff, Ashby, B. H. Banathy, Bertalanffy, Boulding, Checkland, Churchman, Forrester, François, Hall, Klir, Rapoport.

Exhibit 2. Some Thought Leaders on Second-Order Thought-1 (chronologically listed): Aristotle, Abèlard, Leibniz, Alexander Pope, De Morgan, Boole, Cayley, Gibbs, Peirce, Hilbert, Bochenski, Harary

Exhibit 3. Some Thought Leaders on Second-Order Thought-2: Kant, Frege, Ashby, Michel Foucault, George J. Friedman

Exhibit 4. Some Action Leaders in Interactive Management-1: Alberts (USA), Ayiku (Ghana), Batra (India), Berkeley-Hill (England), Broome (USA), Caffarel (and children) (Mexico), Cárdenas (Mexico), Chandy (India), Christakis (USA-Greece)

Exhibit 5. Some Action Leaders in Interactive Management-2: Conaway (USA), Ernzen (USA), Flores (Mexico), Fitz (USA), Gulledge (USA), Harris (USA), Haruna (Japan), House (USA), Janes (England)

Exhibit 6. Some Action Leaders in Interactive Management-3: Jeffrey (USA), Kawamura (USA-Japan), Ma (USA-China), Magliocca (USA), McDonald (USA), Moreno (Mexico), Patkar (India), Perino (USA), Rodger (Canada)

Exhibit 7. Some Action Leaders in Interactive Management-4: Jorge Rodriguez (Mexico), Ricardo Rodriguez (Peru), Roy Smith (England), Staley (USA), Temblador and son (Mexico), Treviño (Mexico), Waller (USA)

Exhibit 8. Thought Leaders on Individual Behavioral Pathologies: Bales, Boulding, M. Foucault, G. A. Miller, H. A. Simon, Sir Geoffrey Vickers

Exhibit 9. Thought Leaders on Group Behavioral Pathologies: Allison, Delbecq, M. Foucault, Hayek, Janis, Kapelouzos, Lasswell, Tuckman, Van de Ven

Exhibit 10. Thought Leaders on Organizational Behavioral Pathologies: Argyris, Boulding, Downs, Lasswell, Lewin, March, Simon

Exhibit 11. Thought Leaders on Language: Lavoisier, Boole, Cayley, Peirce, Cantor, Hilbert, Russell, Krippendorff

Appendix B. List of Axioms

Axiom 1.   The Collaboration Axiom
Axiom 2.   The Behavior Axiom
Axiom 3.   The Design Axiom
Axiom 4.   The Graphics Axiom
Axiom 5.   The Structure Axiom
Axiom 6.   The History Axiom
Axiom 7.   The ISM Software Axiom
Axiom 8.   The Verifiability Axiom
Axiom 9.   The Process Leadership Axiom
Axiom 10   The Undiscovered Actors Axiom
Axiom 11   The Behavioral Pathologies Axiom
Axiom 12   The Necessary Organization Axiom
Axiom 13   The Language Axiom
Axiom 14   The Ownership and Commitment Axiom
Axiom 15.   The Coherent (Virtual) Organization Axiom
Axiom 16.   The Infrastructure Axiom

Linguistic Adjustments: Precursors to Understanding Complexity

With minor editorial changes, this Appendix is reproduced with permission of the publisher, John Wiley and Sons, from the article Warfield, John N. (2004), **"Linguistic Adjustments: Precursors to Understanding Complexity"**, *Systems Research and Behavioral Science* 21(2), 123-145.

ABSTRACT

There is no well-accepted, coherent language of systems science founded in correlated theoretical and empirical results that enables it to fill the requirements for people to work with complexity. A set of linguistic adjustments is proposed as a way of moving from the present state of the language toward a sorely-needed, functional state of discursivity. The goal is to achieve a linguistic state of systems science that is commensurate with the needs of applications in many locales to redesign dysfunctional systems, both small and large, in society. A six-component strategy for achieving this goal is described. The development of discursivity along the proposed lines is keyed to this strategy. Acceptance of these linguistic adjustments could do for systems science what Lavoisier did for chemistry over 200 years ago.

INTRODUCTION

Of the three fundamental components of all science, two can be integrated into systems science by addition; namely thought about thought (which requires accepting the idea that computer support enables the human being to take advantage of what has been learned over the centuries about how to augment human reasoning powers) and the behavioral pathologies (which requires accepting the idea of fallibility of the individual and adopting a willingness to collaborate with others in applying tested methods for enhancing the quality of models). The third component, language, is not so readily dealt with. This component can be compared with the difficulty in clearing up a heavily polluted area. The languages associated with systems and with complexity have become so polluted that a sort of super effort becomes necessary to replace this polluted language before it will be possible to take advantage of the benefits of understanding of thought about thought and of the behavioral pathologies. The polluted language has become ingrained. Words that are necessary to applications in systems science are used with meanings that are not compatible with what is required.

To take just two examples, the word "system" itself has been corrupted by narrowing its meaning, and the word "problem" has been chosen to represent what amounts to a collection of problems which must be dealt with as a collection if appropriate remedies are to be found. Moreover, higher education has collaborated in fostering the polluted language in its textbooks and classrooms, steadily increasing the number of people entering the professional areas that have accepted the polluted language. For these reasons, this book must devote much more space to language than to the other two fundamentals. At the same time it must also give a balanced treatment. Hence the space in the chapters is roughly equally balanced among the three fundamental components, but this Appendix emphasizes language.

History tells us that more than 200 years ago a young law-school graduate decided *not* to make a career in law, but rather to make his career in chemistry. Antoine Lavoisier, faced with a language of chemistry that lacked discursivity, decided that he must first upgrade the language of chemistry. As he proceeded along that line he was drawn into a revision of the entire field. Although he perished at the guillotine during the French Revolution, it is fortunate for posterity that it was not his work in revolutionizing chemistry that was responsible for his execution, but rather a dominant dislike of the upper classes in France. If he had been executed for his work in chemistry perhaps, in collateral actions, all of his work might have been burned, denying it to later investigators!!

Today the field of systems studies suffers from the same lack of discursivity that Lavoisier encountered in his study of chemistry more than 200 years ago. Matters are more severe in the systems area because of the great breadth of the field and the widespread dispersion of people with interests in systems among many governments, industries, and scholarly societies. Yet a compelling need exists for the systematization of systems science, because of the impact that a variety of large systems have upon every individual on the planet. The potential for improvement in many of these systems can be inferred from their mediocre performance. A measure of success for systems science is to attain a level of quality and utility that is adequate to enable it to be drawn upon heavily to redesign such systems for improved performance.

The time has come to work systematically toward the enhancement of systems science. This paper is intended to move in that direction following the lead of Lavoisier, by identifying what will be called "linguistic adjustments" for systems science. In the processes of adjustment, changes will have to take place at both ends of a spectrum bounded on one end by philosophy that is very hard, if not impossible, to translate into practice (*we must do so and so, but we won't tell you how!*) and, on the other end, by methods that are insufficiently general to lend themselves to the beginning stages of description and design of many if not most systems issues of today (*you must use such and such a method, even if your situation can't be formulated in that language!*).

In seeking such changes as are presented here one must constantly keep in mind the pressing need for actionable systems science and use, as a criterion of incorporation in such a science, the *capacity for generic applicability*. Exclusion of a material from systems science can be based on a criterion of *applicability limited to special interests*. A substantial amount of material from areas such as operations research and management science can be omitted, thereby greatly simplifying systems science. But at the same time such materials can be thought to be available for import when application of systems science uncovers a need for some of those materials.

A STRATEGY OF LINGUISTIC ADJUSTMENT[1]

Based on extensive empirical evidence, it is possible to proceed directly to name specific adjustments and to explain why they are required. However a broader plan for arriving at adjustments is first to construct a strategy for how to move forward. Such a strategy will be offered here as a preamble to the specification of specific linguistic adjustments. Six components of a strategy have been identified. . The six components are:

- **Identifying Disciplinary Commonalities.** Look for commonalities of method in various disciplines. While the search for methods was often the only search, one now understands that this is far from sufficient.
- **Identifying Evolutionary Insights.** Look for transferable evolutionary insights from historical development of much older areas of study, e.g., physics, economics, and history.
- **Reconciling Generality and Focus.** Reconcile the tension in the requirements that the language must be very general so that it does not restrict the realm of potential applications, but must be sufficiently focused so it can serve demands of a wide variety of applications.
- **Partitioning the Content.** Distinguish systems science from the "domain of systems science" as a way of diminishing the content of the science proper, while retaining the many imports from other areas of study in the larger *domain of the science.*

---

[1] This strategy and the mode of implementing it is supported by very extensive archival resources. The reader will find an annotated section at the end of this paper labeled "Internet Resources" which identifies relevant Internet sites, available at the time of writing of this paper.

Inventing a Cognitive Infrastructure for Local Applications. It cannot be expected that people at the site of a prospective application of systems science would have to learn systems science before it could be applied to some local problematic situation. Neither should the science be deliberately degraded to make it understandable to any high percentage of potential users. Hence the link between language and infrastructure becomes a critical part of the linguistic adjustment. This link must be compatible with cognitive limitations of humans in a way that does not downgrade the linguistics, but rather supplements the linguistics of systems science with locally generated linguistics of the problematic situation; and that can only happen effectively if the systems science itself provides the machinery for this accomplishment. Cognitive infrastructure must absorb and cushion the space between practitioner and user, in order to enable the user to work effectively and efficiently in resolving the complexity associated with problematic situations.

Justifying Conclusions with Empirical Evidence. Draw on empirical results from more than two decades of testing of "Interactive Management"[2] in a wide variety of problematic situations, involving a wide variety of working groups and organizations, as a way to test conclusions that stem from the other components of the strategy.

Strategy Component 1: Identifying Disciplinary Commonalities

The Search for Commonalities. One of the four activating goals cited at the outset of the *Society for General Systems Research* in the mid 1950's was to discover what commonalities of method could be found in various disciplines, and make these commonalities generally known. One obvious potential benefit of this discovery is to enable people to become more capable of working across disciplines and, presumably, become more effective in various practices that span disciplinary

---

[2] More than two decades of testing of Interactive Management in many applications has shown that it satisfies the various components of the strategy for linguistic adjustments very well, as demonstrated by numerous examples (Warfield, 2002).

domains. Perhaps it has not been adequately recognized that *the achievement of this goal requires linguistic adaptations, as will now be explained.*

If some commonality is found among several disciplines, a very conservative posture would be to call attention to that and move on. But this seems to be an unduly weak approach to the upgrading of inter-disciplinarity. If some commonality is discovered, presumably it would be feasible to adopt the language of one of the disciplines as a general statement, and drop the language of the others. There are at least two objections to this. The first is that certain languages are already embodied in the various disciplines which would not be particularly interested in revising all of their literature to conform to language from another discipline. A second is that, even if a general principle or method is stated, there is every reason to suppose that the individual disciplines could benefit by using *both* the more general statements *and* the specific statements. Even if a general principle can be recognized and applied, it may be advisable to retain the specific ideas of the discipline in order to match requirements of applications that are specific to that discipline.

The generalities may then become part of the framework of systems science; being set forth in a language that is sufficiently broad, yet sufficiently definite, that it becomes broadly serviceable without restrictions imposed by pre-existing, discipline-based linguistics.

Strategy Component 2: Identifying Evolutionary Insights

The early thought of the founders of the *Society for General Systems Research* was represented by a statement of four objectives for that society. Especially, they perceived it as important to study various disciplines and detect those methods that they had in common. Still, it appears that they did not emphasize the idea that scholars of systems might learn something about their own quest by observing experiences in the historical evolution of the separate disciplines.

Work toward the development of a systems science is now about a half-century old. Assessment of progress can be compared with developments in other areas of study. While specific beginning dates are arguable, it would seem that physics and economics, as objects of scholarly writings, are each more than three centuries old. Superficially, at least, it appears that systems science has a long way to go to attain the level of development of these subjects. With a combined six centuries or so of development behind these subjects, there are lessons for systems science to be extracted from experiences in the evolution of physics and economics. History, as a discipline is even older, and offers lessons in method stemming from the prolonged 20th century explorations of the history of thought, carried out by Michel Foucault.

Economics: Parallels. The **parallels** between the evolving discipline of economics and the evolving domain of systems are significant. To mention just a few:

- Systems involves *multiple disciplines*, economics involves *multiple sectors*
- Systems involves *models*, economics involves *models*
- Systems involves *dynamics*, economics involves *dynamics*
- Systems involves *multitudes of variables*, economics often involves *multitudes of variables*
- Systems involves *interpreting complexity*, economics involves *interpreting complexity*

Economics: Differences. In addition to the parallels, there are some major **differences** between systems and economics.

A Self-Sealing Discipline. In a certain sense (supported by empirical evidence), economics is a *self-sealing discipline,* whose language is virtually inaccessible to the lay person or even to potential collaborators from other disciplines. While economists often collaborate with one another, collaboration outside the discipline is rare unless it involves a discipline like statistics, which has really become an integral part of economics. (If these statements are doubted, one need only look at references in economics texts.) *System thinking, on the other hand, loses much of its significance if it is not open to all disciplines.*

Cognitive Limitations and Schools of Thought. There exist both significant anecdotal evidence and a scientific basis for believing that when a large number of schools of thought can be identified in some field of study, one reason (and probably a major reason) for the large number of schools of thought is the effect of cognitive limitations on the individual formulation and group evaluation of a school of thought. *The typical ambient situation from which many schools of thought can emerge is one in which the cognitively-limited single investigator chooses a small number of variables from a larger set, ignoring the rest, and takes a group of followers along in his intellectual wake.* In economics, for example, François Quesnay and his followers took the position that manufacturing and commerce did not add value; and that only agriculture added value. Adam Smith saw self-interest as the ignition of the economy and competition was its governor. Malthus and Ricardo differed on the nature of the value of labor.

While a variety of studies have verified the existence of behavioral pathologies (Warfield, 2002) that affect human behavior when striving to characterize a field of study, consider just two. One is the familiar limitation studied first by George Miller (Miller, 1956) and later by H. A. Simon (Simon, 1974), involving the "span of immediate recall". Miller concluded that the human mind can only bring into short term memory about seven items, and Simon suggested that the number is closer to five than seven. Warfield (1988) then noted that if one brings three items into short-term memory and in the same time period wants to consider the interactions among these three in pairs and as a collective, the entire short-term memory is consumed, since for three items there are four interactions, giving a total of seven ideas.

George J. Friedman, in studying the reason for failure of large defense systems, concluded that cognitive limitations were responsible for most of the failures, brought about by defects in equations used in large system designs, because the developers of those equations limited the number of variables to a number small enough to enable an escape from the cognitive limitations just mentioned (Warfield, 2002).

What can be said about the origins of multiple schools of thought in areas of study?

Suppose a school of thought is defined to be an explanation of a problematic situation based on k variables. Suppose that the problematic situation under study actually involves n variables, where n would generally be more than k. Then by elementary combinatorics, the number $T(n,k)$ of schools of thought that can be formed is given by the well-known formula:

$$T(n,k) = n!/(n-k)!k! \qquad (1)$$

which is the same as the number of combinations of n things, taken k at a time. If all values of k from 1 to n are allowed, the sum over k of $T(n,k)$, which is equal to $2^n - 1$, would give all possible schools of thought. For $n = 7$, this number would be 127.

In striving to apply Equation 1 to actual situations, it can be noted at the outset that if the number of variables exceeds the Miller "magical number", there is no reason to suppose that a valid school of thought would be creatively announced by an isolated investigator, i.e., one who does not collaborate with other investigators, working jointly to consider interactions. Consider two special cases where the number of variables in a problematic situation is 7 (Friedman's studies show that almost all the equations of physics involve 7 or less variables).

Equation 1 can be used to consider two special instances.

Case 1. Interaction-Free Study. The scholar identifies all 7 variables in the situation, and does not consider any interactions. In this instance, there is only one school of thought, involving all of the variables. However this school of thought is likely to be very superficial, valid only for a problematic situation where there are no interactions, an unlikely event in the phenomenological world.

Case 2. Three Variables With Interactions. A certain scholar chooses 3 variables out of the 7 variables, and considers all the interactions among the chosen 3. Another scholar may choose 3 other variables, considering the interactions among them. Other scholars might choose fewer than 3 variables and consider interactions among them. Limiting k to the values 1, 2, and 3, the number of possible schools of thought with 7 variables is given from **Eq. 1** by using the numbers $n = 7$ and $k = 3, 2$, and *1*. Then, applying Eq. 1 to the three instances, we find that the total number of schools of thought involving 3 or fewer variables and their interactions, in a problematic situation involving 7 variables is

$$T(7,3) + T(7,2) + T(7,1) = 63 \qquad\qquad (2)$$

The reader may wonder whether there can be any real connection to actual situations. One of the organizations that is taking a systematic look at the field of economics is the *New School of Social Research,* which has enjoyed and continues to enjoy the services of a number of well-known economists. On their web site they identify 71 schools of thought in economics. Most of these schools relate to macroeconomics; i.e., to aggregate variables, such as total annual consumption in an economy.

A purely mechanical conceptualization would argue that this is evidence that the number of significant variables in macroeconomics is at least 8. This comes about because with 7 variables the number 71 exceeds the number 63 computed in **Eq. 2**. With $n = 8$ and $k \leq 3$, the number of schools of thought that can be formed is 92. This would allow for 71 schools of thought, with room left for invention of 21 more.

Expanding the Number of Possible Schools of Thought. Economists have found ways to extend the number of possible schools of thought. Given that the Bank of Sweden established a Prize in honor of Alfred Nobel for work in economics, should it be true that the number of schools of thought involving macroeconomics is nearing saturation, there would be a limited number of opportunities for developing new schools of thought in economics, if adhering only to macroeconomics along the lines just suggested.

One way to take advantage of the incentives offered by the Prize is to find a way to expand the number of variables n. A way to do this would be to invent new financial instruments, such as yen-carry trade derivatives, gold derivatives, and interest rate derivatives. Left unregulated, as these now-prevalent derivatives are treated by the financial powerhouses of the world, with the steady blessing of Dr. Alan Greenspan, there are abundant opportunities to make new discoveries, thereby opening up substantial opportunities for individuals to qualify for the Prize, that would not be available in an economy having fewer variables. On the other hand, the ability of the lay person to comprehend such a system would be vanishingly small.

Recognizing Ashby's Law. Suppose now that a government determined that it wished to exercise controls over an economy for which the foregoing ideas apply. (The U. S. government has demonstrated clearly its intent to exercise such controls as, for instance, in the Humphrey-Hawkins act, which charges the Federal Reserve to work toward certain goals, which are not necessary compatible). Then immediately the government ought to come to grips with Ashby's Law (Theorem) of Requisite Variety. As scholars of cybernetics and systems are generally aware, this Law states that for effective control, the variety available to the controller should be the same as the variety available to the system to be controlled. There is no evidence that economists pay any attention to Ashby's Law.

Ashby's Law implies that if the economy to be controlled has n variables, the controller must be able to control all n variables in order to avoid the significant risk of leaving some subset of those variables uncontrolled. What this means is that if the government wishes to control the economy, a studious way to proceed would be to determine how many variables there are to be controlled, and then make available that same number of control levers to the controller.

Any invention in the economic system that increased the number of variables from some given level, where the system is understood, to some higher value where the system is not understood, then becomes a matter of major risk for unwary investors everywhere. Certainly the invention of derivatives fits that picture. There is no reason to suppose that any economist understands adequately the economic systems even before the introduction of derivatives (given the 71 schools of thought), but at least some experience was available to assist the cognitive practices of striving to understand interactions within a system. Should there be any arrogance associated with attempts to control an economy, the level of arrogance should diminish substantially if it is not possible to demonstrate that Ashby's Law is being satisfied in those attempts.

When there is a prevailing attempt by powerful groups to "globalize", huge risks are taken because of the uncertainties introduced by combining the addition of new variables to the old while, at the same time, exerting significant pressures to change local cultures in nations to accommodate to the economic requirements of institutions such as the International Monetary Fund and the World Bank. No matter how prominent the managers of these institutions may be, there is no reason to suppose that their cognitive powers exceed those of most human beings, and especially in the light of the increased number of variables incentivized by the Prize.

Not only is the number of variables increased by the presence of derivatives, but they are further increased, both by recognizing that behavior of the aggregate variables differs from one culture to another, and by increasing the number of conceivable interactions, so that over-aggregation to avoid increasing the number of variables still further simply masks significant differences that ought to remain at the macroeconomic level.

There are few instances where governments actually admit to mistakes, and retreat to previous conditions. Still it seems that this is an approach that would be reasonable for governments to take, in the light of Ashby's Law, and the potential disruption that can occur when huge sums are invested in derivatives, such as the trillions in notional value of derivatives attributed to J. P. Morgan Chase Bank, along with lesser amounts in other banks in the United States and Europe.

Lessons from Economics. Systems can learn from economics about the **long time** (centuries) that is required for systems-oriented disciplines to mature; and can also learn from economics that **highly-restrictive language is not conducive to cooperative efforts across disciplines.**

The latter idea reinforces the need for systems to make linguistic adjustments to sustain an open language. The former idea should spur systems scholars to try to avoid the many false starts and diverging schools of thought that characterize economics[3]. Systems can learn the impact of continuing to develop **numerous mutually-inconsistent schools of thought**, the choice of which in applications is highly politicized and frequently unresponsive to or may heavily aggravate local problematic situations.

But perhaps the most important insight that can be extracted from observation of the discipline of economics is that the world-wide recognition given to a highly-publicized incentive to work as an individual rather than a systematically-organized group of colleagues can have negative impacts that go beyond the exaltation of disciplinary achievement. The cognitive requirements of systems science demand that there be, as Peirce insisted, "a community of scholars" who work to test the evolving discipline, and to amend it as found necessary. For this to be effective, it seems most important to combine the general with the focused, rather than to make small changes in one or more of many equations. In doing so, Ashby's Law should inform all decisions involving models.

Finally, the combinatorics of fields of study that involve many variables illustrate how opportune it is to construct distinct schools of thought by virtue of minor changes in underlying assumptions about what is important. The temptation to do this as a necessity in a world of "publish or perish" must be resisted constantly if a high-level discursivity is to be attained in a broad field of study.

Physics: Parallels. There are significant **parallels** between physics and systems.

* Systems involves *multiple disciplines*, physics involves *multiple*

---

[3] In a web site said to be related to the *New School of Social Research* about 70 schools of thought that have developed in the continuing evolution of economics as a discipline are named.

> *types of energy*
- Systems involves *models*, physics involves *models*
- Systems involves *dynamics*, physics involves *dynamics*
- Systems involves *interpreting complexity*, physics involves *interpreting complexity*

Physics: Differences. A major **difference** between systems and physics is that with very few exceptions the fundamental results of physics are presented in equation form, involving just a few variables[4], but systems, on the other hand, even physical systems, may involve hundreds of variables; and sociotechnical systems likewise may involve hundreds of variables. Scholars with physics backgrounds tend to displace their findings in physics or mathematical models into larger arenas without the benefit of empirical evidence that supports such displacement. Hopefully systems science can ascend to the levels of quality required in the generalities that characterize systems science.

Distinctions of Scale. Distinctions of scale in systems have demands that can be compared with those in physics and economics. There is a widespread tendency in economics to split the foundations between sets of equations and the gathering of large amounts of data for statistical processing. But evidence of the general benefits of such procedures is lacking, large expenditures notwithstanding. One could even say that if such procedures were adequate there would be no need for systems science. A similar division among sets of equations and statistical methods occurs in physics as well, where sets of simultaneous equations may be used to describe automatic control systems, but statistical methods (e.g., Fermi-Dirac statistics) are called on to describe behavior in solid state environments (e.g., in transistors). It is possible for systems science to go the same route as economics and physics; i.e.., to develop a two-block partition involving sets of equations on the one hand and statistics on the other hand. But if this partition is warranted, that

---

[4] George J. Friedman studied this in detail for physics, and summarized the results in a one-page communication, reproduced in Warfield (2002).

requirement should flow out of more fundamental, case-based considerations; e.g., logic relationships among elements of a problematic situation.

History: A Major Parallel. A major challenge of the historian is to reconstruct, from fragmentary and sometimes inconsistent information, what occurred on a large scale in the past. A similar situation faces the systems practitioner who is frequently brought into a local problematic situation in which there is only fragmentary and inconsistent information available, with the task of helping to resolve that problematic situation.

History: A Major Difference. A major difference may often be seen between the task of the historian and the task of the systems practitioner. There may be a group of local people available to the systems practitioner who have had experience with the problematic situation, while the historian has no such cadre of potential assistants, and is forced to rely on what others said in the distant past. Locals cannot be expected to be masters of systems science; while the practitioner cannot be expected to be masters of the linguistics of the problematic situation. *Very early in any application the principal challenge will be to find a way to describe that situation where the practitioner is guided by systems science and the local people provide the essential ingredients of description of the problematic situation.*

Foucault's Conclusion: Problemization. The unique contributions of the historian Michel Foucault, in his twentieth-century studies of the history of thought, provide opportunities to learn from the study of history. In his position at the Collège de France, where very heavy emphasis is placed upon research and informal learning exchanges, Foucault was able to concentrate his studies over more than a decade. Several summarizing and integrating concepts were contributed by Foucault in the last year of his life, in interviews with Paul Rabinow and others[5].

---

[5] Paul Rabinow, Ed. (1984) *The Foucault Reader*, New York: Pantheon.

Foucault concluded that **the best way to reconstruct what happened in the past is to carry out problemization** via hypothesizing. In this procedure, the historian notes from fragmentary information that certain activities transpired, and hypothesizes what problems the actors were trying to resolve by virtue of these activities. Given that multiple problems are often envisaged as motives for action, Foucault uses the term "problematique" to convey intuitively the aggregate concept of description of a situation. This idea is very similar to Ackoff's well-known description of a "mess", i.e., a collection of interacting problems.

Foucault's Concept of Scientific Communication. Foucault also talked of "founders of discursivity", apparently believing that linguistic discursivity at a level of quality that is needed is absent from the human sciences. If reconstruction of the past involves problemization, how can this task be integrated with the requirement for a high-quality linguistic discursivity? This is a question to which neither Ackoff nor Foucault offered an answer.

Strategy Component 3: Reconciling Generality and Focus

Combining Generality and Focus. One may conclude from the foregoing that a suitable systems science will not adopt the language of any particular discipline, but rather will invent the encompassing language which can be applied to aggregate disciplinary components. This invention could take place in an evolutionary way as a sequence of individual discoveries over time. Even if it occurred in that way it is unlikely that the collective result would provide the kind of discursivity that is needed for a language of general scientific significance for systems science.

Some kind of aggregating and integrating of the separate discoveries would be required. Following Foucault, this might be done through problemization, assisted by a methodology founded in systems science that took advantage of the knowledge and experience of those who have significant awareness of (and often a significant stake in) a problematic situation. If the systems science provides the means for enabling a thorough problemization to take place through the participation of local people, this organization of the description of the problematic situation may provide the focus for the local discursivity generated by applying a systems science whose own discursivity reflects the importance of enabling this type of local linguistic empowerment.

Even then it would be appropriate to test the discursivity of a systems language so formed to see if it truly met the broad requirements of an integrative science that encompasses and goes beyond multiple existing disciplines.

Then even if it met these requirements, one would hope that it would be conceived in a sufficiently broad way that it could accommodate evolutionary requirements that could include incorporating still newer disciplines as new discoveries are made. In other words, a strategy for developing a language of systems science with evolutionary integrity is beneficial in moving toward a language with appropriate discursivity.

Linguistic Adjustments for Discursivity. It seems, therefore, quite appropriate to examine the linguistic adjustments that would have to be made to provide the discursivity that a mature systems science might exhibit. Evidently if this is to be successful, for reasons already mentioned, the linguistic adjustments must move in two complementary directions at once:

a) Produce general frameworks that are sufficiently broad as to encompass various disciplines without adopting the language of any one, and b) Satisfy the criterion that, when called upon, the frameworks must be smoothly reducible to the language of any particular encompassed discipline, by simple substitutions

Internal Linguistic Adjustments. The presence of a variety of several hundred systems societies, modest in size, producing their own self-sealing publications, testifies silently to the existence of an ad hoc, broadly dysfunctional language of systems comprised of the aggregate of the languages of all of these societies and the languages of their publications. This situation adds new requirements for a language of systems science with appropriate discursivity. Simple aggregation is not likely to be effective. The language of systems dynamics is quite different from the language of Checkland's "soft systems science" for example.

But those conditions already described for various disciplines will have to be satisfied also for these various societies. Anticipating that at least some of these would prefer to be thought of as systems science rather than as a discipline, it is still necessary to visualize them in that way in order to apply the same strategy already mentioned. Linguistic adjustments that apply to the disciplines mentioned earlier must also be invoked across the spectrum of systems societies, and may even be met with greater resistance because of the differences that these societies perceive among themselves.

In other words, internal linguistic adjustments are required *within* as well as *outside* the systems community–a community that is quite disparate in makeup. Getting acceptance will be difficult.

The discursivity of systems science must incorporate the capacity to enable discursivity to be constructed in and for local problematic situations since, without this, sensible discussions cannot yield sensible products, nor produce local consensus on a course of action.

Strategy Component 4: Partitioning The Content

Partitioning of Content: The Fate of Specialized Methods. Does a drive toward linguistic adjustments mean that all of those specialized methods that have, in various ways, become attached to or associated with the systems literature must be discarded? No. Just as the disciplinary languages and structures are not disabled by the superposition of a broader and less-specific language, neither should the specialized methods *that can be imported into* (but are not really a part of) systems science be in some sense rejected, just because systems science cannot cross numerous disciplines while retaining the language of all of them. The term "linguistic adjustments" does not mean to replace existing language indiscriminately in those domains where it is appropriately housed. But it does mean to cover them, much as a roof covers a house, protecting the contents, and offering shelter from storms–shelter of a type that the specific languages cannot provide. An analogy can be drawn with the way "clip art" is used in the construction of texts:

standing in a supportive aggregate, clip art is drawn upon when and only when the need arises, and not used automatically because of some historical legacy. We may speak respectfully of "clip methods", to help cement their place and function in the *domain* of systems science, as opposed to lying within and cluttering the science, thereby making it much more diffuse, hence much more difficult to learn and apply.

Partitioning of Content: Descriptive and Normative Science. Systems science must represent an integration, not only of commonalities from the disciplines, but must be perceived along two more general axes: as a science competent to serve both descriptive and normative purposes in the same context. The normative sciences and their interrelationships have been identified by Charles S. Peirce[6]. The three most commonly identified normative sciences, namely aesthetics, ethics, and formal logic, have been interrelated by Peirce in a manner shown in Figure 1. A very extensive elaboration of Peirce's views has been offered by the late Father Vincent G. Potter[7].

---

[6]   The Peirce Edition Project (1998): T*he Essential Peirce, Selected Philosophical Writings*, Vol. 2 (1893-1913). Chapter 10 elaborates on these ideas, and asserts that even these normative sciences are based on the most fundamental concept of phenomenology. In concluding this Chapter, Peirce writes that "A phenomenology which does not reckon with pure mathematics, a science hardly come to years of discretion when Hegel wrote, will be the same pitiful clubfooted affair that Hegel produced."

[7]   Vincent G. Potter (Edited by Vincent M. Colapietro) (1996): *Peirce's Philosophical Perspectives*, New York: Fordham University Press, American Philosophy Series Number 3.

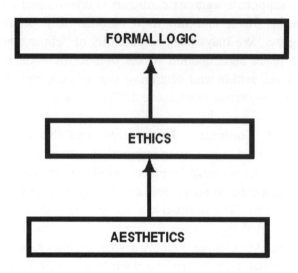

Fig. 1. Aesthetics **informs** Ethics which, in turn, **informs** Formal Logic, insofar as human values are involved in decisions

These views are appropriate in the modern context of economics, but the moral side of economics has largely been relegated to the distant past. (So it came as quite a surprise to economists and others when Amartya Sen received the Nobel award in economics in 1998, re-incorporating a normative perspective in economics.) Hopefully systems science will not allow itself to be detached from human values, but neither will it waste so much time striving to analyze those values that it is distracted from moving ahead with problemization, carried out by the owners of those values who, if asked to analyze their own esthetics and ethics, singly or collectively, might find themselves too busy to do so. They can, however, easily exercise those values in their problem descriptions and choices of design options.

The Unique Role of Formal Logic. Human beings possess inherent powers to intuit esthetics, with results that vary from one individual to another. Human beings have different perceptions of ethics. Only formal logic has the kind of literature base that lends itself to analytical and synthetic systems activity. Peirce, acknowledged to be one of the world's great logicians, had a very clear understanding of the role of logic in human decision-making (which can be interpreted as a component activity of modeling). Peirce stated that:

> *"If we fall into the error of believing that vitally important questions are to be decided by reasoning, the only hope of salvation lies in formal logic, which demonstrates in the clearest manner that reasoning itself testifies to its own ultimate subordination to sentiment. It is like a Pope who should declare ex cathedra and call upon all the faithful to implicitly believe on pain of damnation by the power of the keys that he was **not** the supreme authority."*

Sentiment is the cumulative view of what is ethical in the light of what is esthetic.

While the quotation just cited may appear to assign a weak role to formal logic, the clear intent (in light of the vast body of Peirce's writings) is to inform sentiment wisely by recourse to formal logic. But how to do this? Peirce viewed all of science as a cooperative endeavor. Cooperation, in turn, hinges on commonality of language. Sentiment is not conducive to commonality of language, hence linguistic adjustment must prepare formal logic for application of sentiment in a collective way, where the logical aspects of a situation are jointly formulated without stopping to try to resolve what may be an impossible task: articulating in adequate detail the esthetic and ethical views of every individual. It is through the joint application of individual sentiment that a final formal logic expression can be found that reflects a near-consensus point of view on topics that, at first, seem unreconcilable[8]. It is through this effort that local discursivity becomes achievable.

---

[8] Numerous examples to illustrate this point of view appear in J. N. Warfield (2002) *Understanding Complexity: Thought and Behavior*, Palm Harbor, FL: Ajar Publishing Company (and other sources identified in that book.).

Learning from the Evolution of Physics and Economics: More Differences. Both physics and economics are notable for the attainment of results by individual investigators. These investigators assert basic results, and those who follow apply those results. While the intensity of this statement is not as strong in economics as it is in physics, because of the extensive variation in points of view in economics, the result tends to be the same in applications: results from prior investigators are applied in the new problematic situation.

Seemingly it is not recognized adequately in the systems community that even in applications the actors must begin at a more basic level. That is because the variables in any given situation are likely to be greater in number and variable in extent and interaction than in prior problematic situations. For this reason, if one begins with established equations or statistical results and strives to proceed to a solution, one is at least taking substantial risks.

As the work of the twentieth-century investigators in human behavior in problem-solving situations amply demonstrates, the human cognitive apparatus is not attuned to coping individually with problematic situations. While the Nobel Prize in Physics may go to one or even two or (rarely) more; and while the Bank of Sweden Prize in Economic Sciences in Memory of Alfred Nobel may now and then be split between two or more economists, the cognitive limitations of the individual will generally preclude any such prize in systems; and would do so even if some kind of empirical results could be found to help validate past behavior. (The Nobel Peace Prize is often awarded to people who, after the fact, appear not to have made any significant, positive impact on peace.)

Strategy Component 5: Inventing A Cognitive Infrastructure For Local Applications

Just as Lavoisier recognized the need for linguistic adjustments in chemistry, this paper argues the need for linguistic adjustment in systems science. But further it argues the need for the synthesis of discursivity in each problematic situation where systems science is needed as a basis for resolving complexity. *The discursivity of systems science is the attribute of the linguistic construction of systems science that is required, in order to make it possible for systems science to enable the creative generation of local discursivity focused upon the local problematic situation.*

A standard type of cognitive infrastructure is required that will be applicable in every problematic situation that is encountered. It must, therefore, be linguistically neutral. But it must involve a seamless construction of infrastructure that supports local development of the language needed both to describe a problematic situation and to design a corrective system for resolving that situation.

This cognitive infrastructure benefits from the following components:

- **Well-Equipped Space for Working Groups.** A well-equipped space (situation room) will include a table, chairs, magnetic wall boards for holding lots of information, and computers to enable the information generated to be stored as the work progresses, to be printed at intermediate points, and to provide help to the facilitator of the group by generating the questions to be asked that trigger the discussions which ultimately lead to a discursive language in which the problematic situation is describable and in which a design for resolution is articulated. The room should be free of noise, both from outside sources and from inside equipment such as noisy cooling or heating blowers.
- **Well-Prepared Practitioners.** Well-prepared practitioners understand well the methods that will be used to enable the participants in working groups to be most effective in generating descriptions of the problematic situation. These descriptions will involve problemization, meaning that participants will generate, clarify, and structure problems according to how they interact. The structuring process has been described in several places (Warfield and Perino, 1999; Warfield, 1994). Practitioners will know how to facilitate groups, and will follow the principles set forth in detail (Warfield and Cárdenas, 1994)
- **Skilled Interpreter.** When systems science becomes a basis for describing and designing, with computer assistance in organizing information, the results often appear in structural forms with which

participants are unfamiliar, even though they produced the results as group majority views. Hence a skilled interpreter is required from the practitioner community, who can play back to the group what their work has produced, interpreting skillfully for them what they have collectively produced.

If these conditions are met, the cognitive burden on both participants and practitioners are greatly diminished. By displaying in sequence all of the key group products on the magnetic walls, no one must remember all of those products. By clarifying each element as it is revealed, the extensive misunderstanding that is characteristic of human communication is greatly diminished. By structuring the problems to show how they interrelate, deep insights are gained that are very difficult to achieve without the heavy focus upon relationships. By focusing the discussion on a single relational question at a time, displayed in front of the group under computer control, each potential relationship can be examined in detail. When relationships are aggregated in structural form, the totality can be examined, both to understand how the aggregate has been structured, and to see whether it appears that any amendments should be considered.

By relieving the facilitator of the need to keep setting direction for the group (since the computer does this by its questioning of the group), the facilitator can focus upon group dynamics, helping to establish a healthy pattern of discussion, and avoid the commonplace diversions that take place in group work without professional facilitation. Some facilitators misinterpret their role, and think that they must resolve the problematic situation for the group, after the group has discussed it. This involves ad hoc structuring on the part of the facilitator, which is not needed when the computer does the structuring, based on group inputs.

So cognitive benefits are available to practitioner and participant alike, if the appropriate cognitive infrastructure is established.

Two types of facility are required for best long-term results. The first is the special kind of situation room just mentioned, and another type called the "observatorium". The former is the location where groups develop materials under the guidance of systems practitioners. The latter is where the work of groups is retained through time, as a learning facility for anyone who was not present in the original development work; and as a source where any newly-relevant information is integrated, including any amendments that correct earlier oversights or errors.

Strategy Component 6: Justifying Conclusions With Empirical Evidence

As the reader has probably gathered at this point in the article, extensive empirical testing has been done (extending roughly from 1975 to the present) in which everything alluded to previously in this article has been examined and found to be reliable information. Aside from the discussion of cognitive infrastructure, not discussed so far has been the setting in which practitioners are likely to be operating. These settings are typically within organizations, because it is there that most of the applications of systems science are likely to occur; if for no other reason than that the organization is able to support the work required to resolve complexity. It has been found helpful to have in mind a picture of a "virtual organization"; i.e., *not* a real organization, but rather an organizational model that reflects the most essential responsibilities for action within real organizations. The model that is used to help lend additional insights into the need for linguistic adjustments is referred to as "The Coherent Organization".

The Coherent Organization Model

By definition, complexity exceeds the grasp of the individual. Often the resolution of complexity requires significant resources that are unlikely to be available except in an organization. But even the conventional concept of organization is not adequate as a context for resolving complexity. This is a time of mergers of large organizations, and of task forces formed from a variety of organizations.

It is even possible that the inability of the individual to comprehend complexity, imprisoned by a constraining institutional setting, is responsible for what has been described as a "flight from science and reason" (Gross, et al, 1996) and for the ascendency and popularity of management gurus (Micklethwait and Wooldridge, 1996).

The Coherent Organization is a virtual organization with three organizational levels. Any conventional organization can be thought of as a changing collection of such virtual organizations. Unfortunately neither the components of this collection nor the whole organization fits the definition of "coherent organization". Nor is it likely that practitioners (or even top managers) will be able to gain a working picture of the whole organization. Hence one of the early steps in resolving complexity is to adopt the Coherent Organization Model as the context within which resolution of complexity is attempted. This leaves open the later task of correlating the actual organization with the Coherent Organization Model; something that is best done when sufficient structure has been discovered to make this possible in the context of a particular problematic situation..

The Coherent Organization Model is vertically organized into Levels 1, 2, and 3. The population of this organization is greatest at Level 3, the *Producing Level*, the level in which goods and services are produced. The population is lowest at Level 1, the *Strategic Level*, the level in which broad goals are enunciated, where most of the organizational authority lies, and where the survival and growth of the organization is pondered. The intermediate level, Level 2, is the *Mediating Level*. At this level the Level 3 activities and the Level 1 strategies are mediated. In order for this mediation to be effective, people in the Mediating Level (let us call them "middle managers") must be aware of what is happening at both the lower and the higher level. They must also serve to educate the higher level people (let us call them "top managers") about what the producers are doing and what difficulties they are having. They must convey the organizational vision to the producers, lest they misplace their efforts.

This model of the Coherent Organization is consistent with an older model sometimes applied in organizational planning; where the concept of strategic, tactical, and operational practice has sometimes been useful. However the model of the Coherent Organization was essentially an empirical outgrowth of two investigations that were carried out with Interactive Management (Warfield and Cárdenas, 1994). One of these investigations produced "The Alberts Pattern" (Alberts, 1995), and the other produced "The Cárdenas-Rivas Pattern"(Cárdenas and Rivas, 1995). None of these investigators began with the concept of Coherent Organization; but they developed structural patterns that showed three-level inclusion structures. Moreover, each provided the necessary language to enable coherence among the three levels, using the detailed structures developed at the Producing Level.

The linguistic capability that is developed in such applications provides the organization with the discursivity that is essential to enabling cooperative action among the three levels in the Coherent Organization Model which, after the work is accomplished has been, in effect, embedded within the real organization, where it can be effective in implementing the results of group work.

To carry this discussion further requires linguistic adjustments that enable more details to be advanced.

Implementing the Six-Component Strategy

Up to now in this paper, attention has been focused on a six-component strategy for developing a discursive language for systems science. An implicit assumption has been that one must start with the present state of affairs, and move away from that state toward the level of discursivity that is sought, based on this strategy. Attention is now turned to some specifics that arise from the combination of the strategy and results that have already been attained over the period of more than thirty years in which complexity has been the focus of my research.

Replace "The Problem" with "The Problem Set". Extensive empirical evidence in working with complexity has made clear that the often-repeated statement "let's begin by defining the problem" is the opening scene of an evolving linguistic nightmare. Whenever complexity is involved, hundreds of cases have shown that the producing level in an organization will identify dozens or even hundreds of problems. A "problem", as interpreted here will mean each and all of the following:

a) A **human construct** arising when an individual asserts a condition that the individual finds unsatisfactory, requiring corrective action–a condition which may often be intangible

b) A **component of a set** of problems (which *cannot* also be called "the" problem, if dialog is to be coherent, since one needs to discuss individual problems *and* the set of problems in the same linguistic context, along with relationships among members of the set)

c) A **component of a structure** in which an interrelationship among the problems is shown by means of a graphic called a **problematique** (Warfield and Perino, 1999).

Size of the Problem Set. Results from hundreds of cases indicate that a typical number of problems in such a problem set will be about 100, but the number has varied from about 30 to about 700. In such instances, the word "problem" has to be used consistent with the three attributes cited above. This linguistic adjustment clarifies the urgency of developing and analyzing the set, interrelationships among its members, and options for alleviating individual problems enroute to a larger outcome. Seen against this background of complexity, Ashby's Law of Requisite Variety (Ashby, 1958) becomes more than an intuitively attractive concept, demanding incorporation into activities aimed at resolving complexity, where it serves, at minimum, as a reminder that the variety in the inquiry should be uncovered before striving to design for resolution. .

Replace "Complex Problem" with "Problematique". Having defined "problematique" as a structure showing how a set of problems is interrelated by means of the relationship "significantly aggravates" (Warfield and Perino, 1999), the tendency to use the term "complex problem" to represent what is happening should be suppressed in favor of the term "problematique". This practice inserts into the language the idea that it is now possible to show how the different component problems of what might otherwise be called a "complex problem" are interrelated, leaving aside the human tendency to want to think in terms of a one-element set (e.g., "the problem", free of interacting members). *Then, instead of saying that one wishes to solve a problem, one may say that* *one wishes to resolve a problematic situation. Serviceable language requires attention to detail.*

Replace "Complex System" with "Problematic Situation". The term "problematic situation" (or, in short form, the "situation") brings little constraint to a conversation. It just indicates the recognition that something is wrong, and people are not at all certain of what to do about it. The term "complex system", on the other hand, already implies that there is a "system", and that it has the property of being "complex". Each of these component terms begs the question of what the system is and how it is known to be complex.

Yet when such language is used, it is commonplace to suppose (paradoxically) that everyone knows what *the system* is and knows that it is *complex*; and this knowledge is present, even in the absence of a definition of what the system is in the particular case in point. Also there is no explanation of why a certain system is thought to be complex, while another would not be. Nor is it clear how a tangible system can have the same property as an intangible concept of a possible future system, even though both may be declared to be complex by some. *The linguistic legacy tends to preclude deep investigation because of the suppositions embedded in the received language.*

Replace "Solutions" with "Options". Commonly, software marketers have chosen the word "solution" to represent a software product. This is possibly the most presumptuous linguistic ploy yet devised for marketing purposes (remarkable, given the plethora of marketing ploys!). It presupposes, linguistically, that what the buyer purchases will solve whatever problems the buyer may have (and certainly not introduce new ones!). And later the buyer is told that once he rips open the shrink-wrapped container that holds the compact disc with the software, he is agreeing that the only liability of the seller is to replace the disc if it is mechanically flawed or turns out not to have the software on the disc. Moreover, when the user seeks to install the software, he is once again asked to agree to a statement that relieves the seller of all responsibility for what might ensue if the product is used.

The fact that the term "system" has come to be so widely used to represent "computer system" was strongly disliked by Sir Geoffrey Vickers. He gave his views as follows (Vickers, 1980):

> *"The concept of systemic relations, though not new, has been developed in the last few decades to an extent which should be welcome, since it is the key to understanding the situations in which we intervene when we exercise what initiative we have and especially to the dialectic nature of human history. It has, however, become so closely associated with man-made systems, technological designs and computer science that the word 'system' is in danger of becoming unusable in the context of human history and human culture. I seek to contribute something to its rescue and restoration. For we need it for understanding and for action in human and social contexts..."*

The term "solution", like the term "system" has become so heavily embedded in the language that even when the foregoing argument has been advanced, people continue to stay with that old language. Use of such language often is a form of *linguistic pollution*. The use of the term "solution" before the fact is clearly presumptive, but this does not disturb the entrepreneurial mind. The term "option" is our choice, reflecting the opportunity to make a choice and the uncertainty as to whether future experience will reveal that an option could be converted into a solution.

It is a feature of complexity that no one knows at the beginning of an inquiry what might be done to resolve it. Naming something as a "solution" at the outset of inquiry is both empty and presumptive, and therefore must be ruled out in any work presented as being based in science. Yet if anything is to be done, some options for action must be generated.

An Alternative Is a Set of Mutually-Reinforcing Options. Systems language often displays the terms "option" and "alternative" interchangeably. It should be clear that, when complexity is involved, at least a two-level language is needed. This is recognized when the word "option" is seen as a component of some possible "alternative", e.g., a set of interacting options that could be chosen to try to resolve a problematic situation.

Recognize "Hierarchy" and "Cycle" as Components of a Larger Structure. Structural features of information; i.e., relationship patterns developed during hundreds of case studies, belie the common belief that structure is necessarily hierarchical. On the contrary, purely hierarchical structure is almost as uncommon as just-mined gold nuggets in the mall. A typical structure is comprised of an integrated set of components, some *hierarchical* and some *cyclic* (Zamierowski, et al, 1976). Purely cyclic structures are also seldom found. But the structural statistics coming from the extended period of research mentioned earlier show that about 99% of all problematiques contain at least one cycle. Researchers who discuss only hierarchical structure are automatically to be distrusted. It is incredibly difficult to prove that conceptual structures are free of cycles in any particular instance. When discussing purely hierarchical structure, the better part of valor is to indicate that the presence of cyclic substructures remain to be investigated. This will demonstrate that the inquirer is, at least, aware that such substructures are possible.

Avoid Uncritical Acceptance of Metaphors from Physics and Biology. Disciplinary scholars from physics and biology assert that they are scholars of complexity[9]. Unfortunately neither of these groups knows a lot about complexity[10] even though they may be immersed in it. To understand complexity, at minimum, one must understand thought about thought as provided by scholars from Aristotle to Peirce, with a special stopover at the works of De Morgan and Boole. In the era of complexity,

---

[9] The Santa Fe Institute is widely seen as a major source of complexity *theory* (NOT complexity *science*, since that would involve empirical evidence of the validity of their theory), and the European biologists are following a somewhat similar pattern of exposition. Moreover members of the American management and public policy schools and departments are seizing upon the metaphors emanating from physics and biology as representative of real human organizations.

[10] In several interviews described in the American press, inability to define complexity has been demonstrated by relevant authors. See, e.g., George Johnson (1997), "Researchers on Complexity Ponder What It's All About", *The New York Times*, May 6, 1997, Page C1. Johnson became affiliated with the Santa Fe Institute.

the right to make assertions that ignore the theory of relations, and assert that social systems somehow obey non-linear partial differential equations, is not conferred along with the doctoral diploma or even with a Nobel Prize, popular assumptions notwithstanding!!!

The common metaphors from physics and biology, wherein sublanguage is asserted to occupy a site that ought to be reserved for higher-level, more-encompassing concepts should not be tolerated in the halls of scholars of systems and of complexity. Nor do physicists and biologists have the right to occupy a definitive, overarching place in management theory or in the theory of organizations merely because physical components and biological components display structure, or because solutions to differential equations behave in a certain way. The rise of positivism and its terrible consequences have been well-explained by Hayek in one of his lesser-known, but sterling works (Hayek, 1952, 1979). Very likely few, if any, of the physicists and biologists who write about complexity are aware of this highly-scholarly and well-documented work, or of its implications for those who misplace emphasis.

Linguistic adjustments do not merely substitute one term or phrase for another, but must also purge overblown and inappropriate language from the conversational domain. Language suitable for local purposes should be properly constructed in the confines of the Coherent Organization Model. Overblown language normally enures at Level 1, since it is essentially unserviceable at Levels 2 and 3. If used at Level 1 to reveal strategy, middle managers will be strained to mediate a linkage with the producing level. The most effective language will reverberate among the three levels in the Coherent Organization without losing any utility and without engendering any confusion. *These linguistic attributes are not attained without substantial effort and empirical study of actual situations.*

Expand Attention to Model Consistency.   The act of model development is common to all of the fields of study mentioned in this article. Surely no one wants to be identified as a builder of inconsistent models. *Yet the amount of attention typically given to assuring internal consistency in model development is minuscule.* It is rare to find this subject even mentioned in the literature of modeling.   To assure the empirical justification of the linguistic adjustments mentioned here, it is necessary to have some assurance that the models developed, such as the problematique, have a quality about them that stems from their consistency. This is especially true since the development of such models is a joint activity of a systems practitioner and a group of local people who do not know systems science, but are present because of their common interest in and awareness of some local problematic situation. A systems science that would purport to engage them in the development of models without a discursive language at the base, and without any assurance of model consistency, would be a poverty-stricken systems science indeed. Consistency and linguistic adjustment are two sides of the same coin. Linguistic adjustments in the absence of model consistency are fruitless, and consistency in using language that cannot span the Coherent Organization will not lend itself to success in resolving complexity.

Friedman's Constraint Theory. George Friedman developed a very comprehensive "constraint theory" (Friedman, 1967). One of the most important contributions in this theory is a result that I have named "Friedman's Theorem of Non-Conservation of Model Consistency". Imagine that a group is studying a problematic situation, and that various models have been constructed by subgroups. Suppose that each subgroup's model has been tested and found to be consistent. Then it is proposed to merge these models into a higher level model. Friedman's Theorem can be stated as follows:

When a group of models, each of which is internally consistent, is aggregated into a single composite model; there is no assurance of conservation of consistency. (This applies, e.g., to the aggregation of a group of individually consistent mental models to form a single model.)

Friedman's Theorem tells us what cannot be taken for granted. This Theorem should come to mind any time someone proposes to get several different groups to develop components of a larger model, with the intent of merging their contributions to form a larger model. This would be true, even if each group is a group of one, meaning that each individual develops a piece of a model and the pieces are linked together. In *all* such instances, there is never assurance that the aggregated model is consistent, even when all the parts are consistent.

Harary's Structural Modeling Theory: A Theorem of Assured Model Consistency.   As part of Harary's theory of structural models, he developed a theorem which I refer to as Harary's Theorem of Assured Model Consistency.   This theorem (Harary, et al, 1965) is stated as follows (Few popular systems methods demonstrate awareness of this):

Logical consistency of a set of relations (constraints) represented by a square Boolean matrix M, such that M = M + I, where I is the identity matrix, is assured, provided (a) the relationship represented by M is transitive and (b) the Boolean square of the matrix M is equal to the matrix M. [Note: Most, but not all of the relationships of physics are transitive.]

Harary's Theorem is based in De Morgan's theory of relations and the concept of transitive relationships, topics that are avoided by many authors who may be unaware of their importance. *Yet this particular theorem is probably the single most important one ever developed for constructing logic patterns that illuminate complexity.*   It is for that reason that software, called "Interpretive Structural Modeling (ISM) Software"[11], has been developed which enable individuals or groups to construct patterns using transitive relationships.   Using this software, which is a key component of Interactive Management processes, model consistency is guaranteed.   If Harary's Theorem is ignored, Friedman's Theorem steps into the conceptual breach as the dominant consideration.

Stakeholders Are Necessary, but Not Sufficient.   Victims of bureaucratic insults love to assert how important it is that *stakeholders* be involved in striving to work together to ameliorate or terminate whatever is being done that affects them.   It is *necessary* to involve stakeholders to assure that their needs are adequately described, but *merely* being a stakeholder is not sufficient to qualify someone to take part in the

---

[11] An older, but serviceable, version of this ISM software, along with a User Guide, can be downloaded at no cost, from this web site: http://www.gmu.edu/departments/t-iasis.

necessary discoveries that are involved in working to resolve complexity. Complexity involves great difficulty of comprehension, and merely being a stakeholder provides no assurance of ability to help conceive the essential *discoveries and system designs.* Among other things, representative government has been institutionalized in recognition of the physical impossibility of direct and everyday involvement of all stakeholders. What is important is that the people constructing the models are *both stakeholders and highly informed about what the problems are* that should be in the problem set, and that whatever they produce should be openly visible to all those who are already stakeholders, and those who may become stakeholders when action is initiated to resolve the complexity. The stakeholder who is not competent in description or design may still be in a unique position to *assess* and *critique* descriptions and designs emanating from others. (The impact of implementing inadequate "solutions" has been summarized by a famous American academic, the late W. L. Everitt, who once said "In education, we are constantly recovering from the effects of our last 'solution'"). Solutions that are not highly correlated with problem sets are not desired, but neither are solutions that, while highly correlated with stakeholder desires, are impossible to implement.

Discursivity and Complexity

It is now possible to apply what has been said so far in this article to discuss complexity. Whenever it is intended to understand and resolve complexity, a Coherent Organization is defined, and synthesized as necessary to accommodate the perceived scope of the problematic situation, remembering the distinction between stakeholder and participant.

The problem set to be discovered at a given time is greatest in size at the Producer Level, hence model construction is carried out from a beginning with persons operating at that level and knowledgeable of the problems arising at that level. After the problem set has been identified and the problematique has been constructed, it is normally possible to determine categories for the problems, and the set of categories and the contents of each are passed on from the Producer Level to the Mediating Level. This set of categories, in turn, is further categorized into a set of areas, and the set of areas along with the attached structural information is passed on to the Strategic Level. It is the task of middle management to learn and to mediate any differences in perspective, in order to attain a coherent model. From that point forward in time, incremental changes are made to reflect changing conditions. In this way the Coherent Organization stays coherent through time. Continuing visibility is achieved through the Corporate Observatorium (Warfield, 1996).

Each major problematic situation is dealt with in the same way, with recourse to its own Coherent Organization. Invariably problematiques are produced and interpreted, and options are chosen related to each problem in the problematique in the light of the structural interpretation that can be presented by a person who has mastered the way to interpret problematiques. It is not something that can be casually done, but significant education and experience in interpreting structural models is necessary (Fertig, 1980; Perino, 1999).

It would, of course, be possible to work on a problematic situation merely at one of the three levels. Unfortunately, if that is done, the difficulties of gaining sufficient momentum and understanding in the non-involved levels may mean that the road to implementation will prove to be impossible to navigate. Hence whenever possible the Coherent Organization should be articulated at the beginning of work to help assure that the work will gain continuity and preserve momentum.

DISCUSSION AND SUMMARY: PART 1.

It is now appropriate to strive to integrate all of the foregoing material into a summary discussion. Since much of the integrative thinking appears elsewhere, this discussion and summary will outline what has been accomplished so far in testing the kinds of linguistic adjustments that have been discussed earlier. As mentioned, this testing has been done under the heading of "Interactive Management", a system of management that has been described in detail and extensively tested for more than two decades. The processes of Interactive Management are components of what is called the Work Program of Complexity.

This Work Program of Complexity can be summarily outlined with the aid of the linguistic adjustments set forth. It consists of a sequence of two steps: Discovery and Resolution. The general philosophy underlying it is that since no one understands the complexity, collective discovery is essential. This type of work involves problemization, as described earlier, and yields various interpretive structural models, including problematiques. This Program is based in twenty laws of complexity (Warfield, 1999; Kapelouzos, 1989).

Discovery. Discovery involves two steps: Description and Diagnosis. Description involves preliminary statement of the problematic situation (in general terms, to focus the work), generation of the problem set by an informed group of stakeholders, placement of the members of the problem set into categories (then assigning titles to the categories, for use by the middle managers), and construction of the problematique (assisted by the appropriate software which implements Harary's Theorem of Assured Consistency). All of this is done with the benefit of the infrastructure found in a well-designed situation room. Diagnosis is carried out initially by an individual who is expert in interpreting the problematique, and who then presents it to the developers of the problematique for validation and/or amendment.

Resolution. Resolution involves two steps: Design and Implementation. Design, carried out in the situation room, involves the generation of the options set by an informed group, correlating options with problems and problem categories; followed by the construction of one or more alternatives as collections of options. In matching options with problems, Ashby's Law of Requisite Variety is seen as a governing concept in arriving at design alternatives. Choice of an alternative opens the door to Implementation.

Communication of the results of the group work is carried out in part through the Corporate Observatorium, which houses the group's products for ready review and observation. The Observatorium is kept up to date as Implementation proceeds, and is used to educate people who are engaged in some way with the problematic situation, but who were not present at the original work activity..

Theorem of Necessity. All of the work described is briefly encapsulated by this Theorem of Necessity: **A necessary condition for understanding and resolving complexity is to make certain linguistic adjustments (as described) and to carry out the four components of The Work Program of Complexity** (whether they are named as shown here, or given other names that are less conducive to describing actions that are necessary enroute to the resolution of complexity). Continued reliance on this Theorem requires prolonged empirical testing in real situations, but extensive testing to date supports it.

In order to create a functional state of discursivity for systems science regarding complexity, linguistic adjustments are necessary, to make the language suitable for carrying out the Work Program of Complexity in the virtual "Coherent Organization" The latter serves as the conceptual basis for striving to resolve complexity in problematic situations.

DISCUSSION AND SUMMARY: PART 2

This paper, at root, is designed to amplify three propositions, which are:

- The language of systems science requires linguistic adjustments in order to attain a level of discursivity that is adequate for resolving complexity in a wide variety of local problematic situations.

- Guidance for identifying and justifying the linguistic adjustments is given by the six-component strategy offered here.

- The linguistic adjustments presented here are sufficient to provide the level of discursivity that is lacking in the present language of systems science.

The paper reminds us that a similar requirement for enhanced linguistics was encountered long ago by Lavoisier, whose courageous, precedent-setting activity in chemistry set a standard for developments in systems science.

In taking guidance from the six-component strategy given here, the following summary thoughts were presented:

- Methods that are common across disciplines will retain their language in the separate disciplines, but a broader language that provides a cover for these separate languages is required, and that language is the language of formal logic, in which the problems that those disciplines are striving to solve are articulated, clarified, and organized into problematiques. The role of systems science is *not* to develop such structures for the disciplines; but rather it is to supply the means to enable such developments to take place on a very broad scale in all kinds of local situations where complexity is encountered, through the actions of local people supported by cognitive infrastructure which has been identified, and justified empirically by extensive testing.

- Of the many methods that can be brought to bear on problematic situations, only those that have a suitable combination of generality and focus are appropriate for systems science proper, with all other relevant methods assigned to the domain of systems science, where they are available for importation when application of systems science reveals a need for some of them.

- Insights into the evolution of systems science and, in particular, to the linguistic adjustments required for discursivity, can be found in observing the evolutionary development of other fields of study. In particular, the evolution of economics, physics, and history all shed light upon ways of thinking about the evolution of systems science.

- The evolution of economics tells us that when a large number of variables is involved, there is a strong tendency for individuals to construct and/or accept as valid large numbers of underconceptualized schools of thought which take root in the discipline in various forms. When a powerful incentive, such as a large monetary award, is brought to the discipline, it expands the opportunity to create new schools of thought by introducing new financial instruments that make it much more difficult for the typical investor to play a role in economic development, and much easier for unscrupulous individuals to take advantage of such instruments for their own benefit. This situation ought to encourage systems scientists to become much more concerned with shrinking their science down to the essential components, leaving adjunct methods to the broader domain for importation when required.

- The evolution of economics tells us also that systems science should evolve as a highly collaborative effort among systemists: an effort which can hardly take place on any significant scale in the absence of a language that provides a discursivity amenable to such collaboration.

- The evolution of physics tells us that there is a tendency in disciplines to export their thinking into other realms for which no justification or empirical evidence is offered. Instead, as in economics as well, there is a steady tendency to rely more and more on mathematical models of systems in physics that have no larger parallels in the broader social realm. The incentives that produce this kind of behavior are much weaker in systems science, but are still active, and require a deliberate effort on the part of systemists to avoid such behavior.

- The unique scholarship of the historian Michel Foucault, fortunate to be enabled to study the history of thought for more than a decade in the highly intellectual Collège de France, has produced a strong belief that in reconstructing good descriptions of the past the best approach is problemization. This concept, elaborated, has been developed in a system of management to be applied locally at many levels in society, called "Interactive Management (IM)". This system has been tested in many settings over a period of several decades. It embodies and strengthens the concept of problemization, with the help of "Interpretive Structural Modeling (ISM)".

• In both theory and applications, ISM takes both insight and method from three key theorems: Friedman's Theorem of Non-Conservation of Model Consistency, Harary's Theorem of Assured Model Consistency, and Ashby's Law of Requisite Variety. When integrated into IM, a level of quality control in both linguistics and process is attained that cannot be achieved in frameworks that do not recognize the behavioral import of these contributions.

• Experience with using IM has shown the need for and the value of infrastructure to provide cognitive assistance to both practitioners of systems science and local participants in resolving complexity.

• Specific language that is widely-used in the systems world is shown to be unserviceable for an appropriate level of discursivity, and the necessary linguistic adjustments to replace such language are identified and the rationales for the replacement are given.

In the process of developing the foregoing ideas, it is hoped that the need for linguistic adjustments to bring about a high level of discursivity for the field of systems science has been made clear, and the necessary adjustments have been adequately defined.

REFERENCES[12]

Alberts, H. C. (1995), "Redesigning the United States Defense Acquisition System", Ph. D. Dissertation, Department of Systems Science, The City University, London, U. K.
Ashby, W. R. (1958), "Requisite Variety and its Implications for the Control of Complex Systems," *Cybernetica* 1(2), 1-17.
Cárdenas, A. R. and Rivas, J. C. (1995), "Teaching Design and Designing Teaching", in *Integrated Design and Process Technology* (A. Ertas, C. V. Ramamoorthy, M. M. Tanik, I. I. Esat, F. Veniali, and Taleb-Bendiab, Editors), IDPT-Vol. 1, 111-116.
Fertig, J. A. (1980), "An Inquiry Into Effective Design of Graphicolingual Displays for Systems Engineering", Ph D Dissertation, University of Virginia.

---

[12] Please see also the "Internet Resources" listing which follows the list of References.

Friedman, George J. (1967), "Constraint Theory Applied to Mathematical Model Consistency and Computational Allowability", Ann Arbor, MI: UMI Dissertation Services.

Gross, P. R., Levitt, N., and Lewis, M. W. (Editors) (1996), The Flight from Science and Reason, Vol. 775, *Annals of the New York Academy of Sciences*, New York: New York Academy of Sciences.

Harary, F. R.; V. Norman; and D. Cartwright (1965), Structural Models: An Introduction to the Theory of Directed Graphs, New York: Wiley.

Hayek, F.A. (1952, 1979), The Counter-Revolution of Science: Studies on the Abuse of Reason, Indianapolis: Liberty Fund.

Johnson, George (1997), "Researchers on Complexity Ponder What It's All About ", *The New York Times*, Tuesday, May 6, 1997, beginning on page C1.

Kapelouzos, I. B. (1989), "The Impact of Structural Modeling on the Creation of New Perspectives in Problem-Solving Situations", *Proceedings of the 1989 European Congress on Systems Science*, Lausanne, Switzerland: AFCET, October, 915-932.

Micklethwait, J. and A. Wooldridge (1996), The Witch Doctors: Making Sense of the Management Gurus, New York: Times Books.

Perino, G. H. (1999), "Complexity: A Cognitive Barrier to Defense Systems Acquisition Management", Fairfax: Ph. D. Dissertation, George Mason University.

Rabinow, P. (1984), The Foucault Reader, New York: Pantheon.

Vickers, G. (1980), Responsibility--Its Sources and Limits, Seaside, CA: Intersystems.

Warfield, J. N. and Cárdenas, A. Roxana (1994), A Handbook of Interactive Management, Ames, IA: The Iowa State University Press.

Warfield, J. N. (1996b), "The Corporate Observatorium: Sustaining Management Communication and Continuity in an Age of Complexity", in Tanik, M. M. et al (Eds.), *Integrated Design and Process Technology, Vol. 2* (Proc. Society for Design and Process Science), Austin, TX, 169-172.

Warfield, J. N. (1999), "Twenty Laws of Complexity: Science Applicable in Organizations" *Systems Research* 16(1), 3-40.

Warfield, J. N. and Perino, George, Jr. (1999): "The Problematique: Evolution of an Idea", *Systems Research and Behavioral Science* 16(3), 221-226 .

Zamierowski, E.; D. Hornbach, and R. Fitz (1976), "Ecological Components of Climax Agriculture: An Example of Structuring Complex Feedback Systems", *Proceedings of the International Conference on Cybernetics and Society*, New York: Institute of Electrical and Electronics Engineers, 667-673.

INTERNET RESOURCES

The annotated list of Internet URLs which follows provides an avenue to additional resources that support the arguments and conclusions reached in this paper. The numbering is for convenience only, and carries no connotation of relative importance or utility.

1. **Interactive Management Community.** This web site consists of photographs and brief biographical sketches of individuals who have contributed to Interactive Management in a wide variety of ways. This community is comprised of people from several countries, with diverse disciplinary backgrounds.

http://groups.msn.com/IMCommunity

2. **Questions and Responses.** This web site states a number of questions that have been raised in the past about aspects of the work reported here, along with Warfield's responses to those questions.

http://hometown.aol.com/jnwarfield/myhomepage/index.html

3. **The IASIS File (An 88-page annotated bibliography).** Placed on the Internet by a reader, this web site offers an annotated bibliography of Warfield's research which spans the time period from the mid 1940s until 1993, when this particular bibliography was published by the Institute for Advanced Study in the Integrative Sciences (IASIS) at George Mason University.

http://sunsite.utk.edu/FINS/Technique_Democracy/Fins-TD-05.txt
http://www.thefrontend.org/statewave/tiers_1_4/BIBWARF.htm

4. **The Warfield Special Collection.** In the year 2000, the majority of Warfield's papers, reports, books, videotapes from applications, transparencies (over 700), audio cassettes, and compact disks were donated to the George Mason University Fenwick Library. Located in Fairfax County, Virginia, these materials are open to scholars. The size of the collection is described by the librarian to be approximately 93 linear feet. At this URL one finds a listing of the contents of the collection and the location of the individual items. See Appendix 2 in this book for additional information.

http://www.gmu.edu/library/specialcollections/warfield.htm

5. **The New School of Social Research.** In 1933 the University in Exile was established in New York City for scholars fleeing totalitarianism in Europe. In 1934, this became the graduate faculty of political and social science. At the time of writing, the following web site offered a broad discussion of economics from various points of view, along with other matters related to studies at the New School.

http://cepa.newschool.edu/het/schools/newsch.htm

Appendix 5

The Two Neutral Processes of Systems Science

Sufficiency statement: only two processes are sufficient to satisfy all of the conditions of systems science. Ironically, using these two processes not only satisfies the conditions of systems science, but also provides the evidence to support the sufficiency statement. Hence the individual who doubts the statement will be required either (a) to suspend doubt long enough to test the adequacy in practice, in order to gather the data that validates the statement or (b) to study carefully the results obtained by numerous investigators of the type described in Part 4 of this book.

Two Basic Process Types: Neutral and Specific. Systems processes, i.e., processes that may have some utility in working with systems, can be classified as either neutral or specific. The neutral ones are readily identifiable as those which contain no carry-forward mathematics other than the mathematics of logic; while the specific ones will contain some type of mathematics associated with numerical spaces from which quantitative data such as time, intensity, mass, standard deviation, weight, and reaction factors enter quantitatively into decision-making.

Many authors describe the specific processes as system processes because they are applicable to some kinds of systems. Regrettably these authors almost never provide the inquirer with a means to circumscribe the applications; but rather tend to overstate the realms of application.

The Two Neutral Processes: NGT and ISM. The two neutral processes that have been tested and found to be sufficient for systems science are the truncated[1] Nominal Group Technique (designated here as NGT); and Interpretive Structural Modeling (designated here as ISM).

The Neutral Context: The Problematic Situation. The context for all systems applications is the problematic situation. The implications here are as follows: by "situation" is meant that there is some kind of widespread surround and by "problematic" is meant that aspects of this surround are very troublesome and no one understands fully the nature of the troubles while, at the same time, there is significant desire and motivation to try to understand what has been happening, to apply resources to develop an understanding of it, and to take corrective action based on that understanding.

Relation of Neutral Processes to Specific Processes. The neutral processes are always to be applied first in working to resolve a problematic situation. **In assessing this statement, one should keep in mind that no one understands the problematic situation.** Ultimately the products of application of the neutral processes will lend sufficient insight to reveal to moderately-well-informed practitioners what types of specific processes are likely to be helpful in carrying out the programmatic steps that are required to resolve the problematic situation. Typically some of these processes will be used to estimate time and costs, while others will help to set design parameters of whatever system designs may be required to resolve the problematic situation.

Iteration. If the neutral processes are applied by experienced staff and insightful local individuals with appropriate support, iteration is not likely to be required; but one must understand that both the neutral and the specific methods engender learning, and the insights that are obtained

---

[1] The Nominal Group Technique, as presented by its inventors, included a final step which I have elided because it is not cognitively viable. In contrast with all of the early steps, which are cognitively outstanding, this final step is unsatisfactory. But to honor the inventors of the Nominal Group Technique, I simply make this note here and, hereafter, make no distinction in the notation between the original version and the truncated version. By NGT, I will always mean the truncated version.

by learning will sometimes suggest that iteration is likely to be the most reasonable course to follow until the point of diminishing returns is attained.

The Nominal Group Technique

The Nominal Group Technique (NGT) has the dual function of serving as a progressive component in the development of products enroute to the resolution of the complexity relating to the problematic situation, while at the same time yielding metrics that help enable various judgments to be made having to do with important comparisons. I think it will be useful to pose this duality side by side, although the utility of the metrics may not be clear to the reader who is approaching the NGT for the first time.

STEPS IN NGT

1. **Triggering Question (TQ).** An informed group will be asked to respond: to a "triggering question" which they have seen before they came to the group work; e.g., **"What problems do you anticipate in striving to resolve problematic situation X?"**

Comments on Result 1: The group is precluded from trying to resolve the situation X prematurely before they have gained any kind of common understanding of it.

2. **Silent Writing.** Facilitator asks group members to write responses silently to the TQ.

Comments on Result 2: Typically a group will only need **15 to 25 minutes** to write all the answers they can think of and, in the process will generate between 35 and 150 responses.

3. **Posting Problem Statements.** Facilitator takes one question aloud in turn from each participant, numbers each question and, as each chart is filled, posts it on the wall.

Comments on Result 3: As more and more charts are posted, participants begin to gain insight into the complexity of the situation, seeing why it has been so troublesome. **Up to two hours** may be needed to acquire all of the problem statements.

4. **Clarifying Problem Statements.** Facilitator asks for clarification of each problem statement, resolves overlaps among statements identified, and adds any new problem statements as they surface.

Comments on Result 4: As the group sees how poorly their ideas are understood, they begin to see why no progress has been made, and begin to gain insight into the complexity. **Up to three hours** may be needed to clarify all of the problem statements.

5. **Importance Voting.** Each participant is asked to choose the five most important problems and to rank them as follows:

> 5–most important
> 4–next most important
> 3–next most important
> 2–next most important
> 1–least important of the 5

Comments on Results 5: The staff aggregates the results of the voting, and tabulates the results. The set of problems can then be partitioned into two parts as follows:

Part A. The "Importance Subset". Problems that received at least one vote from at least one participant.

Part B. "The Set-Aside Subset". Problems that received no vote from any participant.

6. **Metrics of Complexity Computed from NGT Results.**

The staff is now in a position to compute some metrics of complexity from the NGT results:

- **The Miller Index**
- **The Spreadthink Index**

The **Miller Index** would be 1 if the group had no more than 7 problems to think about at once and if there were no interactions among the problems. Regrettably this has never been found to be the case; To compute the Miller Index, we add the number of problems in Part A and Part B and divide the result by 7. The larger this number is compared to 1, the greater the complexity, as indicated by the Miller Index.

The **Spreadthink Index** would be 1 if all members agreed on which 5 problems were the most important. Regrettably, this has never been found to be the case. To compute the Spreadthink Index, we divide the number of problems in Part A by 5. The larger this number is, the more the participants differ in their points of view about what is important in the problematic situation.

Hundreds of projects have been carried out using NGT. From all of these projects, there has never been one where the Miller Index has been as low as 3. Moreover, it is always found that the Spreadthink Index is large compared to 1.

From these results and observations of many Interactive Management Workshops, we can say firmly that complexity in problematic situations entails these attributes:

- **Many Constituent Problems.** The problematic situation encompasses many constituent problems, as perceived by those local people who are involved with that situation and who are, so to speak, victims of it.

- **Non-Discursive Local Language.** The local people lack a language that is adequate to discuss the situation, as evidenced by the universal difficulties in communication that are uncovered and partly overcome in the clarification sessions of the NGT.

- **No Local Agreement on Relative Saliency.** There is virtually no agreement among the local people as to what the most important component problems in the situation are.

- **No Focused Local Agreement.** There is seldom even a single component problem which a majority of the local people find to be among the most important.

- **Chaotic Situational Structure.** Such structure as the problematic situation may be said to have can be described as chaotic.

- **Naive Outsiders.** Many outside consultants are not aware of the foregoing, and do not incorporate these insights into their practices.

Interpretive Structural Modeling (ISM)

In Chapter 5 I have described, in reverse order, the history of some of the Thought Explorers, whose ideas culminated in my development of Interpretive Structural Modeling (ISM) in the early 1970s. It is very helpful to understand the evolution of this process in order to get a feeling for its uniqueness.

Now I will place it in the application context, connect it to NGT and, as with NGT, show how it has a duality associated with it in the sense that it both yields products that are effective in helping to resolve the problematic situation while, at the same time, providing evidence to support the sufficiency statement. We may anticipate that the use of ISM will essentially resolve the difficulties stemming from the lack of a discursive local language, produce local agreement on relative saliency, provide focused local agreement, and yield organized local structure; supplanting chaotic conditions with well-organized plans for moving ahead to resolve the complexity.

STEPS IN ISM
Type 1 Session

1. **Objective: Develop Type 1 Problematique.** Choose to develop a "Type 1 Problematique" by entering the Importance Subset Part A from the NGT results, and choosing the generic question "In the context of the problematic situation X that is being explored, Does Problem Y significantly aggravate Problem Z"?

> Comments on Result 1: The Type 1 Problematique will show how the problems in The Importance Subset, Part A of the problem set found in NGT, are related to one another through the chosen relationship; this relationship being displayable in a large wall graphic, where it can be interpreted.

2. **Computer-Sequenced Questioning Session with Facilitator Management of Group Dynamics.** The computer will cycle the group through the entire Importance Subset choosing all of the problems as required, in order to develop the structure of the Type 1 problematique. The computer drives a text display which keeps a question before the group at all times. The facilitator manages the group process, and tallies the votes, striving to make sure that premature voting does not take place (i.e., that people do not vote until they understand fully the question that is being asked).

> Comments on Result 2: The time required to develop the problematique cannot be predicted with much accuracy. It depends on how many problems are involved in Part A, and how much time the group requires to discuss the response to each question. **Times between 2 and 8 hours** are typical of past Interactive Management Workshops.

3. **Computer Calculation of Structure.** The computer recognizes when all the questions have been asked and answered that are required to compute the structure of the problematique. When that is done, it will compute the structural information, and print it out for the facilitator to

use eventually in displaying the structure on the wall. Normally this will take place quite some time after the group has completed the structuring session.

> Comments on Result 3: The Type 1 problematique will usually require about 15 to 20 feet of wall space to display. People can view it both from a distance and up close. They can walk past it in small groups and discuss particular relationships to deal with any questions they may have.

4. **Facilitator Interpretation of Structure.**   At some point (usually a few days later after sufficient time has been allowed for study and materials preparation) the facilitator will interpret the structure for the group to determine if there are any amendments required and to determine if the structure reflects the majority view of the group.

> Comments on Result 4: There is seldom any requirement for any amendments. The structure reflects only majority views on every relationship portrayed on the structure.

- The **De Morgan Index** relates to the number of distinct binary relationships involved in the problematique developed by the group. These distinct relationships are readily counted upon conclusion of the application of the ISM process, whereby members of the group taught each other about the relationships. The aggregate relationships form the problematique, which can be analyzed to produce data for computation of the De Morgan Index and also for the Aristotle Index, to be explained next.

- The **Aristotle Index** relates to the number of syllogisms found in the problematique.

A reference value of 1 can be defined for each of these indexes, with values below 1 indicating absence of complexity, and values above 1 indicating presence of complexity. **In practice, values are inevitably significantly above 1 for both of these indexes.** The use of 1 as the boundary is justified by research showing the limitations of human minds, arising from the behavioral pathologies.

Numerous applications at the Ford Motor Company have generated data on the indexes. A thorough treatment of four of them appeared in a paper from the Ford Scientific Research Laboratories: (Staley, 1995): "Complexity Measurements of Systems Design", in *Integrated Design and Process Technology* (A. Ertas, C. V. Ramamoorthy, M. M. Tanik, L. I. Esat, F. Veniali, and Taleb-Bendiab, Editors), IDPT-Volume 1, Austin, Texas, 153-161.

Reading the Type 1 Problematique. It is generally recognized that many years of formal education are dedicated to teaching prose, and even then college graduates continue to have difficulty in reading and composing prose. It should come as no surprise that highly educated people should have difficulty reading structural graphics, and it has been demonstrated clearly that they do. The Type 1 problematique is a structural graphic. When it became very evident that people who had just completed the development of the Type 1 problematique had difficulty in interpreting it, two developments ensued:

- A specialist role was dedicated to interpreting the structure for those who had created it.
- A research program was initiated by George H. "Tony" Perino[1] to determine statistics on how experienced managers performed when asked to interpret structural graphics.

Both of these initiatives turned out to be very well conceived. It was found that highly-experienced managers not only could not read structural graphics, but were inclined to misinterpret them in ways that were likely to cause significant errors in performance. Moreover an experienced specialist could read and interpret structures regardless of

---

[2] Perino, G. H. (1999),*Complexity: A Cognitive Barrier to Defense Systems Acquisition Management*, Fairfax, VA: Ph. D. Dissertation, George Mason University, with a shortened version in *Acquisition Review Quarterly*.

the topic, because the interpretation hinged much more on the nature of the relationship than upon the nature of what was being related. The collaborative combination of the participants who had developed the relationship in the first place, and the experienced interpreter who understood the nature of the relationship, offered a very powerful way of interpreting the Type 1 Problematique.

This work will go very smoothly provided magnetic wallboards are used with small rubberized magnets available in large quantities. Some of these should have question marks on them, which participants can use to go the wall and place question marks on problem statements where they have questions about placements of problems in categories.

Type 2 Session

Step 1. Objective: Develop Problems Field.
A "Problems Field" is a collection of problems in which each member of a set of problems is placed in one or more named categories of problems. Normally the number of problem categories is much smaller than the number of problems placed in the categories, meaning that it is much easier to work with the categories than with the problems. It is also possible then to work back and forth from problems to categories, depending on what is intended.

To develop the Problems Field, begin by entering the Importance Subset Part A from the NGT results, and choosing the generic question "In the context of the problematic situation X that is being explored, Is Problem Y in the same category as Problem Z"? [Variations of this question have also been used.]

The urge to name categories should be resisted until the categories appear to have stabilized.

Comments on Result: 1: Placing problems in categories invariably involves intuitive replies, and will invariably involve considerable rethinking. The skills of the facilitator come into play as this process proceeds. ISM is best thought of as a big help in getting a "first draft", and as the process proceeds the role of the computer steadily diminishes, and the role of the facilitator steadily increases.

Step 2. Optional. Incorporate Part B from NGT. If there is enough time, items may be distributed to individuals and they may be invited to place problems from Part B into the named categories.

Comments on the Result: 2: Names aren't given to categories until the contents have stabilized. But names may be given before Step 2 begins. New categories are proposed when it appears that some problems don't fit any named categories.

Step 3. Placing Question Marks. If any participant has a question about placement of a problem in a named category a question mark should be placed on that problem. The facilitator should lead a discussion on all items bearing question marks, until all elements have been placed in acceptable categories.

Comments on Results 3. Dimensions. The categories may be called the "dimensions of the situation" for purposes of the design of a system for resolving the problematic situation.

Type 2 Problematique. Historically, some practitioners have chosen to bypass the development of the Type 1 problematique. Instead they have developed the Problems Field, and then proceeded to substitute the problem categories in place of the problems, following the procedures described above under the heading "Type 1 Session", using the categories instead of the problems. While this is not a recommended practice, there may be times when it is appropriate. An example of such a time is the project carried out by Ms. Carol Jeffrey in Liberia with a group of warlords and warriors titled "Disarmament and Demobilization". This project was time-limited and resource-limited, but the prospects for attaining a period of peace in a country troubled with civil war were sufficient to warrant a departure from normal practice. Her work was successful. The report on her work is available in the "Warfield Special Collection" at George Mason University (see Appendix 2).

The Type 2 problematique is typically more superficial than the Type 1. Its best use is as an adjunct to the Type 1 problematique. If both the

Type 1 problematique and the Problem Field are available, the Type 2 problematique can be constructed by inspection directly from the information contained in these two products. To make this easy, the categories are labeled with letters of the alphabet and these letters are placed directly on the Type 1 problematique. Then it can be seen which letters "significantly aggravate" which other letters, and this enables manual construction of the Type 2 problematique. Examples are shown in the book *Understanding Complexity: Thought and Behavior*, including one developed by Carol Jeffrey.

The Type 2 problematique not only helps to understand how the categories are interrelated, but also it helps to correlate problem categories with parts of an organization. For example, some group of people in an organization may have responsibility for work on some category, while a second group may have responsibility for work on some other category. Since the graphical representation of the Type 2 problematique will show how one category is related to another, this carries over directly into a recognition that one part of the organization will be expected to cooperate with another part of the organization in working on the categories of problems shown to be related in the Type 2 problematique. By looking also at the specifics in the Type 1 problematique, further focus is provided to the nature of the cooperative relationship that is to be anticipated.

Options Field; Optionatique. The reader has seen that it is possible to generate, clarify, and partition sets of problems using NGT. Likewise it is possible to do the same with options. In the context of systems science, an option is seen as an action that might ultimately be chosen for implementation in order to help resolve one or more problems that have been discovered to be part of the Problems Field. With the Problems Field available, the group can use NGT to generate options for each individual category, and by this means create an Options Field. We may speak of the dimensionality of the Problems Field as the number of categories found there and we decree that the dimensionality of the Options Field will be the same as that of the Problems Field, in order to be consistent with Ashby's Law of Requisite Variety.

When participants choose at least one option from each dimension of the Options Field they create what is called either (a) an Options Profile or (b) a Design Alternative; the two names being interchangeable. The set of options can then be put in the computer and an ISM session can be run to create an optionatique, using the question: "In the context of the problematic situation X that is being explored, Will achievement of Option Y significantly help us in achieving Option Z"? The structure created in this use of ISM will help provide insight into the sequence of activities that should be carried out, and to the linkages that should be envisaged as the work program progresses toward the resolution of the complexity involved in the problematic situation.

Other Uses of ISM. ISM has been developed to be useful with any relationship that can be seen to have the mathematical property of being transitive. This means that there is a large class of relationships which can be used with this process.

Appendix 6

Statements, Themes, Findings, Structure

It does not seem to be too far-fetched to say that the subject of systems science and its partner, complexity, is somewhat foreboding. Consequently one may be forgiven if an effort is made to portray it in complementary ways, with some redundancy. In this Appendix, three complementary ways are chosen, along with a summarizing structural portrayal: a field type of graphic that is sometimes produced when applying Interactive Management. The complementary ways are: focusing statements, theme analysis, and key findings. These are bound together in the structural portrayal.

Focusing Statements for Systems Science

Focusing Statements. What are some focusing statements that run through systems science? Here are some:

- **Common Scientific Foundations.** All sciences, including systems science, have common foundations.
- **Ubiquity in Application of Systems Science.** Systems science must serve all problematic situations, whatever their nature.
- **Neutrality of Systems Science.** Systems science must be a neutral science in order to serve all problematic situations.
- **Cue to Needed Imports.** After its results have been applied to a particular problematic situation, to structure that situation and to motivate whatever specific followup is warranted, specific results from other sources may be imported from those other sources (whether they be from "sciences" or not).

- **Unbiased Nomenclature of Systems Science**. Because systems science must be neutral, the language of systems science cannot be biased in any direction, except that which arises from the common foundations of all science, and which no science can escape.

- **Two Types of Practitioner.** Because of the wide scope of systems science, its application to a problematic situation requires two types of practitioners: (a) a cadre of people who have learned how to apply systems science in a wide variety of problematic situations (the "systemists") and (b) a cadre of people who are informed about the local problematic situation (the "locals"). Neither type should expect to substitute for the other, except that a small percentage of locals who have had long experience with applications of systems science can "graduate" to become systemists.

- **The Modest System Science Practitioner.** Because of the wide variety to which it must be applicable, it can be expected that the cadre of practitioners of systems science will seldom be knowledgeable of the local conditions from which a particular problematic situation springs. Whatever is learned about such a situation will normally be learned from local people.

- **Generating Local Discursivity.** It cannot be expected that the complexity inherent in a local problematic situation is adequately described by colloquial language arising from multiple, undisciplined sources; therefore the requisite discursivity must be generated locally.

- **Local Discursivity as a Designed-In By-Product.** In the joint interests of effectiveness, efficiency, and parsimonious use of local resources, the necessary local discursivity must arise as a by-product of the processes used in working toward resolution of the situation. This requirement serves as a funnel through which many proposed methods cannot pass, because they do not enable this requirement to be satisfied.

- **Sufficient Processes of Systems Science.** The Nominal Group Technique (NGT) and Interpretive Structural Modeling (ISM) are sufficient (and neutral) processes to implement all aspects of systems science; keeping in mind that after the results of systems science come into view, other (specific) processes can be imported as required, although this may require further help for local practitioners who may be unaware of those processes. Such processes are not part of systems science, and are seldom supported by practitioners of systems science, although they may help local practitioners connect with appropriate persons who can support such processes.

- **Supportive Physical Infrastructure for Systems Science.** Application of systems science is greatly facilitated by using appropriate physical infrastructure; i.e., a "situation room" and an "observatorium".
- **Systems Science Has Nested Sub-Sciences.** The sub-sciences of systems science are: a science of description, a science of generic design, a structure-based science of complexity, and an action science (Interactive Management), these being nested in the sequence stated as parts of systems science.
- **Empirical Support.** Questions of the adequacy and suitability of systems science derive support from the archives of persons who have applied it to a variety of situations in a variety of cultures, as stated in their own words.

Some Themes Involved in Studying Complexity

A. Organizational Themes

1. Organizational Coherence. Given the complexity of many of today's situations, should we expect to find coherence (vertical, horizontal) in the organizations where complexity is troublesome?

2. Processes in Organizations. What is required to assure that good processes are applied in organizations?

3. Time Allotments. Should time allotments for working to resolve complexity be any different than normal time allotments for everyday problem solving?

B. Communication Themes

4. Communicating Outcomes. How can one interpret to non-participants the products of a complexity-resolving process?

5. Language 1. Is ordinary language appropriate to discovery regarding a problematic situation?

6. Language 2. What requirements should language(s) satisfy to be useful in resolving complexity?

7. Language 3. Is a glossary of complexity likely to be useful?

C. Organizational Infrastructure Themes

8. Infrastructure of Implementing Organization. If science is to be useful in studying complexity, is there some infrastructure that would enhance the capacity to **apply science** in the working environments of implementing organizations (local situations)?

9. Situation Room. If a group is to work together to strive to resolve complexity, what kind of physical facility would be beneficial?

10. Observatorium. Should a physical space be dedicated to continuing portrayal of results of studying complexity in a particular local situation?

D. Human Behavior Themes

11. Dysfunctional Behavior. What kind of behaviors work against understanding complexity?

12. Killer Assumptions. What assumptions that govern action are likely to make resolving complexity impossible?

13. Behavior Enhancement. Can one design processes that enhance human behavior in groups?

14. Human Behavior. Are there people who have studied human behavior enough that their ideas might be useful to people today in studying complexity?

E. Process Themes

15. Complexity-Resolving Processes. What kind of processes should be used to resolve complexity?

16. Description Process. When complexity is expected, should the process of **description** go beyond the normal?

17. Diagnosis Process. When complexity is expected, should the process of **diagnosis** go beyond the normal?
18. Design Process. If some process for resolving complexity is to be designed, what process would be useful?

F. Science Themes

19. Demands of Complexity. What is demanded in order to resolve complexity?
20. Formalisms (Algorithms). What kind of computer formalisms would be helpful in studying complexity?
21. Modeling. What criteria should govern model development in studying complexity?
22. Infrastructure of Science. If science is to be useful in studying complexity, is there some infrastructure that would enhance the capacity to **develop science** in that study?
23. Thought Leaders on Thought. Are there any people who have studied thought processes enough that their ideas might be useful to people today in studying complexity?
24. Laws of Complexity. What laws of complexity have been proposed and illuminated?

G. Product Themes

25. Product of Description Process. What should the product of a **description** process look like?
26. Product of Diagnosis Process. What would the product of a **diagnosis** process look like?
27. Product of Design Process. What would the product of a **design** process it look like?
28. Communicating Outcomes. How can one interpret to non-participants products of a complexity-resolving process?

H. Empirical Themes

29. Independent Testing in Applications.

30. System Practitioners.
31. Longevity in Use.
32. Issue Diversity in Applications.
33. Cultural Diversity in Applications.

Key Findings

The following "key findings" are numbered for convenient reference, and also lettered for reference to the two-page summary field drawing (to follow) on which they all appear. The letters point to the categories in which the key findings are located. One may note that there is a total of ten categories for the key findings, these being identified on the two-page summary under the headings A through J.

C. 1-Identification of Laws of Complexity and Their Origins.
Twenty Laws of Complexity have been set forth.
      C. 2-70% of the Laws of Complexity are behaviorally-based
      C. 3-10% of the Laws of Complexity are Media-Based
      C. 4-30% of the Laws of Complexity are mathematics-based

D. 5-Recognition of Inadequacy of Prose. Prose is inadequate to represent complexity.

I. 6-Behavioral Shortcomings in Instruction in Methods. Virtually all of the methods taught in higher education are Behavioral-Pathology Insensitive.

I. 7-Necessity of Behavior-Oriented Methods. Behavioral-Pathology-Sensitive (BPS) methods are essential for working with complexity.

B. 8-Fundamental Nature of Spreadthink. Spreadthink is a defining attribute of complexity.

H. 9-Requirement for Computer Assistance. Computer assistance is required to help structure complexity.

I. 10-Structuring Complexity. Complexity can be structured.

A. 11-Necessity of Group Collaboration. Groups are required to structure complexity.

B. 12-Predictability of Incorrectness. Individuals who push their own ideas to the exclusion of those of others are almost certainly wrong.

C. 13-The Problematic Situation. The "problematic situation" is a fundamental concept.

J. 14-Secondary Status of "Problem". "The problem" recedes as a high-saliency concept because it is a component, one of many.

D. 15-Defense Mechanism. Linguistic pollution is a defense mechanism used by people in the face of complexity.

J. 16-Propagating Killer Assumptions. Killer assumptions propagate into killer frameworks.

J. 17-Quality Control in Modeling. Quality control of modeling recedes in the face of complexity, thereby degrading the products from human activity.

A. 18-Evolution of Second-Order Thought. A 2400-year evolution of second-order thought is a key inheritance.

B. 19-Behavioral Pathologies. Behavioral pathologies represent core concepts in the study of complexity.

F. 20-Metrics of Complexity and Their Origins. Metrics of complexity invariably involve concepts from second-order thought, or from behavioral pathologies, or both.

G. 21-Comprehensive Process. The Work Program of Complexity is highly effective.

J. 22-Display Constraints. Analysts regularly accept inappropriate display constraints, e.g., too small display spaces.

J. 23-Linguistic Constraints. Analysts who use graphics invariably accept inappropriate linguistic constraints; e.g., too few words in a box to convey understanding.

I. 24-Interactive Management. Interactive Management works as a means of carrying out The Work Program of Complexity.

J. 25-The Guru and the Analyst. Analysts find it much easier to accept the work of gurus whose thoughts are not fundamental than to locate the Golden Legacy.

B. 26-Externalizing Costs. Managements love to externalize costs related to Quality Control; costs which should be internalized.

C. 27-A Bipartite Conceptual Space. The Ordinary and the Complex occupy the same conceptual space (like hydrogen and oxygen employ the same physical space in air), but their properties are very different; hence we have the Ordinary Domain and the Domain of Complexity.

D. 28-A Semantic Control. "Complex" should almost never be used as an adjective.

D. 29-Graphical Products. Graphical products are a necessary consequence of high-quality explorations of complexity.

J. 30-Weakness in Interpreting Graphics. Analysts lack skill in reading graphical products stemming from the study of complexity.

J. 31-Ambiguous Graphics. Analysts typically promote the use of ill-defined graphics, which (perforce) are inherently ambiguous.

I. 32-The Graphical Hypothesis. The Work Program of Complexity, when carried out, yields graphical hypotheses that await testing in practice.

J. 33-Confusing Hypotheses With Ultimate Products of Science. Analysts mistakenly think that the Work Program of Complexity should produce scientifically-established results, just as work in the Ordinary Domain produced such results.

E. 34-Narrowness of Higher Education. Higher education is a failure, in terms of education about complexity; trying to draw from the narrow foundations of some established discipline.

I. 35-Origins of Literature of Complexity.   The popular current literature of complexity is mostly produced by theoretical physicists or biologists who continue and promote the practice of developing Behavioral-Pathology-Insensitive (BPI) theories and processes.

D. 36-Advocacy. Founders of discursivity can gain advocates who will follow them for long periods of time, even for centuries. [The social consequences may be called "Clanthink" if many believe the same thing, and if all who do are wrong.]

H. 37-Designed Infrastructure.   Special infrastructure is required for working efficiently with and learning about complexity.

D. 38-Theory of Relations.   The theory of relations (Augustus De Morgan, 1847) is the fundamental mathematics of structure.

J. 39-Analyst Unawareness. The theory of relations remains unknown to most analysts.

I. 40-ISM and the Theory of Relations.   Interpretive Structural Modeling (ISM, 1974-1976) instruments the theory of relations, making it available for practical use in developing those structural graphics that portray complexity and designs for resolving complexity; using ISM software developed specifically for those purposes.

B. 41-Executive Behavior. Top executives may suppress results obtained from applying The Work Program of Complexity, since these results may be perceived as threatening their leadership or autonomy (in Chris Argyris' language, the results may be "undiscussable" and "their undiscussability may be undiscussable").

G. 42-Empirical Evidence. Empirical results have been observed from more than 500 Interactive Management Workshops.

G, J. 43-Impact of Killer Assumptions. Killer Assumptions have taken root in the minds of most analysts, where they become the basis for much of what goes wrong in working with complexity.

D. 44-Single-Relationship Models. Single-relationship models are essential to interpreting complexity, hence they represent key products from applying The Work Program of Complexity.

I. 45-Thinking in Sets. It is necessary to learn to think in sets, otherwise the products of study of complexity will be severely deficient.

A. 46-Historical Neglect. Neglect of the work of relevant thought leaders accounts for many difficulties in working with complexity.

FIELD REPRESENTATION: KEY FINDINGS OF RESEARCH PROGRAM ON SYSTEMS AND COMPLEXITY-I

A. Golden Legacy

• A 2400-year evolution of second-order thought is a key historical inheritance (18)

• Neglect of the work of relevant thought leaders is responsible for many of the difficulties in working with complexity that take place when the Work Program of Complexity is not applied (46)

B. Behavioral Pathologies

• Spreadthink is a defining attribute of complexity (8)

• Individuals who produce their own un-clarified ideas are almost certainly wrong (12)

• Behavioral pathologies are core concepts in the study of complexity (19)

• Managements love to externalize costs related to quality control that should be internal (26)

• Executives frequently suppress results obtained by using the Work Program of Complexity, feeling that their autonomy is threatened (41)

C. Laws of Complexity

• Twenty Laws of Complexity (1)

• 70% of the 20 Laws are behavior-based (2)

• 25% are based in physiology (2)

• 10% are based in media (3)

• 30% are based in mathematics (4)

• The problematic situation is a fundamental concept (13)

• The ordinary and the complex occupy the same conceptual space, like hydrogen and oxygen in air, but their properties are very different, hence we have the ordinary or normal domain and the domain of complexity (27)

F. Metrics

• Metrics of complexity invariably involve concepts from second-order thought or from behavioral pathologies or from both (20)

D. Language

• Prose is inadequate to represent complexity (5)

• Linguistic pollution is a defense mechanism used by people in the face of complexity (15)

• "Complex" should almost never be used as an adjective (28)

• Graphical products are a necessary product of high-quality explorations of complexity (29)

• Founders of discursivity can gain advocates who will follow them for long periods of time, even for centuries (36)

• The Theory of Relations (De Morgan, 1847) is the fundamental mathematical language of structure (38)

• Single-relationship models are essential to interpret complexity, hence they are key products of the Work Program of Complexity (44)

FIELD REPRESENTATION: KEY FINDINGS OF RESEARCH
PROGRAM ON SYSTEMS AND COMPLEXITY-II

G. Empirical Results

- The Work Program of Complexity is highly effective (21)
- Empirical results from more than 500 Interactive Management Workshops have been studied (42)
- "Killer Assumptions" have taken root in the thought of most analysts, where they are responsible for much of what goes wrong in working with complexity (43)

I. Methods

NOTE: BPI refers to Behavioral-Pathology-Insensitive, while BPS refers to Behavioral-Pathology-Sensitive

- Virtually all methods for resolving complexity that are taught in higher education are BPI methods (6)
- BPS methods are essential for working effectively with complexity (7)
- Complexity can be structured (10)
- Interactive Management works as a means of carrying out the Work Program of Complexity (24)
- The Work Program of Complexity yields graphical hypotheses that await testing in practice (32)

I. Methods (continued)

- Theoretical physicists present BPI concepts as definitive with respect to complexity, and circulate this information widely (35)
- Interpretive Structural Modeling (ISM) implements the Theory of Relations (De Morgan, 1847), and makes it available for practical use by people who are in difficult situations (40)
- Scholars who do not learn to think in sets (some who have done so include Hayek, Foucault, and Vickers) typically produce severely deficient work in the domain of complexity (45)

E. Education

- For the most part, institutions of higher education fail to educate about complexity, and where they purport to do so they offer misleading subject matter (34)

H. Infrastructure

- A computer with ISM software is essential to structuring complexity (9)

- Physical infrastructure is vital (37)
- Groups are required to structure complexity (9)

J. Analysts

- The "problem" fails to take a back seat to the "problematic situation" (14)
- Killer assumptions propagate into killer frameworks (16)
- Quality control of modeling is ignored in the face of complexity (17)
- Analysts willingly accept too-small display spaces (22)
- Analysts accept inappropriate linguistic constraints in graphics (23)
- Analysts favor "prestigious" gurus over the Golden Legacy (25)
- Analysts lack skill in reading graphics arising from appropriate study of complexity (30)
- Analysts promote ill-defined, ambiguous graphics (31)
- Analysts misunderstand the role of structural studies, and the power of structural hypotheses (33)
- The Theory of Relations remains unknown to most analysts (39)

Appendix 7

Literacy in Structural Graphics: The Higher Education Imperative

The introduction of systems science in higher education will benefit greatly if it is done in a systematic way. One of the key components of the introduction, one which it is imperative to do well, and one which will yield many benefits, is to enable graduates to become literate in structural graphics.

I have tried to emphasize this requirement in various ways. For example, in my 2002 book *Understanding Complexity*, I dedicated an appendix to the portrayal of a collection of problematiques, illustrating a variety of structural graphics coming from numerous applications in different areas. I wished to show that any time a careful effort is made to describe a problematic situation that extends into the domain of complexity, the result will involve a requirement for structural graphics. This illustration of empirical results was further buttressed by the research of George H. Perino, who showed empirical evidence that highly-trained managers were not able to read and interpret such structures. His work illustrated two points: absence of formal education in structural graphics not only is responsible for inability to read them, but also implicitly encourages managers to misread them, because of the ad hoc nature of their understanding of the graphical structures that they have encountered in their past experience.

I have tried to imagine metaphors that would help drive home the nature of this requirement. Suppose, for example, that you arrive at an airport in a strange country and acquire a rental car. But instead of a road map you receive a thick book filled with nothing but prose descriptions of the roads, cities, populations statistics, locations of tourist sites, etc., with which to guide your travel. Now instead of using a map to take advantage of the scanning ability of the human eye to form quick images to guide your driving through the country to reach a destination, you are forced to stop frequently and thumb through the pages of the book, trying to find scattered bits of text that will help you learn first how to escape from the airport, then how to get pointed in the right direction to wherever your plans take you, and then what turns to make as you proceed. I hope that the point is made here that a graphical presentation which takes advantage of the scanning ability of the human eye to transmit images to the brain for processing offers vastly superior means when compared to the prose representation, whenever structural features of information are critical to understanding. (Nothing I have said denies the value of the prose as a complement to the graphic.)

Yet even if a faculty member should be swayed by the brief argument given here or by the examples referred to above, there may be difficulty in introducing the full powers of the graphical literacy into the academic curriculum. For full benefits, here is a sequence that could be very desirable:

- Identify a problematic situation to be studied as a part of an academic offering
- Form a small group to generate a problem set, using NGT
- Structure the problem set, using ISM
- Construct the structure and display it prominently (e.g., using a large wall space), where the group can all see the structure and discuss it in a group setting
- Test readability as an exercise for an individual, asking a student to interpret the structure, and engaging in a class discussion of the accuracy of the discussion
- If parts of the structure appear to be information-deficient, consider whether those parts could become the topic for research projects (perhaps even thesis material, where the overall structure would form a framework within which the thesis could add new insights embedded in and interpreted in terms of the larger structure)

Variations on this plan could be imagined. Even a creative writing class could take advantage of this scheme. I know an individual who creates structures of his planned books before he begins to write the prose, and who has good success in the marketplace with his books. So if someone imagines that the foregoing concepts are only proposed with schools of business, public policy, or engineering in mind, please allow the mind to roam freely through the academic halls, with the thought that creative use of graphical structure may have many untested applications, even inside academia.

I have proposed the use of graphical structures to describe the various academic disciplines. I believe it is true that most of the disciplines cannot be adequately described with linear prose. But, as the Wandwaver Solution (you can find it in a web search) suggests, many or all of the disciplines can be described by structural models showing the problems that the discipline seems intended to treat as the subject matter and the relationships envisaged among those problems.

From another perspective, the Foucault concept of problemization can be applied not only to writing history as normally conceived, but also to writing history of a discipline, bringing its history up to date, and keeping it up to date as it changes with time. In this way, taking advantage of the kind of overview that can be provided with structural graphics, even the faculty of a discipline can obtain a grasp of that discipline not readily achievable in any other way. (The graphics can give a road map instead of a long and ill-organized collection of texts.)

In other ways, literacy in structural graphics is a new and valuable skill that has served well in a few diverse applications so far. Now it is time to enlarge greatly the scope of its awareness, and higher education offers a wonderful opportunity to bring that about.

Index

394